Daily Planner

Daily Affirmatio...

- ✔ The energy of your area and the peop... ...you. Be an *"energy"* manager.

- ✔ Managing is a people job. Put people first.

- ✔ Managing is what you do *with* people, not *to* people.

- ✔ Walk your talk; back up your words with actions. People believe what they *see* more than what they *hear*.

- ✔ "If it's to be, it begins with me."

- ✔ You *gain* power when you *share* power with your employees.

- ✔ The best business is common sense.

- ✔ Always ask: What do your customers value, and how do you *know* that they value it?

- ✔ The best performance starts with clear goals.

- ✔ You get what you reward.

- ✔ The more mistakes you make, the closer you are to the right answer.

- ✔ If you can't measure performance, you can't manage it.

- ✔ *Remember:* It's not personal, it's business.

- ✔ If you don't like the way things are today, be patient. Everything will change tomorrow.

- ✔ Make work fun. Doing so is good for you *and* for the bottom line.

- ✔ Don't sweat the small stuff (it's all small stuff).

- ✔ The simple approach is often the best approach.

Managing For Dummies®

Quick Reference Card

Ten Ways to Motivate Employees

Employees may not need a pay raise as much as they do personal thanks from their manager for a job well done. Following is the top ten list of motivators for today's employees:

- ✔ Personally thank employees for doing a good job — one on one, in writing, or both. Do it promptly, often, and sincerely.

- ✔ Be willing to take time to meet with and listen to employees — as much time as they need or want.

- ✔ Provide specific feedback about performance of the employee, the department, and the organization.

- ✔ Strive to create a work environment that is open, trusting, and fun. Encourage new ideas and initiative.

- ✔ Provide information about upcoming products and strategies, how the company makes and loses money, and how each employee fits into the overall plan.

- ✔ Involve employees in decisions, especially those decisions that affect them.

- ✔ Encourage employees to have a sense of ownership in their work and their work environment.

- ✔ Create a partnership with each employee. Give people a chance to grow and learn new skills; show them how you can help them meet their goals within the context of meeting the organization's goals.

- ✔ Celebrate successes of the company, the department, and the individuals in it. Take time for team- and morale-building meetings and activities.

- ✔ Use performance as the basis for recognizing, rewarding, and promoting people; deal with low and marginal performers so that they improve their performance or leave the organization.

IDG BOOKS WORLDWIDE

Copyright © 1996 IDG Books Worldwide, Inc. All rights reserved.

Quick Reference Card $2.95 value. Item 858-7.

For more information about IDG Books, call 1-800-762-2974.

For Dummies™: Bestselling Book Series for Beginners

Praise for Managing For Dummies

"Bob Nelson and Peter Economy have demonstrated a rare talent for distilling the most complex and essential elements of good management into an easily digestible, understandable, and practical text. Although intended primarily for new managers, the wise tenets they have selected and carefully explained are as valuable to CEOs of large corporations as they are to novice professionals just beginning their management careers."

— Ron Vukas, Executive Vice President, The Institute of Real Estate Management

"Everywhere I opened this book, I found concepts I could immediately apply in my job and in the job of managing others to get their best performance."

— Bill Taylor, Regional Team Leader, K/P Corporation

"Bob Nelson's *Managing For Dummies* contains sound, practical management advice developed with a pleasing touch of humor. The book avoids traditional management theory in favor of useful, applications-oriented management information and techniques that can be used immediately on the job. 'Dummies' is the way management material should be presented as we move into the 21st century."

— Professor J. Michael Cicero, Coordinator, General Business Program, Highline Community College, Seattle

"This is *the* one handbook that I keep close by as a reference for daily work problems. It serves as both a guide and refresher for a myriad of situations that arise at work."

— Sam Steinhardt, Vice President and CFO, Context Integration, Inc.

"*Managing For Dummies* is dynamite! Whether you are a rookie or management pro, it will help blast you to stellar managerial performance. *Managing For Dummies* has the latest information on the best ways to manage yourself, your subordinates, and your organization to outstanding performance. This extraordinary book is the next best thing to an MBA!"

— Dr. W. Bradley Zehner II, MBA Professor, Pepperdine University

"Every manager will benefit from the sound advice found in *Managing For Dummies;* especially the belief that management can and must be fun."

— Felix Mussenden, Executive Vice President, General Manager, Universal Studios Hollywood

"While it seems that most management fads are here today and gone tomorrow, there are precious few sources that present the essential basics of managing a business in a way that is at once understandable, useful, *and* fun to read. *Managing For Dummies* has a real knack for accomplishing all of these goals."

— William K. VanCanagan, J.D., L.L.M., Partner, Datsopoulos, MacDonald, & Lind

"This book recognizes that it is a new world of management out there. But it takes the best of proven, older principles to apply to the new workplace."

— Dr. Rick Crandall, Speaker and Author, *Marketing Your Service: For People Who HATE to Sell;* Publisher and Editor of *Executive Edge* newsletter

"This is a valuable book for any manager, or any aspiring manager. It provides a useful, easy-to-read description of the tools that an effective manager must draw from. I like its breadth and diversity of topics, from interviewing to budgeting, from technology to teambuilding, from coaching to compensation. They're put together in a practical package that'll make sense to anyone in the world of business."

— Oren Harari, Contributor, Management Review and Professor, McLaren School of Business, University of San Francisco

"Nelson and Economy have crafted the ABC's of MBA! Novice managers will be relieved; experienced managers will be renewed. An excellent and powerful resource for everyone charged with helping others perform effectively."

— Chip R. Bell, Author, *Customers As Partners* and *Managers As Mentors*

Praise for Bob Nelson and 1001 Ways to Reward Employees

"It is amazing to me how Bob Nelson is able to come up with simple, creative ways to motivate average employees to become top performers."

— Dan Stiff, Director, Learning Center, Black & Decker, Towson, MD

"There's a difference between having someone show up for work and bringing out the best thinking and initiative in each person. To do that requires treating employees more as partners, not as subordinates. Being nice isn't just the right thing to do, it's also the economical thing to do."

— *Seattle Post-Intelligencer*

"The most interesting and inventive business book on the market today . . . a publishing phenomenon."

— *Training* magazine

"Welcome to Bob's World: A place of above-average managers and workers, all committed to personal excellence, good will and, of course, company profits. Details how a little praise goes a long way."

— *The Philadelphia Inquirer*

"A must read for anyone in business.""Better than money: Praise and personal gestures motivate workers. Things that don't cost money are ironically the most effective."

— *The Wall Street Journal*

"[Bob Nelson helps managers] take certain rewards and mold them into new management styles at their companies."

— *The New York Times*

"This book should be in the top drawer of every manager's desk!"

— Karl Albrecht, Coauthor of *Service America*

"This blockbuster guide does wonders for morale! . . . use of its ideas is changing the face of rewards and recognition in the workplace."

— *Success* magazine

"A must read for anyone in business."

— *Small Business Forum*

Praise for Peter Economy

"Peter's contemporary management guidelines helped us streamline our small service company's approach, dramatically increasing our return. We thought we were already good managers but, after applying Peter's approaches, our employees began to think so, too."

— W. Lee Hill, Vice President, Verloc Group, Inc.

"I have long been a fan of Peter Economy's books — he has a way of explaining complex business concepts in simple and accessible terms. As the chief executive of a rapidly growing software development firm, I am especially thankful for his solid grasp on the latest developments in computers and information technology."

— Steven Dente, President, Signature Software

Other Books by Bob Nelson

1001 Ways to Reward Employees
Empowering Employees Through Delegation
Delegation: The Power of Letting Go
Decision Point: A Business Game Book
Exploring the World of Business (with Ken Blanchard, Charles Shewe,
     and Alex Hiam)
The Perfect Letter (with Patricia Westheimer)
Better Business Meetings (with Peter Economy)
*We Have to Start Meeting Like This: A Guide to Successful Meeting
     Management* (with Roger Mosvick)
The Presentation Primer: Getting Your Point Across (with Jennifer Wallick)
Making More Effective Presentations
*Louder and Funnier: A Practical Guide to Overcoming Stage Fright
     in Speechmaking*
The Supervisor's Guide to Controlling Absenteeism
The Job Hunt: The Biggest Job You'll Ever Have

...and as a Series Editor

The New Manager's Handbook, by Brad Thompson
Straight Answers to People Problems, by Fred Jandt
Rewarding and Recognizing Employees, by Joan Klubnik
Listen for Success: A Guide to Effective Listening, by Arthur Robertson
Managing Stress: Keeping Calm Under Fire, by Barbara Braham
Managing Your Priorities: From Start to Success, by Bill Bond
The Berkeley Guide to Employment for New College Graduates,
     by James Briggs
Strategic Planning: Selected Readings, by J. William Pfeiffer
Odiorne on Management, by George Odiorne

Other Books by Peter Economy

Better Business Meetings (with Bob Nelson)
Business Negotiating Basics
Negotiating to Win

Managing

FOR

DUMMIES®

by Bob Nelson and Peter Economy

Foreword by Ken Blanchard

IDG
BOOKS
WORLDWIDE

IDG Books Worldwide, Inc.
An International Data Group Company

Foster City, CA ♦ Chicago, IL ♦ Indianapolis, IN ♦ New York, NY

Managing For Dummies®

Published by
IDG Books Worldwide, Inc.
An International Data Group Company
919 E. Hillsdale Blvd.
Suite 400
Foster City, CA 94404
www.idgbooks.com (IDG Books Worldwide Web site)
www.dummies.com (Dummies Press Web site)

Library of Congress Catalog Card No.: 96-76253

ISBN: 1-56884-858-7

Printed in the United States of America

15 14 13

1B/QX/QY/QQ/IN

Distributed in the United States by IDG Books Worldwide, Inc.

Distributed by CDG Books Canada Inc. for Canada; by Transworld Publishers Limited in the United Kingdom; by IDG Norge Books for Norway; by IDG Sweden Books for Sweden; by IDG Books Australia Publishing Corporation Pty. Ltd. for Australia and New Zealand; by TransQuest Publishers Pte Ltd. for Singapore, Malaysia, Thailand, Indonesia, and Hong Kong; by Gotop Information Inc. for Taiwan; by ICG Muse, Inc. for Japan; by Intersoft for South Africa; by Eyrolles for France; by International Thomson Publishing for Germany, Austria and Switzerland; by Distribuidora Cuspide for Argentina; by LR International for Brazil; by Galileo Libros for Chile; by Ediciones ZETA S.C.R. Ltda. for Peru; by WS Computer Publishing Corporation, Inc., for the Philippines; by Contemporanea de Ediciones for Venezuela; by Express Computer Distributors for the Caribbean and West Indies; by Micronesia Media Distributor, Inc. for Micronesia; by Chips Computadoras S.A. de C.V. for Mexico; by Editorial Norma de Panama S.A. for Panama; by American Bookshops for Finland.

For general information on IDG Books Worldwide's books in the U.S., please call our Consumer Customer Service department at 800-762-2974. For reseller information, including discounts and premium sales, please call our Reseller Customer Service department at 800-434-3422.

For information on where to purchase IDG Books Worldwide's books outside the U.S., please contact our International Sales department at 317-596-5530 or fax 317-572-4002.

For consumer information on foreign language translations, please contact our Customer Service department at 1-800-434-3422, fax 317-572-4002, or e-mail rights@idgbooks.com.

For information on licensing foreign or domestic rights, please phone +1-650-653-7098.

For sales inquiries and special prices for bulk quantities, please contact our Order Services department at 800-434-3422 or write to the address above.

For information on using IDG Books Worldwide's books in the classroom or for ordering examination copies, please contact our Educational Sales department at 800-434-2086 or fax 317-572-4005.

For press review copies, author interviews, or other publicity information, please contact our Public Relations department at 650-653-7000 or fax 650-653-7500.

For authorization to photocopy items for corporate, personal, or educational use, please contact Copyright Clearance Center, 222 Rosewood Drive, Danvers, MA 01923, or fax 978-750-4470.

About the Authors

Bob Nelson (San Diego, CA) is founder and president of Nelson Motivation, Inc., an innovative training and consulting firm headquartered in San Diego. As a practicing manager and a best-selling author, Bob is an internationally recognized expert in the areas of employee recognition, rewards, motivation, productivity, supervision, leadership, management, and suggestion systems.

Bob has published 16 books and has been featured extensively in the media: on CNN, PBS, and CNBC; and in *The New York Times*, *The Wall Street Journal*, and *The Philadelphia Inquirer*, among others. He publishes a monthly newsletter called *Bob Nelson's Rewarding Employees* and holds a master's degree in business administration from UC Berkeley. Bob is currently a doctoral candidate in the Executive Management Program at the Claremont Graduate School in Los Angeles.

Bob would be delighted to speak to your next association meeting or management conference. Call Nelson Motivation, Inc., at 800-575-5521, or visit the company Web site (http://www.nelson-motivation.com) for more information on Bob and the full complement of Nelson Motivation, Inc., products and services. Bob's e-mail address is BobRewards@aol.com.

Peter Economy (La Jolla, CA) is a best-selling business writer who is coauthor of Consulting For Dummies with Bob Nelson and At the Helm: Business Lessons for Navigating Rough Waters with Peter Isler. Peter combines his writing expertise with more than 15 years of management experience to provide his readers with solid, hands-on information and advice. He received his bachelor's degree (with majors in economics and human biology) from Stanford University and is currently pursuing his MBA at the Edinburgh Business School. Peter welcomes your questions and comments; you can e-mail him at bizzwriter@stanfordalumni.org.

ABOUT IDG BOOKS WORLDWIDE

Welcome to the world of IDG Books Worldwide.

IDG Books Worldwide, Inc., is a subsidiary of International Data Group, the world's largest publisher of computer-related information and the leading global provider of information services on information technology. IDG was founded more than 30 years ago by Patrick J. McGovern and now employs more than 9,000 people worldwide. IDG publishes more than 290 computer publications in over 75 countries. More than 90 million people read one or more IDG publications each month.

Launched in 1990, IDG Books Worldwide is today the #1 publisher of best-selling computer books in the United States. We are proud to have received eight awards from the Computer Press Association in recognition of editorial excellence and three from Computer Currents' First Annual Readers' Choice Awards. Our best-selling *...For Dummies®* series has more than 50 million copies in print with translations in 31 languages. IDG Books Worldwide, through a joint venture with IDG's Hi-Tech Beijing, became the first U.S. publisher to publish a computer book in the People's Republic of China. In record time, IDG Books Worldwide has become the first choice for millions of readers around the world who want to learn how to better manage their businesses.

Our mission is simple: Every one of our books is designed to bring extra value and skill-building instructions to the reader. Our books are written by experts who understand and care about our readers. The knowledge base of our editorial staff comes from years of experience in publishing, education, and journalism — experience we use to produce books to carry us into the new millennium. In short, we care about books, so we attract the best people. We devote special attention to details such as audience, interior design, use of icons, and illustrations. And because we use an efficient process of authoring, editing, and desktop publishing our books electronically, we can spend more time ensuring superior content and less time on the technicalities of making books.

You can count on our commitment to deliver high-quality books at competitive prices on topics you want to read about. At IDG Books Worldwide, we continue in the IDG tradition of delivering quality for more than 30 years. You'll find no better book on a subject than one from IDG Books Worldwide.

John Kilcullen
Chairman and CEO
IDG Books Worldwide, Inc.

IDG is the world's leading IT media, research and exposition company. Founded in 1964, IDG had 1997 revenues of $2.05 billion and has more than 9,000 employees worldwide. IDG offers the widest range of media options that reach IT buyers in 75 countries representing 95% of worldwide IT spending. IDG's diverse product and services portfolio spans six key areas including print publishing, online publishing, expositions and conferences, market research, education and training, and global marketing services. More than 90 million people read one or more of IDG's 290 magazines and newspapers, including IDG's leading global brands — Computerworld, PC World, Network World, Macworld and the Channel World family of publications. IDG Books Worldwide is one of the fastest-growing computer book publishers in the world, with more than 700 titles in 36 languages. The "...For Dummies®" series alone has more than 50 million copies in print. IDG offers online users the largest network of technology-specific Web sites around the world through IDG.net (http://www.idg.net), which comprises more than 225 targeted Web sites in 55 countries worldwide. International Data Corporation (IDC) is the world's largest provider of information technology data, analysis and consulting, with research centers in over 41 countries and more than 400 research analysts worldwide. IDG World Expo is a leading producer of more than 168 globally branded conferences and expositions in 35 countries including E3 (Electronic Entertainment Expo), Macworld Expo, ComNet, Windows World Expo, ICE (Internet Commerce Expo), Agenda, DEMO, and Spotlight. IDG's training subsidiary, ExecuTrain, is the world's largest computer training company, with more than 230 locations worldwide and 785 training courses. IDG Marketing Services helps industry-leading IT companies build international brand recognition by developing global integrated marketing programs via IDG's print, online and exposition products worldwide. Further information about the company can be found at www.idg.com.   1/26/00

Dedication

To any manager who has struggled to do the job and every employee who has had to live with the consequences.

Acknowledgments

Throughout our careers, we have been fortunate to have had skilled mentors to model the right kinds of management skills and techniques that we advocate in *Managing For Dummies.*

Bob recalls three influential mentors in particular. Jim Reller, a delegator par excellence at Control Data Corporation, often gave out assignments with a disclaimer such as, "I could probably do this task faster than you, but I believe you'll learn a lot from the process." Jim Briggs at the University of California, Berkeley, showed Bob how to avoid becoming bogged down in organizational politics. Finally, Ken Blanchard, also known as *The One Minute Manager,* demonstrated how to get the best efforts from people by using the softer side of management and *never directly telling them what to do.* He lives the values he preaches and serves as a daily inspiration for getting the best results from others by having *their* best interests at heart.

In Peter's case, Richard Vaaler, contracting officer for the Department of Defense, taught the benefits of upholding high ethical standards and making things happen. At Horizons Technology, Inc., CFO Debbie Fritsch demonstrated the importance of hiring and developing superior employees and challenging authority. Pat Boyce, president, taught Peter to look beyond the obvious to ferret out the truth and also showed him the value of becoming one with your customers. Jim Palmer, chairman, embodied the value of painting the big picture — a vision for all employees to strive for.

These people taught more than just the technical skills of assigning work, conducting a performance appraisal, or disciplining an employee, but instead emphasized the people side of management: how to motivate employees by example, reward them when they exceed your expectations, and make each customer feel like he or she is your only customer — even if you have thousands of others.

Bob wants to thank all the great folks at Blanchard Training and Development, Inc., for their support; Peter offers profuse thanks to everyone in the General Services Section of the San Diego Housing Commission; Bob and Peter are both grateful to Dick Roe for helping them get together with IDG Books Worldwide.

Bob and Peter are also especially appreciative of all the folks at IDG Books Worldwide, especially Kathy Welton, Sarah Kennedy, Stacy Collins, and Pam Mourouzis for their infinite wisdom, guidance, and support on this project.

On the personal side, Bob would like to acknowledge the ongoing love and support of his father Edward, his wife Jennifer, and his children Daniel and Michelle. Peter acknowledges his mother Betty Economy Gritis, his wife Jan, and his children Peter J and Skylar Park for their everlasting love and for putting up with his crazy life. *May the circle be unbroken.*

Publisher's Acknowledgments

We're proud of this book; please register your comments through our IDG Books Worldwide Online Registration Form located at: http://my2cents.dummies.com.

Some of the people who helped bring this book to market include the following:

Acquisitions, Development, and Editorial

Project Editor: Pamela Mourouzis

Executive Editor: Sarah Kennedy

Copy Editor: Leah Cameron

General Reviewers: Chad Lewis, Sam Steinhardt, Jennifer Wallick

Editorial Manager: Kristin A. Cocks

Editorial Assistants: Chris Collins, Ann Miller

Special Help

Joyce Pepple, Permissions Editor

Bethany Waddington, Reprint Editor

Production

Associate Project Coordinator: Debbie Sharpe

Layout and Graphics: E. Shawn Aylsworth, Brett Black, Linda M. Boyer, J. Tyler Connor, Cheryl Denski, Maridee V. Ennis, Kelly Hardesty, Todd Klemme, Tom Missler, Anna Rohrer, Brent Savage, Gina Scott, M. Anne Sipahimalani, Deirdre Smith, Kate Snell, Michael Sullivan

Special Art: Shelley Lea

Proofreaders: Kathleen Prata, Christine Meloy Beck, Michelle Croninger, Rachel Garvey, Nancy Price, Dwight Ramsey, Carl Saff, Robert Springer, Karen York

Indexer: Anne Leach

General and Administrative

IDG Books Worldwide, Inc.: John Kilcullen, CEO

IDG Books Technology Publishing Group: Richard Swadley, Senior Vice President and Publisher; Walter R. Bruce III, Vice President and Publisher; Joseph Wikert, Vice President and Publisher; Mary Bednarek, Vice President and Director, Product Development; Andy Cummings, Publishing Director, General User Group; Mary C. Corder, Editorial Director; Barry Pruett, Publishing Director

IDG Books Consumer Publishing Group: Roland Elgey, Senior Vice President and Publisher; Kathleen A. Welton, Vice President and Publisher; Kevin Thornton, Acquisitions Manager; Kristin A. Cocks, Editorial Director

IDG Books Internet Publishing Group: Brenda McLaughlin, Senior Vice President and Publisher; Sofia Marchant, Online Marketing Manager

IDG Books Production for Branded Press: Debbie Stailey, Director of Production; Cindy L. Phipps, Manager of Project Coordination, Production Proofreading, and Indexing; Tony Augsburger, Manager of Prepress, Reprints, and Systems; Laura Carpenter, Production Control Manager; Shelley Lea, Supervisor of Graphics and Design; Debbie J. Gates, Production Systems Specialist; Robert Springer, Supervisor of Proofreading; Trudy Coler, Page Layout Manager; Troy Barnes, Page Layout Supervisor, Kathie Schutte, Senior Page Layout Supervisor; Michael Sullivan, Production Supervisor

Packaging and Book Design: Patty Page, Manager, Promotions Marketing

♦

The publisher would like to give special thanks to Patrick J. McGovern, without whom this book would not have been possible.

♦

Contents at a Glance

Foreword .... *xxv*

Introduction 1

Part I: So You Want to Be a Manager? 7
Chapter 1: You're a Manager — Now What? 9
Chapter 2: Wake Up, Smell the Coffee, and Get Organized! 27
Chapter 3: Delegation: Getting Things Done without Getting Done In 47
Chapter 4: Lead, Follow, or Get Out of the Way 63

Part II: Managing: The People Part 77
Chapter 5: Hiring: The Million-Dollar Decision 79
Chapter 6: Inspiring Employees to Better Performance 95
Chapter 7: When in Doubt, Coach 109

Part III: Making Things Happen 119
Chapter 8: Goal-Setting Made Easy 121
Chapter 9: Measuring and Monitoring Individual Performance 137
Chapter 10: Performance Evaluations: Not Necessarily a Waste of Time 153

Part IV: Working with (Other) People 167
Chapter 11: Getting Your Message Across 169
Chapter 12: It's a Team Thing 189
Chapter 13: Politics in the Office 207

Part V: Tough Times for Tough Managers 227
Chapter 14: Keep Cool! Dealing with Change on the Job and the Stress It Creates 229
Chapter 15: Employee Discipline: Speak Softly and Carry a Big Stick 243
Chapter 16: Too Little, Too Late: Terminating Employees 257

Part VI: Tools and Techniques for Managing 269
Chapter 17: Budgeting, Accounting, and Other Money Stuff 271
Chapter 18: Harnessing the Power of Technology 291
Chapter 19: Developing and Mentoring Employees 303
Chapter 20: Quality and the Learning Organization 315

Part VII: The Part of Tens 329
Chapter 21: Ten Common Management Mistakes 331
Chapter 22: Ten Great No-Cost Ways to Recognize Employees 337
Chapter 23: Ten Classic Business Books You Need to Know About 341

Index 347

Cartoons at a Glance

By Rich Tennant

page 7

page 77

page 119

page 227

page 329

page 269

page 167

Fax: 978-546-7747

E-mail: richtennant@the5thwave.com

World Wide Web: www.the5thwave.com

Table of Contents

· ·

Foreword .... *xxv*

Introduction 1
   Why You Need This Book 1
   How to Use This Book 2
   How This Book Is Organized 3
      Part I: So You Want to Be a Manager? 3
      Part II: Managing: The People Part 3
      Part III: Making Things Happen 3
      Part IV: Working with (Other) People 3
      Part V: Tough Times for Tough Managers 4
      Part VI: Tools and Techniques for Managing 4
      Part VII: The Part of Tens 4
   Icons Used in This Book 4
   Where Do I Go from Here? 5

Part I: So You Want to Be a Manager? 7

Chapter 1: You're a Manager — Now What? 9
   The Different Styles of Management 9
      Tough guy management 10
      Nice guy management 11
      The ideal compromise 11
      Quick fixes don't stick 12
   The Management Challenge 14
      The old rules don't work anymore 15
      The new business environment 15
      It's a new army 17
      Trust is not a four-letter word 17
   The New Functions of Management 19
      Energize 19
      Empower 20
      Support 22
      Communicate 22
   Taking the First Steps toward Becoming a Manager 23
      Look and listen 24
      Do and learn 25

Chapter 2: Wake Up, Smell the Coffee, and Get Organized! **27**

What's That Mess on Your Desk? 27
Get Your Act Together — It All Starts with You! 28
Knowing What's Important and What's Not 30
Personal Planners: Fashion Statement or Necessity? 32
    The low-tech but reliable calendar 33
    The fashionable and functional daily planner 34
    The digital alternative 37
        The electronic organizer: a grown-up calculator or
            a downsized computer? 38
        Personal digital assistants: the future is here, now 39
        Computers: keeping you organized at home, in the office, and
            on the road 40
        When is a watch more than a watch? 42
    Choosing your personal planner 44
Getting a Jump on the Next Crisis 45

Chapter 3: Delegation: Getting Things Done without Getting Done In **47**

Delegating: The Manager's #1 Tool 48
Myths about Delegation 49
    Myth #1: You can't trust your employees to be responsible. 50
    Myth #2: When you delegate, you lose control of a task and
        its outcome. 50
    Myth #3: You are the only one who has all the answers. 51
    Myth #4: You can do the work faster by yourself. 52
    Myth #5: Delegation dilutes your authority. 52
    Myth #6: Your employees will be recognized for doing a good job,
        but you won't. 53
    Myth #7: Delegation decreases your flexibility. 53
    Myth #8: Your employees are too busy. 53
    Myth #9: Your workers don't see the big picture. 54
    You've got to trust your employees 54
The Six Steps of Delegating 55
Good and Bad Things to Delegate 56
    Always delegate these things 56
    Avoid delegating these things 58
        Personal assignments 59
        Confidential or sensitive circumstances 59
Checking Up Instead of Checking Out 59

Chapter 4: Lead, Follow, or Get Out of the Way **63**

The Differences between Management and Leadership 64
What Leaders Do 65
    Inspire action 65
    Communicate 66
    Support and facilitate 67

Leading Leadership Traits 68
    Optimism 70
    Confidence 70
    Integrity 71
    Decisiveness 72
Different Strokes for Different Folks: Situational Leadership 72
    Directing 73
    Coaching 73
    Supporting 74
    Delegating 75

Part II: Managing: The People Part 77

Chapter 5: Hiring: The Million-Dollar Decision 79

Defining the Characteristics of Your New Employees 80
Defining the Job Before You Start 81
Finding Good People 82
You Can Be the Greatest Interviewer in the World 84
    Asking the right questions 85
    Interviewing dos 86
    Interviewing don'ts 87
Evaluating Your Candidates 88
    Checking references 88
    Reviewing your notes 91
    Conducting a second (or third) round 91
Hiring the Best (and Leaving the Rest) 92
    Be objective 92
    Check your bias at the door 93
    Trust your gut 93
    After the offer 93

Chapter 6: Inspiring Employees to Better Performance 95

The Greatest Management Principle in the World 96
    It's not as simple as it looks 96
    Jellybean motivation 97
What Motivates Employees? 98
    Creating a supportive environment 99
    You've got to have a plan 100
What to Reward 101
Start with the Positive 102
Make a Big Deal about Little Things 103
Money Isn't Important (No, Really!) 104
    Compensation is a right 105
    When incentives become entitlements 105
    What motivates today's employees? 106
    You hold the key to your employees' motivation 108

Chapter 7: When in Doubt, Coach 109

Who's a Coach? 110
Coaching: The Short Lesson 112
Coaching: The Daily Search for Turning Points 113
  Making turning points into big successes 114
  Coaching your employees through their turning points 114
The Tools of the Coach 116
Coaching Metaphors for Success in Business 117

Part III: Making Things Happen *119*

Chapter 8: Goal-Setting Made Easy 121

If You Don't Know Where You're Going, How Will You Know
  When You Get There? 122
SMART Goals 124
Setting Goals: Less Is More 126
These Are the Goals (Pass Them On) 128
Juggling Priorities: Keeping Your Eye on the Ball 131
Using Your Power: Making Your Goals Happen 133

Chapter 9: Measuring and Monitoring Individual Performance 137

Keeping Your Eye on the Ball 138
Developing a System for Providing Immediate Performance Feedback 140
  Setting your checkpoints: the milestones 140
  Reaching your checkpoints: the actions 141
  Sequencing your activity: the relationships 142
  Establishing your time frame: the schedules 142
Putting Performance Measuring and Monitoring into Practice 143
  Case 1: World-class performance 143
  Case 2: Helping your employees give 100 percent 145
Gantts, PERTs, and Other Yardsticks 146
  Bar charts 147
  Flowcharts 148
  Software 149
You've Got Their Number: Now What? 150

**Chapter 10: Performance Evaluations: Not Necessarily
a Waste of Time** 153

Performance Evaluations: Why Bother? 154
Introducing Mr. Norms and Ms. Standards 155
The Performance Evaluation Process 157
Common Mistakes That Evaluators Make 159

Why Evaluations Go Bad 160
   Don't drop the ball 161
   Call 911: I've been mugged! 162
For the No-Surprises Evaluation: Prepare 163
Career Planning and Salary Discussions 163

Part IV: Working with (Other) People *167*

Chapter 11: Getting Your Message Across 169

Communication: The Cornerstone of Business 169
The Cutting Edge of Communication 171
   Faster, more flexible, and more competitive 173
   Faxes and electronic mail 174
   Portable computers and personal digital assistants 175
   Voice mail and pagers 176
   Cellular phones and personal toll-free numbers 177
   Videoconferencing and electronic meetings 178
Listening 179
The Power of the Written Word 181
Making Presentations 183
   Preparing to present 183
   A picture is worth a thousand words 184
   Making your presentation 187

Chapter 12: It's a Team Thing 189

The Obsolescence of Hierarchy 190
   The downsizing of corporate America 190
   The move to cooperation 192
Team Empowerment 193
   The value of an empowered workforce 193
   What about quality? 194
Advantages of Teams 194
   Smaller and nimbler 195
   Innovative and adaptable 195
Setting Up and Supporting Your Teams 196
   Formal teams 196
   Informal teams 197
   Self-managed teams 198
   The real world 199
   New technology and teams 200
Meetings: Putting Teams to Work 201
   Effective meetings pay off 202
   What's wrong with meetings? 203
   The eight keys to great meetings 204

Chapter 13: Politics in the Office **207**

Evaluating Your Political Environment 208
    Assessing your organization's political environment 208
    Identifying key players 210
    Redrawing your organization chart 211
Polishing Your Image 213
    Being rational 213
    Being someone who knows 214
    Avoiding emotional displays 215
Communication: What's Real and What's Not? 216
    Believing actions, not words 217
    Reading between the lines 217
    Probing for information 218
The Unwritten Rules of Organizational Politics 218
    Be friendly with all 219
    There's no interest like self-interest 220
    Don't party at company parties 221
    Manage your manager 222
    Move ahead with your mentors 223
    Be trustworthy 223
Protecting Yourself 224
    Document for protection 224
    Don't make promises you can't keep 224
    Be visible 225

Part V: Tough Times for Tough Managers *227*

**Chapter 14: Keep Cool! Dealing with Change on the Job
and the Stress It Creates** **229**

What's the Rush? 230
    Legitimate urgency versus crisis management 231
    Recognizing and dealing with crises 231
Change Happens 232
    The four stages of change 233
    Are you fighting change? 233
Identifying the Symptoms of Stress 236
Managing Your Stress 237
    Changing the things you can change 238
    Accepting the things you can't change 239
    Specific stress reduction exercises 241
When All Else Fails 242

Chapter 15: Employee Discipline: Speak Softly and Carry a Big Stick ... 243

Disciplining Employees 244
Focus on Performance, Not Personalities 246
The Two Tracks of Discipline 247
    Dealing with performance problems: the first track 248
    Dealing with misconduct: the second track 249
Disciplining Employees: A Suite in Four Parts 251
    Describe the unacceptable behavior 251
    Express the impact to the work unit 252
    Specify changes required 252
    Outline the consequences 253
    Putting it all together 253
Making a Plan for Improvement 254
Implementing the Improvement Plan 256

Chapter 16: Too Little, Too Late: Terminating Employees 257

Terminations for Every Occasion 258
    Voluntary terminations 258
    Involuntary terminations 259
        Good reasons for firing your employees 260
        Reasons why some managers avoid the inevitable 261
Conducting a Layoff 262
Warning: Before You Fire an Employee 264
The Big Day: Firing an Employee in Three Steps 266
When Is the Best Time to Terminate? 268

Part VI: Tools and Techniques for Managing 269

Chapter 17: Budgeting, Accounting, and Other Money Stuff 271

The Wonderful World of Budgets 272
Doing a Budget 273
Pulling Rabbits Out of Hats and Other Budget Tricks 276
    Up-front budget maneuvers 277
    Staying on budget 278
The Basics of Accounting 279
    The accounting equation 279
    Double-entry bookkeeping 283
The Most Common Financial Statements 283
    The balance sheet 285
    The income statement 285
    The cash flow statement 287

Chapter 18: Harnessing the Power of Technology 291

Computers: Where the Action Is 292
What do managers do with their computers? 292
Do computers really make your organization more efficient? 293
Parts Is Parts: It's What's Inside That Counts 295
Hardware: Those boxes with the blinking lights and buttons
you can push 295
Software: Those expensive boxes full of air and cheap plastic disks 296
Operating systems 296
Word processors 297
Spreadsheets 297
Personal information management software 297
Presentation software 298
Database programs 298
Communications 298
PC versus Mac 299
Let's Network! 299
Telecommuting: An Idea Whose Time Has Come? 300

Chapter 19: Developing and Mentoring Employees 303

Why Help Develop Your Employees? 304
Creating Career Development Plans 306
Helping Employees to Develop 308
Find a Mentor, Be a Mentor 311
Development and Downsizing 312

Chapter 20: Quality and the Learning Organization 315

The Quality Movement 316
Scientific management 317
Japan: the rising sun 318
Starting a quality improvement program 321
Systems Thinking 323
Obstacles to Learning 324
Creating a Learning Organization 327

Part VII: The Part of Tens *329*

Chapter 21: Ten Common Management Mistakes 331

Not Making the Transition from Worker to Manager 331
Failing to Delegate 332
Not Setting Goals with Employees 332
Failing to Communicate 332
Failing to Learn 333

Resisting Change 333
Not Making Time for Employees 334
Not Recognizing Employee Achievements 334
Going for the Quick Fix Over the Lasting Solution 335
Taking It All Too Seriously 335

Chapter 22: Ten Great No-Cost Ways to Recognize Employees 337

Interesting Work 337
Visibility 338
Time Off 338
Information 338
Feedback on Performance 339
Involvement 339
Independence 339
Celebrations 340
Flexibility 340
Increased Responsibility 340

Chapter 23: Ten Classic Business Books You Need to Know About 341

Managing for Results 341
The Human Side of Enterprise 341
The Peter Principle 342
Up the Organization 342
The One Minute Manager 342
In Search of Excellence 343
The Goal 343
Leadership Is an Art 344
The Fifth Discipline: The Art and Practice of the Learning Organization 344
The Wisdom of Teams 344
The Game of Work 345

Index 347

Foreword

· ·

*W*hen I first heard about *Managing For Dummies,* I have to admit that I was a bit apprehensive. After all, most of the managers I know are far from dummies. In fact, they tend to be highly educated, hard-working, and intelligent — not dumb by any stretch of the imagination.

Then I got a chance to see what was in the book, and my apprehension quickly shifted to enthusiasm. Here was the practice of management simplified to its essential ingredients, presented in a lively, fun, and practical format! This was one-stop shopping at its finest: a step-by-step guide for what you need, when you need it. I said to myself, "Finally, a book on managing that doesn't make you feel like an idiot!"

I suppose I shouldn't have been so surprised. After all, I have worked closely with Bob Nelson for over ten years and have seen firsthand his ability to build a team and get results. His knack for writing about managing in a clear and practical manner has always been evident — from his best-selling trade book on employee recognition, *1001 Ways to Reward Employees,* to his work as one of my coauthors on our recent textbook, *Exploring the World of Business.* Bob has a rare blend for a writer: He is both an astute observer of management *and* a skilled practitioner. You'll find the fruits of his labor with Peter Economy both insightful and highly practical. They have digested management practices, activities, and skills into a what-you-need-to-know, when-you-need-to-know-it format that both works and is fun in the process.

If clarity is a virtue, Bob and Peter should be the patron saints. They have demonstrated this fact and in the process taken the mystery out of managing. And not a minute too soon, given the complexity of the global business environment and the rapid change that is all around us today.

Thank you for this gift to managers everywhere! This is one book I will be delighted to give to those managers I most want to succeed.

— Ken Blanchard, coauthor
  The One Minute Manager

Introduction

$\bullet$

Congratulations! As a result of your astute choice of material, you are about to read a completely fresh approach to the topic of management. If you have already read other books about management, you have surely noticed that most of them fall into one of two categories: (1) deadly boring snooze-o-rama that makes a great paperweight, or (2) recycled platitudes glazed with a thin sugar-coating of pop psychobabble, which sounds great on paper but fails abysmally in the real world.

Managing For Dummies is different. First, this book is *fun*. Our approach reflects our strong belief and experience that management can be fun, too. You can get the job done and have fun in the process. We even help you to maintain a sense of humor in the face of the seemingly insurmountable challenges that all managers have to deal with from time to time. On some days, you *will* be challenged — perhaps to your limit or beyond. However, on many *more* days, the joys of managing (teaching a new skill to an employee, helping land a new customer, accomplishing an important assignment, and so on) will bring you a sense of fulfillment that you never imagined possible.

Second, popular business books seem to be here today and gone tomorrow. Like it or not, many managers (and the companies they work for) seem to be ruled by the business fad-of-the-month. In *Managing For Dummies,* we buck the trend by concentrating on tried-and-true solutions to the most common situations that *real* supervisors and managers face: solutions that stand up over time and can be used in turbulent times. You'll find no mumbo-jumbo here — just practical solutions to everyday problems.

Managing For Dummies breaks the rules. It provides a comprehensive overview of the fundamentals of effective management presented in a fun and interesting format. It neither puts you to sleep nor is so sugarcoated that it rots your teeth. We know from personal experience that managing can be an intimidating job. New managers — especially ones promoted into the position for their technical expertise — are often at a loss as to what they need to do. Don't worry. Relax. Help is at your fingertips.

Why You Need This Book

Why *Managing For Dummies*? To that, we respond that *all* managers (and those of you who are already managers know that we're telling the truth) feel like dummies from time to time.

For Bob, it was when he was giving an important business presentation before a group of international executives — only to be told by one of the executives that his pants zipper was unzipped. Although Bob *did* score bonus points for getting his audience's attention with this novel fashion statement, he could have done so in a more conventional way.

For Peter, it was when he reprimanded an employee for arriving late to work and later learned that the employee was late because she had stopped at a bakery on the way to work to buy Peter a cake in celebration of Boss's Day. Needless to say, the event wasn't *quite* as festive as it could have been!

Face it: Whether you're new to the job or are faced with a new task in an old job, all managers feel overwhelmed sometimes. The secret to dealing with such feelings is to discover what you can do better (or differently) to obtain the results you want, and when you do make a mistake, pick yourself up, laugh it off, and learn from it. We wrote this book to make learning easier so that *you* won't have to learn the hard way.

How to Use This Book

Despite the obvious resemblance of this book to one of the yellow bricks on Dorothy's road to Oz, the proper way to use this book is not as a doorstop or as a makeshift paperweight. You can use this book in one of two ways:

- ✔ If you want to learn about a specific topic, such as delegating tasks or hiring employees, you can flip to that section and get your answers quickly. Faster than you can say "Where's that report I asked for last week?" you'll have your answer.

- ✔ If you want a crash course in management, read this book from cover to cover. Forget going back to school to get your MBA — you can save your money and take a trip to the Bahamas instead. It's all right here. Honest.

Managing For Dummies is perfect for all levels of managers. You new managers and managers-to-be can find everything you need to know to be successful. You experienced managers are challenged to shift your perspectives and to take a fresh look at your management philosophies and techniques. Despite the popular saying about teaching old dogs new tricks, it's never too late to make changes that make your job — and the jobs of your employees — a little bit easier, a little bit more fun, and a *lot* more effective.

How This Book Is Organized

Managing For Dummies is organized into seven parts. The chapters within each part cover specific topics in detail. You can read each chapter without having to read what comes before. Or you can read each chapter without reading what comes after. Or you can read the book backwards or forwards. Or you can just carry it around with you to impress your friends.

Each part covers a major area of management practice. Following is a summary of what you'll find in each part.

Part I: So You Want to Be a Manager?

Successful managers master several basic skills. This part begins with a discussion of what managers are and what they do, and then it looks at the most basic management skills: organization, delegation, and leadership.

Part II: Managing: The People Part

The heart of management boils down to getting things done through others. This process starts with hiring talented workers and extends to motivating and coaching them to go above and beyond expectations.

Part III: Making Things Happen

Making things happen is another important aspect of managing that starts with knowing where you're going and how to tell when you've arrived. In this part, we consider goal-setting, measuring and monitoring employee performance, and conducting performance appraisals.

Part IV: Working with (Other) People

Successful managers have learned that building bridges to other workers and managers — both inside and outside the organization — is important. This part covers communicating, making presentations, building high-performance teams, and dealing with office politics.

Part V: Tough Times for Tough Managers

As any manager can testify, management is not all fun and games. In fact, managing can be downright difficult at times. In this part, we consider some of the toughest tasks of managing: handling change and stress, disciplining employees, and firing employees.

Part VI: Tools and Techniques for Managing

Being a manager requires that you learn and apply certain technical tools and skills. This part discusses guidelines for accounting and budgeting and working with today's technologies.

The most successful managers know that standing still in business is the same as falling behind. Good managers *always* look to the future and make plans accordingly. Developing and training employees and creating a learning workplace are also covered in this part.

Part VII: The Part of Tens

Finally, we include the Part of Tens: a quick-and-dirty collection of chapters that give you ten (or so) pieces of information that every manager needs to know. Look to these chapters when you need a quick refresher on managing strategies and techniques.

Icons Used in This Book

To guide you along the way and point out the information you really need to know, this book uses icons along its left margins. You'll see the following icons in this book:

This icon points to tips and tricks that make managing easier.

If you don't heed the advice next to these icons, the situation may blow up in your face. Watch out!

Remember these important points of information, and you'll be a much better manager.

This icon points out wise sayings and other kernels of wisdom that you can take with you on your journey to becoming a better manager.

Always keep these general rules of management in mind.

This icon flags sidebars (those gray boxes) that give you a mini-quiz on the topics presented in each chapter. If you read a whole chapter and want to see whether you picked up the main points, look to these sections.

We know that not every manager is technically adept — and many of you probably don't care to be, either. But because technology is revolutionizing the business world, you may need to know this stuff someday.

These anecdotes from Bob and Peter and other real-life managers show you the right — and sometimes wrong — way to be a manager.

Where Do I Go from Here?

If you are a new or aspiring manager, you may want to start at the beginning (isn't *that* a novel concept?) and work your way through to the end. Simply turn the page and take your first step into the world of management.

If you are already a manager and are short of time (and what manager *isn't* short of time?), you may want to turn to a particular topic to address a specific need or question. The Table of Contents gives a chapter-by-chapter description of the topics in this book. You can also find specific topics in the index.

Enjoy your journey!

Part I
So You Want to Be a Manager?

The 5th Wave   By Rich Tennant

"His only drawback as a manager was his inability to delegate."

In this part . . .

Before you can become an effective manager, you need to master some basic skills. In this part, we cover some of the most important managing skills, including getting organized, delegating tasks to employees, and becoming a leader.

Chapter 1

You're a Manager — Now What?

· ·

In This Chapter

▶ Figuring out what the heck management is

▶ Moving from a doer to a manager of doers in the new global business environment

▶ Understanding the changing workforce

▶ Defining the key functions of management

▶ Taking the first steps toward becoming a manager

· ·

Congratulations! Because you're reading this book, it's probably safe to assume that you are (1) a manager, (2) a manager-to-be, or (3) an individual who is uncontrollably attracted to books with bright yellow and black covers. Of course, if you are simply curious and want to learn the intimate details about the kinds of management techniques that can help you get the best from your employees every day of the week, then welcome!

Managing is truly a calling — one that the authors as managers are proud to have answered. *We're the few. The proud. The managers.* In the world of business, no place else can you have such a direct, dramatic, and positive impact on the lives of others and on the ultimate success of your enterprise. (Except, perhaps, for the guy who is in charge of fixing the Xerox machine.)

The Different Styles of Management

One definition describes management as *getting things done through others.* Another definition more specifically defines management as *making something planned happen within a specific area through the use of available resources.* Seems simple enough. If it's so simple, however, why do so many bright, industrious people have trouble managing well? And why do so many companies today seem to offer a flavor-of-the-month training program? How often have you been introduced to some hot new management concept — guaranteed to turn your organization around in no time flat — only to watch it fade away within a few months, if not sooner? Of course, as soon as one management fad disappears, another is waiting in the wings to replace it.

What? You didn't catch onto that concept of Quality Circles? That's okay — we decided that they don't really work anyway. Now, we want you to pay close attention to this video on the Science of Chaos — it's the latest thing. The big guy read an article about it in The Wall Street Journal *and wants us to implement it throughout our North American operations right away!*

Unfortunately, good management is a scarce commodity — at once precious and fleeting. Despite years of evolution of management theory and the comings and goings of countless management fads, many workers — and managers, for that matter — have developed a distorted view of management and its practice, with managers often not knowing what to do. As the saying goes, "If it's foggy in the pulpit, it'll be cloudy in the pew."

Have you ever heard any of the following statements at your office or place of business?

- ✔ We don't have the authority to make that decision.

- ✔ She's in charge of the department — fixing the problem is her responsibility, not ours.

- ✔ Why do they keep asking us what we think when they never use anything we say?

- ✔ I'm sorry, but that's our policy. We're not allowed to make exceptions.

- ✔ If my manager doesn't care, I don't either.

- ✔ Working hard here doesn't get you anywhere faster.

- ✔ You can't trust those employees — they just want to goof off.

When you hear these types of statements in the hallway or restroom, after another boring meeting, or at the end of a long day, red lights should be flashing before your eyes, and alarm bells should be ringing in your ears. Statements like this indicate that managers and employees are not communicating effectively, and that employees lack confidence in their managers. If you're lucky, people report these kinds of problems to you while you still have a chance to do something about them. If you're not so lucky, they don't bother — and you're stuck making the same mistakes over and over.

The expectations and commitments that employees carry with them on the job are in large part a product of the way that their managers treat them. Following are the most commonly adopted styles of management. Do you recognize *your* management style?

Tough guy management

What is the best way to make something planned happen? Everyone seems to have a different answer to this question. Some people see management as something you do *to* people — not *with* them. You've probably heard the rallying cry of this kind of manager: "I don't care if you like it or not — that's the way we're going to do it. Understand?" Or perhaps the ever-popular threat: "It had better be on my desk by the end of the day — or else!" If worse comes to worst, a manager can unveil the ultimate weapon, "Mess up one more time, and I'm going to transfer you to Siberia!"

This type of management is often known as *Theory X management,* which assumes that people are inherently lazy and need to be driven to perform. Managing by fear and intimidation is always guaranteed to get a response. The question is, do you get the kind of response that you really want? (***Hint:*** The answer starts with the letter *N.*) When you closely monitor your employees' work, you usually end up with only short-term compliance. In other words, you'll never get the best from others by building a fire under them — you have to find a way to build a fire within them.

Sometimes managers *have* to take command of the situation. If the building is on fire, for example, you're not going to call a meeting to decide who's going to put it out. By the time you can find an opening in everyone's schedule, the building will be nothing but a burned-out shell. Similarly, if a proposal has to go out in FedEx in an hour and your customer just sent you some important changes, you should take charge of the situation to ensure that the right people are on the task — that is, if you're serious about keeping your customer.

Nice guy management

At the other end of the spectrum, some people see management as a nice-guy kind of thing. *Theory Y management* assumes that people basically want to do a good job. In the extreme interpretation of this theory, managers are supposed to be sensitive to the *feelings* of their employees and be careful not to do anything that might disturb their employees' tranquillity and sense of self-worth. *Uh, there's this little problem with your report; none of the numbers are correct. Now, don't take this personally, but we need to consider our alternatives for taking a more careful look at these figures in the future.* Again, managers might get a response with this approach (or they might choose to do the work themselves!), but are they likely to get the *best* possible response? They're more likely to come to be taken advantage of.

The ideal compromise

Good managers realize that they don't have to be tough guys all the time — and that nice guys often finish first. If your employees are diligently performing their assigned tasks and no business emergency requires your immediate intervention, you can step back and let them do their jobs. Not only do your employees learn to be responsible, but *you* are able to concentrate your efforts on the things that are most important to the bottom-line success of your organization.

The *real* job of a manager is to inspire employees to be their best and establish a working environment that allows them to be their best. The best managers make every possible effort to remove the organizational obstacles that prevent employees from doing their jobs and to obtain the resources and training that employees need to do their jobs effectively. All other goals — no matter how lofty or pressing — must take a back seat.

Bad systems, bad policies, bad procedures, and poor treatment of others are organizational weaknesses that managers must be talented at identifying and repairing or replacing. Build a strong organizational foundation for your employees. Support your people, and they will support you. Time and time again, when given the opportunity to achieve, workers in all kinds of businesses — from factories to venture capital firms — have proven this rule to be true. If you haven't seen it at *your* place of business, you may be mistaking your employees for problems. Quit squeezing *them* and start squeezing your organization. The result is employees who want to succeed and a business that flourishes right along with them. Who knows, your employees might even stop hiding when they see you coming their way!

Squeezing employees may be easier than fighting the convoluted systems and cutting through the bureaucratic barnacles that have grown on your organization. You may be tempted to yell, "It's your fault that our department didn't achieve its goals!" Yes, blaming your employees for the organization's problems may be tempting, but doing so isn't going to solve the problems. Sure, you might get a quick, short-lived response when you push your people, but ultimately, you are failing to deal with the organization's *real* problems.

Quick fixes don't stick

Despite what many people would have you believe, management is not prone to simple solutions or quick fixes. Being a manager is *not* simple. Yes, the best management solutions tend to be common sense; however, turning common sense into common *practice* is difficult.

Management is an attitude — a way of life. It's a very real desire to work with people and help them succeed, as well as a desire to help your organization succeed. Management is a life-long learning process that doesn't end when you walk out of a one-hour seminar or finish viewing a 25-minute video. It's like the old story about the happy homeowner who was shocked to receive a bill for $100 to fix a leaky faucet. When asked to explain the basis for this seemingly high charge, the plumber said, "Tightening the nut cost you $5. Knowing which nut to tighten cost you $95!"

Management is a *people* job. If you're not up to the task of working with people — helping them, listening to them, encouraging them, and guiding them — then you shouldn't be a manager.

Because management is such a challenge, management training often focuses on creating instant gratification among the attendees, many of whom have spent hundreds — even thousands — of dollars to be there. "Let's give them so much stuff to use that it will be their fault if they never use any of it!"

Once, Peter went to one of those touchy-feely offsite management meetings meant to build teamwork and communication among the members of the group. Picture this: Just after lunch, a big tray of leftover veggies, bagels, fruit, and such was sitting on a table at the side of the room. The facilitator rose from his chair, faced the group, and said, "Your next task is to split yourselves into four groups and construct a model of the perfect manager by using only the items on that tray of leftovers." A collective groan filled the room. "I don't want to hear any complaints," the trainer said. "I just want to see happy people doing happy things for the next half-hour."

The teams feverishly went about their task of building the perfect manager. With some managers barely throttling the temptation to engage each other in a massive food fight, the little figures began to take shape. A banana here, a carrot stick there . . . and voilà! After a brief competition for dominance, the winners were crowned. The result? We thought you would never ask. Check out Figure 1-1.

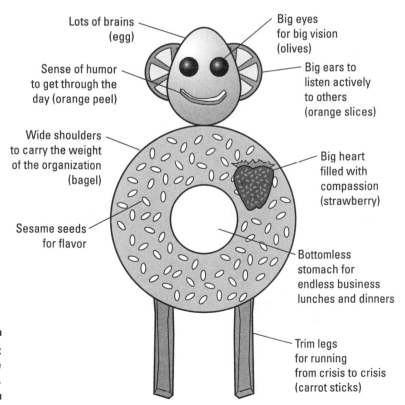

Lots of brains
(egg)

Big eyes
for big vision
(olives)

Sense of humor
to get through the
day (orange peel)

Big ears to
listen actively
to others
(orange slices)

Wide shoulders
to carry the weight
of the organization
(bagel)

Big heart
filled with
compassion
(strawberry)

Sesame seeds
for flavor

Bottomless
stomach for
endless business
lunches and dinners

Figure 1-1:
The veggie
manager.

Trim legs
for running
from crisis to crisis
(carrot sticks)

We have to admit that the result was kind of cute (and kind of tasty, too), but did it really make a difference in the way in which these managers managed their employees when they returned to the office the next day? We don't think so. A nice break from the day-to-day office routine, yes. A meaningful teaching tool with lasting impact, no.

The Management Challenge

When you are assigned a task in a non-management position, completing it by yourself is fairly simple and straightforward. Your immediate results are in direct response to your effort. To accomplish your task, you first review the task, then you decide how best to accomplish it, and then you set schedules and milestones for its successful completion. Assuming that you have access to the tools and resources necessary to accomplish your task, you can probably do it yourself quickly and easily. You are an expert *doer:* a bright, get-things-done type of person.

If you hold a management position, however, you were probably selected because you proved yourself to be very skilled in the areas that you are now responsible for managing. Peter's friend John, for example, was a member of a team of software programmers developing an application for a hand-held computer. When he was a member of the team, everything was fine. He came to work in a T-shirt and jeans — just like the rest of his teammates — and often spent time with his programmer friends after hours. The bond that the team shared changed, however, when John was selected to manage the team.

In his new role of manager, John first changed offices. Instead of sharing an open bay with the other programmers, he moved into his very own office. A secretary was assigned to guard his door. Of course, the jeans and T-shirt had to go — they were replaced with a business suit and tie. Instead of having fun programming, John was now concerned about more serious topics such as cost overruns, schedule delays, and returns on investments. As John's role changed, so did John. And as John changed, so did his relationship with his coworkers. To achieve his goals, John quickly had to make the transition from a doer to a manager of doers.

When you want to get a task done through someone else, you employ an entirely different set of skills than when you do the task yourself. All of a sudden, because of this simple decision to pass the responsibility for comple-tion of a task on to someone else, you introduce an *interpersonal* element into your equation. *Oh, no! You mean I have to actually work with people?* Being good technically at your job is not enough — no matter how good your technical skills are. Now you have to have good planning skills, organization skills, leadership skills, and follow-up skills.

In other words, in addition to being a good doer, you have to be a good *manager* of doers.

The old rules don't work anymore

If this challenge isn't already enough, managers today face yet another challenge — one that has shaken the very foundations of modern business. The new reality is the partnership of managers and workers in the workplace.

The old model of business consists of managers and workers, period, which makes management a pretty straightforward proposition. In this model, the job of the manager is to divide the company's work into discrete tasks, assign the work to individual workers, and then closely monitor the performance of the workers and steer them toward accomplishing their tasks on time and within budget. The old reality of management relies on fear, intimidation, and power over people to accomplish goals. If things aren't going according to management's plan, then management commands its way out of the problem: "I don't care what you have to do to get it done — just get it done. Now!" The line between managers and workers is drawn clearly and drawn often.

The new business environment

What's going on inside the organization is a reflection of what's going on outside the organization. The following factors are creating rapid and constant change in today's new business environment:

- A surge of global competition
- New technology and innovation
- The flattening of organizational hierarchies
- Widespread downsizing, reengineering, and layoffs
- The rise of small business
- The changing values of today's workers
- The increasing demands for ever-better customer service

Sure, managers still have to divide and assign work, but workers are taking on more of that responsibility themselves. Most importantly, managers are learning that they can't *command* an employee's best work — they have to create an environment that fosters their employees' *desire* to do their best work. In short, the new reality is the partnership of managers and workers in the workplace.

Watch out! Technology explosion ahead!

In the new world of information technology, the old ways of doing business are being turned on their sides. With the advent of computer networks, e-mail, and voice mail, the walls that divide individuals, departments, and organizational units are crashing down. In the words of Frederick Kovac, vice president of planning for the Goodyear Tire and Rubber Company, "It used to be, if you wanted information, you had to go up, over, and down through the organization. Now you just tap in. Everybody can know as much about the company as the chairman of the board."

(Source: *Fortune*, Dec. 13, 1993.)

Some of you may recall the words of folk singer and former weather vane of the American social fabric, Bob Dylan. In his song *Ballad of a Thin Man,* Dylan reflected on the changes swirling all around his generation in the '60s.

Similarly, the landscape of American business has changed dramatically over the past couple of decades. If you don't change with it, you are going to be left far behind your competitors. You may think that you can get away with treating your employees like "human assets" or children, but you can't. You can't because your competitors are learning how to unleash the hidden power of their employees. They're no longer just *talking* about it; they're *doing* it! Consider what these business leaders say:

- When asked how Chrysler managed to increase earnings by 246 percent to $3.7 billion, chief executive officer Robert Eaton said, "If I had to use one word, it's empowerment. When decisions are made, they're made by somebody down in the organization who knows a helluva lot more about the issue than I do" (*Fortune,* Mar. 20, 1995).

- Federal Express vice president Dave Rebholz attributes his company's success to its focus on people. "Each and every employee of Federal Express is given the opportunity to be what they dream to be. Federal Express goes to great lengths to make sure people understand that" (*Marketing News,* Aug. 19, 1991).

- Darryl Hartley Leonard, president of Hyatt Hotels Corporation, puts it in more basic terms: "Empowerment is the recognition that employees are not as dumb as employers thought they were" (*The Wall Street Journal,* Mar. 5, 1993).

It's a new army

Bob recently made a presentation to a group of managers in northern California. As he was wrapping up his presentation, he opened the floor to questions. A hand shot up. "With all the downsizing and layoffs that we've endured, people are lucky to get a paycheck, much less anything else. Why do we have to bother to empower and reward employees?" Before Bob had a chance to respond, another manager in the audience shot back, "Because it's a new army."

This response really sums it all up. In business, times are changing. Now that employees have tasted the sweet nectar of empowerment, there's no turning back. Companies that stick with the old way of doing business — the hierarchical, highly centralized model — will lose employees and customers to those companies that institutionalize the new ways of doing business and make them a part of their corporate culture. The best employees will leave the old-model companies in droves, seeking employers who treat them with respect and are willing to grant them greater autonomy and responsibility.

That leaves *you* with the employees who don't want to take risks or rock the boat. You get the yes-men and yes-women. No one will challenge your ideas because they are afraid to. No one will suggest better or more efficient ways to do business because they know that you won't listen or care anyway. Your employees won't bother to go out of their way to help a customer because you don't trust them to make the most basic decisions — the ones that can make the biggest difference to the satisfaction, or the lack thereof, of your precious customers.

Imagine the difference between an employee who tells your key customer, "Sorry, my hands are tied. I am not allowed to make any exceptions to our policies," and the employee who tells that customer, "Sure, I'll do everything in my power to get you your order by your deadline." Whom do you think your customers prefer to do business with? Whom would *you* prefer to do business with? (**Hint:** Don't even *think* about the first alternative!)

Managers used to *rent* behavior. Some workers used to be called "hired hands." Today, hiring your hands is not good enough. You must find a way to capture their souls and bring their best efforts to the workplace each and every day.

Trust is not a four-letter word

Management expert Tom Peters has built an entire industry around the telling and retelling of customer service success stories. His tales of exceptional customer service are legendary. Nordstrom, Union Pacific Railroad, 3M, and many other companies have been the subject of Peters's books. Each tale of success shows certain common characteristics.

Companies that provide exceptional customer service unleash their employees from the constraints of an overly controlling hierarchy and allow front-line workers to serve their customers directly and efficiently. For example, while many companies devote forests of paper to employee manuals, Nordstrom, Inc., devotes exactly one page to its manual. Figure 1-2 shows you what is on that page.

We're glad to have you with our Company. Our number one goal is to provide outstanding customer service.

Set both your personal and professional goals high.

Nordstrom Rules:

Rule #1: Use your good judgment in all situations.

There will be no additional rules. Please feel free to ask your department manager, store manager, or division general manager any question at any time.

Figure 1-2:
Nordstrom's employee manual shows an exceptional amount of trust in employees.

(Source: *Business and Society Review,* Spring 1993, n85)

You may think that a *small* company with five or ten employees can get away with a policy like that, but certainly not a big company like yours. However, Nordstrom is not a small business by any stretch of the imagination — unless you consider a company with 42,000 or so employees and more than $5 billion in sales last year small.

How does management at a large business like Nordstrom get away with such a policy? They do it through trust.

First, they hire good people. Then they give them the training and tools to do their jobs well. Then they get out of the way and let their employees do their work. Nordstrom knows that they can trust their employees to make the right decisions because they know that they have hired the right people for the job and have trained them well.

We're not saying that Nordstrom doesn't have problems — every company does. But they've taken a proactive stance in creating the environment that employees most need and want.

Can you say the same for your organization?

When you trust your employees, they respond by being trustworthy. When you recognize them for being independent and responsive to their customers, they *continue* to be independent and responsive to their customers. And when you give them the freedom to make their own decisions, they *do* make their own decisions. With a little training and a lot of support, these decisions are in the best interests of the company because they are made by the right people at right level of the organization.

The New Functions of Management

Remember the four "classic" functions of management — plan, organize, lead, and control — that you learned in school? These management functions form the foundation from which every manager works. Although these basic functions are fine for taking care of most of your day-to-day management duties, they fail to reflect the new reality of the workplace and the new partnership of managers and workers. What is needed is a new set of management functions that builds upon the four classic functions of management. You're in luck. In the sections that follow, we describe the functions of the new manager in the workplace of the 21st century.

Energize

Today's managers are masters of *making things happen* — starting with themselves. *If it's to be, it's to begin with me.* Think of the best managers you know. What one quality sets them apart from the rest? Is it their organizational skills, their fairness, or their technical ability? Perhaps it's their ability to delegate or the long hours that they keep.

While all these traits may be important to a manager's success, we have not yet named the unique quality that makes a good manager great. This most important management function is to get people excited and inspired.

You can be the best analyst in the world, the most highly organized executive on the planet, or fair beyond reproach, but if the level of excitement that you generate can be likened more to that of a dish rag than to that of a spark plug, then you will always be handicapped in your efforts to create a truly *great* organization. ("Everyone follow me!" she said as her staff went back to sleep.)

Great managers create far more energy than they consume. The best managers are organizational catalysts. Instead of taking energy *from* an organization, they channel and amplify it *to* the organization. In every interaction, effective managers take the natural energy of their employees, add to it, and leave the employees in a higher energy state than when they started the interaction. Management becomes a process of transmitting the excitement that you feel about your organization and its goals to your employees in terms that they can understand and appreciate. Before you know it, your employees will be as excited about the organization as you are, and you can simply allow their energy to carry you forward.

It's said that a picture is worth a thousand words. This statement is as true for the pictures that you paint in the minds of others as it is for the pictures that people paint on canvas or print on the pages of magazines and books. Imagine taking a vacation with your family or friends. As the big day draws near, you keep the goal exciting and fresh in the minds of your family or friends by creating a vision of the journey that awaits you. Vivid descriptions of white sand beaches, towering redwoods, glittering skylines, secluded lakes, hot food, and indoor plumbing paint pictures in the minds of each of your fellow travelers. With this vision in mind, everyone works toward a common goal of having a successful vacation.

Successful managers create compelling visions — pictures of a future organization that inspire and compel employees to bring out their very best performance.

Empower

Have you ever worked for someone who didn't let you do your job without questioning your every decision? Maybe you spent all weekend working on a special project only to have it casually discarded by your boss. "What were you thinking when you did this, Elizabeth? Our customers will never buy into that approach!" Or maybe you went out of your way to help a customer, accepting a return shipment of an item against company policy. "Why do you think we have policies — because we enjoy killing trees? No! If we made exceptions for everyone, we'd go out of business!" How did it feel to have your sincere efforts at doing a great job disparaged? What was your reaction? Chances are, you didn't bother making the extra effort again.

Despite rumors to the contrary, when you empower your employees, you do not stop managing. What changes is the *way* you manage. Managers still provide vision, establish organizational goals, and determine shared values. However, managers must establish a corporate infrastructure — skills training, teams, and so forth — that supports empowerment. And although all your employees may not *want* to be empowered, you still have to provide an environment that supports those employees who *are* eager for a taste of the sweet nectar that comes along with the freedom to apply their personal creativity and expertise to your organization.

What managers really do

With tongue planted firmly in cheek, we pretty much universally agree that all managers perform five functions in an organization. These five functions are as follows:

- **Eat:** Management clearly has its rewards, one of which is an expense account and all the company-paid lunches and dinners you can get away with. And if those yo-yos in accounting dare to question the business purpose of your meals, you can always threaten to leave them off your list of invitees.

- **Meet:** Meetings are truly a perk of management. The higher you rise in an organization, the more time you spend in meetings. Instead of doing productive work, you now spend more time than ever listening to presentations that have no relevance to your department, drinking three-day-old coffee, and keeping close tabs on your watch as your meeting drags on and on — well past its scheduled ending time.

- **Punish:** With so many wayward employees, the best managers learn to punish early and punish often. What better way to show your employees that you care? Punishment also sends a welcome signal to upper management that you will not put up with any nonsense from your employees.

- **Obstruct:** When you ask managers what single achievement makes them most proud, they are likely to bring out policies as thick as the Yellow Pages that were carefully drafted over many years. A close look at the policy might reveal a package of deftly written red tape that does more to prevent good customer service than it does to support it.

- **Obscure:** Managers are masters at the art of miscommunication. No one knows better than a manager that information is power, that an individual who has it has the power, and that an individual who doesn't have it is lost. With potential enemies all around, why give anyone else a chance to get an advantage over you? "Hey! That information is on a need-to-know basis only!" And for heaven's sake, why let your employees in on the inner workings of the organization? They wouldn't appreciate or understand it anyway, right?

Actually, this *isn't* the list of the functions of management. While the list may ring true in many cases, we were just pulling your leg.

Great managers *allow* their employees to do great work. This is a vital function of management, for even the greatest managers in the world can't succeed all by themselves. To achieve the goals of the organization, managers depend on the skills that their employees offer. Effective management is the leveraging of the efforts of every member of a work unit towards a common purpose. If you are constantly doing your employees' work for them, not only have you lost the advantage of the leverage that your employees can provide you, but you are also putting yourself on the path to stress, ulcers, and worse.

However, far worse than the personal loss that you suffer when you don't empower employees is that everyone in your organization loses. Your employees lose because you aren't allowing them to stretch themselves or to show creativity or initiative. Your organization loses the insights that its creative workforce brings with it. Finally, your customers lose because your employees are afraid to provide them with exceptional service. Why should they?

Support

For a long time, the job of managers was to give orders, see that they were followed, and hold people accountable if they didn't comply. Now, all that is changing. A manager's job is no longer that of a watchdog, police officer, or executioner. Increasingly, managers must be coaches, colleagues, and cheer-leaders for the employees they support. The main concern of today's managers needs to be shaping a more supportive work environment that enables each employee to feel valued and be more productive.

When the going gets tough, managers support their employees. Now, this doesn't mean that you do everything for your employees or make their deci-sions for them. It does mean that you give your employees the training, re-sources, and authority to do their jobs, and then you get out of the way. You're always there for your employees to help pick up the pieces if they fall, but fall they must if they are going to learn. The idea is the same as learning to skate: If you're not falling, you're not learning.

The key to creating a supportive environment is establishing *openness* through-out an organization. In an open environment, employees can bring up questions and concerns — in fact, they are encouraged to do so. When the environment is truly open, an individual can express concerns without fear of retribution. Hidden agendas do not exist, and people feel free to say the same things in business meetings that they would say after work. When employees see that their managers are receptive to new ideas, they are more likely to think of more and better ways to improve systems, solve problems, save money, and so forth.

Managers also support each other. Personal fiefdoms, fighting between depart-ments, and withholding information have no place in the modern organization; companies can no longer afford to support these dysfunctional behaviors. All members of the organization — from the top to the bottom — must realize that they play on the same team. To win, team members support each other and keep their coworkers apprised of the latest information. Which team are *you* on?

Communicate

Without a doubt, communication is the lifeblood of any organization, and managers are the element that connects different levels. We have seen firsthand the positive effects on a business and its employees of managers who communi-cate, and the negative effects on a business and its employees of managers who don't. Imagine a football quarterback trying to get the offense to the goal line without calling a play. What would happen after he hiked the ball? Probably nothing — or utter chaos.

Managers who don't communicate effectively are missing out on a vital role of management.

Communication is a key function for managers today. Information is power, and as the speed of business accelerates, information *must* be communicated to employees faster than ever. Constant change and increasing turbulence in the business environment necessitate more communication, not less. Who'll be around five years from now: The manager who has mastered this function or the one who has not?

With the proliferation of e-mail, voice mail, and the other new means of communication in modern business, managers have simply no excuse not to communicate with their employees. Heck, you can even use the telephone or try a little old-fashioned face-to-face talk with your employees and coworkers.

To meet the expectations that you set for them, your employees have to be *aware* of your expectations. A goal is great on paper, but if you don't communicate it to employees and don't keep them up to date on their progress toward achieving that goal, how can you expect them to reach it? Simply, you can't. It would be like training for the Olympics but never being given feedback on how you are doing.

In management, as in life in general, the little things count: An invitation to an upcoming meeting, praise for a job well done, or an insight into the organization's finances. Not only does sharing this kind of information make a business run better, but it also creates tremendous good will and cements the trust that bonds your employees to the organization and to the successful completion of the organization's goals.

Taking the First Steps toward Becoming a Manager

Every manager has faced this problem at one time or another: How do you know the right and wrong ways to manage in this brave new business world?

Believe it or not, many managers are never formally trained to be managers. For many of you, management is just something that is added to your job description. One day, you might be a computer programmer working on a hot new Web browser, and the next day you may be in charge of the new development team. Before, you were expected only to show up to work and create a product. Now you are expected to lead and motivate a group of workers toward a common goal. Sure, you may get paid more to do the job, but the only training you may get for the task is in the school of hard knocks.

Managers (or managers-to-be) can easily learn how to become good managers by following the recommendations in the sections that follow. No one way is absolutely right or absolutely wrong; each has its pluses and minuses.

Look and listen

If you are fortunate enough to have skilled teachers or mentors during the course of your career — people to take you under their wings — you are treated to an education in management that is equal to or better than *any* MBA program. You learn firsthand the right *and* wrong ways to manage people. You learn what it takes to get things done in *your* organization, and you learn that customer satisfaction involves more than simply giving your customers lip service.

Unfortunately, any organization with good management also has living, breathing examples of the *wrong* way to manage employees. You know who we're talking about: the manager who refuses to make decisions, leaving employees and customers hanging. Or the boss who refuses to delegate even the simplest decision to employees. Or the supervisor who insists on managing every aspect of a department — no matter how small or inconsequential: "No, no, no! The stamp goes on the envelope first, and then the address label — not the other way around!" Examples of the *right* way to manage employees are, regrettably, still few and far between.

You can benefit from the behaviors that poor managers model, however. When you find a manager who refuses to make decisions, for example, carefully note the impact that this management style has on workers, other managers, and customers. You can feel your own frustration and make a mental note that says something like, *I'll never, ever demotivate another person like that.* Indecision at the top inevitably leads to indecision within all ranks of an organization — especially when employees are punished for filling the vacuum left by indecisive managers. Employees become confused, and customers become concerned as the organization drifts aimlessly. There are lessons to learn here.

I meet, you meet, we all meet

According to the experts at this sort of thing, managers are attending more meetings than ever. While meetings take up more than 25 percent of an average business person's time, this figure rises to 40 percent for middle managers and up to a staggering 80 percent for executives. What's even more shocking is that about half of every hour spent in meetings is wasted due to the inefficiency and ineffectiveness of the participants.

A world-class teacher

By many measures, Jack Welch is considered to be one of American business's top chief executive officers. Welch, who heads General Electric, has radically transformed his company's culture while dramatically improving its performance.

Although Welch did *many* different things to make this transformation a reality, one of the most telling was his takeover of GE's training facility in Ossining, New York. As Welch realized, designing a new culture is one thing, but getting the word out to employees and making it stick is another thing altogether. By directing the class curricula for all levels of workers, and by personally dropping into the training center every two weeks or so to meet with students, Welch was able not only to determine what message would be communicated to GE employees, but also to ensure that the message was received loudly and clearly. If there was any confusion in the ranks, employees had ample opportunity to ask Welch himself for clarification.

In a gesture that was at once symbolic and real, Welch directed the ceremonial burning of the old-school General Electric "Blue Books." The Blue Books were a series of management training manuals that prescribed how GE managers were to get things done in the organization. Despite the fact that the use of these books for training had been mothballed for some 15 years, they still exerted tremendous influence over the actions of GE managers. Citing the need for managers to write their own answers to day-to-day management challenges, Welch swept away the old order by removing the Blue Books from the organization's culture once and for all. Now, GE managers are taught to find their own solutions rather than to look them up in a dusty old book.

The same goes for the manager who depends on fear and intimidation to get results. What are the *real* results of this style of management? Do employees look forward to coming to the office every day? Are they all pulling for a common vision and goal? Are they extending themselves to bring innovation to work processes and procedures? Or are they more concerned with just getting through the day without being yelled at? Think about what you would do differently to get the results that you want.

You can always learn *something* from other managers — whether they are good managers or bad ones.

Do and learn

Perhaps you are familiar with this old saying (attributed to Lao Tze):

Give a man a fish, and he eats for a day,
Teach a man to fish, and he eats for a lifetime.

Such is the nature of managing employees. If you make all the decisions, do the work that your employees are able to do given the chance, and try to carry the entire organization on your own shoulders, you are harming your employees and your organization far more than you can imagine. Your employees never learn to succeed on their own, and after a while, they quit trying. In your sincere efforts to bring success to your organization, you stunt the growth of your employees and make your organization less effective and vital.

Simply reading a book or watching someone else manage — or fail to manage — is not enough. To take advantage of the lessons that you learn, you have to put them into practice. Keep these key steps in mind:

✔ First, take the time to assess the problems in your organization. Which areas work, and which don't? You can't focus on *all* your problems at one time. Concentrate on a few that are the most important, and solve those problems before you move on to the rest.

✔ Next, take a close look at yourself. What do you do to help or hinder your employees when they try to do their jobs? Do you give them the authority to make decisions? Just as important, do you support them when they go out on a limb for the organization? Study your personal interactions throughout your business day. Do they result in positive or negative outcomes?

✔ Then try out the techniques that you learn from your reading or from observing other managers at work. Go ahead! *Nothing* will change if *you* don't change first. *If it's to be, it's to begin with me. . . .*

✔ Finally, step back and watch what happens. We promise that you'll see a difference in the way you get things done and in the way your customers and employees respond to the needs and goals of your organization.

Test your new-found knowledge

What is management?

A. An excuse to go on lots of business trips to far-off, exotic locations for free

B. A big pain in the neck

C. Making something planned happen

D. Closing your eyes and hoping for the best

What are the new functions of management?

A. Wet hair, apply shampoo, lather and rinse, and then repeat

B. Energize, empower, support, and communicate

C. See how far you can overrun your budget before anyone notices

D. Speak only when you're spoken to

Chapter 2

Wake Up, Smell the Coffee, and Get Organized!

. . . .

In This Chapter

▶ Sorting through that mess on your desk

▶ Getting your act together

▶ Knowing what's important and what's not

▶ Choosing a personal planner

▶ Getting a jump on the next crisis

. . . .

*T*here comes a time when every manager has to face this realization: You can't be an effective manager if you are disorganized. It just doesn't work.

Picture your office. What does it look like? Not the furniture or the picture on the wall of you accepting an award for making the best suggestion of the month (you remember — moving the lunch room closer to your office, resulting in an additional $5,000 of yearly vending machine sales). Take a close look at the top of your desk and at the places where you store your books, files, and other reference materials. If they look like a tornado swept through last night, then you have a *big* problem. Despite fun sayings to the contrary, a messy desk is *not* the sign of a brilliant mind.

Fortunately, disorganization is a problem that *we* can help you solve. How? Just keep reading.

What's That Mess on Your Desk?

It's not just the little things that count. When it comes to getting organized, everything — big, small, and every point in between — can make a tremendous difference in your effectiveness as a manager. When you are organized, you always know where the things that you need to do your job are, and you don't have to waste time searching for them when you need them. Instead of blindly sorting through a veritable blizzard of stick-on notes covering your desk — notes of things to do, phone calls to return, or people to see — you can have all the information immediately available in one place: your desk calendar or planner. You can either maintain your backlog of 40 e-mail messages and your voice mail box that is full to capacity, or choose to *manage* the information that courses through your office.

The Information Age is upon us, and, in case you haven't noticed yet, it's upon us in a *big* way. Managers used to be able to rely on secretaries and assistants to control the information that found its way into their offices. Now, with the impending demise of the secretary (due in part to corporate downsizing and in part to the increased personalization of management communication) and the rise of the computer, business people are bombarded with more information from more people and places than ever before. (Even Bill Gates, the richest man in America, says that he reads every message he gets in his e-mail box at Askbill@microsoft.com.) Modern business people are immersed in an ever-growing flood of near real-time electronic mail from everywhere in the world, live satellite video-conferencing, voice mail, pagers, and cellular phones that can reach them wherever they are 24 hours a day (now even on airplanes!) — whether they want to be reached or not.

Your success as a manager comes down to the difference between managing your work and letting your work manage you. What's it going to be?

Okay, it's time to get *brutally* honest. When you look at your desk, what do you see? Does your desk reflect a manager who is in command of his or her environment and his or her work? To get a truly accurate view, you're going to have to take off your rose-colored glasses for at least a *few* minutes. You may have to momentarily suspend your belief that the disorder reflected throughout your office is the mark of a busy and successful business person. If *you* can't see your desk as it really is, then ask a trusted associate to take a look for you. Bribe that person with lunch if you have to.

Far too many people have desks that are a disorganized mess of reports, notes, scraps of paper, and towering stacks of documents that threaten to topple over and bury them at any moment. What would happen if those stacks *did* fall — with you trapped underneath? How long would it take the search party to find you?

Get Your Act Together — It All Starts with You!

So who's to blame for your disorganized mess? We know that blaming someone else for an inability to stay organized is easy. You might say, "It's my boss's fault — she gives me too much work, and I just don't have enough time to keep up with everything." Or maybe, "I'm just not the tidy type. Anyway, tidiness is the mark of a sick mind." Or, "If my desk is *too* organized, my boss will think that I don't have enough work to do."

Listen, if your business life is a disorganized mess, you can't go through life blaming the mess on everyone else. At some point, if you want to be successful, you have to step up to the plate and commit to getting your affairs in order. Take the pledge. Right here. Right now. Repeat after us:

> *From this day forward*
> *I promise to get my act together*
> *To take every opportunity*
> *To pass on those things that do not require my personal attention*
> *To record all appointments, meetings, and assignments in my calendar*
> *Religiously and with great frequency*
> *To keep a neat and tidy office, everything in its place*
> *To use stick-on notes only in case of extreme emergency*
> *And, when in doubt, to throw it out*
> *And, when in doubt, to throw it out.*

Congratulations! You've taken the pledge to get your business life in order. Now what? Depending on the state of your mess — mild or wild — getting organized may or may not be a daunting task. If your situation is particularly bad (you know, you lost your assistant in your office for three hours last Tuesday), then take on your task one step at a time. To help get the ball rolling, start with some simple enhancements — ones that you can complete quickly and easily but that offer a noticeable improvement in your organizational state of affairs.

- **Find your appointment calendar or daily planner.** Are all your scheduled meetings and appointments duly noted within its pages? Do you even have an appointment calendar? If not, do not pass Go, do *not* collect $200, and report directly to the next section of this book.

- **Use your planning tool!** Gather all the schedule-related notes scattered around your desk, in your pockets, in your briefcase, or stuck to your forehead and immediately transfer them to your appointment calendar or personal planner. From this day forward, promise to carry your calendar with you wherever you go and to make notes directly in it instead of writing on scraps of paper that may very well get lost — or worse, end up cluttering your planner.

- **Organize your workspace.** Try tackling one of the many piles of paper that litter your desk. Which items can you file away? Which can you pass on to others in your organization or delegated to your staff? For the stuff that remains, give it the final test of necessity: *If I throw this document away, would anyone miss it?* If the answer is no, then pitch away. Try to touch each piece of paper only once!

Let's go! We'll have no backsliding here! From now on, you are duly sworn to avoid the temptation to scribble meeting dates and times on the back of your hand. Further, you *will* refuse to fall prey to the easy habit of using stick-on notes to record your appointments and then sticking them all over your office — and all over yourself. You *will* note each appointment immediately — not two days after the meeting. Finally, you will refrain from using every available work surface in your office as an impromptu filing cabinet.

Believe us when we tell you that the rewards of getting organized are many and varied. Not only do you have all your vital business information at your fingertips — instantly and easily accessible — but you are able to sleep well at night knowing that *you* are in control of your business life. Who knows — you might even find a few bucks worth of nickels and dimes in the process, and even get the opportunity to dispose of a few old coffee cups half-filled with viscous, months-old brown liquid and quaint mini-forests of green and black flora. Yum!

Knowing What's Important and What's Not

Managers today are bombarded with a flood of information that can easily overwhelm even the most organized and diligent people. Not only do you still get good, old-fashioned letters (You *do* get old-fashioned letters, don't you? Or is most of it junk mail?), memos, and other correspondence by the truckload through the standard distribution channels, but now you also have a whole new world of information sources to deal with.

Fax machines, pagers, cellular phones, FedEx packages, and the like conspire to rob you of the time you need to think, plan, or just relax. Instead of acting, you find yourself reacting to the deluge of information that threatens to swallow you whole and then spit you out — your priorities lost, your goals diffused, and your neat and tidy attempts at organization shattered.

These new sources of information — and the increased speed and frequency with which they find their way to your desk — have made sorting out what's important from what's not more difficult than ever. The activity trap — keeping busy without achieving much — just got deadlier.

With telephone voice mail, people can leave you messages whenever they want — even in the middle of the night or over the weekend — and they can be fairly sure that you'll get it. After you receive a message, you can respond to it, forward it to others, slice it, dice it — whatever you want. Before you know it, your voice mail box can overflow with messages. "I'm sorry, but that mailbox is full," said the cold electronic voice that was at once apologetic and final.

The Internet: Land of opportunity?

The wonder of the Internet has introduced managers to a whole new universe of opportunities to receive hundreds of electronic mail messages from all over the world — and to waste untold hours in the process. If Peter's America Online e-mail in-box is an accurate reflection of most business users on the Internet, 95 percent of those messages are pure *junk*. Invariably, junk e-mail messages first apologize for taking up your precious time, and then they proceed to do just that. Here are some real winners from Peter's Internet e-mail in-box:

First let me apologize for this brief interruption. After you read this message, you'll thank me for the intrusion. A dream home, a new car, $25,000 cash, and more are all yours with my awesome new network marketing program. Oh yeah, you can retire in 18 months with a lifetime retirement. GUARANTEED!!!

Yeah. And chickens have lips. If that doesn't convince you to quit your 9-to-5 job, how about this irresistible offer?

$$$Make big bucks in CASINOS$$$ Earn a $2,500 daily cash income at the roulette wheel with my proprietary system. You'll be amazed! I guarantee that you'll win 9 out of 10 sessions. Write me to find out how!

If this system is so successful, then why hasn't this guy retired yet? This next one is bound to bring you around to the wonders that await you on the Internet.

FIRE YOUR BOSS! My husband and I grossed over $100,000 last year. We'll send you our free "Fire Your Boss" T-shirt with the HOME-BASED ENVELOPE STUFFER audio tape to get you started. Only $25 shipping and handling.

Maybe if they sell enough "free" T-shirts, they won't have to advertise anymore. As more business people and product marketers get wise to the ways of the Internet, expect to get *very* wet as you wade through the flood in your mailbox.

And just try to tell us that you haven't been tempted to listen to your messages on weekends at home or when you're on vacation. So much for your time off! Remember when people worried that our biggest problem with technology would be what to do with all our leisure time? *Yeah, right!*

The point is that you have lots more ways to waste time than ever before. At the same time, you are expected to be far more productive than you were last year, or five or ten years ago. So how do you sort through all the junk and all the distractions and concentrate only on the things that are important to you and your organization? As you review the paper that spills out of your in-box, your voice mail and electronic mail messages, and the requests of customers and coworkers to schedule a piece of your limited time, consider the following:

✔ **What is the impact to the bottom line of your organization?** If the task is a high-payoff one — that is, if it significantly increases your ability to meet your organization's goals — then it is a high priority. If the task is a low-payoff one — that is, it does not significantly increase your ability to meet your organization's goals — then it is a low priority, and you should treat it as such.

✔ **Can you delegate the task or item to another employee?** If another employee can review or act on the item, then by all means assign it to that employee. Don't waste your time doing things that your employees can do for you. Save your time for the things that you are uniquely qualified to do.

✔ **Someone else's emergency is not necessarily *your* emergency.** Don't let someone else's lack of planning or foresight short-circuit your plans or priorities.

Always make an exception to this rule, however, when your *customer* has an emergency. Bailing your customers out of tough situations should be your number one, drop-everything-else priority. If they can depend on you in times of crisis, they will be sure to take care of you when things aren't quite so hectic.

For a more in-depth discussion on the value of getting organized and a variety of different approaches for taking charge of your business life, pick up a copy of Jeffrey Mayer's *Time Management For Dummies* (IDG Books Worldwide, Inc.). In this book, Mayer does a super job of laying out the best ways to make you a more efficient and effective time manager. You always have room to improve, and in his easy-to-read style, Mayer helps you do so better than anyone else.

Personal Planners: Fashion Statement or Necessity?

Sometimes you've got to wonder: What's with these daily planners that everyone seems to be carrying around all of a sudden? Franklin Day Planner systems, Day-Timers, Day Runners, and the like seem to have taken managers by storm.

And you pioneering types who prefer a dose of electricity to help prod your efforts at organizing your business lives can find a tremendous variety of tools available. Electronic organizers, personal digital assistants (PDAs), and other tools allow you not only to keep track of phone numbers, appointments, and things to do, but also to send and receive electronic mail and perform basic word processing and spreadsheet tasks. Light years beyond the simple calendars and appointment books that people formerly relied on to keep track of their schedules, daily planners and electronic organizers promise to do much, much more. They tell you what day it is, and they can bring order and structure to your personal and business life. At least that's how they're *supposed* to work.

There's only one catch. For a daily planner to be useful, you have to *use* it. Religiously. Doing so is not *quite* as easy as you might think. As the sections that follow explain, daily planners have grown tremendously in complexity, as well as in popularity. While additional features make them much more comprehensive, and ultimately much more useful, than simple calendars for a wide variety of management tasks, daily planners require *lots* of ongoing, day-to-day maintenance. For busy managers — already burdened with a full day's work and then some — setting aside the time necessary every day to maintain a planner requires no small measure of discipline.

In the following sections, we review some of the key features, advantages, and disadvantages of each major type of daily planner.

The low-tech but reliable calendar

Formerly the mainstay of every busy manager's system of organization, calendars have been largely supplanted by "sexier," bulkier, and much more expensive planning *systems* such as those offered by Franklin Covey Co. Calendars are most useful for recording the basic information that is beneficial to a manager. Meeting schedules, employee days off, project due dates, appointments, and such can all be quickly, easily, and efficiently recorded on a calendar. What? Your 9:00 a.m. Friday appointment needs to reschedule to the following Tuesday? No sweat. Simply grab an eraser and pencil in the new date and time. While plain-old calendars may not be very sexy, they certainly are easy to use.

On the plus side, calendars come in just about every size and shape. You need something you can carry around in your pocket? No problem. You can get anything from miniature wallet-sized to larger briefcase-sized versions. At the other end of the spectrum, do you want a calendar that you can post on the wall for all to see — even those with 20/400 vision at 100 paces? Good news — you're covered. Any office supply store can guide you through a shockingly diverse collection of calendars to meet your *every* desire.

Some key advantages of calendars are

- The batteries never run out.
- You can use your calendar to count down the days until you retire.
- Modern calendars reflect the individuality and self-image of their owners. For example, calendars with photos of teddy bears, jellyfish, or famous dictators tell you a *lot* about their owners.

Another advantage of calendars is the very reason that many managers still prefer them over their more recent siblings: their simplicity. On a desk calendar that shows an entire month at a time, what could be simpler than jotting a name and time in the big block devoted to January 21?

Most important, like cockroaches, calendars have stood the test of time. Since the earliest versions that were hand-crafted in stone thousands of years ago by the industrious and business-visionary Aztecs, people have relied on calendars to tell them what day today is and what day tomorrow is.

With a good, reliable calendar at your side, you need never worry about your batteries dying or about a *no hard drive found* error message staring you down as you try to access your appointments for the week. Long after your PDA has faded into obsolescence, and your bulky daily planner has been relegated to a bookshelf in your office (to help collect dust and to continue to exude some small amount of *l'essence de management*), your calendar continues to be the reliable workhorse that it has always been, keeping track of your schedule one day at a time.

The fashionable and functional daily planner

If you find calendars to be too limiting — or too old-fashioned and un-hip — the daily planner offers something for everyone. Over the past decade, companies like Franklin Covey Co. and Day Runner, Inc., have presided over an industry whose growth mushroomed virtually overnight. From its inception in 1983 as The Franklin Institute, Franklin Covey Co. has grown into a vast management planning empire with sales in excess of $550 million. With more than 80 Franklin Covey retail outlets strewn across the American business landscape, Franklin Covey Co. dominates the paper-based personal planner market — estimated at about $900 million in sales per year.

What exactly is a daily planner? A daily planner is essentially a calendar on steroids. And not just any steroids. We're talking big-league, Olympic-career-ending steroids here. (See Figures 2-1 and 2-2.)

A daily planner can be anything you want it to be. In many companies, the conversion of managers into the ranks of *believers* has taken on an almost religious zeal. Management training sessions on using the planners can re-semble old-time revival meetings, as true believers testify as to how their planners saved them from business and personal failure and eternal doom. Managers are awarded planners in elaborate rites of passage, and the chosen ones carry them through their organizations as leather-like vinyl badges of honor.

Before I got my planner, I was a lamb that had lost its way. My life was a disorga-nized mess until I found the answer to my prayers. Priorities were forgotten, phone numbers were misplaced, and — sin of sins — Secretaries' Day passed unacknowl-edged! I was lost, but now I'm found. Hallelujah! I have seen the light!

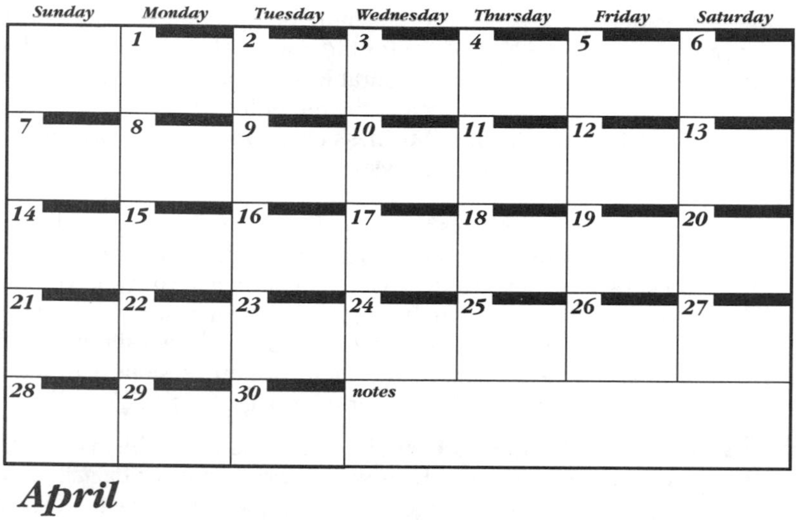

Sunday	Monday	Tuesday	Wednesday	Thursday	Friday	Saturday
	1	2	3	4	5	6
7	8	9	10	11	12	13
14	15	16	17	18	19	20
21	22	23	24	25	26	27
28	29	30	notes			

Figure 2-1:
This is your calendar.

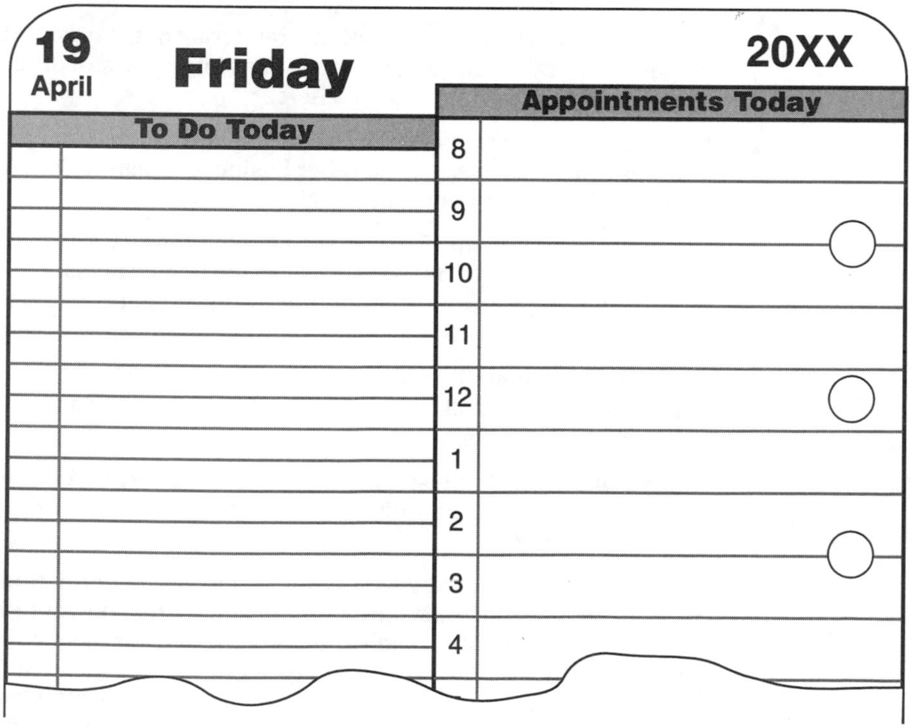

April

19 April — **Friday** — **20XX**

To Do Today

Appointments Today

8	
9	
10	
11	
12	
1	
2	
3	
4	

Figure 2-2:
This is your calendar on steroids.

And considering the expense of the more comprehensive systems, which range in price from about $25 to $300+ for the ones with all the bells and whistles, daily planners better have a measurable and positive benefit to a company's bottom line. To give you an idea of the incredible universe of features and options available to the busy business user, following is a brief guided tour of the Franklin Covey day planner system:

- **Binder:** The binder sets the stage for all the delights that lie within its covers. Not only do binders come in four different sizes — from the pocket-sized *Pocket* to the royal-sized *Monarch* (the one you have to hire someone to carry for you!) — but binders also are available in vinyl, simulated leather, and real leather versions. The fashion-conscious can purchase tapestry cloth and woven calfskin versions with matching checkbook covers and designer handbags. *Très chic!*

- **Prioritized Daily Task List:** The task list is really the heart of the Franklin Covey planning system. Here you record and prioritize all your daily tasks. Simply cross off the task after you complete it. Carry the task over to the next day if you aren't able to finish it. Or just act like you finished it. You're a manager now — the choice is *yours*.

- **Appointment Schedule:** A traditional rendering of the classic daily appointment calendar. Meeting times, appointments, and other significant events (insignificant ones, too) go here.

- **Daily Expense Record:** Use the Daily Expense Record to keep track of business lunches, mileage, and other business expenses. You never know when Uncle Sam will come knocking!

- **Daily Record of Events:** Fortunately, Franklin Covey Co. provides an entire page for recording events — plenty of space to take notes, doodle, or practice writing out your new title when you get that promotion you've been pushing for.

- **Address/Telephone Directory:** Names. Phone numbers. Addresses. Fax numbers. Zip codes. All alphabetized. All available with a flick of your wrist. Think of the possibilities.

- **Values and Goals:** Not just for today, but for the rest of your life. Take your time here; this is serious stuff. Maybe "Ending world hunger" or "Finding a cure for cancer"?

- **Tabs, tabs, and more tabs:** In addition to the basic information management system, you get tabs for recording information on your personal finances; key information such as blood type and car mechanic; ready reference charts for metric conversions, time zones, and area codes; a monthly calendar to record an entire month's worth of stuff; and future planning calendars (to note events such as oil changes up to six years into the future). If that's not enough to keep you busy for the next couple of years, you can choose from many other options including contact logs, menu planner/shopping lists, check registers, meeting planners, client files, and personal communication planners.

Coupled with training sessions such as the Franklin Covey proprietary *TimeQuest* time management seminars that are available now at a city near you, you'll never have an excuse to be disorganized again!

Unfortunately, the advantages of daily planners — their comprehensiveness, flexibility, and expansion options — can also be their biggest detriment. There is no denying that having your calendar; address book; appointments; priorities; daily, weekly, monthly, annual, and five-year goals; lists of birthdays and anniversaries; and other significant information all in one place is tremendously useful. But to be frank (or should we be Bob?), some daily planners can become tremendous burdens to their users, in both their physical weight and their ongoing requirements for updating and maintenance.

And heaven forbid that you should ever *lose* your planner. When used properly, your planner becomes an indispensable repository for every possible piece of business information that you need to survive in your business world. Lose it, and you're dead meat. Unlike a computer file, you can't just press a button to back up your information to a floppy disk or tape drive for archiving.

Don't forget that your employer can seize calendars and planners if you quit or are fired, and a court can subpoena them for evidence if you or your company are ever sued. Would that possibility cramp your style or have a negative effect on the kinds of information that you record in your planner? Perhaps soon you will be able to buy lost planner insurance. Imagine the ads: *Did you lose your life when you lost your planner? Feel secure even when it's out of your hands.*

The digital alternative

Although electronic organizers, personal digital assistants, and personal information management software still have a long way to go before they win widespread acceptance, more managers are beginning to rely on these tools to organize their business lives. Computerized alternatives to the old-fashioned, dead-tree counterparts offer an increasingly viable alternative for busy managers who are ready to jump on the wave of new information technology.

If you thought that personal planners offered lots of options, you haven't seen anything yet. When considering the digital alternative for self-organization, first ask yourself these questions:

✔ **What do I want this thing to do for me?** Asking this question is important because each product offers its own, generally unique mix of benefits and limitations. Would you like a system that allows you to keep track of your appointments? No problem. How about an alarm to remind you to make that call to your customer in France? Easy. Send and receive faxes? Hmmm. *That* is a little more difficult. Send and receive e-mail messages worldwide over a standard phone line? A much smaller group of products can do this. What if you want self-contained cellular telephone transmission capabilities along with digital paging and built-in handwriting or voice recognition? The group is smaller still.

✔ **How big do I want it to be?** Although information technology keeps getting smaller, more capable, and more affordable, size is still an issue for many products. Electronic products range in size from a wristwatch that receives and displays appointment and other information downloaded from your personal computer to highly capable — and rather bulky — laptop or desktop computers running personal information management software. Although you can't *always* make this assumption, the smaller the product, the fewer features it generally offers. Conversely, the more features you demand of your electronic partner, the less convenient it is to carry around as its size increases proportionately.

✔ **How much do I want to spend?** This is the proverbial $64 question (although, good luck finding *any* electronic organizer for a price *that* low). For only a couple hundred bucks, you can buy a simple but relatively powerful electronic organizer. For a couple hundred bucks more, you can buy a full-fledged personal digital assistant that can send and receive electronic mail remotely on your company's computer network or through the Internet and perform other computing tasks. For a few hundred bucks more, you can buy a basic laptop computer that does all of the above and more. At $6,000+ are the most powerful laptop computers — which can do everything but cook your dinner and take the dog out for a walk. You clearly have many possibilities to consider.

Now that you have some idea of the constraints that guide your search for an electronic planning system, take a look at the many different ways in which manufacturers remove your hard-earned money from your wallet and insert it in theirs.

The electronic organizer: a grown-up calculator or a downsized computer?

Electronic organizers have been around for some time now. During the past decade, calculators produced by companies such as Casio, Hewlett-Packard, and Texas Instruments have become more and more capable. Formerly miniature adding machines, these products evolved into a class of microprocessor-based, palm-sized devices that incorporate alphanumeric input and output, communications, contact management capabilities, and more. Such products have blurred the sharp line that once separated calculators and computers.

Most of these personal electronic organizers — like the Franklin Rex line — allow you to keep track of appointments, phone numbers, schedules, and financial information; take notes; and perform other basic organizing tasks. Some even send and receive faxes and perform limited word processing and spreadsheet functions.

As technology and user interfaces continue to improve, managers are discovering the versatility, ease of use, and cost effectiveness of these products. According to Hewlett-Packard electronic organizer user Lori Burke, director of communications for the New England Shelter for Homeless Veterans, "Finally there's an easy way to keep track of my work-related and personal information — including my budgets — without having to spend a fortune or take a course on how to do it." With their intuitive, graphically based operating systems, applications are only a few keystrokes or the touch of a pen away.

On the plus side of the equation, electronic organizers are compact and increasingly powerful. At a fraction of the price of personal digital assistants (see the following section) or laptop computers, many managers find them to be indispensable business tools.

On the minus side, the tiny keyboards built into most of these units are painfully inadequate for any amount of serious data entry. To get around this problem, some systems offer connectivity options allowing you to hook up your organizer to your personal computer. These options make life *much* easier — especially if you have long lists of phone numbers and addresses to incorporate into your organizer.

Personal digital assistants: the future is here, now

The recent development of *personal digital assistants* — miniature, hand-held computers that offer pen-based input — is the most exciting development on the management organization front since daily planners ascended to the throne several years ago. Now, you can not only keep track of your calendar, but you can also perform a wide variety of amazing tasks with true portability and almost unlimited flexibility — anywhere, anytime.

The Palm Computing series of PDAs are prime examples of just how far personal planning technology has come. If these features don't get your adrenaline pumping and make your heart skip a beat or two, then we don't know what will. You can

- Plan your daily calendar
- Manage business contacts
- Send and receive wireless electronic messages
- Send messages to fax machines
- Use built-in networking
- Check airline schedules and stock quotes
- Look up the capital of Guam

What could be cooler or more effective and efficient than collecting all your information and portable communications into a single electronic device? With its built-in cellular phone technology, the 4-ounce Palm PDA can truly free you from the chains of your office. ¡Viva la revolucion!

Computers: keeping you organized at home, in the office, and on the road

Personal computers have become fixtures in offices and homes throughout the nation and around the world. Whether your computer is a Macintosh or an IBM PC-compatible, or big or small, chances are that you depend on it to get your work done. If so, a wide variety of personal information management software is available for your use. You can purchase some — like ACT, the popular contact manager that Jeffrey Mayer features in *Time Management For Dummies* — as stand-alone packages. Others — like Outlook, which is a part of the Microsoft Office suite — are bundled into software packages. Even Franklin Covey Co. has jumped into this market with its Franklin Planner software for Windows package, an electronic version of its ever-popular line of personal planners.

While desktop computers are most useful for performing organizing tasks at a fixed location — you can update your schedules and contacts and then print them out to carry with you in your briefcase — laptop computers have revolutionized the global business landscape. Laptops match the power of desktop computers, and they can run for several hours on battery power alone. With built-in modems, remote networking capability, and the capacity to run sophisticated business software, laptop computers allow business people to bring their offices with them wherever they go — on the road, at a client's office, or in a hotel room, across town or across the ocean.

Take a moment to review the features of Microsoft Outlook, a typical personal information management software package. Although the exact features of individual software programs vary from vendor to vendor, the features contained in Outlook are common to most.

- ✔ To-do lists
- ✔ Appointment tracking
- ✔ Task tracking
- ✔ Contact manager
- ✔ Mail merge
- ✔ Address book
- ✔ E-mail
- ✔ Meeting scheduling

According to Microsoft, the idea behind Outlook is to make viewing appointments, managing tasks, and keeping track of key contacts easy for business users. Furthermore, Microsoft developed Outlook with portability in mind.

You can easily transfer files from a desktop to a laptop computer or electronic organizer — making it possible to keep track of important business information anywhere, anytime. (See Figure 2-3.)

With a click of your computer's mouse, you can choose to view your schedule on a daily, weekly, or monthly basis. Need to reschedule an appointment? No sweat — just click and drag the appointment to whatever day and time you want. Your contact manager allows you to record names, phone, fax, and cellular numbers, and other important information, including your clients' birthdays and the names of their spouses.

You can quickly schedule meetings with coworkers on the same computer network by using a special "Meeting Wizard," and you can send out advance copies of meeting agendas along with your meeting request. And if your meeting attendees are located on a different coast or in a different country, Schedule+ automatically adjusts meeting times for your recipients to their local time zones.

Bob Nelson		S	M	T	W	T	F	S
		S	1	2	3	4	5	6
Tuesday, April 16, 20XX		7	8	9	10	11	12	13
		14	15	16	17	18	19	20
		21	22	23	24	25	26	27
		28	29	30				

8:00	Breakfast meeting with Boswell @ Hyatt
:30	
9:00	
:30	
10:00	Management team meeting
:30	
11:00	
:30	
12:00	
:30	Pick up dry cleaning

Figure 2-3: With the Outlook daily schedule, even you know what you're doing today.

A PDA scenario

You're scheduled for a lunch meeting to discuss new product delivery problems with one of your best customers. That morning, you pull up your daily schedule and note the time and place for the meeting. Just in case you forget, you set an alarm to go off exactly one hour before the appointed time. In a cab on the way to the meeting, you review the notes that you prepared for your discussion, and you quickly scan through your priorities for the day and the rest of the week. Taking advantage of the short trip across town, you hand-write a note to check on your staff's progress on the Ohio project development plan.

When you arrive at the meeting, you slip your PDA into your briefcase and pull up a chair at your client's table. As he regales you with his tale of woe and sorrow, you reach for your PDA and scribble notes on its surface. After creating a memo detailing your client's concerns, you fire it off to the shipping and customer service departments via electronic mail. You perform this task in minutes via the cellular phone built into your PDA — without ever leaving the table. Completing the task takes only a few taps of your pen. Before dessert arrives, you receive an e-mail from shipping detailing their plan to correct the problems. After reviewing the memo with your client, you offer to fax it to his office — he'll have it on his desk when he gets back.

Wow! Let's see that old calendar on your desk do that!

Outlook makes managing tasks easy. Not only can you keep track of your tasks, but your computer also can remind you when a task is overdue. You can organize tasks by project and prioritize them, too. (See Figure 2-5.)

According to Microsoft, the capability to print in various ways was the number one request of Outlook users. In response to this request, Microsoft built in more than 1,500 ways to print such things as personal schedules, tasks, and lists of contacts. Finally, as the next section explains, Outlook can download selected information directly to the Timex Data Link watch. Now your personal information manager can be with you wherever you go.

When is a watch more than a watch?

A watch is more than a watch when it's a personal organizer that just happens to be a watch, too. Born out of a partnership of long-time watch manufacturer Timex and software giga-giant Microsoft, the Data Link watch does much more than your average timepiece.

Bob Nelson		S	M	T	W	T	F	S
		S	1	2	3	4	5	6
Tuesday, April 16, 20XX		7	8	9	10	11	12	13
		14	15	16	17	18	19	20
		21	22	23	24	25	26	27
		28	29	30				

Figure 2-5:
No more
excuses
with the
Outlook task
schedule
feature.

To Do List (All):

1

1 Conduct performance appraisals starts on Sat 4/20/XX, ends on Tue 4/30/XX.

2

2 Liquidate asset accounts starts on Fri 4/19/XX, ends on Fri 4/19/XX.

3

3 Draft letter to Agency contact starts on Fri 5/3/XX, ends on Fri 5/3/XX.

Using a special photo-receptor, the Data Link watch can receive and display Microsoft Outlook information directly from your desktop or laptop computer screen. No wires or other hardware are necessary. Just push a button, and you transmit 70 or so of your appointments, phone numbers, anniversaries, and to-do lists to your watch — plenty for up to a week away from your office.

So how does the watch work in the real world? According to Peter, who conducted extensive field testing of the Data Link for this book, the watch is "definitely cool."

For the busy business person on the run, this gizmo may be just the ticket. No bulky planners to carry around, no rinky-dink keyboard to try to hunt-and-peck your messages into. Just set up your schedules on your desktop or laptop computer, download the data to your watch, and you're all set. Of course, you can't take notes, and you can't change the schedules programmed into your watch when you are away from your desktop computer, but that's a small price to pay for *total* portability. Hey — these watches *look* cool, too. Now, if you could just program them to fill in for you at your weekly staff meetings, you would *really* have something.

Choosing your personal planner

Selecting a personal planner is a personal choice. What's best for one person most certainly isn't best for another. But instead of overanalyzing the available choices, pick an option and jump right in. You're a manager now. You have the right to change your mind and your approach as quickly and as often as you like. The fact is, most business people still rely on a paper-based planning system — despite the proliferation of electronic alternatives. According to Day-Timer Technologies, 85 percent of business people using computerized personal information managers are *also* using paper-based planners.

The point is this: Getting a system — any system — and beginning to use it right away is better than neglecting this vital management task. With all the options available, *something* has to fit both your personality *and* your pocketbook. Clearly, whichever planner you choose — whether it is old- or new-fashioned, low-tech or high-tech, in style or out of style — you have absolutely *no* excuse for not getting organized. Right now!

Getting a Jump on the Next Crisis

In management, as in war and many other activities, you're only as good as your last success. Just as you've got to always be on the lookout for the next opportunity, you also have to be on the alert for the next crisis. That's what being organized is all about. You don't want to waste your time with useless trivia when important issues that have significant impact on your customers or your organization deserve your attention.

While literally hundreds of different techniques and products are available to make your time productive (we review the most important ones in this chapter), none of them is worth a dime if you can't keep the people and things that waste your precious time to a minimum. Every day, you are bombarded with all sorts of potential ways to waste time — unscheduled appointments, meetings that run over their allotted time, junk mail, a coworker who wants to complain about his or her paycheck, and trivial tasks that do nothing to improve your bottom line. All these things conspire to make you an ineffective manager.

What seems like a small problem today can quickly become tomorrow's disaster — and it *will* if you don't identify its importance early on and deal with it right away. Make prioritizing everything you do your number one priority — every day of your working life. And after you set your priorities, work on the *highest priority items* first. Finally, at all costs, refuse the temptation to allow other, less important tasks to get you off track. The simple fact is, if you don't create and enforce your priorities, someone else will decide your priorities for you. *People who don't have goals are controlled by others who do.*

Despite all this doom and gloom, there *is* hope! You *can* take charge of your business life. In summary, you need a system of organizing and keeping track of the important things while you filter out the unimportant things. Whatever form your system takes, and however you decide to implement it, make sure that you follow these general guidelines:

- ✔ **Buy a planning calendar and keep it up to date.** Whether the calendar is simply an old-fashioned desk calendar or the latest and greatest electronic gizmo is not so important. The important thing is that you get *something* and use it religiously.

- ✔ **Set aside 20 minutes at the beginning of your business day to set your priorities for the day.** Take time to save time. Make this time yours and yours alone by forwarding your phone to voice mail and by keeping your schedule clear. If you have a hard time setting this time aside, reserve the time by making a daily appointment with yourself in your calendar.

- ✔ **Do your highest priority first and your lowest priority last.** This tip may seem obvious, but doing the quick and easy, low-payoff tasks first and saving the more difficult, high-payoff tasks for later is far too tempting. Unfortunately, after spending the day taking care of everything else, later never comes — until it's too late.

- ✔ **If you have an assistant, assign him or her the task of intercepting and destroying all your junk mail.** Even better, head it off at the pass before it hits your desk. Contact the producers of this junk and tell them to take you off their mailing lists. If they give you a hard time, tell them that you're going to put them on *your* mailing list!

- ✔ **Set aside at least 20 minutes at the end of your business day to tie up loose ends.** Go through your remaining work and make assignments to employees, forward information to coworkers as necessary, file away things that you need to keep, and toss anything you don't need into the trash. Finally, quickly review your appointments for the next day.

By taking charge of your business life, you are always in control of your priorities and your schedule. While crises or emergencies that you *can't* control will always arise, you can at least be on top of the things you *can* control. Not only that, but you are better able to deal with the inevitable crisis when it does arrive. You owe it to yourself, your employees, and your organization.

Don't forget that you took a pledge to get organized and stay organized. *We* haven't forgotten, and we're going to hold you to it! Getting organized is probably the most important thing that you can do to improve your effectiveness as a manager. *You can't manage others until you can manage yourself.* It will make a tremendous and measurable difference in your business life — we guarantee it!

Test your new-found knowledge

How many times should you touch a document?

A. At least ten times before it's filed

B. Once

C. It depends on how much coffee gets spilled on it

D. The more times the merrier

What's the best personal planner?

A. The one covered in fine Corinthian leather

B. The one that makes the most noise when you throw it against the wall

C. Whichever one is most impressive to your boss and coworkers

D. It's a personal choice — whichever one works best for you

Chapter 3

Delegation: Getting Things Done without Getting Done In

In This Chapter

▶ Managing through delegation

▶ Debunking the myths about delegation

▶ Putting delegation to work

▶ Choosing which tasks to delegate

▶ Checking up on your employees

*T*he power of effective management comes not from your efforts alone (sorry to burst your bubble) but from the sum of all the efforts of the members of your work group. If you were responsible for only a few employees, with extraordinary effort, you perhaps could do the work of your entire group if you so desired.

However, when you are responsible for a much larger organization, you cannot be an effective manager by trying to do all the work of your group. More likely, you'll be viewed as a *micromanager* — a manager who gets too involved in the petty details of running an organization — with more time for other people's work than for your own. Worse yet, your employees may take less responsibility for their work because you are always there to do it (or check it) for them.

Managers assign the responsibility for completing tasks through *delegation*. As we explain in this chapter, simply assigning tasks and then walking away is not enough; you may hear such comments as, "Uh, Sharon, what am I supposed to do next?" For delegation to be effective, managers must also give authority to their employees and ensure that employees have the resources necessary to complete tasks effectively. Finally, managers who have learned to delegate like experts monitor the progress of their employees towards meeting their assigned goals.

Delegating: The Manager's #1 Tool

Now that you're a manager, you are required to develop skills in many different areas. Not only do you need good technical, analytical, and organizational skills, but most important, you also must have good people skills. Of all the people skills, the one skill that can make the greatest difference in your effectiveness is the ability to delegate well. Delegating is a manager's #1 management tool, and the inability to delegate well is the leading cause of management failure.

So why is delegating so hard for managers? A variety of reasons exist:

- You're too busy and just don't have enough time.

- You don't trust your employees to complete their assignments correctly or on time.

- You don't know how to delegate effectively.

Or perhaps you're still not convinced that it's a good idea for managers to delegate at all. If you're a member of this large group of reluctant managers *(Hey! You there in the back! Yeah, you know who you are!)*, then here's why you should let go of your preconceptions and inhibitions and start delegating today:

- **Your success as a manager depends on it!** Managers who can successfully manage a team of workers — each of whom has specific responsibilities for a different aspect of the team's performance — prove that they are ready for bigger and better challenges. Bigger and better challenges are often accompanied by bigger and better titles, paychecks, and the other niceties of business life, such as offices with windows and office machines that actually work on occasion.

- **You can't do it all.** No matter how great a manager you are, carrying the entire burden of achieving your organization's goals by yourself is not in your interest unless you want to work yourself into an early grave. Besides, wouldn't it be nice to see what life is like outside the four walls of your office? At least every once in a while?

- **Your job is to concentrate your efforts on the things that you can do and your staff can't.** That's why they're paying you the big bucks — to be a manager — not a programmer, an accounting clerk, or a customer service representative. Do *your* job, and let your employees do theirs.

- **Delegation gets workers in the organization more involved.** When you give responsibility and authority to employees to carry out tasks — whether individually or in teams — they respond by becoming more involved in the day-to-day operations of the organization. Instead of being mere drones with no responsibility or authority, they are vital to the success of the work unit and the entire organization. *You mean that if I succeed, we all succeed?* Yep.

✔ **Delegation gives you the chance to develop your employees.** If you make all the decisions and come up with all the ideas, your employees never learn how to take initiative and be responsible for seeing tasks through to successful completion. And if they don't learn, guess who's going to get stuck doing things forever? (***Hint:*** Take a look in the mirror.)

As a manager, *you* are ultimately responsible for all your department's responsibilities. However, for most managers, personally executing all the tasks necessary for your department to fulfill its responsibilities and for you to achieve your organizational goals is neither practical nor desirable.

Say, for example, that you are the manager of the accounting department for a software development firm. When the firm had only five employees and sales of $500,000 a year, it was no problem for you to personally bill all your customers, cut checks to vendors, do payroll, and take care of the company's taxes every April. However, now that employment has grown to 150 employees and sales are at $50 million a year, you can't even pretend to do it all — you don't have enough hours in the day. (The last time we checked, there were still only 24 hours in a day — they're not making any more.) Now you have employees who take care of accounts payable, accounts receivable, and payroll, and you have farmed out the completion of income tax work to a CPA.

Each employee that you have assigned to a specific work function has specialized knowledge and skills in his or her area of expertise. Sure, you could personally generate payroll if you had to, but why would you want to? Your payroll clerk is probably a lot better and quicker at it than you are.

On the other hand, you are uniquely qualified to perform numerous responsibilities in your organization. These responsibilities might include developing and monitoring your operations budget, conducting performance appraisals, helping to plan the overall direction of your company's acquisitions, and selecting the flavor of the coffee that your department stocks in the coffee pool. Later in this chapter, we tell you which tasks to delegate to your employees and which ones to retain. First, however, consider some of the popular misconceptions about delegation.

Myths about Delegation

You may have many different reasons to rationalize to yourself why you *can't* delegate work to your employees. Unfortunately, these reasons are guaranteed to get in the way of your ability to be an effective manager. Do any of the following myths sound familiar to you? *Now tell the truth!*

Myth #1: You can't trust your employees to be responsible.

If you can't trust your employees, who can you trust? Assume that you were responsible for hiring at least a portion of your staff. Now, forgetting for the moment the ones you didn't personally hire, you likely went through quite an involved process to recruit your employees. Remember the mountain of resumes that you had to sift through and then divide into *winners, potential winners,* and *losers?* After hours of sorting and then hours of interviews, you selected the best candidates — the ones with the best skills, qualifications, and experience for the job.

You selected your employees because you thought that they were talented people deserving of your trust. Now your job is to give them your trust without strings attached.

You usually reap what you sow. The members of your staff are ready, willing, and able to be responsible employees; you just have to give them a chance. Sure, not every employee is going to be able to handle every task that you assign. If that's the case, find out why. Does he or she need more training? More time? More practice? Maybe you need to find a task that is better suited to his or her experience or disposition. To get responsible employees, you have to give responsibility. It's that simple.

Myth #2: When you delegate, you lose control of a task and its outcome.

If you delegate correctly, you *don't* lose control of the task or its outcome. What you lose control of is the way that the outcome is reached. Picture a map of the world. How many different ways are there to get from San Francisco to Paris? One? One million? Some ways are quicker than others. Some are more scenic, and others require a substantial resource commitment. Do the differences in these ways make any of them inherently wrong? No. (See Figure 3-1.)

In business, you have countless ways to get a task done. Even for tasks that are spelled out in highly defined steps — *we've always done it that way* — you should always leave room for new ways to make a process better. Why should your way be the *only* way to get the task done? *Because I'm the boss!* Sorry, wrong answer. Your job is to describe to your employee the outcomes that you want and then to let them decide how to accomplish them. Of course, you need to be available to coach and counsel them so that they can learn from your past experience if they want, but you need to let go of controlling the *how* and instead focus on the *what* and the *when*.

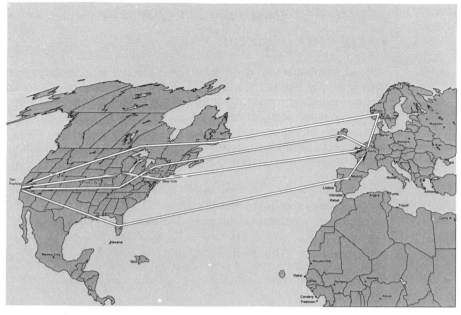

Figure 3-1:
There are
many ways
to get
from San
Francisco to
Paris.

Myth #3: You are the only one who has all the answers.

You're joking, right? If you think that you alone have all the answers, have we got a thing or two to tell you! As talented as you may be, unless you are the company's only employee, there's no way that you can have the only answer to every question in your organization — it's just not possible.

On the other hand, a certain group of people deal with an amazing array of situations every day. They talk to your customers, your suppliers, and each other — day in and day out. Many members of this group have been there far longer than you, and many of them will be there long after you are gone. Who are these people? They are your employees.

Your employees are a wealth of experience and knowledge about your business contacts and the intimate, day-to-day workings of the organization. They are often closer to the customers and problems of the company than you are. To ignore their suggestions and advice is not only disrespectful but also short-sighted and foolish. Don't ignore this resource. You're already paying for it — whether you use it or not!

Myth #4: You can do the work faster by yourself.

You may think that you're completing tasks faster when you do them yourself than when you assign them to others, but this belief is merely an illusion. Yes, discussing and assigning a task to one of your employees may require slightly more time when you first delegate that task, but if you delegate well, the second through *n*th times take substantially less time. Not only does doing the task yourself actually cost you more time, but you are robbing your employees of a golden opportunity to develop their work skills.

Sure, teaching one of your employees how to do a task takes longer, but what happens when you do it yourself instead of delegating it? When you do the task yourself, you are forever doomed to doing the task — over and over and over. When you teach someone else to do the task and then assign him or her responsibility for completing it, you may never have to do it again. Not only that, but your employee may come to do it faster than you can. Who knows, he or she may even *improve* on the way that you have always done it.

Myth #5: Delegation dilutes your authority.

Actually, delegation does exactly the opposite — it *extends* your authority. You are only one person, and you can do only so much. Imagine all 10, 20, or 100 members of your team working toward your common goals. You still set the goals and the timetables for reaching them, but each employee chooses his or her own way of getting there.

Do you have less authority because you delegate a task and transfer authority to an employee to carry out the task? Clearly, the answer is no. What do you lose in this transaction? Nothing. Your authority is undiminished — regardless of how much you extend to your employees. This is the wonder of authority. The more authority you give to employees, the more your entire *work unit* has.

In this transaction, you gain an efficient and effective workforce — employees that are truly empowered, turned on by their jobs, and working as team players — and the ability to concentrate on the issues that deserve your undivided attention.

Myth #6: Your employees will be recognized for doing a good job, but you won't.

Letting go of this belief is one of the biggest difficulties in the transition from being a doer to being a manager of doers. When you're a doer, you are rewarded for writing a great report, developing an incredible market analysis, or writing an amazing piece of computer code. When you become a manager, the focus of your job shifts from your performance in completing individual tasks to your performance in reaching an overall organizational or project goal through the efforts of others. While you may have been the best darn data entry operator in the world, all of a sudden, that talent doesn't matter anymore. Now you're expected to develop and lead a *team* of the best darn data entry operators in the world. The skills required are quite different, and your success is a result of the indirect efforts of others and your behind-the-scenes support.

Wise managers know that when their employees shine, they shine, too. The more you delegate, the more opportunities you give your employees to shine. Give your workers the opportunity to do important work and to do it well. And when they do well, make sure that you tell everyone about it. Give your employees credit for their successes publicly and often, and they will be more likely to want to do a good job for you on future assignments. Don't forget, you are being measured on the performance of your *team* — not what you are *personally* able to accomplish. Chapter 6 covers everything you ever wanted to know about employee motivation and rewards.

Myth #7: Delegation decreases your flexibility.

When you do everything yourself, you have complete control over the progress and completion of tasks, right? *Wrong!* How can you when you are balancing multiple priorities at the same time that you are dealing with the inevitable crisis *du jour?* Being flexible is pretty tough when you're doing everything yourself. Concentrating on more than one task at a time is impossible. While you are concentrating on that one task, you put all your other tasks on hold. Flexibility? *Nyet!*

The more people you delegate to, the more flexible you can be. As your employees take care of the day-to-day tasks necessary to keep your business running, *you* are free to deal with those surprise problems and opportunities.

Myth #8: Your employees are too busy.

If that belief isn't a cop out, we don't know what is! What exactly are your employees doing that they don't have the time to learn something new — something that could make your job easier at the same time that it could boost the performance of your work unit?

Think about yourself for a moment. What about your job makes you want to return day after day? No, we're not talking about your paycheck or the lunch truck. We're willing to bet that it's the satisfaction you feel when you take on a new challenge, meet it, and succeed.

Now consider your employees — their job satisfaction is no different from yours. They want to test themselves against new challenges and succeed, too. But how can they if you don't delegate new tasks to them? Too many managers have lost good employees because they failed to meet employees' needs to stretch and to grow in their jobs. And too many employees have become mindless drones because their managers refuse to encourage their creativity and natural yearning to learn. Don't learn this lesson the hard way!

Myth #9: Your workers don't see the big picture.

How can your employees see the big picture if you won't share it with them? Your employees are often specialists in their jobs or fields of expertise. They naturally develop severe cases of tunnel vision as they pursue the answers to their assignments or process their routine transactions. As we discuss in Chapter 1, your job is to provide your employees with a vision of where you want to go.

Unfortunately, many managers withhold vital information from their employees — information that could make them much more effective in their jobs — in hopes that by doing so, they can maintain a close rein on their behavior. By keeping their employees in the dark, these managers don't create the better outcomes that they hope for. Instead, they cripple their organization and their employees' ability to learn, grow, and become a real part of the organization.

You've got to trust your employees

These myths aside, delegation *can* be a scary thing to do, at least at first. But like anything else, the more you do it, the less scary it gets. When you delegate, you are putting your trust in another individual. If that individual fails, then you are ultimately responsible — regardless of who you give the task to. A line like this probably won't go very far with your boss: *Yeah, I know that we were supposed to get that proposal to the customer today, but Joe dropped the ball.* When you delegate tasks, you don't automatically abdicate your responsibility for its successful completion.

Beginning to delegate tasks to your employees is sort of like bungee jumping for the first time: You jump off that little platform hundreds of feet above the ground and hope that the cord doesn't break. And don't forget that your employees may be a little nervous, too. The thought of taking on a new task may cause some hesitance on their part. This hesitance requires more support from you as your employees learn to become comfortable with their new roles.

The Six Steps of Delegating

Delegation doesn't just happen. Just like any other task that you perform as a manager, you have to work at it. The six steps to effective delegation are the following:

1. **Communicate the task.** Describe exactly what you want done, when you want it done, and what end results you expect.

2. **Furnish context for the task.** Explain why the task needs to be done, its importance in the overall scheme of things, and possible complications that may arise during its performance.

3. **Determine standards.** Agree on the standards that you will use to measure the success of a task's completion. These standards should be realistic and attainable.

4. **Grant authority.** You must grant employees the authority necessary to complete the task without constant roadblocks or standoffs with other employees.

5. **Provide support.** Determine the resources necessary for your employee to complete the task and then provide them. Successfully completing a task may require money, training, advice, and other resources.

6. **Get commitment.** Make sure that your employee has accepted the assignment. Confirm your expectations and your employee's understanding of and commitment to completing the task.

Clearly, delegation benefits both workers *and* managers alike when you do it correctly. So why aren't you delegating more work to your employees? Maybe you aren't sure *what* to delegate. While a manager can delegate almost any task to a worker, some things should be routinely delegated to employees, and some things should never be delegated to employees.

Good and Bad Things to Delegate

Theoretically, you can delegate anything to your employees. Of course, if you delegate *all* your duties, then why should your company bother to pay *you?* Clearly, you have tasks that you should always make an effort to delegate to your employees and tasks that you should retain for yourself. There's a reason, after all, that *you* are a manager and your employees aren't.

When you delegate, begin with simple tasks that don't substantially impact the firm if they aren't completed on time or within budget. As your employees gain confidence and experience, delegate higher-level tasks. Carefully assess the level of your employees' expertise, and assign tasks that meet or slightly exceed that level. Set schedules for completion and then monitor your employees' performance against them. After you get the hang of it, you find that you really have nothing to be afraid of when you delegate.

Always delegate these things

Certain tasks naturally lend themselves to being delegated. As a manager, you should take every possible opportunity to delegate the following kinds of work to your employees.

Detail work

Truly, the devil is in the details. As a manager, you have no greater time-waster than getting caught up in details — you know, tasks such as double-checking pages and pages of figures, spending days troubleshooting a block of computer code, or personally auditing your employees' timesheets. The old saying says that 20 percent of the results come from 80 percent of the work — which illustrates why you were originally selected to be a manager. You can no doubt run circles around almost anyone on those detailed technical tasks that you used to do all the time.

But now that you're a manager, you're being paid to orchestrate the workings of an entire team of workers toward a common goal — not just to perform an individual task. Leave the detail to your employees. Concentrate your efforts on tasks that have the greatest payoff and that allow you to most effectively leverage the work of all your employees.

Information gathering

Browsing the World Wide Web for information about your competitors, spending hours pouring over issues of *Fortune* magazine, or moving into your local library's reference stacks for weeks on end is not an effective use of your time as a manager. Despite this fact, most managers get sucked into the trap. Not only is reading through newspapers, reports, books, magazines, and the like fun, but it also provides managers with an easy way to postpone the more difficult tasks of management. You're being paid to look at the big picture — to gather a variety of inputs and make sense of them. You can do so much more efficiently when someone else gathers needed information, which frees you to take the time you need to analyze the inputs and to devise solutions to your problems.

Repetitive assignments

What a great way to get routine tasks done: assign them to your employees. *Here you go — this should keep you busy for the next few years.* Many of the jobs in your organization occur again and again; drafting your weekly production report, reviewing your biweekly report of expenditures versus budget, and approving your monthly phone bill are just a few examples. Your time is much too important to waste on routine tasks that you mastered years ago.

If you find yourself involved in repetitive assignments, first take a close look at their particulars. How often do the assignments recur? Can you anticipate the assignments in sufficient time to allow an employee to be successful in completing it? What do you have to do to train your employees in completing the tasks? After you figure all this out, develop a schedule and make assignments to your employees.

Surrogate roles

Do you have to be everywhere all the time? Not only *can't* you be everywhere all the time, but you *shouldn't* be everywhere all the time. Every day, your employees have numerous opportunities to fill in for you. Presentations, conference calls, client visits, and meetings are just a few examples. In some cases, such as in budget presentations, you may be required to attend. However, in many other cases, whether you attend personally or send someone to take your place really doesn't matter.

The next time someone calls a meeting and requests that you attend, send one of your employees to attend in your place. This simple act benefits you in several different ways. Not only do you have an extra hour or two in your schedule, but your employee can summarize the results of the meeting for you and present you with only the important outcomes. If no outcomes came forth, at least you didn't waste your personal time in yet another useless meeting. In any case, your employee has the opportunity to take on some new responsibilities, and you have the opportunity to spend the time you need on your most important tasks.

Future duties

As a manager, you should always be on the lookout for opportunities to train your staff in their future job responsibilities. For example, one of your key duties might be to develop an annual budget for your department. By allowing one or more of your employees to assist you — perhaps in gathering basic market or research data — you can give your employees a taste of what goes into putting together a budget.

And don't fall into the trap of believing that the only way to train your employees is to sign them up for an expensive class taught by someone with a slick, color brochure who knows nothing about your business. Opportunities to train your employees abound within your *own* business. An estimated 90 percent of all development occurs on the job. Not only is this training free, but by assigning your employees to progressively more important tasks, you build their self-confidence and help to pave their way to progress in the organization.

Avoid delegating these things

Some tasks are part and parcel of the job of being a manager. By delegating the following work, you fail to perform your basic management duties.

Long-term vision and goals

As a manager, you are in a unique position. Your position at the top provides you with a unique perspective on the needs of the organization. As we discuss in Chapter 1, one of the key functions of management is vision. While employees at any level of a company can help provide you with input and make suggestions that help to shape your perspectives, developing an organization's long-term vision and goals is up to *you*. Simply, every employee can't decide for himself or herself in which direction the organization should move. An organization is much more effective when everyone moves together in the same direction.

Performance appraisals, discipline, and counseling

In the modern workplace, intimacy between manager and employee is often hard to come by. Most managers are probably lucky to get off a quick "good morning" or "goodnight" between the hustle and bustle of a typical workday. Given everyone's hectic schedules, you may have times when you don't talk to one or more of your employees for days at a time. *Oh, hello. Haven't we met each other before? You seem so familiar.*

However, sometimes you absolutely *have* to set time aside for your employees. When you discipline and counsel your employees, you are giving them the kind of input that only *you* can provide. You set the goals for your employees, and you set the standards by which you measure their progress. Inevitably, *you* decide whether your employee has reached the marks you have set or whether he or she has fallen short. You cannot delegate away this task effectively — everyone loses as a result.

Politically sensitive situations

Some situations are just too politically sensitive to assign to your employees. Say, for example, that you are in charge of auditing the travel expenses for your organization. The results of your review show that a member of the corporation's executive team has made several personal trips on company funds. Do you assign the responsibility for reporting this explosive situation to a worker? *Gee, Susan, I was hoping that you could present this information to the Board — I don't think I want to be around when the news hits!* No!

Not only do such situations demand your utmost attention and expertise, but placing your employee in the middle of the line of fire in this potentially explosive situation is also unfair. Being a manager may be tough sometimes, but *you* are paid to make the difficult decisions and to take the political heat that your work generates.

Personal assignments

Occasionally, your boss assigns a specific task to you with the intention that you will personally perform it. He or she may have very good reasons for doing so: You may have a unique perspective that no one else in your organization has, or you may have a unique skill that needs to be brought to bear to complete the assignment quickly and accurately. Whatever the situation, if a task is assigned to you with the expectation that you, and only you, will carry it out, then you should not delegate it to your staff. You may decide to involve your staff in gathering input, but you must retain the ultimate responsibility for the final execution of the task yourself.

Confidential or sensitive circumstances

As a manager, you are likely privy to information that your staff is not. Wage and salary figures, proprietary data, and personnel assessments are all examples of the kinds of information that managers are often uniquely aware of. Release of this information to the wrong individuals could be very damaging to an organization. Salary information should be kept confidential, for example. Similarly, if your competitors could get their hands on some secret process that your company has spent countless hours and money to develop, the impact on your organization could be devastating. Unless your staff has a compelling need to know, then you should retain assignments involving these types of information yourself.

Checking Up Instead of Checking Out

Now delegation gets tough. Assume that you've already gotten through the initial hurdles of delegation — you assigned a task to your employee, and you are anxiously waiting to see how she performs. You defined the scope of the task and gave your employee the adequate training and resources to get it done. Not only that, but you told her what results you expect and exactly when you expect to see them. What do you do next?

Here's one option: An hour or two after you make the assignment, you check on its progress. In a couple more hours, you check again. As the deadline rapidly approaches, you increase the frequency of your checking until finally, your employee spends more time answering your questions about the progress she has made than she spends actually completing the task. Not only that, but every time you press her for details about her progress, she gets a little more distracted from her task and a little more frustrated with your seeming lack of confidence in her abilities. When the appointed hour arrives, she submits the result on time, but it is inaccurate and incomplete.

When delegation goes wrong

Sometimes delegation goes wrong — way wrong. How can you identify the danger signs before it is too late, and what can you do to save the day? You can monitor the performance of your workers in several ways:

- **A formalized tracking system:** Use a formal system to track assignments and due dates. The system can be manual or computerized.

- **Personal follow-up:** Supplement your formal tracking system with an informal system of visiting your workers and checking their progress on a regular basis.

- **Sampling:** Take periodic samples of your employees' work and check to make sure that the work meets the standards you agreed to.

- **Progress reports:** Regular progress reporting from employees to you can give you advance notice of problems *and* successes.

If you discover that your employees are in trouble, you have several options for getting things back on track:

- **Counseling:** Discuss the problems with your employees and agree on a plan to correct them.

- **Rescinding authority:** If problems continue despite your efforts to resolve them through counseling, you can rescind your employees' authority to complete the tasks independently. (They still work on the task, but under your close guidance and authority.)

- **Reassigning activities:** The ultimate solution when delegation goes wrong. If your employees cannot do their assigned tasks, give them to workers who are better suited to perform them successfully.

Here's another option: After you make the assignment to your employee, you do nothing. Yes, you heard right. You do nothing. Instead of checking on your employee's progress and offering your support, you assign the task and move on to other concerns. When the appointed hour arrives, you are surprised to discover that the task is not completed. When you ask your employee why she didn't meet the goal that you had mutually agreed upon, she tells you that she couldn't obtain some information and, rather than bother you with this problem, she decided to try to construct it for herself. Unfortunately, this slight diversion required an additional two days of research before she found the correct set of numbers.

Clearly, neither extreme is a productive way to monitor the delegation process. However, in between lies the answer to how to approach this delicate but essential task.

Each employee is unique. One style of monitoring might work with one employee but not work with another. New or inexperienced employees naturally require more attention and hand-holding than employees who are seasoned at their jobs —

whether they realize it or not. Veteran employees do not need the kind of day-to-day attention that less experienced employees need. In fact, they may resent your attempts to closely manage the way in which they carry out their duties.

Effective monitoring of delegation requires the following:

✔ **Tailor your approach to the employee.** If your employee performs his or her job with minimal supervision on your part, then establish a system of monitoring with only a few, critical checkpoints along the way. If your employee *needs* more attention, create a system that incorporates *lots* of checkpoints along the way to goal completion.

✔ **Diligently use a written or computer-based system for tracking the tasks that you assign to your employees.** Use the daily planner, personal digital assistant, or time management software program that you ran out and bought after your read Chapter 2 to keep track of the what, who, and when of task assignments. Figure 3-2 pictures the task-tracking module from the Microsoft Outlook software program. Making a commitment to get organized is important. Do it!

✔ **Keep the lines of communication open.** Make sure that your employees know that you *want* them to let you know if they can't surmount a problem. Find out whether they need more training or better resources. Finding out too early — when you can still do something about it — is better than finding out too late.

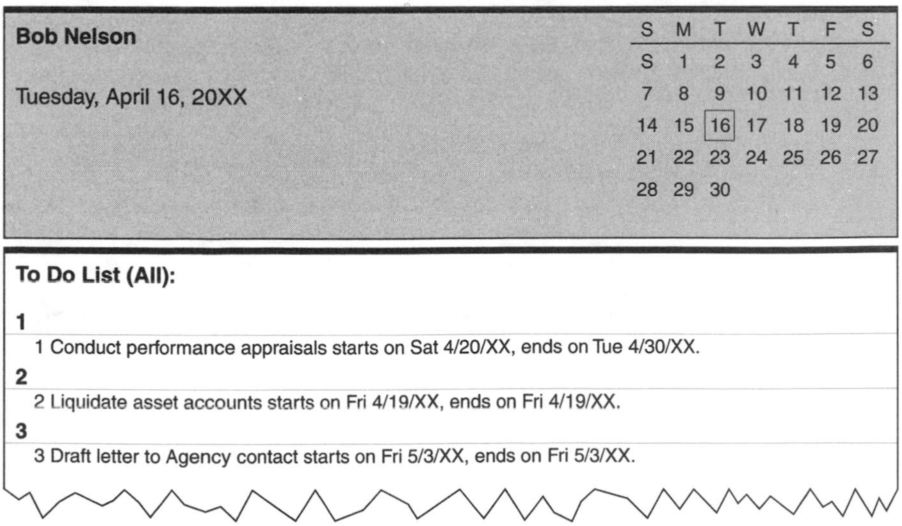

Bob Nelson		S	M	T	W	T	F	S
		S	1	2	3	4	5	6
Tuesday, April 16, 20XX		7	8	9	10	11	12	13
		14	15	16	17	18	19	20
		21	22	23	24	25	26	27
		28	29	30				

To Do List (All):

1
  1 Conduct performance appraisals starts on Sat 4/20/XX, ends on Tue 4/30/XX.
2
  2 Liquidate asset accounts starts on Fri 4/19/XX, ends on Fri 4/19/XX.
3
  3 Draft letter to Agency contact starts on Fri 5/3/XX, ends on Fri 5/3/XX.

Figure 3-2: A Microsoft Outlook task module.

✔ **Follow through on the agreements that you make with your employees.** If a report is late, then find out why. Despite the temptation to let these failures slip *(Gee, he's had a rough time at home lately)*, ignoring them does both you *and* your employees a disservice. Make sure that your employees understand the importance of taking personal responsibility for their work and that the ability of your group to achieve its goals depends on their meeting commitments.

✔ **Reward performance that meets or exceeds your expectations, and counsel performance that falls below your expectations.** If you don't let your employees know when they fail to meet your expectations, then they may continue to fail to meet your expectations. Do your employees, your organization, and yourself a *big* favor and bring attention to both the good things *and* the bad things that your employees do. You can find many more details about counseling employees in Chapters 7 and 10.

Test your new-found knowledge

What are some of the key benefits of delegating work to your employees?

A. You get increased employee motivation and a more efficient and effective work unit.

B. You get to take longer lunches.

C. You can blame your employees when things go wrong and take credit when things go right.

D. You are able to retire without having to leave the organization and take a pay cut.

Should you use a formal system for tracking employee task assignments?

A. No, you can remember every assignment that you make to your staff and when those assignments are due.

B. No, you don't want your employees to think that you are too autocratic.

C. Yes, a formal system for tracking employee task assignments helps you ensure that all tasks are completed on time.

D. No, after you make an assignment you should assume that your employees have taken care of it.

Chapter 4

Lead, Follow, or Get Out of the Way

● ●

In This Chapter

▶ Comparing leadership and management

▶ Becoming a leader

▶ Zeroing in on key leadership traits

▶ Adapting your leadership style

● ●

*W*hat makes a leader? Countless books have been written, endless videos have been produced, and interminable seminars have been taught on the topic of leadership. Still, leadership is a quality that eludes many who seek it.

Studies show that the main traits that all effective leaders have in common are optimism and confidence. That is, they have a positive outlook and are sure of themselves and their ability to influence others and impact the future. Although similar, leadership and management are different; leadership goes far above and beyond management. A manager can be organized and efficient at getting things done without being a leader — someone who inspires others to achieve their best. According to management visionary Peter Drucker, leadership is the most basic and scarcest resource in any business enterprise. According to our informal research on this topic, we concur wholeheartedly.

Everyone in an organization wants to work for leaders. Workers want the men and women they work for to exhibit leadership. *I wish that my boss would just make a decision — I'm just spinning my wheels until she does. I guess I'll just wait here until she lets me know what she wants me to do.* And wait they do — until the boss finally notices that the project is two months behind. Top executives want the men and women who work for them to exhibit leadership. *You need to take responsibility for your department and pull the numbers into the black before the end of the fiscal year!* And employees want their peers to show leadership. *If he's not going to straighten out that billing process, then I'll just have to work around it myself!*

A leader is many things to many people. In this chapter, we discuss the key skills and attributes that make good managers into great leaders. As this chapter explains, leadership requires the application of a wide variety of skills — no single trait, when mastered, suddenly makes you an effective leader. *You mean that I can't become a great leader just from watching this video?* However, you may notice that some leadership skills that follow are also key functions of management today — ones that we review in Chapter 1. This is no coincidence.

The Differences between Management and Leadership

Being a good manager is quite an accomplishment. Management is by no means an easy task, and mastering the wide range of varied skills that are required can take many years. The best managers get their jobs done efficiently and effectively — with a minimum of muss and fuss. Like the person behind the scenes of a great performance in sports or the theater, the best managers are often those whom you notice the least.

Great managers are experts at taking their current organizations and optimizing them to accomplish their goals and get their jobs done. By necessity, they focus on the *here and now* — not on the tremendous potential of what the future can bring. Managers are expected to make things happen *now* — not at some indefinite, fuzzy point in the future. *Smeed! Don't tell me what you're going to do for me next year or the year after that! I want results, and I want them now!* Having good managers in an organization, however, is not enough.

Great organizations need great management. However, great management does not necessarily make a great organization. For an organization to be great, it must also have great *leadership*.

Leaders have vision. They look beyond the here and now to see the vast potential of their organizations. And while great leaders are also effective at getting things done in their organizations, they accomplish their goals in a way different from managers.

Managers use policies, procedures, schedules, milestones, incentives, discipline, and other mechanisms to *push* their employees to achieve the goals of the organization. *What? You missed the March project milestone? You know that we can't afford to be late — the marketing campaign has already started. Please review this schedule and have a detailed report explaining how you're going to get back on track on my desk first thing in the morning.* And if another milestone is missed, the threat of discipline or termination is always a very real tool in a skilled manager's bag of tricks.

Leaders, on the other hand, *challenge* their employees to achieve the goals of the organization by creating a compelling vision of the future and then unlocking their employees' potential. Think about great leaders of recent times. President John F. Kennedy challenged the American people to land a man on the moon. We did. Lee Iacocca challenged the management and workers of the Chrysler Corporation to bring their company out of the clutches of financial disaster and to build a new corporation that would lead the way in product innovation and profitability. They did. Jack Welch of General Electric challenges his workers to help the company attain first or second place in every business that it owns. They do.

All these leaders share a common trait. They all painted compelling visions that grabbed the imagination of their followers and then challenged them to achieve these visions. Without the vision that leaders provide and without the contributions of their followers' hard work, energy, and innovation, the United States would never have landed a man on the moon, the name Chrysler would have slipped quietly into history, and General Electric wouldn't be the hugely successful firm that it is today.

What Leaders Do

The skills required to be a leader are no secret; it's just that some managers have learned to use them and others haven't. And while some people seem to be born leaders, anyone can learn what leaders do and how to apply these skills themselves.

Inspire action

Despite what some managers believe, there are few workers who don't want to feel pride for their organization and who, given the chance, wouldn't give their all to a cause they believe in. A tremendous well of creativity and energy is just waiting to be tapped in every organization. Leaders use this knowledge to inspire their employees to take action and to achieve great things.

Leaders know the value of employees and their critical importance in achieving the goals of a company. Do the managers in *your* company know the importance of *their* employees? Check out what these managers had to say in Bob Nelson's *1001 Ways to Reward Employees*:

✔ Chairman and CEO of the Ford Motor Company Harold A. Poling says, "One of the stepping stones to a world-class operation is to tap into the creative and intellectual power of each and every employee."

✔ According to Paul M. Cook, founder and CEO of Raychem Corporation, "Most people, whether they're engineers, business managers, or machine operators, want to be creative. They want to identify with the success of their profession and their organization. They want to contribute to giving society more comfort, better health, [and] more excitement."

✔ Hewlett-Packard cofounder and leader Bill Hewlett says, "Men and women want to do a good job, a creative job, and if they are provided the proper environment, they will do so."

Unfortunately, few managers reward their employees for being creative or for going beyond the boundaries set by their job descriptions. Too many managers search for workers who do exactly what they are told — and little else. This practice is a *tremendous* waste of worker creativity, ideas, and motivation.

Use your influence as a manager to help your employees *create* energy in their jobs instead of draining it from them with bureaucracy, red tape, policies, and an emphasis on avoiding mistakes.

Leaders are different. Instead of draining energy from their employees, leaders unleash the natural energy within all employees. They do so by clearing the roadblocks to creativity and pride from the paths of their workers and by creating a compelling vision for their employees to strive for. They help employees to tap into energy and initiative that they didn't know they had.

Create a compelling vision for your employees and then clear away the roadblocks to creativity and pride. Your vision must be a *stretch* to achieve, but not so much of a stretch that the vision is *impossible* to achieve.

Communicate

Leaders make a commitment to communicate with their employees and to keep them informed about the organization. Employees want to be an integral part of their organizations and want their opinions and suggestions to be heard. Great leaders earn the commitment of their workers by building communication links throughout the organization — from the top to the bottom, from the bottom to the top, and from side to side.

So how do you build communication links in *your* organization? Consider the experiences of the following business leaders as listed in Bob's *1001 Ways to Reward Employees*:

✔ According to Donald Petersen, President and CEO of Ford Motor Company, "When I started visiting the plants and meeting with employees, what was reassuring was the tremendous, positive energy in our conversations. One man said he'd been with Ford for twenty-five years and hated every minute of it — until he was asked for his opinion. He said that question transformed his job."

✔ Andrea Nieman, Administrative Assistant with the Rolm Corporation, summarizes her company's commitment to communication like this: "Rolm recognizes that people are the greatest asset. There is no 'us' and 'them' attitude here; everyone is important. Upper management is visible and accessible. There is always time to talk, to find solutions and to implement changes."

✔ Says Robert Hauptfuhrer, Chairman and CEO of Oryx Energy, "Give people a chance not just to do a job but to have some impact, and they'll really respond, get on their roller skates, and race around to make sure it happens."

When Bob became a department manager at Blanchard Training and Development, he made a commitment to his team of employees to communicate with them. To make his commitment real, Bob added specifics: He promised that he would report the results of every executive team meeting within 24 hours. Bob's department valued his team briefings because, through this communication, he treated all individuals as colleagues — not as underlings.

Great leaders know that leadership is not a one-way street. Leadership in the '90s is a two-way interchange of ideas where leaders create a vision and workers throughout an organization develop and communicate ideas of how best to reach the vision. The old one-way, command-and-control model of management doesn't work anymore. Commanding workers may work all right in the Army, but as a daily means of managing a company, it doesn't work well at all. Most employees are not willing to simply take orders and be directed all day long. If you think that they are, you are only fooling yourself.

Support and facilitate

Great leaders create environments in which employees are safe to speak up, to tell the truth, and to take risks. It's incredible how many managers punish their employees for pointing out problems that they encounter, disagreeing with the conventional wisdom of management, or merely saying what is on their minds. It's even more incredible that many managers punish their employees for taking risks and losing, instead of helping their employees win the next time around.

Great leaders support their employees and facilitate their ability to get things done. The head of an organization where Peter once worked did just the opposite. Instead of leading his employees by force of vision and inspiration, he pushed them with the twin cattle prods (120 volts DC!) of fear and intimidation. The management team members lived in constant fear of his temper, which could explode without warning and seemingly without reason. More than a few managers wore the psychological bruises and scars of his often public outbursts. Instead of contributing to the good of the organization, some managers simply withdrew into their shells and said as little as possible in this leader's presence. Consider these managers' statements in *1001 Ways to Reward Employees*:

✔ Catherine Meek, president of compensation consulting firm Meek and Associates, says, "In the twenty years I have been doing this and the thousands of employees I have interviewed in hundreds of companies, if I had to pick one thing that comes through loud and clear it is that organizations do a lousy job of recognizing people's contributions. That is the number one thing employees say to us. 'We don't even care about the money; if my boss would just acknowledge that I exist. The only time I ever hear anything is when I screw up. I never hear when I do a good job.'"

✔ According to Lonnie Blittle, an assembly line worker for Nissan Motor Manufacturing Corporation U.S.A., "There was none of the hush-hush atmosphere with management behind closed doors and everybody else waiting until they drop the boom on us. They are right down pitching in, not standing around with their hands on their hips."

✔ James Berdahl, vice president of marketing for Business Incentives, says, "People want to feel empowered to find better ways to do things and to take responsibility for their own environment. Allowing them to do this has had a big impact on how they do their jobs, as well as on their satisfaction with the company."

Instead of abandoning their employees to the sharks, great leaders throw their followers life preservers when the going gets particularly rough. Although leaders allow their employees free rein in how they achieve their organizations' goals, leaders are always there in the background — ready to assist and support workers whenever necessary. With the added security of this safety net, employees are more willing to stretch themselves and to take chances that can create enormous payoffs for their organizations.

Leading Leadership Traits

Today's new business environment is constant, unrelenting change. About the only thing you can be sure of anymore is that *everything* will change. And after it changes, it will change again. And again. And again. (Oops, sorry! The keyboard got stuck for a moment there.)

You had better get used to it now, because this is *the* way of life in business for the foreseeable future. However, while so much in business is changing, great leadership remains steadfast — like a sturdy rock standing up to the storms of change. Numerous traits of great leaders have remained the same over the years and are still highly valued today. The following sections discuss the leading leadership traits.

Key business trends to watch out for

According to Stanley Bing, the incredibly insightful columnist for *Fortune* magazine, many trends are sweeping the business landscape. One major trend is the necessity for managers to *talk the talk* and *walk the walk*. While talking the talk means to *sound* like you know what you are doing, walking the walk takes this a step further and requires that you also *look* like you know what you're doing — whether you do or not.

As the related graph shows, the percentage of executives who can talk the talk and those who can walk the walk has been increasing since 1970. However, the ability of managers to talk the talk *and* walk the walk at the same time has steadily declined from its peak some 20 years ago. Here is some advice from Bing regarding these critical leadership skills:

- "First, always talk the talk, even when others don't seem to understand what you're saying. It's all about consistency and perception — so keep it up!

- Second, if you're not in a position to talk the talk, either because someone superior is doing so or because you've got your mouth full, default to walking the walk exclusively, thereby projecting the necessary executive qualities in dignity and silence.

- Third, don't try doing both together until you're very good at it. There's nothing more pathetic than somebody attempting to walk/talk concurrently and getting his ankles all bollixed up while irreverent employees stand around chortling. So practice!"

(Source: *Fortune,* Sep. 18, 1995)

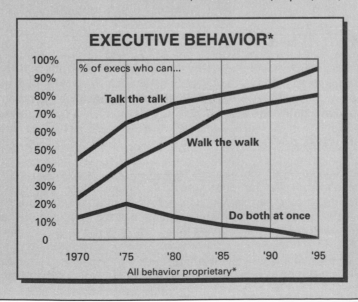

Optimism

To great leaders, the future is always a wonderful place. While they may find much adversity and hard work on the way to achieving their goals, leaders always look forward to the future with great promise and optimism. This optimism becomes a glow that radiates from all great leaders and touches all those who come into contact with them.

People want to feel good about themselves and their futures, and they want to work for winners. Workers are therefore naturally attracted to people who are optimistic rather than pessimistic. Who wants to work for someone who enjoys nothing more than spouting doom and gloom about the future of a business? Leaders like this only demotivate their employees and coworkers and lead workers to spend more time polishing their resumes than they do concentrating on improving their organizations.

Optimism is infectious; before long, a great leader can turn an organization full of naysayers into one that is overflowing with positive excitement for the future. This excitement results in greater worker productivity and an improved organizational environment. Morale increases, and so does the organization's bottom line.

Be an optimist. Let your excitement rub off on those around you.

Confidence

Great leaders have no doubt that they can accomplish any task that they set their minds to — at least not in public. What? A 10,000 foot-high mountain is in the way? No problem — we'll climb it. You say that a vast ocean is separating us from our goal? No sweat — we'll swim it. Hmmm . . . a bottomless crevasse blocking our path? Fine — we'll leap it. Whatever the challenge may be, we'll find a way to surmount it.

Confident leaders make for confident followers, which is why organizations led by confident leaders are unstoppable. An organization's employees mirror the behavior of their leaders. When leaders are tentative and unsure of themselves, so are workers (and the bottom-line results of the organization). When leaders display self-confidence, workers follow suit, and the results can be astounding.

Be a confident leader. You inspire the best performance of your employees at the same time as you help them to become more confident in their *own* abilities.

Integrity

One trait that sets great leaders apart from the rest of the pack is integrity: ethical behavior, values, and a sense of fair play. Honest people — and that means *you* — want to follow honest leaders. In a recent survey, integrity was the *most* desired trait that employees wanted from their leaders. When an organization's leaders conduct themselves with integrity, the organization can make a very real and positive difference in the lives of its employees, its customers, and others who come in contact with it. This, in turn, results in positive feelings about the organization.

Most working Americans devote a third (or more) of their waking hours to their jobs. Whether the organization makes light fixtures, disposes radioactive waste, develops virtual reality software, or delivers pizzas, people want to be part of an organization that makes a positive difference in people's lives. Sure, money is important — people have to make car payments and buy baby shoes — but few would not count this *extrinsic* reward a secondary consideration to the *intrinsic* rewards that they derive from their work.

PEARL OF WISDOM

The five principles of ethical power for organizations

In their book *The Power of Ethical Management,* Ken Blanchard and Norman Vincent Peale present five principles to gain ethical power in any organization. As the authors note in the book's introduction, "We believe that a strong code of morality in any business is the first step toward its success. We believe that ethical managers are winning managers."

Blanchard and Peale say that the five principles of ethical power for organizations are

- ✔ **Purpose:** The mission of our organization is communicated from the top. Our organization is guided by the values, hopes, and a vision that helps us to determine what is acceptable and unacceptable behavior.

- ✔ **Pride:** We feel proud of ourselves and of our organization. We know that when we feel this way, we can resist temptations to behave unethically.

- ✔ **Patience:** We believe that holding to our ethical values will lead us to success in the long term. This involves maintaining a balance between obtaining results and caring how we achieve these results.

- ✔ **Persistence:** We have a commitment to live by ethical principles. We are committed to our commitment. We make sure our actions are consistent with our purpose.

- ✔ **Perspective:** Our managers and employees take time to pause and reflect, take stock of where we are, evaluate where we are going, and determine how we are going to get there.

Decisiveness

The best leaders are decisive. If any complaint is heard from employees time and again, it's that their bosses won't make decisions. Despite the fact that making decisions is one of the key reasons that people are hired to be managers, too few are willing to risk the possibility of making a *wrong* decision. Instead of making wrong decisions — and having to face the consequences — many so-called leaders prefer to indefinitely postpone making a decision, instead continually seeking more information, alternatives, and opinions from others. They hope that, eventually, events may overtake the need to make the decision, or perhaps that someone else may step up to the plate and make the decision for them.

Great leaders make decisions. Now, this doesn't mean that they make decisions in a shoot-from-the-hip, cavalier, gotta-do-it-right-now fashion. No, great leaders take whatever time is necessary to gather whatever information, people, or resources they need to make an informed decision within a reasonable time frame. If the data is immediately available, so be it. If not, then a leader carefully weighs the available data versus the relative need of the decision and then acts accordingly.

Be decisive. Don't wait for the course of events to make decisions for you. Sometimes making a decision — even if it's the wrong decision — is better than making no decision at all.

Different Strokes for Different Folks: Situational Leadership

Using a single style of leadership to manage employees is no longer enough. Not only have downsizing, increased global competition, and other factors radically changed the work environment over the past couple decades, but the workforce itself also has changed. If you want to be an effective manager, you can no longer use only one style of leadership. Instead, you must apply different styles of leadership to match the differing needs of your employees.

Ken Blanchard's Situational Leadership is discussed in *Leadership and The One Minute Manager*. The concept suggests that managers must adapt their leadership style to match the development level of the employee for each assigned task. The end result is the belief that no one best way to manage people exists. A leadership style that works for a new, inexperienced employee will likely fail with an experienced worker. And within a group of seemingly identical workers, each employee has his or her own unique needs.

In Situational Leadership, three factors interact to determine a given result:

- ✔ The amount of direction that a leader provides to employees
- ✔ The amount of support that a leader provides to employees
- ✔ The ability of employees to perform tasks, functions, or objectives

Leadership involves four distinct styles. These four styles depend on whether a leader exhibits low or high directive behavior and whether a leader exhibits low or high supportive behavior. Each style is appropriate according to the particular needs of those being led.

Directing

Directing is the manifestation of a high directive, low supportive leadership behavior. Leaders in directing mode tell their workers exactly what they want done, when they want it done, where they want it done, and how to do it. This style is appropriate for new employees or for employees who have been assigned a new task. These *enthusiastic beginners* bring energy and excitement to a new job or task, but they need clarity in work direction. This style is *not* appropriate for experienced employees, who may associate their bosses' directing behavior with a lack of trust in the employees' abilities.

For an example of what we're talking about: Suppose that you have a couple of new employees who have been assigned to assemble a complicated product — perhaps a super-deluxe, professional-strength widget. This product is *so* complicated to assemble that you have a 5-page, 47-step procedure for doing the deed. Clearly, if you simply sit your new employees at their designated work stations, give them copies of the procedure, and leave them to fend for themselves, you'll have some frustrated new employees and some pretty lousy super-deluxe, professional-strength widgets.

A far better strategy is to apply *directive* leadership. Take the time to sit down with your new employees and give them clear direction, working through the process with them. Or ask one of your best assemblers to train the new employees in the process. If the new employees make a mistake, correct them — immediately. At this point in their learning, your new employees must strictly follow your instructions. This is not a time for your new employees to get creative. After they master the task, then they can work to improve it.

Coaching

When a leader applies high directive, high supportive behavior, the leader is doing what is called *coaching.* This style is best used when an employee still needs direction in learning a task but needs increasing support and encouragement to get the task done. In this situation, an employee is having problems in mastering a task and, in the process, has lost enthusiasm for doing the task. In other words, the honeymoon is over and the employee has become a *disillusioned learner.*

To see how coaching works, consider our example of the employees who are learning to assemble the super-deluxe widget. Your employees have followed your direction, and they are now trying to assemble the widgets on their own. They work and work at putting the widgets together, but because of the complexity of the 47-step procedure, they still have problems completing the assembly on their own.

As a coach, you need to check up on your new employees often to see how they are doing. When you see that they need help to successfully complete their task, your job is to coach them by providing encouragement and direction. You may need to walk them through the procedure again step by step, or you may need only to clarify one or two particular questions. Don't wait for your employees to ask to be coached! They may not even realize that they need to be coached, or they may be too embarrassed to ask.

One thing to remember is that whether in sports or in business, coaches lead their teams, but they *don't play in the game.* They provide training, guidance, clear direction, and strong support, but while their teams make it happen, the job of the coach requires that he or she watch from the sidelines.

Supporting

Leaders who exhibit high supportive, low directive behavior are *supporting* their employees. You use supportive leadership when employees have learned and demonstrated the skills necessary to carry out the desired task but still lack the confidence to do so consistently. Employees in this state of development are called *cautious contributors.* Their leaders need to encourage them to continue to do a good job.

Back to our new widget assemblers. Actually, they aren't quite so new anymore. They are starting to get the hang of their job, and they usually get it right. As their performance improves, they begin to gain mastery of the task and, as a result, start thinking about alternate approaches to doing the job.

The role of the leader now changes again. Instead of providing the high level of direction that he or she provided in the coaching style of management, the leader now concentrates on supporting employees. The employees are not looking for direction in meeting their challenges, but they do need additional support — someone to listen to them and help to build their confidence. Supporting managers provide support wherever necessary until their employees are confident in their own skills and abilities.

Solicit ideas and suggestions from your employees for better approaches to getting the job done. When you ask your employees to contribute, you create a learning opportunity for your employees by asking them to think about the details of how they do their jobs and how they can improve them. You reinforce their developing self-confidence by demonstrating that you trust their opinions.

Some of your employees' new ideas may be great — and others not so great. By explaining to your employees exactly why a new idea will or won't work, you teach them even more about their work processes and about the decision-making process that you use to evaluate new ideas. This learning is invaluable to them as they become more independent of your day-to-day supervision.

Delegating

Finally, *delegating* happens when leaders provide low direction and low support to their employees. This style of leadership works best with employees who are both skilled and confident in carrying out their duties. Such individuals are known as *peak performers* and can be given considerable responsibility to carry out tasks with little direction or support from leaders.

Now our super-deluxe widget assemblers can do their jobs independently and with little or no supervision. They do their jobs well, and if you allow them to implement improvements in the way they do their jobs without your explicit permission, they will do so. Along the way, your new employees have found ways to make the assembly process more efficient. Now, instead of a 47-step procedure to assemble a widget, the procedure may take only 35 steps — saving your firm time and money while improving the quality of the finished product.

Examples of these employees are undoubtedly all around you. Perhaps your sales manager consistently meets the goals that you set — on time, every time. Or maybe the mailroom clerk does a great job day in and day out without any direction from you. It could be the program manager who independently meets with customers, sets milestone schedules for project completion, and monitors the team's progress towards its goals.

Moving as many of your employees as possible through the various stages to become peak performers as quickly as possible is in your interest as a leader. Although you don't want to rush your employees into roles for which they are unprepared, the sooner you can delegate tasks to them, the more time you have to concentrate on the tasks that you are uniquely qualified to perform.

Test your new-found knowledge

What are the three most important things that leaders do?

A. Meet and eat

B. Pick up the tab at business lunches, issue important pronouncements, and keep tabs on employee attendance

C. Inspire action, communicate, and support and facilitate

D. Dress for success, go to all the right schools, and climb the corporate ladder

What are the four phases of Situational Leadership?

A. Directing, controlling, punishing, and terminating

B. Actually, there are only three phases of situational leadership.

C. Directing, coaching, supporting, and delegating

D. None of the above

Part II
Managing: The People Part

The 5th Wave   By Rich Tennant

@RICHTENNANT

Teamwork OR ELSE	Productivity OR ELSE	Attitude OR ELSE
Goals OR ELSE	Results OR ELSE	Challer OR ELS
Effort OR ELSE	Motivation OR ELSE	Winni OF

"FOR A MORE AGGRESSIVE APPROACH, WE HAVE OUR 'OR ELSE' SERIES OF MOTIVATIONAL POSTERS."

In this part . . .

1 f nothing else, managing is a *people* job. The best managers work well with people of all kinds. In this part, we show you how to hire great employees, inspire employees to achieve their best performance, and coach employees.

Chapter 5

Hiring: The Million-Dollar Decision

• •

In This Chapter

▶ Determining your needs

▶ Recruiting new employees

▶ Interviewing dos and don'ts

▶ Evaluating your candidates

▶ Making the big decision

• •

Good employees are hard to find. If you've had the recent privilege of advertising for a job opening, you know this to be the case. Here's the scenario: You place the advertisement and then wait for the resumes of the best and brightest candidates to find their way into your mailbox. In just a couple days, you are pleased beyond your wildest dreams as you see the stack of resumes awaiting your review. How many are there — 100? 200? Wow! What a response!

Your glee quickly turns to disappointment, however, as you begin your review. *"Why did this guy apply? He doesn't have half the required number of years of experience!" "What? She has never even done this kind of work before." "Is this guy joking? He must have responded to the wrong advertisement!"*

Finding and hiring the best candidates for a job has never been easy. Unfortunately, with all the streamlining, downsizing, and rightsizing going on in American business nowadays, a *lot* of people are looking for work. Your challenge is to figure out how to pluck the best candidates out of the sea strewn with the flotsam and jetsam of corporate reengineering. The lifetime earnings of the average American worker are calculated at approximately $1 million. Hiring really *is* a million-dollar decision!

Your mission, should you decide to accept it, is to locate the most highly qualified candidates for your job opening. You will have a wide range of tools at your disposal, but your budget is limited. You will have to use cunning and you will have to be resourceful but, above all, you will have to keep your wits about you at all times. Once you have located your candidates, your task is to narrow your selection down to one person and to ensure that the recruitment is executed with his or her successful entry into the firm. You must succeed in your mission — we cannot afford the alternative. Good luck. This tape will self-destruct in five seconds.

Defining the Characteristics of Your New Employees

Employers look for many qualities in candidates. What do *you* look for when you interview? The following list gives you an idea of the qualities that employers consider most important when hiring new employees. Other characteristics, such as good golfing skills, limited social life, or whatever, may be particularly important to you.

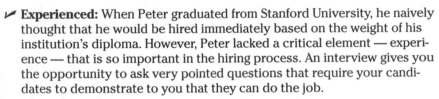

- ✔ **Hard working:** Hard work can often overcome a lack of experience or training. You want to hire people who are willing to do whatever it takes to get the job done. Conversely, no amount of skill can make up for a lack of initiative or work ethic. Although you won't know for sure until you make your hire, careful questioning of candidates can give you some idea of their work ethic (or, at least, what they want you to *believe* about their work ethic).

- ✔ **Good attitude:** While what constitutes a "good" attitude is different for different people, a positive, friendly, willing-to-help perspective makes life at the office much more enjoyable and makes *everyone's* job easier. When you interview candidates, consider what they'll be like to work with for the next five or ten years.

- ✔ **Experienced:** When Peter graduated from Stanford University, he naively thought that he would be hired immediately based on the weight of his institution's diploma. However, Peter lacked a critical element — experience — that is so important in the hiring process. An interview gives you the opportunity to ask very pointed questions that require your candidates to demonstrate to you that they can do the job.

- ✔ **Stable:** You don't want to hire someone today and then find out that he or she is already looking for the next position tomorrow. You can get some indication of a person's potential stability (or lack thereof) by asking how long he or she worked with his or her previous employer and why he or she left. Not only that, but you can enjoy listening to your candidates explain, in intimate detail, how they have finished sowing their wild oats and are now ready to settle down.

- ✔ **Smart:** Smart people can often find better and quicker solutions to the problems that confront them. In the world of business, *work* smarts are more important than *book* smarts. Unless, of course, you work for a publisher.

- ✔ **Responsible:** You want to hire people who are willing to take on the responsibilities of their positions. Questions about the kinds of projects that your candidates have been responsible for, and their exact roles in them, can help you determine this important quality. Little things, like showing up for the interview and wearing the same color socks, can also be key indicators of your candidates' sense of responsibility.

Hiring the right people is one of the most important tasks that managers face. Unfortunately, managers traditionally give short shrift to this task — devoting as little time as possible to preparation and to the actual interview process. As in much of the rest of your life, the results that you get from the hiring process are usually in direct proportion to the amount of time that you devote to it. If you devote yourself to finding the best candidates for a position, you are much more likely to find them. If you rely on chance to bring them to you, you may be disappointed by what and whom you find.

Defining the Job Before You Start

Is the position new, or are you filling an existing one? In either case, before you start the recruiting process, you need to know exactly what standards you are going to use to measure your candidates. The clearer you are about what you need, the easier and less arbitrary your selection process becomes.

If the job is new, now is your opportunity to design your ideal candidate. *Dr. Frankenstein, I presume?* Draft a job description that fully describes all the tasks and responsibilities of the position and the minimum necessary qualifications and experience. If the job requires expertise in C++ programming, then say so. Don't be shy! You're not going to fill the position with a C++ expert if you don't make it a key part of the job description. The more work you put into the job description now, the less work you have to do after you make your hire.

If you're filling an existing position, review the current job description closely and make changes where necessary. Again, the job description should reflect exactly the tasks and requirements of the position. When you hire someone new to fill an existing position, you start with a clean slate. For example, you may have had a difficult time getting a former employee to accept certain new tasks — say, taking minutes at staff meetings or filing travel vouchers. By adding these new duties to the job description before you open recruitment, you make the expectations clear, and you won't have to struggle with your new hire to do the job.

Finally, before you start recruiting, use the latest and greatest job description to outline the most important qualities that you are seeking in your new hire. Use this outline to guide you in the interview process. If you stick to the position's requirements as your guide, you're sure to get the kind of employee that you seek.

Making an interview outline carries an additional benefit: You can easily document why you didn't hire the candidates who didn't qualify for your positions. Pay close attention here. If you are ever sued by disgruntled job candidates for not hiring them, and such lawsuits are more common than you might suspect, you'll be eternally thankful that you did your homework in this area of the hiring process.

Finding Good People

People are the heart of every business. The better the people running your business, the better the business you will have. Some people are just meant to be in their jobs. You may know such individuals — someone who thrives as a receptionist or someone who lives to sell. Think about how great your organization would be if you staffed *every* position with people who lived for their jobs.

Likewise, bad hires can make working for an organization an incredibly miserable experience. The negative impacts of hiring the wrong candidate can reverberate throughout an organization for years. If you, as a manager, ignore the problem, you put yourself in danger of losing your good employees. We cannot overemphasize the importance of hiring the right people. Do you want to spend a few extra hours up front to find the best candidates, or would you rather devote countless hours trying to straighten out a problem employee?

Of course, as important as the interview process is to selecting the best candidates for your jobs, you won't have anyone to interview if you don't have a good system for finding good candidates. So where can you find the best candidates for your jobs?

The simple answer is *everywhere*. Sure, some places are better than others — you probably won't find someone to run your lab's fusion reactor project by advertising on the backs of matchbooks — but you never know where you'll find your next star programmer or award-winning journalist. Who knows, he or she may be working for your competitors right now! (See Figure 5-1.)

Figure 5-1:
An ad like this probably won't get you very far in the hiring process.

"You can have an exciting career in nuclear physics. Simply send for our booklet..."

The sections that follow present some of the best ways to find candidates for your positions. Your job is to develop a recruitment campaign that can find the kinds of people that you want to hire. And don't rely solely on your human resources department to develop this campaign for you; you probably have a better understanding of where to find the people you need (no offense to human resource departments!). Make sure that your input is heeded.

- **Taking a close look within:** In most organizations, the first place to look for candidates is within the organization. If you do your job in training and developing employees, then you should have plenty of candidates to consider for your job openings. Only after you exhaust your internal candidates should you look outside your organization. Not only is hiring people this way cheaper and easier, but you get happier employees, improved morale, and have *new hires* who are already familiar with your organization to boot.

- **Personal referrals:** Whether from coworkers, professional colleagues, friends, relatives, or neighbors, you can find great candidates by referrals. Who better to present a candidate than someone whose opinion you already value and trust? You get far more insight about the candidates' strengths and weaknesses from the people who refer them than you ever get from resumes alone. When you are getting ready to fill a position, make sure that you let people know about it.

- **Temporary agencies:** Hiring *temps,* or temporary employees, has become routine for many companies. When you simply *have to* fill a critical position for a short period of time, temporary agencies are the way to go — no muss, no fuss. And the best part is that when you hire temps, you get the opportunity to try out employees before you buy them. If you don't like the temps you get, no problem. Simply call the agency, and they send replacements before you know it. But if you like your temps, most agencies allow you to hire them at a nominal fee or after a minimum time commitment. Either way, you win.

- **Professional associations:** Most professions have their accompanying associations that look out for their interests. Whether you're a doctor (and belong to the American Medical Association), or a truck driver (and belong to the Teamster's Union), you can likely find an affiliated association for whatever you do for a living. There are even associations of associations. Association newsletters, journals, and magazines are great places to advertise your openings when you are looking for specific expertise, because your audience is already prescreened for you.

- **Employment agencies:** If you are filling a particularly specialized position, are recruiting in a small market, or would simply prefer to have someone else take care of recruiting and screening your applicants, employment agencies are a good alternative. While employment agencies can usually locate qualified candidates in lower-level or administrative positions, you may need help from an executive search firm or *headhunter* for your higher-level positions.

✔ **The Internet:** Every day, more and more companies discover the benefits of using the Internet as a hiring tool. While academics and scientists have long used Internet newsgroups to advertise and seek positions within their fields, corporations are now following suit. The proliferation of corporate World Wide Web pages has brought about an entirely new dimension in recruiting. Web pages let you present almost unlimited amounts and kinds of information about your firm and about your job openings — in text, audio, graphic, and video formats. Your pages work for you 24 hours a day, 7 days a week.

For an example of a particularly effective recruiting Web site, point your browser to `http://www.qualcomm.com` and click on the Employment Opportunities button.

✔ **Want ads:** Not only are want ads relatively inexpensive, but they're an easy way to get your message out to a large cross-section of potential candidates. You can choose to advertise in your local paper or in nationally distributed publications such as the *Wall Street Journal.* On the downside, you may find yourself sorting through hundreds or even thousands of unqualified candidates to find a few great ones. But that's what your human resources department is for, right?

You Can Be the Greatest Interviewer in the World

What kind of interviewer are you? Do you spend several hours preparing for interviews — reviewing resumes, looking over job descriptions, writing and rewriting questions until each one is as finely honed as a razor blade? Or are you the kind of interviewer who, busy as you already are, starts preparing for the interview when you get the call from your receptionist that your candidate has arrived?

The secret to becoming the Greatest Interviewer in the World is to spend some *serious* time preparing for your interviews. Remember how much time you spent preparing for your current job? You didn't just walk in the door, sit down, and get offered the job, did you? You probably spent hours researching the company, their products and services, their financials, their market, and other business information. You probably brushed up on your interviewing skills and may have even done some role playing with a friend or in front of a mirror. Don't you think that you should spend at least as much time getting ready for the interview as the people whom you are going to interview?

Asking the right questions

More than anything else, the heart of the interview process is the questions that you ask and the answers that you receive in response. You get the best answers when you ask the best questions. Lousy questions often result in lousy answers — answers that don't really tell you whether the candidate is going to be right for the job.

A great interviewer asks great questions. "How do I ask great questions?" you ask. According to Richard Nelson Bolles, author of the perennially popular job hunting guide *What Color Is Your Parachute?*, you can categorize all interview questions under one of these four headings:

- ✔ **Why are you here?** Really. Why is the person sitting across from you going to the trouble of interviewing with you today? You have just one way to find out — ask. You may assume that the answer is because he or she wants a job with your firm, but you may be surprised at what you find.

  Bruce Hatz, corporate staffing manager for Hewlett-Packard, tells the story of an interviewee who forgot that he was interviewing for a job with Hewlett-Packard. During the entire interview, the applicant referred to Hewlett-Packard by the name of one of its competitors. (Source: *San Jose Mercury-News* on America Online, downloaded 12/6/95.)

- ✔ **What can you do for us?** Always an important consideration! Of course, your candidates are all going to dazzle you with their incredible personalities, experience, work ethic, and love of teamwork — that almost goes without saying. However, despite what many job seekers seem to believe, the question is not, "What can your firm do for me?" — at least not from *your* perspective. The question that you want an answer to is, "What can you do for us?"

  Martha Stoodley, former recruiter for Advanced Micro Devices, Inc., tells about the job applicant who slammed his hand on her desk and demanded a signing bonus. And this was before the interview had even started! We're not surprised that this particular candidate landed neither the job *nor* the bonus! (Source: *San Jose Mercury-News* on America Online, downloaded 12/6/95.)

- ✔ **What kind of person are you?** Few of your candidates will be absolute angels or demons, but don't forget that you'll spend a *lot* of time with the person that you hire. You want to hire someone whom you enjoy being with during the many work hours, weeks, and years that stretch before you — and the holiday parties, company picnics, and countless other events that you're expected to attend. (Okay, at least someone you can tolerate being with for a few hours every once in a while.) You also want to confirm a few other minor issues: Are your candidates honest and ethical? Do they share your views in regards to work hours, responsibility, and so forth? Are they responsible and dependable employees?

✔ **Can we afford you?** It does you no good if you find the perfect candidate but, at the end of the interview, you bring up the topic of pay and find out that you are so far apart that you're actually in a different state. Keep in mind that the actual wage you pay to workers is only part of an overall compensation package. Although you may not be able to pull together more money for wages for particularly good candidates, you may be able to offer them better benefits, a nicer office, a more impressive title, or a key to the executive sauna.

Interviewing dos

So what should you do to prepare for your interviews? The following handy-dandy checklist gives you ideas on where to start:

✔ **Review the resumes of each interviewee the morning before interviews start.** Not only is it extremely poor form to wait to read your interviewees' resumes during the interview, but you miss out on the opportunity to tailor your questions to those little surprises that you invariably discover in the resumes.

✔ **Become intimately familiar with the job description.** Are you familiar with *all* the duties and requirements of the job? *Really?* Telling interviewees that the position requires duties that it really doesn't is poor form. It's *definitely* poor form to surprise new hires with duties that you *didn't* tell them about in the interview — especially when they are major duties.

✔ **Draft your questions before the interview.** Make a checklist of the key experience, skills, and qualities that you seek in your candidates and use it to guide your questions. Of course, one of your questions may trigger other questions that you didn't anticipate. Go ahead with such questions as long as they provide you with additional insights regarding your candidate and help to illuminate the information that you've outlined on your checklist.

✔ **Select a comfortable environment for *both* of you.** Your interviewee will likely be uncomfortable regardless of what you do. *You* don't need to be uncomfortable, too. Make sure that the interview environment is well-ventilated, private, and protected from interruptions. You definitely don't want your phone ringing off the hook or employees barging in during your interviews. You get the best performance from your interviewees when they aren't thrown off track by distractions.

✔ **Avoid playing power trips during the course of the interview.** Forget the old games of shining bright lights in your interviewees' eyes, turning up the heat, or cutting the legs off their chairs (yes, *some* managers still do this!) to gain an artificial advantage over your candidates. Get real — it's the 21st century, for heaven's sake!

✔ **Take lots of notes.** Don't rely on your memory when it comes to interviewing candidates for your job. If you interview more than a couple of people, you can easily forget who said exactly what and what were your impressions of their performances. Not only are your written notes a great way to remember who's who, but they're also an important tool to have when you are evaluating your candidates. Plus, they look impressive when you route them to your boss.

As you have no doubt gathered by now, interview questions are one of your best tools for determining whether a candidate is right for your company. Although some amount of small talk is appropriate to help relax your candidates *(as sweat poured down the candidate's face, the interviewer asked the opening question with razor-like sharpness: "Hot enough for you?")*, the heart of your interviews should focus on answering the questions just listed. Above all, don't give up! Keep asking questions until you're satisfied that you have all the information you need to make your decision.

And don't forget to take lots of notes as you interview your candidates. Try to avoid the temptation to draw pictures of little smiley faces or that new car you have been lusting after. Write the key points of your candidates' responses and their reactions to your questions. For example, if you ask why your candidate left her previous job, and she starts getting *really* nervous, you should make a note about this reaction. Finally, note your own impressions of the candidates:

✔ "Top-notch performer — the star of her class."

✔ "Fantastic experience with developing applications in a client-server environment. The best candidate yet."

✔ "Geez, did this one just fall off the turnip truck?"

Interviewing don'ts

The topic of interviewing don'ts is probably worth a chapter of its own. If you have been a manager for any time at all, you know that you can run into tricky situations during an interview and that certain questions can land you in *major* hot water if you make the mistake of asking them.

Some interviewing don'ts are merely good business practice. For example, accepting an applicant's invitation for a date is probably not a good idea. After a particularly drawn-out interview at Hewlett-Packard, a female interviewer was asked out on a date by a male candidate. The interviewer considered her options and declined the date; she also declined to make Prince Charming a job offer. (Source: *San Jose Mercury-News* on America Online, downloaded 12/6/95.)

Then you have the blunders of the *major legal type* — the kind that can land you and your firm in court. Interviewing is one area of particular concern in the hiring process as it pertains to the possibility of discrimination. For example, although you can ask applicants whether they are able to fulfill job functions, you cannot ask them whether they are disabled. Because of the critical nature of the interview process, you must know the questions that you absolutely should never ask a job candidate. Here is a brief summary of the kinds of topics that *may,* depending on the exact circumstances, get you and your firm into trouble:

- ✔ Applicant's race or skin color
- ✔ Applicant's national origin
- ✔ Applicant's sex
- ✔ Applicant's marital status
- ✔ Applicant's religion (or lack thereof)
- ✔ Applicant's arrest and conviction record
- ✔ Applicant's height and weight
- ✔ Applicant's debts
- ✔ Applicant's disability

The point is that *none* of the preceding topics are necessary to determine the ability of applicants to perform their jobs. You should therefore ask only questions that are directly related to the candidates' ability to perform the tasks required of them. To do otherwise could put you at definite legal risk.

Evaluating Your Candidates

Now comes the really fun part of the hiring process — evaluating your candidates. If you have done your homework, then you already have an amazing selection of candidates to choose from, you've narrowed your search down to the ones showing the best potential to excel in your position, and you've interviewed them to see whether they can live up to the promises that they made in their resumes. Before you make your final decision, you need a little bit more information.

Checking references

Wow! What a resume! What an interview! What a candidate! Would you be surprised to find out that this shining employee-to-be didn't really go to Yale? Or that he really wasn't the account manager on that nationwide marketing campaign? Or that his last supervisor was not particularly impressed with his analytical skills?

Five steps to better interviewing

Every interview consists of five key steps. They are

1. Welcome the applicant.

Greet your candidates warmly and chat with them informally to help loosen them up. Questions about the weather, the difficulty of finding your facility, or how they learned about your position are old standbys.

2. Summarize the position.

Briefly describe the job, the kind of person you are looking for, and the interview process that you use.

3. Ask your questions.

Questions should be relevant to the position and should cover the applicant's work experience, education, and other related topics.

4. Find out the candidate's strengths and weaknesses.

Although asking your candidates to name their strengths and weaknesses may seem cliched, the answers can be very revealing. Go ahead, ask them. We dare you.

5. Conclude the interview.

Allow your candidates the opportunity to offer any further information that they feel is necessary for you to make a decision. Thank them for their interest and let them know when they can expect your firm to contact them.

A resume and interview are great tools, but a reference check is probably the only chance you have to find out whether your candidates are who they say they are before you make a hiring decision. Depending on your organization, you may be expected to do reference checks. Or maybe your human resources department takes care of that task. Whichever the case, never hire new employees without first doing an *exhaustive* check of their backgrounds.

The twin goals of checking references are to verify the information that your candidates have provided and to gain some candid insight into who your candidates really are and how they really behave in the workplace. When you contact a candidate's references, limit your questions to those that are related to the work to be done. As in the interview process, asking questions that could be considered discriminatory to your candidates is not appropriate.

✔ **Check academic references.** A surprising number of people exaggerate or tell outright lies when reporting their educational experience. This is the first place to start your reference check. If your candidates didn't tell the truth here, you can bet that the rest of their experience is suspect, too, and you can toss the candidate into the discard pile before you proceed any further.

✔ **Call current and former supervisors.** Getting information from employers is getting harder. Many business people are rightfully afraid that they may be sued for libel or defamation of character if they say anything negative about current or former subordinates. Still, it doesn't hurt to try. You get a much better picture of your candidates if you speak directly to their current and former supervisors instead of to their firms' human resources departments — especially if the supervisors you speak to have left their firms. The most you are likely to get from the human resources folks is a confirmation that the candidate worked there during a specific period of time.

✔ **Check your network of associates.** If you are a member of a professional association, union, or similar group of like-minded careerists, you have the opportunity to tap into the rest of the membership to get the word on your candidates. For example, if you are a CPA and want to find out about a few candidates for your open accounting position, you can check with the members of your professional accounting association to see whether anyone knows anything about them.

✔ **Enlist the aid of a professional psychic.** Just joking here, although, to listen to the raving testimonials on the late-night TV psychic hotline infomercials, you'd think that you should never make a step without first consulting your psychic or astrologer. (See Figure 5-2.) And you can simply charge your call to your VISA or Mastercard. If this method was good enough for former First Lady Nancy Reagan, maybe it's good enough for you, too.

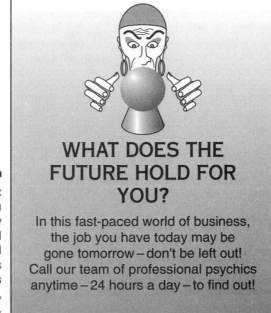

WHAT DOES THE FUTURE HOLD FOR YOU?

In this fast-paced world of business, the job you have today may be gone tomorrow – don't be left out! Call our team of professional psychics anytime – 24 hours a day – to find out!

Figure 5-2:
You probably won't find good candidates with this method, either.

Reviewing your notes

You *did* take interview notes, didn't you? Now is the time to drag them back out and look them over. Review the information package for each candidate — one by one — and compare your findings against your predetermined criteria. Take a look at the candidates' resumes, your notes, and the results of your reference checks. How do they stack up against the standards that you set for the position? Do you see any clear winners at this point? Any clear losers? Organize your candidate packages into the following stacks:

- **Winners:** These candidates are clearly the best choices for the position. You wouldn't hesitate hiring any one of them.

- **Potential winners:** These candidates are questionable for one reason or another. Maybe their experience isn't as strong as that of other candidates, or perhaps you weren't impressed with their presentation skills. Neither clear winners or clear losers, you'll likely consider these candidates for hire only after further investigation or if you are unable to hire anyone from your pool of winners.

- **Losers:** These candidates are clearly unacceptable for the position. There is no way that you would consider hiring any of them.

Conducting a second (or third) round

When you are a busy manager, you have pressure to get things done as quickly as possible, and you're tempted to take shortcuts to achieving your goals. It seems that everything has to be done yesterday — or maybe the day before. When do you have the opportunity to *really* spend as much time as you would like to complete a task or project? Time is precious when you have ten other projects crying for your attention, and it's even more valuable when you are hiring for a vacant position that is critical to your organization and needs to be filled *right now*.

Hiring is one area of business in which you cannot take shortcuts. Finding the best candidates for your vacancies requires a very real investment of time and resources to be successful. Your company's future depends on it.

Depending on your organization's policies or culture, or because you are undecided as to the best candidate, you may decide to bring candidates in for several rounds of interviews. In this kind of system, initial screening interviews are conducted by lower-level supervisors, managers, or interview panels. Candidates who pass this round are invited back for another interview with a higher-level manager. Finally, the best two or three candidates interview with the organization's top manager.

The ultimate decision on how many rounds and levels of interviews to conduct will depend on the nature of the job itself. If the job is simple or at a relatively low level in the company, a single phone interview may be sufficient to determine the best candidate for a job. However, if the job is complex or at a relatively high level in the organization, several rounds of testing and personal interviews may be required to determine the best candidate.

Hiring the Best (and Leaving the Rest)

The first step in making a hiring decision is to rank your candidates within the groups of winners and potential winners that you established during the evaluation phase of the hiring process. You don't need to bother ranking the losers because you wouldn't hire them anyway — no matter what. The best candidate in your group of winners would be first, the next best would be second, and so on. If you have done your job thoroughly and well, the best candidates for the job should be readily apparent at this point.

The next step is get on the phone and offer your first choice the job. Don't waste any time — you never know whether your candidate has interviewed with other employers. It would be a shame to invest all this time in the hiring process only to find out that she just accepted a job with one of your competitors. If you can't come to terms with your first choice in a reasonable amount of time, then go on to your second choice. Keep going through your pool of winners until you either make a hire or exhaust the list of candidates.

The following sections give you a few tips to keep in mind as you rank your candidates and make your final decision.

Be objective

In some cases, you may prefer certain candidates because of their personalities or personal charisma — regardless of their abilities or work experience. Sometimes the desire to like these candidates can obscure their shortcomings, while a better qualified, albeit less socially adept candidate may fade in your estimation.

Be objective. Consider the job that is to be done and consider the skills and qualifications that being successful requires. Do your candidates have these skills and qualifications? What would it take for your candidates to be considered fully qualified for the position?

Don't allow yourself to be unduly influenced by your candidates' looks, champagne-like personalities, high-priced hairstyles, or dangerously named colognes. It's unlikely that any of these things will tell you how well your candidates will perform the job. The facts are there for you to see in your candidates' resumes, interview notes, and reference checks. If you stick to the facts, you can't go wrong.

Check your bias at the door

Not only is discrimination illegal, but it is just bad business practice. We could go on for pages about this topic, but, instead, we'll keep it simple and brief.

Talent knows no boundaries. It knows no color, race, gender, physical disability, religion, creed, or country of origin. If you ignore talent because of the package in which you find it, then you lose, and your organization loses. Period.

Trust your gut

Sometimes you are faced with a decision between two equally qualified candidates, or with a decision about a candidate who is marginal but shows promise. In such cases, you have weighed all the objective data, and you have given the analytical side of your being free rein, but you still have no clear winner. What do you do in this kind of situation?

Listen to yourself. It's time to unlock your heart, your feeling, and your intuition. What do you feel in your gut? Not nausea, we hope. Although two candidates may seem equal in skills and abilities, do you have a feeling that one is better suited to the job than the other? If so, go with it. As much as you may want your hiring decision to be as objective as possible, whenever you introduce the human element into the decision-making process, a certain amount of subjectivity is naturally present.

If, after all this, you are still in a quandary, then flip a coin and see who wins. If you are happy with the results of the toss, then you have made the right decision. If you're unhappy with the result, then you know that the other candidate is the one for you.

After the offer

What do you do if, heaven forbid, you are unable to hire anyone from your group of winners? This is a tough call, but no one said that management is an easy task. Take a look at your stack of potential winners. What would it take to make your top potential winners into winners? If the answer is as simple as a training course or two, then you should give these candidates serious consideration — with the understanding that you'll schedule them for the necessary training soon after hire. Perhaps they just need a little more experience before you would put them in the ranks of the winners. You can make a judgment call as to whether you feel that their current experience is sufficient to carry them through until they gain the experience you are looking for. If not, you may want to keep looking for the right candidate. After all, this person may be working with you for a long time — waiting for the best candidate only makes sense.

If you are forced to go to your group of almost winners, and no candidate really seems up to the task, then don't hire someone simply to fill the position. If you do, you'll probably be making a *big* mistake. Hiring employees is far easier than *un*hiring them. The damage that an inappropriate hire can wreak — on coworkers, your customers, and your organization — can take years and considerable amounts of money to undo. Not only that, but it can be a really big pain in your neck! Other options are to redefine the job, reevaluate other current employees, or hire on a temporary basis to see whether a risky hire works out.

CONCEPT CHECK

Test your new-found knowledge

Where's the first place to look for qualified candidates for your job vacancies?

A. The *National Enquirer* want ads

B. Within your organization

C. Call your competitors.

D. Take out an ad on the side of the Goodyear Blimp.

Which questions should you never ask in an interview?

A. That's a nice yarmulke — are you Jewish?

B. What a beautiful smock — are you pregnant?

C. Smashing kilt! Were you born in Scotland?

D. All of the above

Chapter 6

Inspiring Employees to Better Performance

In This Chapter

▶ Presenting the Greatest Management Principle in the World

▶ Finding out what motivates employees

▶ Deciding what behaviors to reward

▶ Starting with the positive

▶ Rewarding the little things

▶ Using nonmonetary rewards

*T*he question of how to motivate employees has loomed large over managers ever since management was first invented. (Substantial anthropologic evidence indicates that it was invented at about the time of Fred Flintstone and Barney Rubble.) Ultimately, much of the people side of management comes down to mastering skills and techniques for motivating people — to make them better, more productive employees who love their jobs more than anything else in the world. Okay — maybe you'd be happy if they just *liked* their jobs and didn't complain too much.

Most managers recognize two ways to motivate employees: reward and punishment. If employees do what you (their manager) want them to do, you reward them with things that they desire: money, awards, recognition, important titles, and so on. Alternatively, if employees don't do what you want them to do, you punish them with things that they don't desire: warnings, reprimands, demotions, firings, and so on. By nature (human, that is), employees are drawn to things that are pleasing and shy away from things that are punishing. Theories of employee motivation and reward come and go, but the practice of employee motivation still comes down to these two basic tactics.

This chapter deals with the positive side of employee motivation: rewards. We're sorry if you're eager to read about the punishment side, but we cover that in Chapter 15. Besides, 200 years of research in behavioral science and extensive studies at Ohio State University show that, in the long run, you get much better performance from your employees when you use positive motivation techniques instead of negative behavioral consequences. As the saying goes, "You catch more flies with honey than with vinegar."

We are not saying that there isn't a place for punishment; sometimes you have no choice but to punish, reprimand, or even terminate employees. However, before you resort to that, make every effort to use positive recognition, praise, and rewards to encourage the behaviors you seek. As a result, your company will be a much better place to work.

By leading with *positive reinforcers,* not only can you inspire your employees to do what you want them to do, but you can develop happier, more productive employees in the process — and *that* combination is tough to beat!

The Greatest Management Principle in the World

We're about to let you in on the Greatest Management Principle in the World. This simple rule can save you countless hours of frustration and extra work, and it can save your company many thousands, or perhaps even millions, of dollars. Sounds pretty awe inspiring, doesn't it? Are you ready? Okay, here it is:

You get what you reward.

It's not as simple as it looks

Now, don't let the seeming simplicity of this statement, fool you — great depth is hiding behind the two dimensions of this printed page. Here's why: You may think that you are rewarding your employees to do the things that you want them to do — but are you really?

Consider the following example. You have two employees: Employee A is incredibly talented and Employee B is a marginal performer. You give similar assignments to both employees. Employee A completes the assignment before it is due and turns it in with no errors. Because Employee A is already done, you give him two additional assignments. Meanwhile, Employee B is not only late, but when he finally turns in the report you requested, it is full of errors. Because you are now under a time crunch, you accept Employee B's results and then correct them yourself.

What's wrong with this picture? Who is actually being rewarded: Employee A or Employee B?

If you answered Employee B, you're right! This employee has learned that submitting work that is substandard and late is okay. Not only that, but he sees that you (the manager) will personally fix it! That's quite a nice reward for an employee who clearly doesn't deserve one. (Employee B certainly has you trained!)

On the other hand, by giving Employee A more work for being a diligent, outstanding worker, you are actually punishing him. Even though you may think nothing of assigning more work to Employee A, he's no dummy. When Employee A sees that all he gets for being an outstanding performer is *more* work (while you let Employee B get away with doing *less* work), he's not going to like it one little bit. And if you end up giving both employees basically the same raise (and don't think they won't find out), you make the problem even worse.

If you let the situation continue, *all* your top performers eventually realize that doing their best work is not in their best interest. As a result, they leave their position to find an organization that values their contribution, or they simply kick back and forget about doing their best work. Why bother? No one (that means you, the manager) seems to care anyway!

Jellybean motivation

Whenever you give everyone the same incentive — whether it's the same salary increase, equal recognition, or even equal amounts of your time — we call that *jellybean motivation*. Although this treatment may initially sound fair, it isn't.

Nothing is as unfair as the equal treatment of unequal performers.

Bob tells a great story about a large, California aerospace manufacturer that decided to be nice and thank *all* its employees at Christmas with a turkey to take home for the holidays. Sounds good so far, doesn't it? Here's the problem: Some employees noticed that their turkeys were smaller than those of their coworkers. Soon, the complaints reached the executive suites — employees with the smaller turkeys thought that they were being punished for poor performance.

Of course, management couldn't continue to have this misconception. The order went out to the supplier of the Christmas turkeys the next year — all turkeys *must* have the same weight. Unfortunately, the turkey supplier had to inform the aerospace manufacturer that, despite rumors to the contrary, the Lord didn't create all turkeys equal and supplying thousands of identical-weight turkeys would be impossible. Faced with this dilemma, management did what only management could do — it accompanied each Christmas turkey with a printed note that stated, "The weight of your turkey does not necessarily reflect your performance over the last year." Hmmm.

Complaints continued and the situation only got worse. Some employees said that they should have a choice between turkey and ham; others wanted a fruit basket; and so on. As the years went by, management found it necessary to hire a full-time turkey administrator! Finally, the annual Christmas turkey program came to a crashing halt when management discovered that certain employees were so disillusioned that they were dumping the turkeys out of their boxes, filling the boxes with company-owned tools, and then sneaking them past security.

Did the company achieve its goal of equal reward for all? Obviously not. Even though the Christmas turkey program cost quite a bit, it did not boost employee performance or morale, but instead, it caused a new set of management problems.

Don't forget the Greatest Management Principle in the World — You Get What You Reward. Before you set up a system to reward your employees, make sure that you know exactly what behaviors you want to reward and then align the rewards with those behaviors.

After you put your employee reward system into place, you need to check periodically to see that it is having the results that you want. If it isn't, change it!

What Motivates Employees?

Now we're going to tell you a *big* secret. This secret is the key to motivating your employees and getting them to do what you want. You don't need to attend an all-day seminar or join the management-video-of-the-week club to discover this secret: We are letting you in on it right here and right now at no extra charge!

What motivates some employees doesn't motivate other employees.

In other words, no single prescription can help you motivate all your employees. Each employee has his or her own unique motivators, and *your* job is to figure out what they are. Although this idea is easy enough to understand, determining the motivators may not be quite as easy. Because it's unlikely that your employees are going to walk into your office tomorrow, sit down across from you, and tell you what motivates them, *you* must set the stage to find out exactly what motivates each of your employees.

The simplest way to find out how to motivate your employees is to *ask them.* Often managers assume that their employees want only money. These same managers are surprised when their employees tell them that *other* things — such as being recognized for doing a good job, being allowed greater autonomy in decision making, or having a more flexible work schedule — may be much more motivating than cash.

You are a concerned manager; you want to find out what motivates your employees and then use this information as the basis of your employee rewards program. Consider the following as you begin setting the stage for your efforts:

- ✔ First, create a supportive environment for your employees.

- ✔ Next, draw up your plan to design and implement your rewards program.

- ✔ Finally, be prepared to make changes to your plan, based on what works and what doesn't.

Creating a supportive environment

The new business realities of the 21st century bring with them a need to find new ways to motivate employees. Motivation is no longer an absolute, *my way or the highway* proposition. The incredible acceleration of change in business and technology today is coupled with greatly expanded global competitive forces. With these forces pressing in from all sides, managers can have difficulty keeping up with what employees need to do, much less figure out what to tell them to do. In fact, a growing trend is for managers to manage individuals who are doing work that the managers themselves have never done. (Fortunately, given a little time and a little trust, most employees can figure out what needs to be done by themselves.)

Inspiring managers must embrace these changing business forces and management trends. Instead of using the power of their *positions* to motivate workers, managers must use the power of their *ideas.* Instead of using threats and intimidation to get things done, managers must create environments that support their employees and allow creativity to flourish.

You, as a manager, can create a supportive workplace in the following ways:

- ✔ **Make your employees feel safe.** Are your employees as comfortable telling you the *bad* news as they are telling you the *good* news? If the answer is *no,* you have not created a safe environment for your employees. *Everyone* makes mistakes; that's how people learn. If you want employees who are motivated, make it safe for them to take chances and to let you know the bad along with the good. You can do this by avoiding the urge to punish them when they make a mistake. At least be thankful that they are doing *something!*

✔ **Open the channels of communication.** The ability of *all* your employees to communicate openly and honestly with one another is critical to the ultimate success of your organization and has a major role in employee motivation. Today, the quick and efficient communication of information throughout your organization can be the main thing that differentiates you from your competition. Encourage your employees to speak up, to make suggestions, and to break down the organizational barriers — the rampant departmentalization, turfism, and similar roadblocks — that separate them from one another: where and whenever they find them.

✔ **Build and maintain trust and respect.** Employees who are trusted and respected by their managers are motivated to perform their best. By including employees in the decision-making process, today's managers get better ideas (that are easier to implement), and at the same time, they improve employee morale, loyalty, and commitment. *I'll bet our sales clerks can come up with the best way to handle this problem.*

✔ **Develop your greatest asset: your employees.** By helping to meet the needs of your employees, you are also meeting the needs of your organization. Challenge your employees to improve their skills and knowledge and provide them with the support and training that they need to do so. Concentrate on the positive progress that they make and recognize and reward it whenever possible.

You've got to have a plan

Motivated employees don't happen by accident — you've got to have a plan to reinforce the behavior that you want. In general, employees are more strongly motivated by the potential to earn rewards than they are by the fear of punishment. Clearly, a well thought-out and planned rewards system is important to creating a motivated, effective workforce. Here is a short course in setting up a system of rewards in *your* organization:

✔ **Link rewards to organizational goals.** To be effective, rewards need to reinforce the behavior that leads to attainment of an organization's goals. Rewards should be structured to increase the frequency of desired behavior and decrease the frequency of undesired behavior. Make sure that they do!

✔ **Define parameters and mechanics.** After you identify the behaviors that you want to reinforce, you need to develop the specifics of your reward system and create rules that are clear and easily understood by all employees. Make sure that targets are attainable and that all employees have a chance to obtain rewards. For example, your clerks also should have a shot at the rewards — not just salespeople or assemblers.

✔ **Obtain commitment and support.** Of course, you must communicate your new rewards program to your employees. Many organizations publicize their programs in group meetings; they present the programs as positive and fun activities that benefit both the employees and the companies. To get the best results, plan and implement your rewards program with the direct involvement of employees.

✔ **Monitor effectiveness.** Is your system of rewards getting the results that you want? If not, take a another look at the behaviors you want to reinforce and make sure that your rewards are closely linked. Even the most successful rewards programs tend to lose their effectiveness over time as employees begin to take them for granted. Keep *your* program fresh by discontinuing rewards that have lost their luster and bringing in new ones from time to time.

What to Reward

Most managers reward the wrong things — if they reward their employees at all. This tendency has led to a crisis of epic proportions in the traditional system of incentives and motivation in American business. Consider these statistics quoted in *Management Accounting:*

✔ Only 3 percent of base salary separates average from outstanding employees in American companies.

✔ 81 percent of American workers report that they would not receive rewards for increasing their productivity.

✔ 60 percent of American managers say that they would not receive increases in their compensation for increasing their performance.

Yikes! *Houston, we have a problem here!* If American managers and workers aren't being rewarded for increasing their productivity and performance, what *are* they being rewarded for? As we point out in our prior example of the Christmas turkey program, employees are often rewarded just for showing up for work. Isn't *that* why you give your employees their paychecks?

For an incentive program to have meaningful and lasting effects, it has to focus on *performance.* Nothing less and nothing more.

"But wait a second," you say, "that isn't fair to the employees who aren't as talented as my top performers." If that's what you think, we'll straighten out *that* particular misunderstanding right now. *Everyone,* regardless of how smart, talented, or productive they are, can improve their performance.

Suppose that Employee A can produce 100 widgets an hour and stay at that level of performance day in and day out. On the other hand, Employee B produces 75 widgets an hour but improves output to 85 widgets an hour. Who should you reward? *Employee B!* This example embodies what you want to reward: the efforts that your employees make to *improve* their performance, not just to *maintain* a certain level (no matter how good that level is).

The following are examples of *performance-based measures* that any manager should recognize and reward. What measures should *you* be monitoring, measuring, and rewarding in *your* organization? Don't forget, just showing up for work *doesn't* count!

- ✔ Defects decrease from 25 per 1,000 to 10 per 1,000.
- ✔ Annual sales increase by 20 percent.
- ✔ The department records system is reorganized and color-coded to make filing and retrieval more efficient.
- ✔ Administrative expenses are held to 90 percent of the authorized budget.
- ✔ The organization's mail is distributed in 1 hour instead of $1^1/_2$ hours.

Start with the Positive

As we noted at the beginning of this chapter, you are more likely to lead your employees to great results by focusing on their positive accomplishments than by finding fault with and punishing their negative outcomes. Despite this fact, many managers' primary mode of operation is correcting their employees' mistakes instead of complimenting their successes.

In a recent study, 58 percent of employees reported that they seldom received a personal thank-you from their managers for doing a good job even though they ranked such recognition as their most motivating incentive. They ranked a *written* thank-you for doing a good job as motivating incentive Number 2; 76 percent said that they seldom received these. Perhaps these statistics show why a lack of praise and recognition is one of the leading reasons why people leave their jobs today.

Years of psychological research have clearly shown that positive reinforcement works better than negative reinforcement for several reasons. Without getting too technical, the reasons are that positive reinforcement: (1) *increases* the frequency of the desired behavior, and (2) creates good feelings within employees.

On the other hand, negative reinforcement may decrease the frequency of undesired behavior, but doesn't necessarily result in the expression of desired behavior. Instead of being motivated to do better, employees who receive only criticism from their managers eventually come to avoid their managers whenever possible. Furthermore, negative reinforcement (particularly when manifested in ways that degrade employees and their personal sense of worth) can create tremendously bad feelings with employees. And employees who are unhappy with their employers have a much more difficult time doing a good job than do those who are happy with their employers.

The following ideas can help you seek out the positive in your employees and reinforce the behaviors that you want:

- ✔ **Give your employees the benefit of the doubt.** Do you really think that your employees want to do a *bad* job? Unless they are consciously trying to sabotage your firm, no one wants to do a bad job. *Your* job is to figure out what you can do to help them do a good job. Additional training, encouragement, and support should be among your first choices — not reprimands and punishment.

- ✔ **Have high expectations for your employees' abilities.** If *you* believe that your employees can be outstanding, soon they will believe it, too. When Peter was growing up, his parents rarely needed to punish him when he did something wrong. He needed only the words "we *know* that you can do better" to get him back on course.

- ✔ **Catch your employees doing things right.** Although most employees do a good job in most of their work, managers naturally tend to focus on the things that employees do wrong. Instead of constantly catching your employees doing things wrong, catch them doing things right. Not only can you reinforce the behaviors that you want, but you can make your employees feel good about working for you and for your firm.

Make a Big Deal about Little Things

Okay, here's a question for you: "Should you reward your employees for their little day-to-day successes, or should you save up rewards for when they accomplish something really major?" The answer to this question lies in the way that most of us get our work done on a daily basis.

The simple fact is this: For 99.9 percent of people in business, work is not a string of dazzling successes that come one after another without fail. Instead, the majority of work is made up of routine, daily activities — employees perform most of these quietly and with little fanfare. A manager's typical work day, for example, might consist of an hour or two of reading memos and e-mail messages, listening to voice mail messages, and talking to others on the phone. The manager spends another couple of hours in meetings and perhaps another hour in one-on-one discussions with staff members and coworkers. With another couple of hours spent on preparing reports or filling out forms, the manager actually devotes precious little time to decision-making — the activity that has the greatest impact on an organization.

AmEx recognizes great performers

If you could increase your organization's net income by 500 percent in a decade's time, would you take the time to recognize your great performers? The Travel Related Services division of American Express did by creating its "Great Performers" program to recognize and reward exceptional employee performance. The program accepted nominations from employees, supervisors, and even customers. Winners of the Great Performers award were eligible for selection by a worldwide governing committee to become Grand Award recipients. In addition to an all-expenses-paid trip for two to New York City, Grand award winners received $4,000 in American Express traveler's checks, a platinum award pin, and a certificate.

(Source: Nelson, *1001 Ways to Reward Employees*.)

For a line worker, this dearth of opportunities for dazzling success is even more pronounced. If the employee's job is assembling lawnmower engines all day (and she does a good, steady job of it), when does she have an opportunity to be outstanding in the eyes of her supervisor?

We've taken the long way around to say that major accomplishments are usually few and far between — regardless of your place in the organizational chart. Work is a series of small accomplishments that eventually add up to big ones. If you wait to reward your employees for their big successes, you may be waiting a *long* time.

Therefore, it is *absolutely* critical that you reward your employees for their small successes as well as for their big successes. You may set a lofty goal for your employees to achieve — one that stretches their abilities and tests their resolve — but remember that praising your employees' progress toward the goal is as important as praising them when they finally reach it.

Money Isn't Important (No, Really!)

You may think that money is the ultimate incentive for your employees. After all, who isn't excited when they receive a cash bonus or pay raise? *As visions of riches beyond her wildest dreams danced through her head, she pledged her eternal devotion to the firm.* The problem is that money really *isn't* a top motivator for employees — at least not in the way that most managers think.

Compensation is a right

Money is clearly important to your employees. They need money to pay bills, buy food and clothes, rent a video on Friday night, put gas in their cars, and afford the other necessities of life. People *are* very motivated to make enough money to pay for their basic needs. However, after your employees have enough money to pay for these basic needs, additional money becomes less motivating, and other incentives — surprisingly, noncash incentives — become more important.

That is, most employees consider the money that they receive on the job (whether it comes in the form of pay or cash bonuses) to be a fair exchange for the labor that they contribute to their organizations. Compensation is viewed as a *right* by today's employees. Recognition, on the other hand, is a *gift,* and using it helps you, as a manager, get the best effort from each employee.

When incentives become entitlements

In particular, employees who receive annual bonuses and other periodic, money-based rewards quickly come to consider them part of their basic pay. Peter once worked at a company where he received an annual bonus that amounted to approximately 10 percent of his annual pay. The first time he received the bonus, he was very excited by it. His motivation skyrocketed, and he pledged his eternal loyalty to the firm.

However, after Peter realized that receiving the bonus was going to be an annual event, he quickly took it for granted. In his mind, he converted the reward (for work above and beyond his basic job description) into a part of his basic compensation package. As far as Peter was concerned, his annual salary was really the amount of his basic pay *plus* the annual bonus. He even centered his holiday spending plans around the assumption that the bonus would arrive on or about a certain date — and it always did.

Of course, if there was ever a year when the bonus was not to be paid, disappointment and open hostility would erupt in its absence.

Two decades ago, management expert Peter Drucker hit the nail on the head when he pointed out in his book *Management: Tasks, Responsibilities, Practices,* "Economic incentives are becoming rights rather than rewards. Merit raises are always introduced as rewards for exceptional performance. In no time at all, they become a right. To deny a merit raise or to grant only a small one becomes punishment. The increasing demand for material re-wards is rapidly destroying their usefulness as incentives and managerial tools."

The ineffectiveness of money as a motivator for employees is a good news/bad news kind of thing. We'll start with the bad news first. Many managers have thrown lots of money into cash reward programs, and for the most part, these programs really didn't have the positive effect on motivation that the managers wanted. Although we don't want to say that you *waste* your money on these programs, we believe that you can use it more effectively. In fact, with other programs, you may achieve better results with far fewer dollars!

Now you get the good news: Because you know that money is not an effective motivating tool, you can focus on using tools that *are* effective — and the best are rewards that cost little or no money!

What motivates today's employees?

According to Dr. Gerald Graham of Wichita State University, the most motivating incentives (as reported by employees today) are

- ✔ **Manager initiated:** Instead of coming from some nebulous ad-hoc committee, "corporate," or completely out of the blue, the most valuable recognition comes directly from one's supervisor or manager.

- ✔ **Based on performance:** Employees want to be recognized for *the jobs they were hired to do.* The most effective incentives are therefore based on job performance and not on nonperformance-related things such as attendance, attire, or drawing the lucky number out of a hat at the monthly sales meeting.

So you're a busy manager. Cash rewards are convenient because you simply fill out a check request once a year to take care of all your motivation for the year. This manager-initiated, based-on-performance stuff sounds like a lot of work! To be frank, running an effective rewards program does take more work on your part than running a simple, but ineffective one. But as we show you, the best rewards can be *quite* simple — and after you get the hang of using them, you can easily integrate them into your daily routine. *Doing so is part of the job of managing today.*

Don't forget that recognition shouldn't be saved up for special occasions only. Your employees are doing good things — things that you want them to do — every day. Catch them doing something right and recognize their successes regularly and often!

The following incentives are simple to execute, take little time, and are among the most motivating for employees:

✔ Personal or written congratulations from you (the manager) for a job well done

✔ Public recognition, given visibly by you (the manager), for good job performance

✔ Morale-building meetings to celebrate successes

✔ Time off

✔ Asking employees their opinions and involving them in decision-making

For unbelievably comprehensive listings of incentive ideas that *really* work, check out Bob's bestselling book *1001 Ways to Reward Employees*.

Top ten ways to motivate employees

#1 Personally thank employees for doing a good job — one on one, in writing, or both. Do it timely, often, and sincerely.

#2 Be willing to take the time to meet with and listen to employees — as much as they need or want.

#3 Provide employees specific and frequent feedback about their performance. Support them in improving performance.

#4 Recognize, reward, and promote high performers; deal with low and marginal performers so that they improve or leave.

#5 Provide information on how the company makes and loses money, upcoming products, and services and strategies for competing. Explain the employee's role in the overall plan.

#6 Involve employees in decisions, especially as those decisions affect them. Involvement equals commitment.

#7 Give employees a chance to grow and learn new skills; encourage them to be their best. Show them how you can help them meet their goals while achieving the organization's goals. Create a partnership with each employee.

#8 Provide employees with a sense of ownership in their work and their work environment. This ownership can be symbolic (for example, business cards for *all* employees, whether they need them to do their jobs or not).

#9 Strive to create a work environment that is open, trusting, and fun. Encourage new ideas, suggestions, and initiative. Learn from, rather than punish for, mistakes.

#10 Celebrate successes — of the company, of the department, and of individuals in it. Take time for team- and morale-building meetings and activities. Be creative and fresh.

You hold the key to your employees' motivation

In our experience, most managers believe that their employees determine how motivated they choose to be. Managers tend to think that some employees naturally have good attitudes, that others naturally have bad attitudes, and that they (as managers) can't do much to change these attitudes. *I'm getting really tired of your negative attitude. Unless you change it, you'll never get anywhere in this company!*

As convenient as blaming your employees for their bad attitudes may be, looking in a mirror may be a more honest approach. Studies show that *managers* have the biggest influence on how motivated their employees are. Do managers recognize their employees for doing a good job? Do they provide a pleasant and supportive working environment? Do they create a sense of joint mission and teamwork in the organization? Do they treat their employees as equals? Do they avoid favoritism? Do they make time to listen when employees need to talk?

For the most part, *you* determine how motivated your employees are. And when the time comes to recognize your employees, you are the best person to do it — and to reward them fairly and equitably.

When you give out rewards, keep in mind that employees don't want handouts, and they *hate* favoritism. Don't give recognition when none is warranted. Not only do you cheapen the value of the incentive with the employee who received it, but also you lose credibility in the eyes of your other employees. *Credibility* with your employees is one of the most important qualities that you can build; if you lose it, you risk losing everything.

Test your new-found knowledge

What are the two best ways to motivate employees?

A. Reward and punishment

B. Fear and intimidation

C. Money and more money

D. Ridicule and public humiliation

What is the Greatest Management Principle in the World?

A. No pain, no gain.

B. Divide and conquer.

C. You get what you reward.

D. Buy low; sell high.

Chapter 7

When in Doubt, Coach

In This Chapter
▶ Understanding what makes a coach
▶ Developing basic coaching skills
▶ Identifying turning points in coaching
▶ Considering the links between sports and business

*A*s you refer to various parts of this book, you may notice common themes running through it. These themes are the heart and soul of today's new management reality.

One recurring theme is the new role of managers as people who support and encourage their employees, instead of telling them what to do (or simply expecting them to perform). The best managers are *coaches* — that is, individuals who guide, discuss, and encourage others on their journey. With the help of coaches, employees can achieve outstanding results, organizations can do better than ever, and you can sleep well at night, knowing that everything is A-Okay.

In Chapter 4, we discuss Ken Blanchard's *Situational Leadership.* Situational Leadership is the adaptation of a manager's leadership style to match the development level of the employees that they are managing. Of the four styles in the situational leadership model — directing, coaching, supporting, and delegating — the first- and fourth-level styles are the quickest and, therefore, the most tempting to overuse. Busy managers are apt to (1) tell an employee exactly what to do (direct) or (2) have an employee do a task entirely on his or her own (delegate).

The second- and third-level styles — coaching and supporting — take more time and effort and, consequently, can be more easily ignored or underused. Not that *you* would neglect to coach and support, of course! In this chapter, we combine the coaching and supporting leadership styles under the overall label of *coaching*.

For employees who are developing in their skills, knowledge, and self-confidence, coaching is a critical part of their learning process. Your employees don't learn effectively when you simply tell them what to do. In fact, they usually don't learn at all.

As the maxim goes . . .

> Tell me . . . I forget.
>
> Show me . . . I remember.
>
> Involve me . . . I understand.

Neither do your employees learn effectively when you throw a new task at them with no instruction or support whatsoever. Sure, good employees can eventually figure things out, but they waste a *lot* of time and energy in the process. *What the heck is this all about?! I guess I'll just stumble along until I get the hang of it!*

Between these two extremes — being told what to do and being given no support whatsoever — is a happy medium where employees can thrive and the organization can prosper. It's a happy land where everyone lives in peace and harmony. *[Offstage, the chorus swells: "I'd like to sing the world a song in perfect harmony . . ."]* This happy medium happens with coaching.

Who's a Coach?

We assume that you have a pretty good sense of what it means to be a manager, but do you *really* know what it means to be a coach? A coach is a colleague, counselor, and cheerleader, all rolled into one. Based on that definition, are *you* a coach? How about your boss? Or your boss's boss? Why or why not?

We bet that you're familiar with the role of coaches in other nonbusiness activities. A drama coach, for example, is almost always an accomplished actor or actress. The job of the drama coach is to conduct tryouts for parts, assign roles, schedule rehearsals, train and direct cast members throughout rehearsals, and support and encourage the actors and actresses during the final stage production. These roles aren't all that different from the roles that managers perform in a business, are they?

Coaching a team of individuals is not easy, and certain characteristics make some coaches better than others. Fortunately, as with most other business skills, you can learn, practice, and improve the traits of good coaches. You can always find room for improvement, and good coaches are the first to admit it. The list that follows highlights important characteristics of coaching:

> ✔ **Coaches set goals.** Whether an organization's vision is to become the leading supplier of logic boards in the world, to increase revenues by 20 percent a year, or simply to get the break room walls painted this year, coaches work with their employees to set goals and deadlines for completion. They then go away and allow their employees to determine *how* to accomplish the goals.

✓ **Coaches support and encourage.** It's easy for employees — even the best and most experienced — to become discouraged from time to time. When employees are learning new tasks, when a long-term account is lost, or when business is down, coaches are there — ready to step in and help the members of their team through the worst of it. *That's okay, Kim. You've learned from your mistake, and I know that you'll get it right next time!*

✓ **Coaches emphasize team success over individual success.** The overall performance of the team is the most important concern, not the stellar abilities of a particular team member. Coaches know that no one person can carry an entire team to success — winning takes the combined efforts of all members of a team. The development of teamwork skills is a vital step in an employee's progress in an organization.

✓ **Coaches can quickly assess the talents and shortfalls of team members.** The most successful coaches can quickly determine their team members' strengths and weaknesses and, as a result, tailor their approach to each. For example, if one team member has strong analytical skills but poor presentation skills, a coach will concentrate on providing support for the employee's development of better presentation skills. *You know, Mark, I want to spend some time with you to work on making your viewgraph presentations more effective.*

✓ **Coaches inspire the members of their team.** Through their support and guidance, coaches are skilled at inspiring the members of their team to the highest levels of human performance. Teams of inspired individuals are willing to do whatever it takes to achieve the goals of their organization.

✓ **Coaches create environments that allow individuals to be successful.** Great coaches ensure that their workplaces are structured to let team members take risks and stretch their limits without fear of retribution if they fail.

Coaches are always available to advise their employees or just to listen to their problems if need be. *Carol, do you have a minute to discuss a personal problem?*

✓ **Coaches provide feedback.** Communication and feedback between coach and employee is a critical element of the coaching process. Employees must know where they stand in the organization — what they are doing right, and what they are doing wrong. It is equally important that employees let their coaches know when they need help or assistance. And both parties need this dialog in a timely manner, on an ongoing basis — not just once a year in a performance review.

Pink slips do *not* constitute effective feedback. If given without proper warning, they can even blow up in your face. *I guess this means you didn't like the job I was doing? See you in court!*

Transforming Kodak's corporate culture

Although long the world's leader in traditional photographic technology, Kodak has recently been in danger of being left behind as digital imaging technology takes hold and firms such as Sony, Hewlett-Packard, and Casio grab market share. Despite billions of dollars spent over the past decade for research and development and numerous restructurings, Kodak earned more in 1982 than it did in 1993. In a bid to turn the company around, Kodak hired George Fisher away from his post as CEO of Motorola in late 1993 to take the reins at Kodak.

Besides selling off Kodak's health and household products divisions for $7.9 billion, Fisher took aim at transforming Kodak's corporate culture. According to Fisher, "There are textbook types of things that are wrong with this company. Decisions are too slow. People don't take risks." Where past CEOs at Kodak have tended to be autocratic and strictly hierarchical, Fisher is fostering a more informal environment where employees are encouraged to communicate with each other and take risks. Fisher, who can be found most mornings having breakfast in the company cafeteria with Kodak employees, rarely raises his voice in anger and he encourages employees to send him computer e-mail messages. Fisher responds to the 30 or so messages he receives each day by personally handwriting notes on them and returning them to the senders.

(Source: *Business Week,* Feb. 13, 1995.)

Coaching: The Short Lesson

Besides the obvious coaching roles of supporting and encouraging employees in their quest to achieve an organization's goals, coaches also teach their employees *how* to achieve an organization's goals. Drawing from their experience, coaches lead their workers step by step through work processes or procedures. After the workers learn how to perform a task, the coach delegates full authority and responsibility for its performance to them.

For the transfer of specific skills, you can find no better way of teaching, and no better way of learning, than the *show-and-tell* method. Developed by a post-World War II American industrial complex desperate to quickly train new workers in manufacturing processes, show and tell is beautiful in its simplicity and effectiveness.

Show-and-tell coaching has three steps:

1. *You do, you say.* **Sit down with your employees and explain the procedure in general terms while you perform the task.**

In Peter's office, as in many businesses nowadays, computers are a critical tool for getting work done. When Peter needs to coach a new employee in the use of an obscure word processing or spreadsheet technique, the first thing he does is to explain the technique to the employee while he demonstrates it. "I click my left mouse button on the Insert command on the toolbar and pull down the menu. Then I point the arrow to Symbol and click again. I choose the symbol I want from the menu, point my arrow to it, and click to select it. I then point my arrow to Insert and click to place the symbol in the document; then I point my arrow to Close and click again to finish the job."

2. ***They do, you say.*** **Now, have the employees do the same procedure as you explain each step in the procedure.**

"Click your left mouse button on the Insert command on the toolbar and pull down the menu. Okay, good. Now point your arrow to Symbol and click again. Super! Choose the symbol you want from the menu and point your arrow to it. Now click to select it. All right — point your arrow to Insert and click to place the symbol in the document. Okay, you're almost done now. Point your arrow to Close and click again to finish the job. There you are!"

3. ***They do, they say.*** **Finally, as you observe, have your employees perform the task again as they explain to you what they are doing.**

"Okay, Yinka, now it's your turn. I want you to insert a symbol in your document and tell me what you are doing."

"All right, Peter. First, I click my left mouse button on the Insert command on the tool bar and pull down the menu. Then I point the arrow to Symbol and click again. I decide which symbol I want from the menu, point my arrow to it, and click to select it. Next, I point the arrow to Insert and click to place the symbol in the document. Finally, I point my arrow to Close and click again to finish the job. I did it!"

Coaching: The Daily Search for Turning Points

Despite popular impressions to the contrary, 90 percent of management isn't the *big* event — the blinding flash of brilliance that creates markets where none previously existed, the magnificent negotiation that results in unheard of levels of union-management cooperation, or the masterful stroke that catapults the firm into the big leagues. No, 90 percent of a manager's job is made up of the daily chipping away at problems and the shaping of talents.

The best coaches are constantly on the lookout for *turning points* — the daily opportunities to succeed that are available to all employees.

Making turning points into big successes

The big successes — the wins against competitors, the dramatic surges in revenues or profits, the astounding new products — are typically the result of building a foundation of countless small successes along the way. Making a voice mail system more responsive to your customers' needs, sending an employee to a seminar in time management, writing a great sales agreement, conducting a meaningful performance appraisal with an employee, meeting a prospective client for lunch — each is a turning point in the average business day. Although each event may not be particularly spectacular on its own, when aggregated over time, they can add up to *big* things.

This is the job of a coach. Instead of using dynamite to transform the organization in one fell swoop (and taking the chance of destroying it, their employees, or themselves in the process) coaches are like the ancient stone masons who built the great pyramids of Egypt. (See Figure 7-1.) The movement and placement of each individual stone may not have seemed like a big deal when considered as a separate activity. However, each was an important step in the achievement of the ultimate result: the construction of awe-inspiring structures that have withstood thousands of years of war, weather, and tourists.

Figure 7-1:
The Egyptian pyramids.

Coaching your employees through their turning points

Coaches focus daily on spending time with employees to help them win — to assess their progress and to find out what they can do to help the employees capitalize on the turning points that present themselves every day. Coaches complement and supplement the abilities and experience of their employees by bringing their own abilities and experience to the table. They reward positive performance and they help their employees learn important lessons from making mistakes — lessons that, in turn, help the employees to improve their future performance.

For example, suppose that you have a young and inexperienced, but bright and energetic, sales trainee on your staff. Your employee has done a great job contacting customers and making sales calls, but she has yet to close her first deal. When you talk to her about this, she confesses that she is *very* nervous about her own personal turning point: She's worried that she might become confused in front of the customer and blow the deal at the last minute. She needs your coaching.

The following guidelines can help you, the coach, handle any employee's concerns:

- ✔ **Meet with your employee.** Make an appointment with your employee as soon as possible for a relaxed discussion of the concerns. Find a place that is quiet and free of distractions and put your phone on hold or forward it to voice mail.

- ✔ **Listen!** Avoid instant solutions or lectures. Before you say a word, ask your employee to bring you up to date with the situation, his concerns, and any possible approaches or solutions he's considered. Let *him* do the talking while *you* do the listening.

- ✔ **Reinforce the positive.** Begin by pointing out the things that your employee did *right* in the particular situation. Let your employee know when he is on the right track. Give him positive feedback on his performance.

- ✔ **Highlight areas for improvement.** Point out the things that your employee needs to do to improve and tell what you can do to help. Agree on the assistance that you want to provide, whether it is further training, an increased budget, more time, or whatever is necessary. Be enthusiastic about your confidence in the employee's ability to do a great job.

- ✔ **Follow through.** After you determine what you can do to support your employee, do it! Periodically check up on the progress that your employee is making and offer your support as necessary.

Above all, be patient. Coaching is something that you can't accomplish on *your* terms alone. At the outset, understand that everyone is different. Some employees catch on sooner than others, and some employees need more time to develop. Differences in ability don't make certain employees any better or worse than their coworkers — they just make them different. Just as you need time to build relationships and trust in business, your employees need time to develop skills and experience.

The Tools of the Coach

Coaching is not a one-dimensional activity. Because every person is different, the best coaches tailor their approach to the specific needs of each team member. If one team member is independent and needs only occasional guidance, the coach should recognize where the employee stands and provide that level of support. This support might consist of an occasional, informal progress check while making the rounds of the office. If, on the other hand, another member of the team is insecure and needs *lots* of guidance, the coach recognizes this employee's position and assists as needed. In this case, support might consist of frequent, formal meetings with the employee to assess progress and to provide advice and direction as needed.

Although every coach has his or her own style, the best coaches employ certain techniques to elicit the greatest performance from their team members:

✔ **Make time for team members.** Managing is primarily a people job. Part of being a good manager and coach is being available to your employees when they need your help. If you're *not* available, your employees may seek out other avenues to meet their needs — or simply stop trying to work with you. Always keep your door open to your employees and remember that *they* are your #1 priority. Manage by walking around — that is, regularly get out of your office and visit your employees at *their* work stations. *Do I have a minute, Elaine? Of course, I always have time for you and the other members of my staff.*

When the coach needs a coach

Sometimes even coaches need to be coached. Scott McNealy, the 42-year-old CEO of Sun Microsystems, has used a combination of drive, passion, and tough financial controls to shepherd his company from $39 million in sales in 1984, when he took over, to $6 billion in sales in fiscal year 1995. Calling the stand-alone personal computer a "hairball on the desktop," McNealy has pushed the concept of network computing for years — long before the Internet became the "in" place to be. Sun now controls 35 percent of the world market in World Wide Web servers, and Sun's Internet-ready networks are being adopted for internal use by an increasing number of companies, including Gap, Federal Express, and AT&T Universal Card Services.

However, despite his success, Scott McNealy hired a "CEO coach" to help him become even more effective. The coach, Chuck Raben of Delta Consulting Group, Inc., asked McNealy's managers to report areas where they thought their boss could improve. Raben compiled the surveys and summarized the responses. The result was that, according to Sun's management team, McNealy needs to become a better listener. So McNealy now carries with him a reminder to respond to the points that his managers raise in meetings.

(Source: *Business Week,* Jan. 22, 1996.)

✓ **Provide context and vision.** Instead of simply telling employees *what* to do, effective coaches explain the *why*. Coaches provide their employees with context and a *big picture* perspective. Instead of spouting long lists of do's and don'ts, they explain how a system or procedure works and then define their employees' parts in the scheme of things. *Chris, you have a very important part in the financial health and vitality of our company. By ensuring that our customers pay their invoices within 30 days after we ship their products, we are able to keep our cash flow on the plus side, and we can pay our obligations such as rent, electricity, and your paycheck on time.*

✓ **Transfer knowledge and perspective.** A great benefit of having a good coach is the opportunity to learn from someone who has more experience than you do. In response to the unique needs of each team member, coaches transfer their personal knowledge and perspective. *We faced the exact situation about five years ago, Dwight. I'm going to tell you what we did then, and I want you to tell me whether you think that it still makes sense today.*

✓ **Be a sounding board.** Coaches talk through new ideas and approaches to solving problems with their employees. Coaches and employees can consider the implications of different approaches to solving a problem and role-play customer or client reactions before trying them out for real. By using active listening skills, coaches can often help their employees work through issues and come up with the best solutions themselves. *Okay, David, you've told me that you don't think your customer will buy off on a 20 percent price increase. What options do you have to present the price increase, and are some more palatable than others?*

✓ **Obtain needed resources.** Sometimes, coaches can help their employees make the jump from marginal to outstanding performance simply by providing the resources that their employees need. These resources can take many forms: money, time, staff, equipment, or other tangible assets. *So, Gene, you're confident that we can improve our cash flow if we throw a couple more clerks into collections? Okay, let's give it a try.*

✓ **Offer a helping hand.** For an employee who is learning a new job and is still responsible for performing his or her current job, the total workload can be overwhelming. Coaches can help workers through this transitional phase by reassigning current duties to other employees, authorizing overtime, or taking other measures to relieve the pressure. *John, while you're learning how to troubleshoot that new network server, I'm going to assign your maintenance workload to Rachel. Let's get back together at the end of the week to see how you're doing.*

Coaching Metaphors for Success in Business

In business, we are often reminded that, when it comes to coaching and teamwork, the metaphor of company as a winning sports team is *very* strong. In many organizations, CEOs hire professional athletes and coaches to lecture their employees on the importance of team play and winning; managers are given the label of *coaches* or *team leaders;* and workers are given the labels *players* or *team members*.

This being the case, ignoring the obvious parallels between coaching in sports and in business would be difficult. So we're going to get this out of our system once and for all and refrain from linking coaching in sports and business anyplace else in this book after the following list of quotes from Gerald Tomlinson's book, *Speaker's Treasury of Sports Anecdotes, Stories, and Humor.* We *promise.*

- ✔ Lou Holtz, head coach of the Notre Dame football team, had this to say about his approach to coaching: "I don't think discipline is forcing someone to do something. It's showing them how this is going to help them in the long run."

- ✔ According to former Dartmouth lacrosse coach Whitey Burnham, "Good judgment comes from experience, and experience comes from bad judgment."

- ✔ Former Houston Oilers head coach Bum Phillips's theory of football coaching might apply equally well in business: "Two kinds of football players ain't worth a damn: the one that never does what he's told, and the other that never does anything *except* what he's told."

- ✔ The phenomenally successful UCLA basketball coach John Wooden once said, "If you're not making mistakes, then you're not doing anything. I'm positive that a doer makes mistakes."

- ✔ Former head coach of the Oakland Raiders football team John Madden summed up his coaching philosophy as this: "I didn't want a big play once in a while, I wanted solid play every time."

Test your new-found knowledge

What are the three key functions of coaching?

A. Setting goals, coaching, and providing feedback

B. Motivating, intimidating, and blaming

C. Punishing, procrastinating, and apple polishing

D. None of the above

What are the three steps in show-and-tell coaching?

A. I show; you tell; we do.

B. You show; they tell; we coach.

C. Huey, Dewey, and Louie.

D. You do, you say; they do, you say; and they do, they say.

Part III
Making Things Happen

The 5th Wave   By Rich Tennant

FRANKENSTEIN, INC.

"As a team you've done a crackup job collecting body parts. There's just one thing-and maybe I wasn't clear enough about this, but I notice you're all bringing me the SAAAME body part."

In this part . . .

Employees without goals are employees without direction. And after you set goals with employees, you have to be able to measure employee progress against them. In this part, we address setting goals with employees, measuring employee performance, and conducting performance appraisals the *right* way.

Chapter 8

Goal-Setting Made Easy

- -

In This Chapter

▶ Linking goals to your vision

▶ Creating SMART goals

▶ Concentrating on *fewer* goals

▶ Publicizing your goals

▶ Following through

▶ Determining sources of power

- -

Ask any group of workers, "What is the primary duty of management?" The answer *setting goals* is likely to be near the top of the list. If setting goals appears near the bottom of the list, you *know* there's a problem! In most companies, top management sets the overall direction of the organization. Middle managers (those who are left, anyway) then get the job of developing goals and plans for achieving the direction set by top management. Managers and employees work together to set goals and develop schedules for attaining them.

As a manager, you are probably immersed in goals — not only for yourself but for your employees, your department and your organization. This flood of goals can overwhelm you as you try to balance the relative importance of each one. *Should I tackle my department's goal of improving turnaround time first, or should I get to work on my boss's goal of finishing the budget? Or maybe the company's goal of improving customer service is more important. Well, I think I'll just wrap up the division goal of implementing a new system of quality improvement.*

As you discover in this chapter, sometimes having too *many* goals is as bad as not having any goals at all.

Goals provide direction and purpose. Don't forget: If you can *see* it, you can *achieve* it. Goals help you see where you're going and how you can get there.

If You Don't Know Where You're Going, How Will You Know When You Get There?

Did you realize that Lewis Carrol's *Alice in Wonderland* offers lessons that can enhance your business life? If you read this book when you were a child, you might recall the exchange between Alice and the Cheshire Cat about the importance of setting goals. Consider the following passage from Carrol's book, in which Alice asks the Cheshire Cat for advice on which direction to go.

"Would you tell me please, which way I ought to go from here?"

"That depends a good deal on where you want to go," said the Cat.

"I don't much care where — " said Alice.

"Then it doesn't matter which way you go," said the Cat.

" — so long as I get *somewhere*," Alice added as an explanation.

"Oh, you're sure to do that," said the Cat, "if you only walk long enough."

It takes no effort at all to get *somewhere*. Just do nothing, and in a moment, you're there. However, if you want to get somewhere *meaningful*, you first have to know where you want to go. And after you decide where you want to go, you need to make plans on how to get there. This practice is as true in business as it is for you in your everyday life.

For example, suppose that you have a vision of starting up a new sales office in Chicago so that you can better service your Midwestern accounts. How would you go about achieving this vision? You have three choices: (1) an unplanned, non-goal-oriented approach, (2) a planned, goal-oriented approach, and (3) a hope and a prayer. Which choice do *you* think is most likely to get you to your goal? Go ahead, take a wild guess!

If you guessed the unplanned, non-goal-oriented approach to reaching your vision, shame on you! Please report to study hall — your assignment is to write 500 times: *A goal is a dream with a deadline.* Now, no talking to your classmates and no goofing off. We've got our eyes on you!

If you guessed the planned, goal-oriented approach, you have earned a big gold star and a place in the *Managing For Dummies* Hall of Fame! We'll be glad to send you your gold star if you drop us a line in care of the publisher. Congratulations!

Following are the main reasons why you should set goals whenever you want to accomplish something significant:

- ✔ **Goals provide direction.** For our preceding example (starting up a new sales office in Chicago), you could probably find a million different ways to better service your Midwestern business accounts. However, to get something done, you have to set a definite vision — a target to aim for and to guide the efforts of you and your organization. You can then translate this vision into *goals* that take you where you want to go. *Without* goals, you are doomed to waste countless hours going nowhere. *With* goals, you can focus your efforts and the efforts of your staff on only the activities that move you toward where you're going — in this case, opening a Chicago sales office.

- ✔ **Goals tell you how far you have traveled.** Goals provide milestones along the road to accomplishing your vision. If you determine that you must accomplish seven separate goals to reach your final destination and you complete three of them, you know that you have four goals remaining. That is, you know exactly where you stand and how far you have yet to go.

- ✔ **Goals help to make your overall vision attainable.** You can't reach your vision in one big step — you need many small steps to get there. If, again, your vision is to open a new sales office in Chicago, you can't expect to proclaim your vision on Friday and walk into a fully staffed, fully functioning office on Monday. You must accomplish many goals — from shopping for office space, to hiring and relocating staff, to printing stationery and business cards — before you can attain your vision. Goals enable you to achieve your overall vision by dividing your efforts into smaller pieces that, when accomplished individually, add up to big results.

- ✔ **Goals clarify everyone's role.** When you announce your vision to your employees, they may have *some* idea of where you want to go but *no* idea of how to go about getting there. As your well-intentioned employees head off to help you achieve your vision, some employees may duplicate the efforts of others, some tasks may be ignored, and some employees may simply do something else altogether (and hope that you won't notice the difference). Setting goals with employees clarifies what the tasks are, who does which tasks, and what is expected from each employee.

- ✔ **Goals give people something to strive for.** Without getting into a deep discussion of philosophy or theology, we believe that people are more motivated when challenged to attain a goal that is beyond their normal level of performance. Not only do goals give people a sense of purpose, but also they relieve the boredom that can come from performing a routine job day after day.

For goals to be useful, they have to link directly to the vision that is at the end of the road. To stay ahead of the competition, or simply to remain in business, organizations create compelling visions and then management and employees work together to set and achieve the goals to reach those visions. Look over these examples of compelling visions that drive the development of goals at several successful enterprises:

✔ Samsung is the $54 billion, Korean-based manufacturer of electronics, chemicals, and heavy machinery, as well as the purveyor of insurance, credit card, and other financial services. At Samsung, management has created a clear and compelling vision that drives the goals of the organization. Samsung's vision is to become one of the world's ten largest "technological powerhouses."

✔ Motorola, long known for its obsession with quality, has set a truly incredible vision for where it wants to be in the next decade. Motorola has set a target of no more than two manufacturing defects per billion by the year 2000.

✔ Almost a century ago, the chairman of AT&T created this vision for the organization: the dream of good, cheap, and fast worldwide telephone service. Now, with the explosion of information technology creating incredible new opportunities for the telecommunications industry, AT&T has had to create a new vision. AT&T's new vision is to be a "major factor in the worldwide movement and management of information."

(Source: James Stoner, R. Edward Freeman, and Daniel Gilbert, Jr., *Management.*)

SMART Goals

You can find all kinds of goals in all kinds of organizations. Some goals are short-term and specific (*starting next month, we will increase production by two units per employee per hour*), and others are long-term and nebulous (*within the next five years, we will become a learning organization*). Some are easily understood by employees (*line employees will have no more than 20 rejects per month*), but others can be difficult to fathom and subject to much interpretation (*all employees are expected to show more respect to each other in the next fiscal year*). Still others can be accomplished relatively easily (*reception staff will always answer the phone by the third ring*), but others are virtually impossible to attain (*all employees will master the five languages that our customers speak before the end of the fiscal year*).

How do you know what kind of goals to set? The whole point of setting goals, after all, is to *achieve* them. It does you no good to go to the trouble of calling meetings, hacking through the needs of your organization, and burning up precious time, only to end up with goals that aren't acted on or completed. Unfortunately, this scenario describes what far too many managers do with their time.

The best goals are *smart* goals — well, actually *SMART* goals is more like it. SMART is a handy shorthand for the five characteristics of well-designed goals.

✔ **Specific:** Goals must be clear and unambiguous; vagaries and platitudes have no place in goal setting. When goals are specific, they tell employees exactly what is expected, when, and how much. Because the goals are specific, you can easily measure your employees' progress toward their completion.

✔ **Measurable:** What good is a goal that you can't measure? If your goals are not measurable, you never know whether your employees are making progress toward their successful completion. Not only that, but it's tough for your employees to stay motivated to complete their goals when they have no milestones to indicate their progress.

✔ **Attainable:** Goals must be realistic and attainable by average employees. The best goals require employees to stretch a bit to achieve them, but they aren't extreme. That is, the goals are neither out of reach nor below standard performance. Goals that are set too high or too low become meaningless, and employees naturally come to ignore them.

✔ **Relevant:** Goals must be an important tool in the grand scheme of reaching your company's vision and mission. We've heard that 80 percent of worker productivity comes from only 20 percent of their activities. You can guess where the other 80 percent of work activity ends up! This relationship comes from Italian economist Vilfredo Pareto's 80/20 rule. This rule, which states that 80 percent of the wealth of most countries is held by only 20 of the population, has been applied to many other fields since its discovery. Relevant goals address the 20 percent of worker activities that has such a great impact on performance and brings your organization closer to its vision.

✔ **Time-bound:** Goals must have starting points, ending points, and fixed durations. Commitment to deadlines helps employees to focus their efforts on completion of the goal on or before the due date. Goals without deadlines or schedules for completion tend to be overtaken by the day-to-day crises that invariably arise in an organization.

SMART goals make for smart organizations. In our experience, many supervisors and managers neglect to work with their employees to set goals together. And in the ones that do, goals are often unclear, ambiguous, unrealistic, unrelated to the organization's vision, unmeasurable, and demotivating. By developing SMART goals with your employees, you can avoid these traps while ensuring the progress of your organization and its employees.

Although the SMART system of goal setting provides guidelines to help you frame effective goals, you have additional considerations to keep in mind. These considerations help you ensure that the goals, which you and your employees agree to, can be easily understood and acted on by *anyone* in your organization.

✔ **Ensure that goals are related to your employees' role in the organization.** Pursuing an organization's goals is far easier for employees when those goals are a regular part of their jobs. For example, suppose you set a goal for employees who solder circuit boards to "Raise production by 2 percent per quarter." These employees spend almost every working moment pursuing this goal, because it is an integral part of their job. If, however, you give the same employees a goal of "Improving the diversity of the organization," what exactly does that have to do with your line employees' role? Nothing. The goal may sound lofty and may be important to your organization, but because your line employees don't make the hiring decisions, you're wasting your time and their time with that particular goal.

✔ **Whenever possible, use values to guide behavior.** What is the most important value in your organization? For General Electric, it is probably that the company will be ranked Number 1 or Number 2 in sales in every business that they are in.

This value, translated into a goal for all employees, is something that every employee can understand and be a part of. Whether the employee is a corporate vice president or a receptionist, adherence to the corporate value is a part of his or her goal. This common focus clarifies whether the organization is achieving its goal and whether the employee is doing his or her part to help.

✔ **Simple goals are better goals.** The easier your goals are to understand, the more likely the employees are to work to achieve them. Goals should be no longer than one sentence, and they should be concise, compelling, and easy to read and understand.

Goals that take more than a sentence to describe are actually *multiple* goals. When you find multiple-goal statements, break them into single, one-sentence goals. Goals that take a page or more to describe aren't really goals; they are books. File *them* away in the library and try again.

Setting Goals: Less Is More

Peter remembers the scene as if it were yesterday. His organization had determined that it needed to develop a long-range, strategic plan. (Strategic planning was *in* at the time and seemed like a good thing to do.) The entire management team was marshaled for this effort — they scheduled several all-day planning sessions, retained a high-priced consultant, and pronounced to the workers that something was brewing at the top.

The management team threw itself wholeheartedly into the planning effort. Why did the organization exist? Who were its customers? What were its values? What was its mission? What were its goals? How would they know when they achieved them? Session after session, great idea after great idea. Before long, more than 12 poster-sized flip chart pages were taped to the walls of the meeting room, each brimming with goals for the organization. *Improve customer service. Provide quicker project turnaround. Fix the heating and air conditioning system at corporate headquarters.* And many more — in all, more than 200!

As the last planning meeting ended, the managers congratulated each other over their collective accomplishment and went back to their regular office routines. Before long, the goals were forgotten — the pages on which they were recorded neatly folded and stored away in someone's file cabinet. Meanwhile, business went on as usual, and the long-range planning effort went into long-term hibernation. Soon, the organization's employees — who had been told that the management team had embarked on a momentous process of strategic planning — finally tired of asking about it. *Must have been another one of those management fads.* Yup.

Sure, some items eventually found their way out of the room, but most of the goals created by management were promptly forgotten, ignored, or overtaken by other priorities. In our experience, the main reason this happens is that managers — in their well-meaning efforts to fix *every* organizational problem as quickly as possible — create too *many* goals.

Why isn't it always better to have more goals? The greater the number of goals, the less you can focus on any one of them and the less you actually get done. No matter how great a manager or employee you are, you can't focus on everything at once. It's sort of like trying to juggle balls in the air. Most anyone can juggle one or two balls at the same time — you toss one ball in the air and catch it; you toss another ball in the air and catch it. Concentrating on throwing and catching only a couple of balls is relatively easy.

Imagine what happens when you throw a few more balls into the mix — are you starting to have problems keeping all the balls in the air? Are you dropping some of your balls yet? Now, let's spice things up a bit. As you desperately try to keep all your balls in the air, someone tosses you a monkey wrench. *The phone system just went down and our vendor says they can't get out here to fix it until next week!* Of course, that's not the end of it. While you're trying to juggle the monkey wrench — all the while dropping balls — your boss throws in a couple of red hot potatoes for you to add to your act. *These sales contracts have to go out tonight! Mr. Crank is waiting for your call.* Boom! Even the *best* managers can't keep all the balls in the air —*plus* take care of the monkey wrenches and hot potatoes — without dropping a few.

This illustration shows why managers who set too many goals for their organizations often find their best-laid plans pushed aside as employees are overwhelmed by competing organizational needs. In the eyes of busy workers, having too many goals quickly becomes the same as having no goals at all. *Why bother? I can't really make much progress anyway.*

When it comes to goal setting, less *is* more.

The following are guidelines to help you select the right goals — and the right number of goals — for your organization:

- ✔ **Pick two to three goals to focus on.** You can't do everything at once, and you can't expect your employees to either. A few goals are the most you should attempt to conquer at any one time. Picking too many goals dilutes the efforts of you and your staff and can result in a complete breakdown in the process.

- ✔ **Pick the goals with the greatest relevance.** Certain goals take you a lot farther down the road to attaining your vision than do other goals. Because you have only so many hours in your workday, it clearly makes sense to concentrate your efforts on a few goals that have the biggest payoff — rather than on a boatload of goals with relatively less payoff.

- ✔ **Focus on the goals that tie most closely to the mission of your organization.** You can be tempted to take on goals that are challenging, interesting, and fun to accomplish but that are far removed from the mission of your organization. Don't.

- ✔ **Periodically revisit the goals and update them as necessary.** Business is anything but static, and periodically assessing your goals is important to making sure that they are still relevant to the vision you are trying to achieve. If so, great — carry on. If not, meet with your employees to revise the goals and the schedules for attaining them.

In your zeal to get as many things done as quickly as you can, avoid taking on too many goals. Too many goals can overwhelm you, and they can overwhelm your employees, too. You are far better off if you set a few, significant goals and then concentrate your efforts on attaining them. Don't forget that management is not a game of huge success after huge success. Instead, it is a daily meeting of challenges and opportunities — gradually, but inevitably, improving the organization in the process. Keep this in mind and set your goals accordingly.

These Are the Goals (Pass Them On)

Having goals is great, but how do you get the word out to your employees? As you know, goals grow out of an organization's vision. Establishing goals helps you ensure that employee efforts focus on achieving that vision in the desired time frame. You have many possible ways to communicate goals to your employees, but some are better than others. In every case, you must communicate goals clearly, the receiver must understand the goals, and they must be followed through on.

The power of the annual goal at Marmot Mountain

In 1991, when Steve Crisafulli was brought on as president of Marmot Mountain, a Colorado-based producer of super high-quality outdoor clothing, he quickly discovered that Marmot was in *big* trouble. According to Crisafulli, Marmot "had no credit records, an unusable computer inventory system, and financial statements that were six months late. I had never before seen a company this screwed up from an operational standpoint." Crisafulli's plan was to develop specific goals to lead the company to his vision of profitability. However, the job would be done not all at once, but one step at a time. Says Crisafulli, "The way to run a small business is to concentrate on one or two small things."

The first problem to receive Crisafulli's attention was the firm's traditional difficulties making deliveries to customers on time. In one particularly bad example of Marmot's problems in this area, the entire 1989 winter clothing line — due to stores by Labor Day — were not delivered until January 1990. As a result, business dropped precipitously. In late 1991, Crisafulli made timely delivery of Marmot products the firm's Number 1 priority. Employees agreed to a goal of 1992's winter clothing line no later than mid-September 1992. To meet the goal, daily management team meetings were implemented, managers began to communicate with each other and with workers, quality control inspectors were sent out of the plant to check on key suppliers, and marketing budgets were increased.

Says Crisafulli, "Most of what you lack in a small business is resources. People often say, 'I don't have enough money,' but the real thing you lack is time. People are doing a once-over-lightly on too many things. Trying to advance on too broad a front, they don't go anywhere."

To make a long story short, not only did Marmot achieve its goal, but the entire winter clothing line was shipped out two weeks ahead of the deadline of mid-September 1992. Sales have grown from approximately $5 million in the early '90s to $11 million in 1994 with projections for 40 percent growth through the end of the decade. Still, the company and its president retain the single-mindedness that delivered it from the brink of disaster. At its annual strategic meeting, Marmot's management team decides on *one* goal for the following year. According to Crisafulli, "It hasn't failed to work yet. That's the beauty of the system: if you focus on only one thing, it's not difficult to achieve. It's much easier than trying to meet 20 different goals." Amen.

(Source: *Inc. Magazine,* August 1995.)

Communicating your organization's vision is as important as communicating specific goals. You should communicate the vision in every way possible, as often as possible, throughout your organization and to significant others such as clients, customers, suppliers, and so forth. And you need to be aware of possible obstacles to this communication: Often an organization's vision is pounded out in a series of grueling management meetings that leave the participants (you, the managers!) beaten and tired. By the time they reach their final goal of developing a company's vision, the participants are sick of it and ready to go on to the next challenge.

Many organizations drop the ball at this crucial point and are thereby slow to communicate the vision. Also, each succeeding layer of an organization has the natural tendency to draw some of the energy from the vision so that, by the time it filters down to the frontline employees, the vision has become dull and lifeless.

When you communicate vision and goals, do it with energy and with a sense of urgency and importance. This is the future of your organization and your employees we are talking about here — not chopped liver! If your employees don't think that *you* care about the vision, why should they? Simply put, they won't.

Companies usually announce their visions with much pomp and fanfare. The following are different ways that companies commonly announce and communicate their vision:

✔ By conducting huge employee rallies where the vision is unveiled in inspirational presentations.

As spotlights criss-cross the auditorium and balloons cascade from the ceiling, the chairman rises to address the throng. "Ladies and gentlemen, I am proud to unveil the company's new statement of vision: A penny saved is a penny earned."

✔ By printing their vision on anything possible — business cards, letterhead stationery, massive posters hung in the plant, newsletters, employee name tags, and more.

✔ By encouraging managers to "talk up" the vision in staff meetings or other verbal interactions.

When you communicate your organization's vision, clearly, more is merrier — the how is not so important. Make sure that you communicate the vision early and often.

Goals, on the other hand, are much more personal, and the methods you use to communicate them must be much more formal and direct. The following guidelines can help you out:

✔ Make sure that the goals are written down.

✔ Always conduct one-on-one, face-to-face meetings with your employees to introduce, discuss, and assign the goals.

If physical distance prohibits or, for any reason, you can't conduct a face-to-face meeting, conduct your meeting over the phone. The point is to make sure that your employees receive the goals, understand them, and have the opportunity to ask for clarifications.

✔ Call your team together to introduce team-related goals.

You can assign goals to teams instead of to individuals. If this is the case, get the team together and explain the role of the team and each individual in the successful completion of the goal. Make sure that all team members understand exactly what they are to do. Get them fired up and then let them have at it. We discuss the function of teams in more detail in Chapter 12.

✔ Gain the commitment of your employees, whether individually or on teams, to the successful accomplishment of their goals.

Ask your employees to prepare and present plans and milestone schedules explaining how they will accomplish the assigned goals by the deadlines that you agreed to. After your employees embark on the pursuit of their goals, regularly monitor their progress to ensure that they are on track and meet with them to help them overcome any problems.

Juggling Priorities: Keeping Your Eye on the Ball

Now that you have decided the goals that are important to you and to your organization, we have come to the difficult part. How do you maintain the focus of your employees — and your own focus, for that matter — on achievement of the goals that you have set?

Hallmark communicates its goals in many different ways

The management of Hallmark Cards, Inc., the world's largest producer of greeting cards, firmly believes in the value of communicating the organization's vision, goals, and vital business information to its employees. Hallmark's president and CEO, Irvine O. Hockaday, Jr., says, "The only sustainable edge for a corporation is the energy and cleverness of its people. To tap that, a chief executive must craft a vision, empower employees, encourage teamwork, and kindle the competitive fires" *Chief Executive*, March 1993.

To back up its commitment to getting the word out to employees, Hallmark developed an elaborate portfolio of formal employee publications. In addition to publishing a daily newsletter, *Noon News*, for all employees, Hallmark publishes *Crown*, a bimonthly magazine for employees, and a newsletter for managers titled *Directions*. However, Hallmark's commitment to communicating doesn't end with newsletters and magazines — Hockaday regularly invites workers from throughout the organization to join him for a meal to share information.

The process of goal setting usually generates a *lot* of excitement and energy within employees — whether the goals are set in large group meetings or in one-on-one encounters. This excitement and energy can quickly dissipate as soon as everyone gets back to his or her desk. You, the manager, must take steps to ensure that the organization's focus remains centered on the goals and not on other matters (which are less important but momentarily more pressing). Of course, this task is much easier said than done.

Staying focused on goals can be *extremely* difficult — particularly when you are a busy person and the goals are added *on top of* your regular responsibilities. Think about situations that fight for your attention during a typical day at work:

- How often do you sit down at your desk in the morning to plot out your priorities for the day only to have them pushed aside five minutes later when you get a call from your boss?

  Mike, I need you to drop everything and get to work on a report for the general manager right away! She has to have it on her desk by 3:00 p.m. today.

- How many times has an employee come to you with a problem?

  Sorry, Mike, but I think you had better hear about this problem before it gets any worse. Jenny and Tony just had a fight and Jenny says she's going to quit. We can't afford to lose Jenny — especially not right now. She's the key to the development project. What are we going to do?

- Do you remember getting caught in a 15-minute meeting that drags on for several hours?

  Are there any questions on steps 1 through 14 of the new recruitment process? Fine, now let's get started on steps 15 through 35.

In unlimited ways, you or your employees can get off track and lose the focus that you need to get your organization's goals accomplished. One of the biggest problems that employees face is confusing *activity* with *results*. Do you know anyone who works incredibly long hours — late into the night and on weekends — but never seems to get anything done? Although this employee always seems to be busy, the problem is that he or she is working on the *wrong* things. As referenced in Chapter 2, this is called the *activity trap,* and it is very easy for you and your employees to fall into. *Help, I've fallen and I can't get out!*

We previously mentioned the rule of thumb that says that 80 percent of worker productivity comes from 20 percent of their activity. The flip side of this rule is that only 20 percent of worker productivity comes from *80 percent* of their activity. This statistic illustrates the activity trap at work. What do *you* do in an average day? More important, what do you do with the 80 percent of your time that results in so few results? You *can* get out of the activity trap and take control of your schedules and priorities. However, you have to be *tough*, and you have to be *single-minded* in pursuit of your goals.

Achieving your goals is all up to you — no one, not even your boss (perhaps *especially* not your boss), is going to make it any easier for you to concentrate on achieving your goals. *You* have to take charge, and you have to take charge *now*! If *you* aren't controlling your own schedule, you are simply letting everyone else control your schedule for you.

Following are some tips to help you and your employees get out of the activity trap:

- ✔ **Do your #1 priority first!** With all the distractions that compete for your attention, with the constant temptation to work on the easy stuff first and save the tough stuff for last, and with people dropping into your office just to chat or to unload their problems on you, concentrating on your #1 priority is *always* a challenge. However, if you don't do your #1 priority first, you're almost guaranteed to find yourself in the activity trap. That is, you're almost guaranteed to find the same priorities on your list of things to do day after day, week after week, and month after month.

- ✔ **Get organized!** Refer to Chapter 2 for a complete diatribe on why getting organized and managing your time effectively are important. For our purposes here, suffice it to say that, if you are organized, you can spend less time trying to figure out what you *should* be doing and more time *doing* what you should be doing.

- ✔ **Just say no!** If someone tries to make *their* problems *your* problems, just say no! If you are a manager, you probably like nothing more than taking on new challenges and solving problems. The conflict arises when solving somebody else's problems interferes with solving your own. You've got to constantly be on guard and fight the temptation to fritter your day away with meaningless activities. Always ask yourself, "How does this help me achieve my goals?" Be single-minded in your focus on your *own* goals and refuse to let others make their problems your own.

Using Your Power: Making Your Goals Happen

So now that you have created a wonderful set of goals with your employees, how do you make sure that they get done? How do you make *your* priorities your *employees'* priorities? The best goals in the world mean nothing if they aren't achieved. You can choose to leave this critical step in the process to chance, *or* you can choose to get involved.

You have the power to make your goals happen.

Power has gotten a bad rap of late. In reaction to the autocratic leadership styles that often ruled the roost in many American corporations until recent years, employees have increasingly demanded, and organizations have increasingly provided, management that is principle-centered and that has a more compassionate, human face.

We believe that nothing is inherently wrong with power — we all have many sources of power within us. And not only do we have power but we exercise power to control or influence people and events around us on a daily basis. Generally, power is a positive thing in our lives. However, power *can* be a negative thing when it is abused. Manipulation, exploitation, and coercion have no place in the modern workplace.

You can use the positive power within you to your advantage — and to the advantage of those around you — by tapping into it to help achieve your organization's goals. People and systems often fall into ruts or into nonproductive patterns of behavior that are hard to break. Power properly applied can jump start these people and systems and move them in the right direction — the direction that leads to accomplishment of goals.

Everyone has five primary sources of power, and each of us has specific strengths and weaknesses related to these sources. It's important to recognize our strengths and weaknesses and to use them to our advantage. As you review the five sources of power that follow, consider your own personal strengths and weaknesses.

- ✔ **Personal power:** This is the power that comes from within your character. Your passion for greatness, the strength of your convictions, your ability to communicate and inspire, your personal charisma, and your leadership skills all add up to personal power.

- ✔ **Relationship power:** We all have relationships with others at work. These interactions contribute to the relationship power that we wield in our offices. Sources of relationship power include close friendships with top executives, partners, or owners, people who owe you favors, and coworkers who provide you with information and insights that you would normally not get through your formal business relationships.

- ✔ **Position power:** This kind of power derives strictly from your rank or title in the organization and is a function of the authority that you wield to command human and financial resources. Although the position power of the receptionist in your organization is probably quite low, the position power of the president or owner is at the top of the chart.

- ✔ **Knowledge power:** To see knowledge power in action, just see what happens the next time your organization's computer network goes down! Then you'll see who *really* has the power in an organization (in this case, your computer network administrator). Knowledge power comes from the special expertise and knowledge that you have gained during the course of your career. Knowledge power also comes from obtaining academic degrees (think *MBA*) or special training.

> ✓ **Task power:** Task power is the power that comes from the job or process that you perform at work. As you have undoubtedly witnessed on many occasions, people can facilitate or impede the efforts of their coworkers and others through the application of task power. For example, when you submit a claim for payment to your insurance company and months pass with no action (*Gee, we don't seem to have your claim in our computer — are you sure you submitted one? Maybe you should send us another one just to be safe!*), you are on the receiving end of task power.

If you are weak in certain sources of power, you can increase them if you want. For example, work on your weakness in relationship power by making a concerted effort to get to know your coworkers better and to cultivate relationships with higher ranking managers or executives. Instead of passing on the invitations to get together with your coworkers after work, join them — have fun and strengthen your relationship power at the same time.

If you want to increase your personal power, you can find many ways to improve in this area. You can join Toastmasters — a nonprofit group devoted to helping people improve their public speaking skills — or you can enroll in a self-improvement program such as those offered by the Dale Carnegie Institute, Blanchard Training and Development, the Institute for Principle-Centered Leadership, and many others.

Be aware of the sources of your power and use it in a positive way to help you and your employees accomplish the goals of your organization. For getting things done, a little power can go a *long* way.

Test your new-found knowledge

What are the characteristics of SMART goals?

A. They are specious, moneymaking, attractive, regular, and tiny.

B. They are successful, mediating, attuned, reactive, and total.

C. They are superficial, meditative, altruistic, rare, and tubular.

D. They are specific, measurable, attainable, relevant, and time-bound.

What are the five sources of power in an organization?

A. The president of the corporation and her four vice presidents.

B. That depends.

C. Personal, relationship, position, knowledge, and task.

D. None of the above.

Chapter 9

Measuring and Monitoring Individual Performance

● ●

In This Chapter

▶ Quantifying your goals

▶ Developing a performance feedback system

▶ Putting your system into practice

▶ Charting your results graphically

▶ Making the most of your data

● ●

*I*n Chapter 8, we discuss the whys and wherefores of setting goals. Setting goals in an organization is extremely important — goals for individuals, goals for teams, and goals for the overall organization. However, ensuring that the organization is making progress toward the successful completion of goals (in the manner and time frames agreed to) is equally important. The performance of the organization depends on the performance of each individual who works within it. Achieving goals is what this chapter is all about.

Measuring and monitoring the performance of individuals in your organization is like walking a tightrope: You don't want to overmeasure or overmonitor your employees. Doing so only leads to needless bureaucracy and red tape which can negatively affect the ability of your employees to perform their tasks. Neither do you want to undermeasure or undermonitor your employees. This lack of watchfulness can lead to nasty surprises when a task is completed late, over budget, or not at all. *What?! The customer database conversion isn't completed yet? I promised the VP of sales that we would have that job done two weeks ago! Heads are going to roll now — it's been nice working with you, George!*

Please keep in mind that (as manager) your primary goal in measuring and monitoring the performance of employees is not to punish them for making a mistake or missing a milestone — it is to help your employees stay on schedule and to find out whether they need additional assistance or resources to do so. Few employees like to admit that they need help getting an assignment done — whatever the reason. Because of their reluctance, it's critical that *you* systematically check on the progress of your employees and regularly give them feedback on how they are doing.

If you don't monitor it, you won't achieve it. Don't leave achieving your goals to chance; develop systems to monitor progress and ensure that your goals are achieved.

Keeping Your Eye on the Ball

The first step in checking your employees' progress is to determine the key indicators of a goal's success. If you follow the advice in Chapter 8, you set goals with your employees that are concise and few in number. And because they are *SMART* goals (specific, measurable, attainable, relevant, and time-bound), they are measurable and have clear deadlines.

When you quantify a goal in precise numerical terms, your employees have no confusion over how their performance is measured and when their performance is adequate (or less than adequate). If you measure performance in terms of the quantity of sprockets produced per hour, your workers know exactly what you mean. If the goal (that you're measuring for) is to produce 100 sprockets per hour, with a reject rate of one or less, your employees clearly understand that producing only 75 sprockets per hour with 10 rejects is unacceptable performance. Nothing is left to the imagination, and the goals are not subject to individual interpretation or to the capricious whims of individual supervisors or managers.

How you measure and monitor the progress of your employees toward completion of their goals depends on the nature of the goals. You can measure some goals, for example, in terms of time, others in terms of units of production, and others in terms of delivery of a particular work product (such as a report or a sales proposal). The following are examples of different goals and the ways you can measure them:

- ✔ **Goal:** Plan and implement a company newsletter before the end of the second quarter of the current fiscal year.

  Measurement: The specific date (for example, June 30) that the newsletter is mailed out (time).

- ✔ **Goal:** Increase the number of mountain bike frames produced by each employee from 20 to 25 per day.

  Measurement: The exact number of mountain bike frames produced by the employee each day (quantity).

- ✔ **Goal:** Increase profit on the project by 20 percent in fiscal year 2005.

  Measurement: The total percentage increase in profit from January 1, 2005, through December 31, 2005 (percentage increase).

Although noting when your employees attain their goals is obviously important, recognizing your employees' *incremental progress* toward attaining their goals is just as important. For example:

- ✔ The goal for your drivers is to maintain an accident-free record. This is an ongoing goal with no deadline. To encourage them in their efforts, you prominently post a huge banner in the middle of the garage that reads "153 Days Accident Free." And you increase the number for each day of accident-free driving.

- ✔ The goal of your fiscal clerks is to increase the average number of transactions from 150 per day to 175 per day. To track their progress, you publicly post a summary of each employee's daily production counts at the end of each week. As production increases, you praise the progress of your employees towards the final goal.

- ✔ The goal set for your reception staff is to improve the percentage of "excellent" responses on customer feedback cards by 10 percent. You tabulate the monthly counts for each receptionist and announce the results at department staff meetings. The receptionist with the highest total each month gets treated to lunch by the department manager.

The secret to performance measuring and monitoring is the power of positive feedback. When you give positive feedback (increased number of units produced, percentage increase in sales, and so on), you encourage the performance of the behavior that you want. However, when you give negative feedback (number of errors, number of work days lost, and so on) you aren't encouraging the behavior you *want;* you are only discouraging the behaviors that you *don't want.* There is a *big* difference.

- ✔ **Instead of measuring this:** Number of defective cartridges

  Measure this: Number of correctly assembled cartridges
- ✔ **Instead of measuring this:** Number of days late

  Measure this: Number of days on time
- ✔ **Instead of measuring this:** Quantity of backlogged transactions

  Measure this: Quantity of completed transactions

You may wonder whether the feedback that you provide to employees regarding their performance should be public or private. What do you think? Do you put the information out for everyone to see, or do you get a better response by making the information confidential?

From our experience as managers, we find that you are much more likely to get the results you want when you put performance measures out in the open for everyone to see. Nothing else is quite like the natural tendency of employees to compete against one another to motivate them to boost performance. When performance data is hidden, your employees don't know how they're doing relative to anyone else, and they have little incentive to improve their performance — despite your ongoing encouragement. However, when they see their weekly or monthly performance results ranked against those of their coworkers, all of a sudden, they want to be at the top of the list and their performance increases as a result. You *don't* want to encourage destructive rivalries; you *do* want to encourage a striving for excellence.

The absolute, best, bar-none way to get results is to make the data on your employees' incremental progress a part of their everyday consciousness. That is, publish the performance data of all your employees and then post it where everyone can see it.

What? You're concerned that your employees may be embarrassed when you post their performance data? This is sort of the point. Although you don't want your employees to be humiliated in front of their peers, you want to tap into the strong power that peer pressure can wield on your behalf. Unless the employees at the bottom of your weekly standings absolutely just don't care, they are going to do whatever it takes to move up. This pushes your top performers even harder to stay ahead. Before you know it, you've got a whole group full of high performers.

Developing a System for Providing Immediate Performance Feedback

You can measure an infinite number of behaviors or performance characteristics. What you measure and the values that you measure against are up to you and your employees. In any case, you should keep certain things in mind when you design a system for measuring and monitoring the performance of your employees. Build your system on the *MARS* system. MARS is an acronym for *milestones, actions, relationships,* and *schedules;* we describe each element of the MARS system in the following sections.

Setting your checkpoints: the milestones

Every goal needs a starting point, an ending point, and points in between to measure progress along the continuum. Milestones are the checkpoints, events, and markers that tell you and your employees how far along you are on the road to reaching the goals that you've set together.

For example, suppose that you establish a goal of finalizing corporate budgets in three months time. The third milestone along the way to your ultimate goal is that draft department budgets be submitted to division managers no later than the June 1. If you check with the division managers on June 1 and they haven't submitted the draft budgets, you quickly and unambiguously know that the project is behind schedule. If, however, all the budgets are in on May 15, you know that the project is ahead of schedule and that you may reach the final goal of completing the corporate budgets sooner than you originally estimated.

Reaching your checkpoints: the actions

Actions are the individual activities that your employees perform to get from one milestone to the next. To reach the third milestone in your budgeting project, your employees must undertake and complete several actions after they reach the second milestone in the project. In this example, these actions may include the following:

- Review prior year expenditure reports and determine the relationship, if any, to current activities.

- Review current year-to-date expenditure reports and project final, year-end numbers.

- Meet with department staff to determine their training, travel, and capital equipment requirements for the new year.

- Review possible new hires, terminations, and pay raises to determine the impact on payroll cost.

- Create a computerized draft budget spreadsheet using numbers developed in the preceding actions.

- Print the draft budget and manually double-check the results. Correct entries and reprint if necessary.

- Submit the draft budget to the division manager.

Each action gets your employees a little farther along the way toward reaching the third milestone in the project — completion of draft corporate budgets by June 1 — and is therefore a critical element in the performance of your employees. When developing a plan for completion of a project, note each action in writing. Doing this makes focusing easier for your employees because they know exactly what they must do to reach a milestone, how far they have gone, and how much farther they have to go.

Sequencing your activity: the relationships

Relationships are how milestones and actions interact with one another. Relationships proscribe and define the proper sequencing of activities that lead you to the successful, effective accomplishment of your goals. Although sequence doesn't *always* matter, it is usually more effective to perform certain actions before others and to attain certain milestones before others.

For example, in the prior list of actions needed to achieve the third project milestone — submitting draft corporate budgets by June 1 — trying to perform the fifth action before the first, second, third, or fourth is *not going to work!* If you haven't figured out the right numbers to put into your spreadsheet before you fill in the blanks, your results are going to be meaningless.

However, keep in mind that there may be more than one way to reach a milestone and give your employees the latitude to find their own ways to reach their goals. Doing so empowers your employees to take responsibility for their work and to learn from their mistakes and successes. The results are successful performance and happy, productive employees.

Establishing your time frame: the schedules

How do you determine how far apart your milestones should be and how long project completion should take? You do this by estimating the schedule of each individual action in your project plan. How long does it take to review current year-to-date expenditure reports and project final, year-end numbers? A day? A week? How long does it take you to meet with all the members of your staff to assess their needs?

Using your experience and training to develop schedules that are realistic and useful is important. For example, you may know that if everything goes perfectly, meeting with all your employees will take exactly four days. However, you also know that if you run into problems, the process could take as long as six days. Therefore, for planning purposes, you decide that five days is an appropriate schedule to apply to this particular action. This schedule allows for *some* variability in performance while ensuring that you meet the milestone on time.

Application of each characteristic — milestones, actions, relationships, and schedules — results in goals that you can measure and monitor. If you can't measure and monitor your goals, chances are that your employees will never achieve them and you won't know the difference. And wouldn't that be a shame?

Learning to measure instead of count

According to management guru Peter Drucker, most business people spend too much time counting and too little time measuring the performance of their organizations. What does Drucker mean by this? Drucker is talking about the tendency of managers to be shortsighted in their application of management controls such as budgets. For example, most budgets are meant to ensure that company funds are spent *only* where they are authorized. They are control mechanisms that prevent spending from going out of control unnoticed by counting the number of dollars spent for a particular activity. However, Drucker suggests that, instead of using budgets only to count, they should be used to measure. Managers could do this by relating

proposed expenditures to *future* results and by providing follow-up information to show whether the desired results were achieved.

Drucker likens counting to a doctor using an X-ray machine to diagnose an ill patient. Although some ailments — broken bones, pneumonia, and such — show up on an X-ray, other, more life-threatening illnesses such as leukemia, hypertension, and AIDS won't. Similarly, most managers use accounting systems to X-ray the financial performance of their organizations. However, accounting systems won't measure a catastrophic loss of market share or a failure of the firm to innovate until it's already too late and the patient has been damaged — perhaps irretrievably.

Putting Performance Measuring and Monitoring into Practice

Theory is nice, but practice is better. So far we've discussed the theory of measuring and monitoring employee performance, but now we must get into the practice of making it happen. Following are a couple of real-life cases for your reading pleasure. Each case takes a different path to achieve the same ends: successful employee performance.

Case 1: World-class performance

A couple of years ago, Bob took over his company's product customization department. At the time, the department was in shambles — project management was haphazard at best, there was no clear system of organization, and customers had to wait weeks or even months to receive their customized products, which often came to them with countless errors. Clearly, a change was needed, and Bob was given the task of straightening things out.

After reviewing the operations of the department and collecting data from internal and external customers, Bob worked up a checklist of things that would need to be done to bring the organization up to a world-class level of performance. At the heart of Bob's plan was a complete revamping of the department's system of measuring and monitoring performance.

Step 1: Setting goals with employees

The first two things Bob did after drafting a checklist of what he wanted to accomplish were to talk to the employees in his new department and to interview users. And were they ever ready to talk! By the time he had finished collecting everyone's feedback, Bob had filled several pages with negative comments about the department, work processes, procedures, and more. An example of the kind of problems that Bob's employees talked about was vividly illustrated on his first day in the office when a company salesperson called in some urgently needed changes to one of the projects completed the day before only to find out that the software was lost! Ouch!

All performance starts with clear goals. After Bob figured out exactly what was interfering with his employees' ability to do a good job, he discussed department needs and changes with them. The result of these discussions was a set of mutually acceptable goals and a game plan for the department. Together, Bob and the employees set the stage for the next step in achieving world class performance.

Step 2: Change the performance monitoring system

When he reviewed the department's systems for measuring and monitoring employee performance, Bob quickly noticed that the measurements were all *negative*. All the talk was about problems: late projects, the number of mistakes, backlogged orders, etc. There was no tracking of any *positive* performance measure.

Bob wanted to start some positive tracking to establish a baseline for performance and to build a positive momentum. He installed a new system that focused on only *one* performance measure — a positive one — the number of on-time projects. From only a few on-time projects when Bob took over, the department racked up an amazing 2,700 on-time projects (in a row!) by the end of two years. Not only did this tremendous increase in performance make Bob happy, but the difference in the morale of his employees was like night and day. Instead of dreading the requests for customized products — and never having their efforts appreciated or "good enough" — they looked forward to the challenge of exceeding the high standards of performance that they had set for themselves.

Step 3: Revising the plan

As project performance improved, Bob pushed for other improvements: 24-hour project quotes, project indexing, software storage, streamlining of royalty and invoicing systems, and more. At the same time that the improvements were planned and implemented, Bob walked a tightrope between balancing the long-term needs of system improvements with the short-term needs of getting the work done.

Before long, top management noticed what was going on in Bob's department. As the department's performance continued to improve, the work of the department went from being a liability to the firm (that many salespeople refused to use) to being a major competitive advantage in the marketplace. By this time, the department completed 80 percent of its projects within two weeks after receipt.

Case 2: Helping your employees give 100 percent

You may not always measure the results you want for your organization in terms of the number of widgets produced or the percentage increase in an employee's contributions to profitability. Sometimes you simply want your employees to show up on time and to at least *seem* to enjoy the eight or nine hours that they spend at work each day. If the *morale* of your employees is poor, their productivity is likely to be poor, too.

A survey of employees at Diamond Fiber Products, Inc., that is cited in Bob's *1001 Ways to Reward Employees* showed that 79 percent of employees felt they weren't being rewarded for a job well done, 65 percent felt that management treated them disrespectfully, and 56 percent were pessimistic about their work. Not exactly the formula for a great company! Fortunately, company managers recognized that they had a problem (to say the least) and here is what they did to fix it.

Step 1: Create a program based on the behaviors you want

The first step the management of Diamond Fiber Products took was to create a brand new club in the company. They developed the 100 Club to reinforce the behaviors that management wanted to promote throughout the organization. These behaviors were

- Attendance
- Punctuality
- Safety

The plan was to award points to employees based on certain measurable criteria related to these behaviors. Any employee attaining a total of 100 points would then receive an award — in this case, a nylon jacket with the Diamond Fiber logo and the words *The 100 Club* imprinted on it.

Step 2: Assign points to the desired behaviors

The next step was to assign points to each desired behavior. Depending on whether employees exhibit the desired behavior (or not), they can either receive points or have them taken away. For example, employees receive 25 points for a year of perfect attendance. However, for each full or partial day of entire year without formal disciplinary actions receive 20 points, and employees who work for a year without injuries resulting in lost time receive 15 points. Employees can also receive points for making cost-saving suggestions, safety suggestions, or participating in community service projects such as Red Cross blood drives or the United Way.

In assigning points to each behavior, management made sure that the number of points was proportionate to the behavior's importance to the organization. Further, management ensured that, although the numeric goals weren't too easy to attain — that is, employees would have to stretch themselves to reach them — they wouldn't be impossible to reach and thereby be demotivating.

Step 3: Measure and reward employee performance

Measurement and reward of the desired employee behavior are the heart of Diamond Fiber's program. Supervisors and managers closely track the performance of their employees and assign points for each of the factors. When employees reach the coveted 100 point level, they are inducted into the 100 Club, and the jacket is theirs.

You might think that this program is trivial — who would *really* care about getting a jacket with a company logo and three words, *The 100 Club,* printed on it? *Your* employees, that's who! A local bank teller tells a story about a Diamond Fiber employee who once visited the bank to proudly model her new 100 Club jacket to bank customers and employees. According to the woman, "My employer gave this to me for doing a good job. It's the first time in the 18 years that I've been there that they've recognized the things I do every day."

Even more telling, in the first year of the program, Diamond Fiber saved $5.2 million, increased productivity by $14\frac{1}{2}$ percent, and reduced quality-related mistakes by 40 percent. Not only that, but 79 percent of employees said that the quality of their work concerned them more now than before the program started; 73 percent reported that the company showed concern for them as people; and an amazing 86 percent of employees said that the company and management considered them to be either "important" or "very important." Not bad results at all for a $40 baby blue jacket!

Gantts, PERTs, and Other Yardsticks

In some cases, measuring your employees' progress toward achieving a goal doesn't really take much. For example, if the goal is to increase the number of widgets produced from 100 per hour to 125 per hour, a simple count can tell you whether your employees have achieved that goal. *Sorry Stella, you're still averaging 120 widgets per hour!* However, if the goal is to fabricate a prototype electric-powered vehicle in six months' time, the job of measuring and monitoring individual performance gets much more complicated and confusing.

Although you may decide to write out all the different milestones and actions (as we did in the corporate budgeting example earlier in this chapter), reading and understanding a graphical representation of the project is often much easier for complex projects. PERTs, Gantts, and other yardsticks perform this vital service for businesspeople around the world 24 hours a day, 7 days a week. *[Offstage, the music swells as cannons fire a 21-gun salute, troops pass in review, and high-octane fighter planes thunder over the throng.]*

Bar charts

Bar charts, also known as *Gantt charts* (named for that famous [*who?*] industrial engineer, Henry L. Gantt), are probably one of the simplest and most common means for illustrating and monitoring project progress. With a quick glance, a manager can easily see exactly where the project should be at any given date and can compare actual progress against planned progress.

The three key elements of bar charts are the following:

- ✔ **Time line:** The time line provides a scale with which you measure progress. You can express the time line in any units you want: days, weeks, months, or whatever is most useful for managing the project. In most bar charts, the time line appears along the horizontal axis (the *x-axis* for you math majors out there).

- ✔ **Actions:** Actions are the individual activities that your employees perform to get from one milestone to the next. In a bar chart, each action is listed — usually in chronological order — vertically along the left side of the chart (that's the *y-axis*, math experts!).

- ✔ **Bars:** Now, what would a bar chart be without bars? An *unbar* chart perhaps? Bars are the open blocks that you draw on your bar chart to indicate the length of time that a particular action is estimated to take. Short bars mean short periods of time; long bars mean long periods of time. What's really neat about bars is that, as an action is completed, you can fill in the bar — providing a quick visual reference of complete and incomplete actions.

We use our prior example again to illustrate the use of a bar chart. Figure 9-1 shows a typical bar chart; in this case, the chart illustrates the actions that lead up to the third milestone in the corporate budgeting example.

As Figure 9-1 shows, the time line is along the top of the bar chart — just as we said it would be. In this example, the time line stretches from April 15 to June 1, with each increment representing one week. The seven actions necessary to reach the third milestone are listed vertically along the left side of the bar chart. Finally, you see those neat little bars that are really the heart and soul of the bar chart. Leave the bars unfilled until an action is completed; you may color them in now if you like.

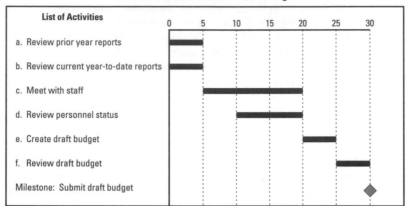

Figure 9-1:
A bar chart illustrating actions leading up to the third milestone.

If all actions are completed according to the bar chart, the third milestone will be reached on June 1. If some actions take longer to complete than estimated, it's quite possible that the milestone will not be reached on time and *someone* may end up in hot water. Conversely, if some actions take less time than estimated, the milestone can be reached *early* (sounds like a bonus is in order!).

The advantages of the Gantt chart are its simplicity, ease of preparation and use, and low cost. Although fine for a simple project such as preparing a budget, Gantt charts are generally unsuitable for large, complex projects such as building a space shuttle or doing your taxes.

Flowcharts

When the going gets tough, the tough get going — and they reach for their flowcharts. Although bar charts are useful for simple projects, they do not illustrate the sequential flow of actions in a project (and, therefore, aren't as useful for complex projects). On the other hand, flowcharts do a good job of illustrating this sequential flow. Although flowcharts look completely different than bar charts, they also have three key elements:

✔ **Actions:** In the case of flowcharts, actions are indicated by arrows. Arrows lead from one event to the next on a flowchart until the project is completed. The length of the arrows do not necessarily indicate the duration of an action. The primary purpose of the arrows in a flow chart is to illustrate the sequential relationship of actions to one another.

✔ **Events:** Events, represented in flowcharts by numbered circles, signify the completion of a particular action.

> ✔ **Time:** Time estimates are inserted alongside each action (arrow) in the flowchart. By adding the number of time units along a particular path, you can estimate the total time for the completion of an action.

Figure 9-2 shows a flowchart of the corporate budgeting example illustrated in Figure 9-1. As you can see, the flow chart shows exactly how each action relates to the others. By following the *longest* path in terms of time, you can determine the *critical path* of the project. This kind of analysis is called the *critical path method (CPM)* and assumes that the time to complete individual actions can be estimated with a high degree of certainty. The critical path method highlights the actions that determine the soonest that a project can be completed — in this case, 30 days.

PERT, short for *program evaluation and review technique,* is a variation of CPM used when the time to complete individual actions *cannot* be estimated with a high degree of certainty. Using some very interesting statistical techniques (zzzzz . . .), PERT averages a range of possible times to arrive at an estimate for each action.

Software

Fortunately for those of you who missed out on taking calculus in 12th grade, the wonderful world of computers and software has now touched project monitoring and measurement. What you used to do with hours of drawing, erasing, redrawing, and so on, you can now accomplish with only a few well-placed keystrokes.

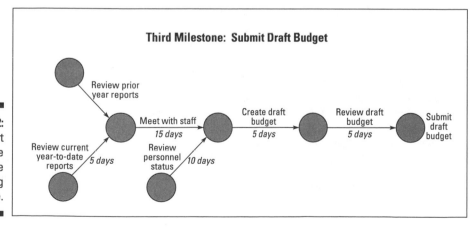

Figure 9-2:
A flowchart for the corporate budgeting example.

Microsoft Project, one of the foremost project-planning software packages on the market today, enables you to create and revise project schedules quickly and easily. Setting up a project with Microsoft Project is as easy as 1, 2, 3:

- ✔ Enter the actions to be completed.
- ✔ Enter the sequence of the actions and their dependencies on other actions.
- ✔ Enter the resources (people and money) required to complete the action.

As a project progresses, you can input data such as actual start and completion dates, actual expenditures, and more to get a realistic picture of where the project is at any time. You can print out these results in the form of tables, charts, or graphs — whatever your preference — and then save them for future reference.

You've Got Their Number: Now What?

You've set up your goals, you've set performance measures, and you've obtained pages of data for each of your employees. Now what? Now you determine whether the expected results were achieved.

- ✔ **Compare results to expectations:** What is the expected goal? Suppose that the goal is to complete the cost-benefit analysis by November 1. When was the cost-benefit analysis completed? It was completed on October 17 — well ahead of the deadline. Super! The mission was accomplished with time to spare.

The Six Phases of a Project

Some management techniques are so popular that they are photocopied and passed from employee to employee and from company to company in an informal system of communication that outperforms the *formal* communication system of many organizations. These tongue-in-cheek lists, diagrams, and cartoons help many employees find humor in their own workplaces and brighten up their days. The following Six Phases of a Project list has been floating around for years — our copy looks like it's at least fifth generation:

1. Enthusiasm

2. Disillusionment

3. Panic

4. Search for the Guilty

5. Punishment of the Innocent

6. Praise and Honors for the Non Participants

✔ **Record the results:** Make note of the results — perhaps put them in the files that you maintain for each employee or print them out on your computer and post them in the work area.

✔ **Praise, coach, or counsel your employees:** If the job was done right, on time, and within budget, congratulate your employees for a job well done and reward them appropriately: a written note of appreciation, a day off with pay, a formal awards presentation — whatever you decide.

However, if the expected results were *not* achieved, find out why and what you can do to ensure that the expected results *are* achieved the next time. If the employees need only additional support or encouragement, coach them to better performance. You can listen to your employees, refer them to other employees, or provide your own personal examples. If the poor results stem from a more serious shortcoming, counsel or discipline your employees. (More on this subject in Chapter 15.)

Test your new-found knowledge

What are the four parts of the MARS system of measuring and monitoring performance?

A. Monitored, active, related, and scheduled

B. Milestones, actions, relationships, and systematic

C. Milestones, actions, relationships, and schedules

D. None of the above

What is the critical path?

A. The soonest that a project can be completed

B. The path of least resistance

C. The maximum amount of time to complete a project

D. The most difficult approach to a project

Chapter 10

Performance Evaluations: Not Necessarily a Waste of Time

- -

In This Chapter

▶ Considering the importance of performance evaluations

▶ Introducing norms and standards

▶ Developing performance evaluations

▶ Avoiding evaluation mistakes

▶ Making evaluations better

▶ Discussing pay and career plans

- -

*T*imely and accurate performance evaluations are an extremely important tool for *every* business manager or supervisor. So if performance evaluations are so important to the successful management of employees, why do most managers and supervisors *dread* doing them, and why do so many employees *dread* receiving them? According to studies on the topic, 40 percent of all American workers *never* receive performance evaluations. And for the 60 percent of the workers who *do* receive performance evaluations, most are poorly done. Very few employees actually receive regular, formal performance evaluations that are thoughtfully and completely done.

Ask *any* manager, supervisor, or employee: Are formal performance evaluations *really* necessary? The answer you get will likely be a resounding *yes!* However, if you look a little below the surface, the reality may echo something quite different. Although most managers consider performance evaluations an important and necessary tool in developing their employees, reinforcing good performance, and correcting poor performance, these evaluations are often too little, too late. They often miss the mark as tools for developing employees. If performance evaluations are done poorly, managers are better off not doing them at all — especially if the alternative is more frequent coaching.

In the sections that follow, we consider the benefits of performance evaluations and explore the right ways and the wrong ways to do them.

Performance Evaluations: Why Bother?

You can find many very good reasons for conducting regular formal performance evaluations with your employees. Formal performance evaluations are just one part of an organization's system of delegation, goal setting, coaching, motivating, and ongoing informal and formal feedback on employee performance. If you don't believe us, try a few of these positive elements of performance evaluations on for size:

- ✔ **A chance to summarize past performance and establish new performance goals:** All employees want to know whether they are doing a good job. Formal performance evaluations *force* managers to communicate performance results — both good and bad — to their employees and to set new goals. In many organizations, the annual performance evaluation is the only occasion when supervisors and managers speak to their employees about performance expectations and the results of employee efforts for the preceding evaluation period.

- ✔ **An opportunity for communication:** It's a fickle thing. You need to constantly compare expectations. In fact, try this with *your* manager. List your ten most important activities. Then ask your *manager* to list what he or she considers to be your ten most important activities. Surprise! Chances are, your lists are quite different. On average, business people who do this exercise find that their lists overlap only 40 percent at best. Performance evaluations help the employer and employee to compare notes and make sure that assignments and priorities are in order.

- ✔ **A forum for career development:** In many organizations, career development takes place as a part of the formal performance evaluation process. Managers and employees are all very busy folks and often have difficulty setting aside the time to sit down and chart out the steps that they must take to progress in an organization or career. Although career development discussions should generally take place in a forum separate from the performance evaluation process, combining the activities does afford the opportunity to kill both birds with the same stone, or something like that.

- ✔ **A formal documentation of employee performance:** Most employees get plenty of *informal* performance feedback — at least of the negative kind. *You did what? Are you nuts?!* Most informal feedback is verbal and, as such, undocumented. If you are trying to build a case to give your employee a promotion, you can support your case much easier if you have plenty of written documentation (including formal performance evaluations) to justify your decision.

The preceding list gives very important reasons for conducting regular formal performance evaluations. However, consider this: Many companies have paid a *lot* of money to employees and former employees who have successfully sued them for wrongful termination or for other, biased employment decisions. Imagine how lonely *you* would feel on the witness stand in the following scene, a scene that's replayed *for real* time and again in American courts of law:

Lawyer: So, Manager Framus, would you please tell the court exactly why you terminated Employee Dingdong?

Manager Framus (You): Certainly, I'll be glad to. Employee Dingdong was a very poor performer — clearly the worst in my department.

Lawyer: During the five years that my client was with your firm, did you ever conduct formal performance evaluations with Employee Dingdong?

Manager Framus (You): Uhhh . . . well, no. I meant to, but I'm a very busy person. I was never quite able to get around to it.

Lawyer: Manager Framus, do you mean to say that, in all the time with your firm, Employee Dingdong never received a formal performance evaluation? Exactly how was my client supposed to correct the alleged poor performance when you failed to provide Employee Dingdong with the feedback needed to do so?

Manager Framus (You): Uhhhhh. . . .

Introducing Mr. Norms and Ms. Standards

Now that you are convinced that you should conduct formal performance evaluations, you might ask, "Exactly what am I supposed to evaluate?" We're glad you asked. *Ladies and gentlemen, we now have the honor to introduce to you Mr. Norms and Ms. Standards.*

Norms and standards comprise the rules of the road in any organization, and they are the bases for your employee evaluations.

Norms are the informal behaviors that are considered to be generally acceptable in a workplace. For example, the fact that all the male managers in your company feel compelled to wear jackets and ties and all the female managers feel compelled to wear suits is a norm. Although no formal rule *requires* managers to dress this way, they do anyway. Not only do they do so willingly, but they would probably feel quite naked without their self-imposed "uniforms."

Standards are the formal requirements of a workplace. Standards include a company's rules, policies and procedures, performance goals, and other formally established guidelines — whether written or verbal. An example of a standard is a company's policy against sexual harassment. If it is written well, the policy clearly describes to employees the bounds of acceptable behavior as well as the consequences of stepping out of bounds. Then if an employee acts in conflict with the policy, the resulting discipline (or even termination) of the offending employee comes as no surprise.

Even though norms and standards are both used to evaluate employee behavior, knowing the differences between the two and applying each appropriately is important.

Standards are generally clear and unambiguous. If your department has established the standard that workers will produce a minimum of 200 widgets an hour, then determining whether employees have met the standard is quite easy. If employees only produce 100 widgets an hour, then they have clearly not met the standard. If they produce 300 widgets an hour, then they have clearly over-met the standard *(and you should set a higher standard!)*. If your company policy says that employees are supposed to work five days a week, Monday through Friday excepting holidays, then employees who show up only three days a week have clearly not met the required standard.

Because *good* (note the operative word: *good*) standards are clear and unambiguous, it is simple for you (the manager) to use them to measure employee performance and to base promotion, discipline, and other performance-related decisions on them.

However, norms are another animal altogether (a giraffe, perhaps?). Because norms are not written in stone as formal policies, rules, or procedures, they are harder to identify, and they are *much* more subjective than standards. Because of this, managers find that using norms as a yardstick (or *dipstick,* for you car fanciers) to measure employee performance is harder. Take for example a company's norm to treat coworkers with respect — a norm that is growing in popularity along with the proliferation of diversity programs throughout many organizations. Exactly how do you measure respect? Is respect an "either/or" kind of thing or are there degrees of respect that can be quantified and reported? Where do you draw the line between respect and disrespect?

As you can see, the problem with using norms to measure employee performance is that they are situational — identical behavior that may be considered acceptable to one manager may not be acceptable to another. Alternatively, behavior that a manager considers to be acceptable from one employee (perhaps the teacher's pet) may be considered unacceptable by the same manager when manifested by another employee.

We're not saying that norms are any less important than standards. The fact is that violation of an organization's norms can have as much impact as a violation of its standards. Have you ever had an employee who was very talented, but a *royal pain in the neck* to work with? Peter has had one or two assistants whose performance exceeded all the standards, but whose behavior wreaked utter havoc throughout the organization. A week didn't go by without Peter's receiving a call from an employee who had been offended or insulted by one of these assistants. Peter began to spend more time trying to patch up the damage from these ongoing violations of the organization's norms. When this happened, he knew that he had to make the violations a performance issue and counsel his employees about the problem.

Some pain in your neck (that is, violation of norms) is okay and to be expected. But when the pain gets so severe that it interferes with the performance of other employees, that's where you have to draw the line.

The Performance Evaluation Process

As with anything else in life, there is a right way and a wrong way to conduct performance evaluations. Considering the importance of the performance evaluation process to you, your employees, and your organization, doing it the *right* way is likely in your best interest.

Many managers tend to see the performance evaluation process in very narrow terms: How can I get this thing done as quickly as possible so I can get back to my *real* job? (Whatever their *real* job *is* as managers.) In their haste to get the evaluation done and behind them, many managers merely consider a few examples of recent performance and base their entire evaluation on them. And because few managers give their employees the kind of meaningful, ongoing performance feedback that they need to do their jobs better, the performance evaluation can become a dreaded event — full of surprises and dismay. Or it can be so sugar coated that it becomes a meaningless exercise in management. *This* scenario is not the *right* way to evaluate your employees!

The performance appraisal process is *much* broader than just the formal, written part of it. Here are five steps that help you encompass the broader scope of the process; follow them when you evaluate your employees' performance:

1. **Set goals, expectations, and standards.**

   Before your employees can achieve your goals, or perform to your expectations, you have to set goals and expectations with them and develop standards to measure their performance. And after you've done all this, you have to *communicate* them — *before* you evaluate your employees — not *after*. In fact, the performance review really starts on the first day of work! Tell your employees right then how you evaluate them, show them the forms to be used, and explain the process.

   Make sure that job descriptions are clear and unambiguous, and that you and your employees understand and agree to the standards you have set for them. This is a two-way process. Make sure that employees have a voice in setting their goals and standards.

2. **Give continuous and specific feedback.**

   Catch your employees doing things right — every day of the week — and tell them about it then and there. And if you catch them doing wrong (nobody's perfect!), then let them know about *that*, too. Feedback is *much* more effective when you give it regularly and often than when you save it up for a special occasion (also known as *gunnysacking,* if the feedback is negative). The best formal performance evaluations contain the fewest surprises.

3. Prepare a formal, written performance evaluation.

Every organization has different requirements for the formal performance evaluation. Some evaluations are simple, one-page forms that only require checking off a few boxes — others are multipage extravaganzas that require extensive narrative support. Regardless of the requirements of your particular organization, the formal performance evaluation should be a summary of the significant events of the evaluation period — events that you have discussed previously with your employees. Support your words with examples and make evaluations meaningful to your employees by keeping your discussion relevant to the goals, expectations, and standards that you developed in step 1.

As a reality check, have the employee fill out his or her *own* performance evaluation. Then compare your (the manager's) comments with the employee's comments; the differences that you find become topics of discussion.

4. Meet personally with your employees to discuss the formal performance evaluation.

There's nothing quite like the personal touch to get your message across to your employees. Set aside some *quality* time to meet with your employees to discuss their performance evaluation. This *does not* mean five or ten minutes, but *at least* an hour — maybe more! When you plan formal performance meetings, less is definitely *not* more. Pick a place that is comfortable and free of distractions. Meetings should be positive and upbeat. Even when you have to discuss performance problems, center your discussions on ways that you and your employees can work *together* to solve them.

5. Set new goals, expectations, and standards.

The formal evaluation meeting gives you and your employees the opportunity to step back from the inevitable daily issues for a moment and to take a look at the big picture. You both have an opportunity to review and discuss the things that worked well and the things that, perhaps, didn't work so well. Based on this assessment, you can then set new goals, expectations, and standards for the next review period. The last step of the performance evaluation process becomes the first step, and you start all over again.

Although most formal performance evaluations happen on an annual or semi-annual basis, as a manager, you should give your employees informal feedback on their performance early and often. If you catch your employees doing something right, then tell them so — right then and there! Don't wait for a year to tell them about it. Similarly, if your employees drop the ball, let them know your concerns while the behavior is still fresh in your mind.

Above all, don't save instances of poor performance in a gunnysack, only to dump them on your employees at some distant point in the future. Not only does gunnysacking have little effect on getting the performance that you want out of your employees, but it can cost you their respect in the process.

Common Mistakes That Evaluators Make

Evaluators can easily fall into certain traps in the evaluation process. To avoid making a misstep that could result in getting your foot stuck in one of these traps (ouch!), keep in mind these common mistakes that evaluators make:

> ✔ **The halo effect:** This happens when an employee is so good in a particular area of their performance that you ignore problems in other areas of their performance. For example, you might give your star salesperson (who your firm desperately needs to ensure continued revenue growth) a high rating (a halo) despite the fact that she refuses to complete and submit paperwork within required time limits.

Turning the tables: upward and 360-degree evaluations

In recent years, a new kind of performance evaluation has emerged. Instead of the typical *downward* evaluation where manageres review the performance of their workers, the *upward* evaluation process stands this convention on its head by requiring workers to evaluate the performance of their managers. If you think that getting a performance evaluation from your manager is uncomfortable, you haven't seen anything yet. There's nothing quite like the feeling you get when a group of your employees gives you direct and honest feedback about the things you do that make it hard for them to do a good job. Ouch!

However, despite the discomfort that you might feel, the upward evaluation is invaluable — who better to assess your *real* impact on the organization than your employees? The system works *so* well that Fortune 500 companies such as Federal Express and others have institutionalized the upward evaluation and made it a part of their corporate cultures. In a recent survey, almost 15 percent of American firms are using some form of the upward performance evaluation to assess the performance of their managers.

Also popular is the 360-degree evaluation which is used by companies such as Levi Strauss & Co. and Boeing Co. Levi's 360-degree evaluation process dictates that all employees are evaluated by their supervisors *and* by their underlings and peers. The results can be quite a surprise to the lucky employee who is the subject of the evaluation who may find that other employees see him or her as less caring and visionary than he or she thought.

✔ **The pitchfork effect:** The opposite of the halo effect, the pitchfork effect happens when you allow an instance of poor performance to adversely affect your assessment of an employee's overall performance. For example, your administrative assistant has done a very good job for you in the months preceding his evaluation, but last week he missed a customer's deadline for submission of a proposal to continue with their advertising account. Your firm lost the account and you gave your assistant a scathing performance evaluation as a result.

✔ **Stereotyping:** This occurs when you allow preconceived notions about your employees dictate how you rate them. For example, you may be convinced that women make better electronic parts assemblers than do men. As a result, your stereotyping automatically gives female employees the benefit of the doubt and higher ratings, while men have to prove themselves before you take them seriously.

✔ **Comparing:** Often, when you rate two employees at the same time, you can be tempted to compare their performances. If one of the employees is a particularly high performer, your other employee may look bad in comparison — despite his or her individual level of performance. Conversely, if one of the employees is a particularly low performer, the other employee may look really good in comparison. Your assessment of the performance of an individual employee should stand on its own two feet and not be subject to how good or bad your other employees are.

✔ **Mirroring:** Everyone naturally likes people who are most like themselves. That's why you can easily fall into the trap of rating highly those employees who behave most like you and rating lowly those employees who behave least like you. While this is great for the employees who you favor, it's not so great for the ones you don't. Take some advice. Don't do it.

✔ **Nice Guy/Gal:** One reason that many managers dread doing performance evaluations is that it forces them to acknowledge the failings of their employees and then talk to their employees about them. Few managers *enjoy* giving their employees bad news, but it is quite important for employees to get the bad news as well as the good (just be ready to duck when you give them the *bad* news). Otherwise, they won't know where they need to improve. And if they don't know where they need to improve, you can bet they won't.

Why Evaluations Go Bad

From our experience, few employee evaluations are done well. Not only are they often poorly written — lacking in meaningful examples and insights — but the main process of the performance evaluation, the *discussion,* is rarely given the time and attention that it deserves. As a result, performance evaluations often fail to have the kind of impact that the managers and supervisors who gave them intended.

Real apprehension can surround the evaluation process — from both sides of the equation. Often, managers don't feel adequate to the task, and workers don't get the kind of timely and quality feedback that they need to do the best job possible. On top of all this, an underlying tension often accompanies the performance evaluation process and comes from the fact that most companies tie money and pay raises to performance evaluations. Evaluations that focus on the pay instead of on the performance, or the lack thereof, are not uncommon.

Why do so many performance evaluations go bad?

Don't drop the ball

To begin, although the performance evaluation process itself is pretty simple, a *lot* more goes into it than filling out a three-page form you get once a year and then meeting with your employees for 15 minutes to give them the results of your assessment. The performance evaluation process begins on the day that your employees are hired, continues each and every day that they report to you, and doesn't end until, through transfer, promotion, or termination, they move out of your sphere of responsibility.

The *entire* process consists of setting goals with your employees, monitoring their performance, coaching them, supporting them, counseling them, and providing continuous feedback on their performance — both good and bad. If you have been doing these things before you sit down for your annual or semi-annual performance evaluation session with your employees, you're going to find reviews a pleasant wrap up and review of past accomplishments instead of a disappointment for both you and your employees.

Don't be among the many managers who fail to give their employees ongoing performance feedback and, instead, wait for the scheduled review. Despite your best intentions, and the best efforts of your employees, assignments can easily go astray. Schedules can stretch, roadblocks can stop progress, and confusion can wrap its ugly tentacles around a project. However, if you haven't set up systems to track the progress of your employees, you probably won't figure this out until too late. You end up mad, and your employees get black eyes because of their mistakes.

Even worse than not giving your employees feedback until they've failed is to save up *all* the failures and then to dump them on your employees all at once. This technique, called *gunnysacking,* is *not,* we repeat, is *not* the right way to conduct performance evaluations. Instead of an making incremental course corrections along the way, offending managers ambush their employees with weeks, months, and even years of problems that they have been saving up for a special occasion. And instead of helping to reinforce the *good* behaviors and performance of their employees, gunnysacking managers leave their employees dazed and confused — wondering what hit them.

Call 911: I've been mugged!

Peter will long remember one particularly large gunnysack that a manager dropped on *him* one bright and sunny morning. One day — a day that started out like any other — Peter picked up a folder from his in box. The folder was stapled tightly shut, not uncommon in this organization, where all personnel actions were routed in folders. Still, the extra five or ten staples securing this particular folder *did* seem a bit much. Peter eagerly tore the folder apart to get to the pages that were nestled within its crimson leaves. Inside was a memo listing numerous examples of Peter's alleged dereliction of duty: projects completed late, errors that had brought the organization to a screeching halt, and other serious transgressions of his manager's expectations. Horrors!

After Peter recovered from the initial shock of getting mugged by the memo (all the while refraining from the overwhelming urge to dial 911), he noticed an interesting pattern. This pattern illustrates the shortcomings of the gunnysack method:

- First, the memo neglected to mention — even in passing — the 99 percent of the things that Peter and his department did *right* and *on time* day in and day out.

- Second, in the cases where projects were not completed to his manager's expectations, Peter's manager had not spelled out *any* expectations — either in advance or during the projects' course. It was the old "I'll let you know if that's not what I wanted" approach to management. Peter didn't know that he hadn't met his manager' expectations until after the fact, when it was too late to do anything about it. The body was already cold, and there was nothing left to do but bury it.

- Third, Peter's manager dropped the bomb and then went on to other things. No follow-up meeting was scheduled; no expectations were set. Nothing. Nada. The die was cast for the next round of unfulfilled expectations. Here we go again: *management by ambush!*

Instead of checking up on Peter's progress along the way and coaching and supporting his efforts, Peter's manager instead chose to save up these alleged misdeeds and dump them squarely on Peter's head all at once. Although this ambush clearly took a lot less time to accomplish than would setting up and administering an ongoing system of performance monitoring, evaluation, and feedback — or even a discussion, for that matter — the results were likely not what Peter's manager intended. Not only were the manager's expectations unmet (*how could they be met if they weren't communicated?*), but no changes were made to ensure that the expectations would be met in the future.

For the No-Surprises Evaluation: Prepare

If *you* are doing *your* job as a manager, there should be *no* surprises for your employees. Following the lead of the best managers: Keep in touch with your employees and give them continuous feedback on their progress. Then, when you *do* sit down with them for their formal performance evaluation, the session is a recap of the things that you have already discussed during the evaluation period, instead of an ambush. Keeping up a continuous dialog lets you use the formal evaluation to focus on the positive things that you and your employees can work on *together* to get the best possible performance.

Above all, *be prepared* for your employee evaluations!

Like interviews, many managers leave their preparation for performance evaluation meetings for the last possible minute — often just before the employee is scheduled to meet with them. *Oh, oh. Cathy is going to be here in five minutes. Now, what did I do with her file? I know it's here somewhere!*

Performance evaluation is a *year-round* job. Whenever you recognize a problem with your employees' performance, mention it to them, make a note of it, and drop it in your employees' files. Similarly, whenever your employees do something great, mention it to them, make a note of it, and drop it in their files. Then, when you're ready to do your employees' periodic performance evaluations, you can pull their files and have plenty of documentation available on which to base the evaluations. Not only does this practice make the process *easier* for you, but it makes the evaluation a *lot* more meaningful and productive for your employees.

Career Planning and Salary Discussions

Common practice in many organizations supplements formal performance evaluations (as if there weren't enough to talk about already!) with career planning discussions and — the real icing on the cake — the (hopefully) good news on a raise for your hard-working employees. This approach to conducting performance evaluations has just a *few* problems. Well, okay, maybe more than just a few!

First, despite the practice of most companies to link formal performance evaluations, career planning, and pay increases, each topic is independent of the others, and they each require separate consideration and action. However, managers (with their hectic schedules) are a tough bunch to tie down for more than a few minutes at a time. Many companies take the opportunity to get the most mileage possible out of the few minutes that they *can* squeeze out of the schedules of their busy managers. Thus, we have this regular *managementfest* of activities centered around the formal performance evaluation.

The Net speaks

In the following discussion, conducted within the Managing People board of *Inc.* magazine's service on America Online, participants consider the pluses and minuses of different kinds of performance evaluations.

Bizzwriter (Peter Economy): What is your opinion on that necessary evil of management, performance appraisals?

Fizza (Arthur Manuel, Industrial Engineering/ Assembly Manager, Keithley Metrabyte Division of Keithley Instruments): I must say that the type of review that has had the biggest impact on me was a review system called "Managing for Performance" (MFP). This type of review was done by getting input from my peers. Getting input from people on the same level is eye opening to say the least. You get a real feel for what kind of manager you are and what people think of your performance. The biggest problem with this type of review system is that it takes time to do.

Bizzwriter: Peer reviews can indeed be *very* powerful as you have seen.

Abben (James Dierberger, Owner, Synergetics): As a project engineer I once asked my supervisor why we didn't have subordinates evaluate their manager's skills at leadership. He said there wouldn't be anything to learn by doing such a 'reverse' appraisal. Time marched on . . . I began having my staff do self-appraisals about three years before it was required. I did one and each of them did one. Then we went one-on-one and compared the two reviews. It was excellent! This isn't rocket science. All it takes is a little ingenuity and creativity and the interest in getting the best from your people.

Bizzwriter: Thanks for your input, Abben. It sounds like the reverse performance reviews have worked very well for you and your organization.

MWEISBURGH (Mitchell Weisburgh, President, Personal Computer Learning Centers): A few things to watch out for, though, is that sometimes there is a popularity contest. A manager may go out of the way to get employees to give him/her a good rating. Also, no matter how well you spell things out, each person grades on their own scale, so one group of people may think a 3 is really good, while another may regard anything less than a 4 as being poor. Finally, we tried having managers evaluated by other managers. This was a disaster. The responses indicated a real hidden agenda. More like, "How will my career benefit if I rate this person well, or how if I rate this person poorly?"

Bizzwriter: Your points are well taken about the dangers of popularity contests and hidden agendas.

Second, by directly linking pay increases to the formal performance appraisal, you are creating a situation where your employees are potentially so anxious about the size of their hoped-for pay raise that they don't even hear what you have to say about their performance. *Oh boy — I really need a raise this year so we can afford to buy that new house!* Sure, you get lots of nods of their heads and "*Oh, I see,*" but their focus is understandably on the bottom line — not on all the "fluff" that precedes it. Heaven forbid that you forget to bring up the subject of a pay increase after all the torture your employees have had to endure to get through their performance evaluations!

Third, giving your employees bad financial news causes them to discount any good performance news. *Gee, Sarah, you're head and shoulders above the rest of the department, but my hands are tied. I wish I could give you a raise but I can't.* What kind of message do you think your employee will get from that? We guaranteed that you'll have one dejected employee. We also guaranteed that your star employees will wonder whether they really ought to work so hard. Why bother? They got the same pay raise as their coworkers who retired in place five years ago — *nothing*!

Fourth, as with giving performance feedback, career planning is a process that shouldn't wait to be done only once or twice a year. You and your employees should constantly be on the alert for opportunities to improve your employees' skills and to develop their abilities. Let's say that you get information on a series of classes that would be perfect for your assistant a couple of months after you completed his last formal performance evaluation. Are you going to hold on to the information until the *next* evaluation, nine months hence, or are you going to get with your employee *right now* to discuss it. You better not have chosen the first answer!

Finally, the formal performance evaluation process and meetings require the full attention of both you and your employees. Cluttering them up with other topics, other agendas, and other information — no matter how timely or well intended — only distracts all parties from the real reason for the meeting: to communicate the results of the formal performance evaluation and to develop strategies to improve future performance. Anything else just gets in the way.

Test your new-found knowledge

What are norms?

A. The informal behaviors considered generally acceptable in a workplace

B. Whatever your manager likes

C. Formal behaviors that guide employee actions

D. The best ways of getting things done

What is the first step in the performance evaluation process?

A. Decide your employee's rating

B. Set goals, expectations, and standards

C. Go to lunch with your employee

D. None of the above

Part IV
Working with (Other) People

The 5th Wave — By Rich Tennant

"TECHNICALLY HE'S A WIZARD, BUT AS A MANAGER HE LACKS PEOPLE SKILLS."

In this part . . .

No manager is an island. Managers work with other people — clients, teams, coworkers, and higher-ups, to name a few — all the time. In this part, we introduce some key skills for communicating effectively with others, working with teams, and dealing with politics in the office.

Chapter 11
Getting Your Message Across

● ●

In This Chapter

▶ Valuing informal communication over formal communication

▶ Discovering new ways to communicate

▶ Listening to others

▶ Communicating your thoughts in writing

▶ Making presentations

● ●

*H*ow important is getting your message across to your employees, peers, boss, clients, and customers? *Very!* You can't be a manager today without being able to communicate, and communicate effectively (well, at least not a very *good* manager).

You have more ways to communicate today than ever before, and it appears that many more are on the way. Only a couple of decades ago (yes, we *do* vaguely recall that ancient time), you had only a few different communications skills to master. Telephones, letters, face-to-face conversations, and the occasional speech or presentation were about it.

Now, however, you have all kinds of exciting and new ways to tell your counterpart on the other side of the world to take a hike. There's computer e-mail — both on local networks within companies and on the Internet — voice mail, voice pagers, conference calls, teleconferencing, faxes, cellular phones, satellite uplinks, satellite downlinks, and on and on. In fact, certain airlines now allow you to make telephone calls to individuals *at their seats!*

This chapter is about communicating with others and, in particular, the *way* in which you do it.

Communication: The Cornerstone of Business

Communication is all-important for the growth and survival of today's organizations. How big or how small the organization is doesn't matter — communication must be the cornerstone of every organization.

In business, communication takes place in a variety of formats. Table 11-1 shows you the order in which the bulk of business communication occurs. However, we find that the formal training that American people receive in school *reverses* this order. Table 11-2 illustrates the focus of formal communication training.

Table 11-1	The Format of Business Communications
Communication Format	**Frequency of Use**
Listening	Most frequent
Speaking/Presentation	Next most frequent
Writing	Next most frequent
Reading	Least frequent

Table 11-2	Our Formal Training in Communications
Communication Format	**Training Provided**
Reading	4 years English
Writing	4 years English
Speaking/Presentation	Optional class
Listening	Little formal training offered

As you can see, *informal* communication — not *formal* communication — is most important in business. Many managers fail because they don't understand this critical point. It's not the occasional speeches that you make, it's not how many beautifully crafted memos you write, and it's not how many articles on chaos theory that you read. It's the talking to your employees one-on-one, face-to-face — day in and day out. It's listening to them and *really* hearing what they have to say. Is it any wonder that most primary and secondary school systems fail to prepare students for business?

Over the past couple of decades, a fundamental change in the *style* of business communication has occurred. Long ago, most business communication — whether verbal or in writing — was very formal and constrained. This style came out of the old view of business, and the workers within it, as a vast machine (or at least hierarchical and proper). In this obsolete view of business, the formal hierarchy was *everything*. If a line worker had an idea that could make life better for a company's customers and save some money to boot, that worker had a *right* way and a *wrong* way to communicate the idea.

The *right* way was to write a formal memorandum to your boss. If your boss liked the idea, then he or she would pass it up to the next level, and so on until it found its way to the top of the organization. If the big boss liked the idea, then the memo — probably rewritten several times by each manager along the way — would get the stamp of approval and be passed back down the line for implementation. The process was slow; the procedure "proper."

The *wrong* way was to jump any of the steps in the formal hierarchy or to make the change without the explicit approval of the powers that be. Woe to the employees who strayed outside the approved lines of communication. They were renegades who were bucking the status quo.

Today, the way that business people communicate has changed. In fact, the *wrong* way is now the *right* way. Business communication today is, above anything else, informal and nonhierarchical. Fast and furious. Quick and dirty. Sure, formal communication still has its place — contracts, licensing agreements, and nasty letters to wayward suppliers, for example. After all, three-quarters of a million American lawyers can't be wrong! (Or can they?)

The Cutting Edge of Communication

The explosion in information technology has brought with it numerous, often surprising and powerful new ways to communicate. Whether you like them or not, they're here, and they're here to stay. Not only that, but more are on the way. You can choose to ignore them and be left behind, or you can choose to leverage these new technologies to your advantage. What's it going to be for you?

For today's manager, it's no longer necessary to be in an office to communicate with your clients and coworkers. You can be anywhere — using your cellular phone while at a restaurant or in your car, or dialing into the Internet while in bed at a remote cabin in the woods. All it takes is the right tools. (And this is not some sort of Buck Rogers fantasy!) The future is here — now. Do you remember those AT&T advertisements that ended with the tag line, "Someday you will," as a business person sent a fax from the beach via his laptop computer? While you may not have a burning desire to send a fax from the beach, affordable, easy-to-use technologies to do just that exist now. Someday you will — and that day is today.

Not only can you communicate anywhere you want, you can communicate *anytime* you want. Regular business hours used to be just that — regular. The office opened at 9:00 a.m. and it closed at 5:00 p.m., Monday through Friday. Until the fairly recent introduction of the answering machine and voice mail, if you called outside those regular business hours, you were greeted by a phone that rang and rang or by an answering service.

With the advent of microprocessor-based tools such as electronic mail (e-mail), voice mail, fax machines, and overnight air delivery services, business is rapidly becoming a 24-hour-a-day affair. Now, not only can you leave a message at any time of the day or night at most any business across the nation, but if you are a voice-mail user, you can access your date and time-stamped messages remotely — from anywhere in the world that you can make a phone call. Then you can reply to them, forward them to coworkers, or archive them for future reference.

While many corporations are beginning to outfit their employees with cellular phones, pagers, portable computers, and such, they aren't doing so just to make life more convenient for their employees. It's no accident that employees who have such equipment spend more of their personal time doing work for their employers. A recent study of individuals whose company provides them with telecommunications equipment indicates that these individuals work 20 to 25 percent more hours *on their own time*.

Hotels, airlines, and even car rental agencies have jumped on the bandwagon of universal communication, providing the tools and facilities for business travelers to stay connected with their clients. An example is the Hyatt Business Plan offered by the Hyatt Hotel chain. For $15 over the standard room rate, the well-connected business person gets a personal work space and desk phone with no phone access charges, an in-room fax machine, and 24-hour access to photocopiers and computer printers. To sweeten the deal, Hyatt even throws in an express breakfast and morning newspaper.

Communicating your way to bankruptcy

Sometimes formal communication can be a bad thing — particularly when it is the result of a bloated bureaucracy. In his book *The Tom Peters Seminar,* Tom Peters presents a great example of how formal communication in the extreme can choke the life out of a business.

At Union Pacific Railroad, the organization had settled into a finely tuned hierarchy that threatened to send it the way of the Tyrannosaurus rex. It seems that when track inspectors found a problem with customer-owned rail sidings, instead of approaching the customer directly, they had to present the problem to the yardmaster, who passed it up to the assistant trainmaster, who then brought it to the trainmaster. The trainmaster forwarded the problem to the division superintendent for transportation, who passed it up to the division superintendent, who carried it to the regional transportation superintendent, who then brought it up to the assistant general manager, and then to the general manager. Now that the problem had finally made its

way to the top of the operations side of the organization, it was passed laterally to the assistant vice president of sales, who headed the sales and marketing organization within Union Pacific, then down to the regional sales manager, and next the district sales manager. *Finally,* the sales representative was given the problem and, if the customer hadn't yet gone out of business (no joke!), then the sales pitch was made. Ouch!

This sad state of affairs continued until Mike Walsh was appointed CEO in the late '80s. Within 120 days of his arrival, Walsh cut six layers out of the operations hierarchy — two-thirds of the total operations workforce. Now, when track inspectors find problems with customer-owned rail sidings, they simply notify the customers themselves. Most of the time, the customers agree, and Union Pacific makes the needed repairs. No muss, no fuss.

This story shows how a little common sense, and a very sharp knife, can get an organization back on the right track.

Faster, more flexible, and more competitive

The manager of the 21st century is a master of time and space. You know the old saying: *You can't be in two places at once.* While this statement may have been true years ago, the Information Revolution has brought about changes that have turned this worn-out cliché on its head. A manager, by using readily available, microprocessor-based tools, can be anyplace, anytime he or she wants.

Want to schedule meetings with customers in five different states, confirm their attendance, enter the meetings into your personal calendar, check all your notes, and then be reminded half an hour before each meeting — all while you relax in your hotel room in Miami? Piece of cake. Just tap out a message on your wireless Palm Computing electronic organizer, touch the on-screen icon, and you're on your way.

Cyrix Corporation, a manufacturer of microprocessors that compete directly with those designed and manufactured by Intel, has a sales force of only 20 people. However, Cyrix has found a way to multiply the effectiveness of its sales force many times over. Each Cyrix salesperson works out of his or her home and has a full array of the most current information technology at his or her fingertips. Cyrix outfits its salespeople with pagers, notebook personal computers, and cellular phones and has installed a sophisticated order-processing system to allow them to check product availability instantly. Instead of tying up its sales force with meetings, paperwork, and other red tape, Steve Domenik, marketing vice president for Cyrix, says in a recent issue of *Business Week* that "by eliminating all this goofing around, we can compete with companies with 200 salespeople."

According to *Business Week,* technological innovation gives small businesses the edge over their larger competitors. As we show you, many of these advantages are a direct result of the innate ability of small firms to work *faster* than larger firms.

- Unfettered by bureaucracy and expensive existing information systems, small companies can implement new technologies more rapidly and effectively than their larger counterparts.

- As companies become electronically linked, outsourcing of functions, from accounting to product development, by large companies creates many opportunities for highly skilled small shops.

- Electronic bulletin boards and online data services give small companies access to more market data and business opportunities than ever before, allowing them to quickly attack new opportunities.

- Cheap computer-aided design and manufacturing software and flexible factories let small companies crank out multiple prototypes quickly and cheaply without large product development labs.

> ✔ Groups of small companies can easily use information links to form "virtual corporations," gaining market heft while enabling each to concentrate on what it does best.
>
> ✔ Mobile computing lets small companies compete around the world without setting up expensive branch offices.

Use the latest advances in computing and telecommunications technology to make your organization faster and more flexible. The faster that information is distributed and acted on within your organization, the more competitive and successful your business is.

Faxes and electronic mail

The *facsimile machine,* also known as a *fax,* has quickly become a necessity for every serious business enterprise. A fax machine digitally transmits documents such as letters, reports, and photographs to another fax machine that then prints out a copy of the original document. The two communicating fax machines can be across the hall or halfway around the world from each other — it doesn't matter. Fax technology has now migrated to personal computers. Instead of printing a document first and then faxing it, you can now transmit and receive documents directly from personal computer to personal computer.

Electronic mail, also known as *e-mail,* is similar to voice mail but is a text-driven message system instead of a voice-driven message system. With e-mail, users on a computer network can send and receive messages to and from each other and can attach document files to their e-mail messages. For example, if you are working on a draft report on product sales for your boss, you can attach a copy for her to review to an e-mail message that informs her of your progress to date. She can then make changes to the text file and return it to you along with a note thanking you for your hard work.

E-mail allows business people to be much more responsive than they ever dreamed possible by using the U.S. Postal Service. It's no accident that the online community refers to the U.S. Mail as *snail* mail. While it might take several days for a standard letter to be delivered by the Postal Service from a city on the west coast of the United States to a city on the east coast, it only takes the push of a button, and a few seconds, for an e-mail message to be delivered to its destination.

Use fax machines and e-mail to make the transmission of information instantaneous. Your organization will be faster and more responsive to client needs as a result.

According to Andrew S. Grove, chief executive officer of Intel, "Companies that use e-mail are much faster, much less hierarchical. There are two companies — one that operates this way and one that doesn't . . . you're either going to do it or you disappear" (*Business Week,* May 18, 1994).

That Internet thing

On September 2, 1969, the group of 40-plus people crowded in a lab in Boelter Hall at UCLA had no idea that they were witnessing the birth of a vast communications network that would some 25 years later span all the continents and consist of millions of individual computers worldwide.

The Internet is a network of approximately 3 million host computers located in educational institutions, businesses, and research laboratories worldwide. Without question the largest computer network in the world, the Internet is used by up to 20 million individuals to send e-mail, weather maps, video clips, photographs, and a wide variety of other information to each other. What makes the Internet unique is that it is not the property of any one person or entity. Rather, it exists because of the investment in computer resources of numerous organizations and the volunteer efforts of thousands of individuals and organizations who act as system managers.

Despite all the media attention, the Internet is not the be-all, end-all of the Information Super-highway. Other computer networks exist, and have for some time. CompuServe, America

Online, and Prodigy are all commercial networks, also known as *online services,* that allow users to tap into vast databases of information and chat live with other users worldwide. Each service has its own distinct personality — Prodigy, for example, features commercial advertisements in a box at the bottom of the screen—that attracts different users depending on their personal tastes or information needs.

Each service is vying to offer the most attractive package of services for its users. As such, online services are quickly becoming essential to today's businessmen and businesswomen. America Online, for example offers a wide variety of topics, electronic magazines, reference materials, and bulletin boards of interest to business people. Some of the current offerings include *Business Week* magazine online, The Nightly Business Report, and a complete area dedicated to small businesses. This area contains information about starting a business, obtaining financing and assistance from the Small Business Administration, and bulletin boards to share information and advice with other small business owners.

Portable computers and personal digital assistants

Personal digital assistants, or *PDAs,* combine the features of a computer, a fax machine, a modem, wireless communication, and handwriting recognition into a small (about the same size as a paperback book) battery-operated package. Instead of having to deal with the standard typewriter keyboard of most computers, PDAs allow you to write your input on the work surface with a special stylus. As the first digital tool to combine all the best elements of the Information Age along with true portability, the personal digital assistant has opened new avenues for the business person on the move.

What is bringing the ultimate communication device even closer is the continued integration of all the aforementioned systems — personal computers, fax, e-mail, cellular phones, and so on — into a coherent business system where the whole is much greater than the sum of its parts. The *connectivity* of computers and other digital devices is bringing business to a new level of sophistication as information can be generated, edited, transmitted, reviewed, and acted upon — through a wide variety of platforms — without ever being printed onto paper. Connectivity is the capability of different electronic devices to interface and communicate with each other. The clearly defined distinctions that separated different platforms (like computers from phones) are blurring and become increasingly meaningless.

For example, Peter's IBM ThinkPad laptop computer combines all of the following functions into a 4½-pound battery-operated package that is about the same size as a personal planner: computer, fax machine, telephone, voicemail center, word processor, e-mail box, personal calendar/scheduler, contact manager, and (Peter's personal favorite) 3-D pinball machine. If Peter needs to fax a document or connect to the Internet, no problem: he simply plugs in a phone cord, touches a button or two, and the computer does the rest. Anywhere, anytime.

With portable computers and personal digital assistants, you can take your office with you — anywhere you want it to be. Use portable computers and personal digital assistants to get your employees out of *their* offices and into your *customer's* offices, where they can have the greatest impact on your organization's bottom line.

Voice mail and pagers

Answering machines are such a ubiquitous part of our culture that, although having one was once considered a novelty, *not* having answering machine is now the novelty. The revolution in information technology has taken the basic idea of the answering machine and increased its power a thousand fold. The result is *voice mail*. Voice mail is a computer-based digital system that allows a telephone caller to leave messages and allows the user to extensively manage those messages. For example, the user of a voice mail system has the ability to take a phone message and forward it, along with a personal message, to another voice mail user. If the caller is also on the voice mail system, the user can send a verbal response directly to the caller's own mailbox, and even record and broadcast messages to lists of selected voice mail boxes.

Most of the recent excitement in the new era of telecommunications has centered on *wireless communications*. Wireless communications systems work by utilizing radio, infrared, or other electromagnetic frequencies to transmit and receive information. Although wireless communication is not a new concept — radio and television have been around for decades — the conversion of devices such as telephones, computers, and other business staples into digital wireless communications tools has generated the most excitement.

The *pager* is one of the first digital wireless communications devices to gain widespread acceptance in the business world. A pager is a small radio receiver — smaller than a deck of playing cards — that displays the phone number of a caller. To complete the communication, the pager owner then calls the phone number displayed on the pager. More advanced (and more expensive) models can also display a caller's message or record voice messages. Pagers are very portable, and with the use of an array of satellites circling the earth, can receive messages almost anywhere. Particularly interesting are the latest generation of pagers that can both receive *and* send messages.

Voice mail and pagers allow you to send and receive messages anywhere, anytime and be notified whcn *you* receive messages. Use these systems to keep your employees in better touch with their coworkers and your clients.

Cellular phones and personal toll-free numbers

Increasingly, communication between devices is being conducted without wires. According to AT&T product manager Lisa Pierce, "Right now we have a physical wire from phone company to house, and that wire does one thing at a time. It does that one thing at a relatively low speed." Wireless communication bypasses the physical limitations of wires and allows for a brave new world of offerings by service providers. As Kenneth S. Forbes III, president and CEO of MobileDigital Corporation of Alameda, California observes in the May 1993 issue of *Nation's Business,* "I think wireless communications is probably the last communications breakthrough in our lifetimes. The ability to reach anyone while I'm mobile in real time without it being intrusive is the closest to thought projection we're going to get."

The *cellular telephone* advanced the progress of wireless communications considerably. A cellular telephone is a portable, battery-operated device that broadcasts on a special high frequency radio band. While cellular phones were once little more than expensive status symbols, prices have plunged, and cellular phones are now essential tools to the mobile business person.

Although cellular phones have been commercially available only for the past decade, the industry has shown meteoric growth. The cellular industry now boasts $15 billion-plus in annual sales and more than 11 million customers in the U.S. alone. The cellular phone brought more than just another gadget into the lives of the modern business person — it brought freedom, too. Freedom to conduct business outside of the constraints of the normal office environment — unchained from our desks, our phones, and our old, worn-out paradigms. Says Mark Adler, a Washington, D.C. publishing agent, "It lets me have my office anywhere I happen to be" (*Business Week,* May 18, 1994). According to Adler, he once used a cellular telephone to close a publishing deal while watching his daughter play at a local playground.

You already know how useful 800 numbers can be. Your clients and employees can call you toll free from anyplace. 800 numbers have become *so* popular that the phone companies have almost run out of them. A new toll-free calling prefix — 888 — is now joining the venerated 800 prefix as a way to communicate. As more companies and individuals obtain toll-free phone numbers, new toll-free prefixes are undoubtedly right around the corner.

Cellular phones and toll-free numbers can make you more accessible to your coworkers and clients. Make sure that your employees have these tools so that they can communicate easily and affordably with business associates.

Videoconferencing and electronic meetings

Not too many years ago, if you wanted to have a meeting with members of your design team in Cambridge, production engineers in Pittsburgh, and vendors scattered all about the countryside, you had to all fly or drive to a central location for the meeting. Hours of travel and thousands of dollars later, you all would be in the same place at the same time. Heaven help you if you left something important back at the office!

Once again, computers have saved the day. With a computer, a video camera, and some special software, you can create your very own videoconference — live and in living color! Phones are okay for conducting business, but sometimes you need to be able to *see* what your client is trying to describe to you. And sometimes your counterpart needs to *see* what the heck you're trying to say. Thus the miracle of videoconferencing. Which do *you* prefer, Option A or Option B?

- **Option A:** "Okay, Bob, I just made the changes to the sales figures and printed out a new graph. Now, sales rose 39.5 percent in 2005 — to $45.5 million. This surge was led by our Northwestern sales office. In the first quarter of 2006 we saw a decline to an annualized figure of $39.1 million in sales, primarily due to weak sales out of the South Central and North Central sales offices which were off target by a combined total of $4.2 million. The second quarter looks a lot better. It looks like we're back on track with an annualized number of $44.7 million. Did you get all that, Bob?"

- **Option B:** "Okay, Bob, I just made the changes to the sales figures and printed out a new graph — you should be able to see it now on your computer monitor. Do you have any questions?"

Similarly, you can link together large groups of individuals into *virtual* meetings, where everyone can see and speak to each other in real time. Now you'll never have to get stuck in another airport waiting for your late flight or endure another night on a lumpy mattress in some nameless town in the middle of nowhere. Unless, of course, that's your idea of fun. Just turn on your computer, fire up the video camera, and meet to your heart's content!

Videoconferences are rapidly becoming more common as computers and telecommunications systems become more powerful. Use them to set up meetings of employees at different locations — whether across town or around the world. You can save substantial amounts of both time and money.

Listening

The communication equation has two sides. We've already discussed the side that most people think about when they hear the word *communication:* the doing side. However, just as important is the other side of the equation: the listening side.

You're a busy person. You probably have 10 million things on your mind at any given time: the proposal you have to get out before 5:00 p.m. today; the budget spreadsheets that don't seem to add up; lunch. And if that isn't enough already, someone is in your office gibber-jabbering about the latest rumors at corporate. *Did you hear that Sandy is on the way out?* With all the distractions, it's probably not too surprising that you have made a habit of tuning out your coworkers. *Huh? Sandy just got promoted?*

Stop!

When you don't give the person on the other side of your desk your *full* attention, you are shortchanging both yourself *and* the other person. Not only do you miss out on getting the message, but your inattention sends its own special message: *I don't really care what you have to say.* Is that the message that you really want to convey? When you listen actively, you increase the likelihood that you understand what the other person is saying. Depending on what you're talking about, understanding can be *quite* important.

Don't leave listening to chance. Communication is a two-way street and you have to do your part. Be an active listener. When someone has something to say to you, make a decision to either participate in the communication, or let the other person know that you are busy and will have to get back to him or her later. *Sorry, Tony, I've got to get these numbers together before lunch. Can we get together later this afternoon?* If you decide to communicate, then clear your mind of all its distractions. Forget for a moment the proposal that has to go out in a few hours, the spreadsheets, and that growling in the pit of your stomach. Give the other person your full attention.

Of course, this is easier said than done. How can you focus on the other person and not get distracted by all the people and things that compete for your attention? It's a tough job, but someone has to do it. And that someone is *you*!

✔ **Express your interest:** One of the best listening techniques is to be interested in what your counterpart has to say. For example, give your counterpart your full attention and ask questions that clarify what he or she has to say. You might say, "That's really interesting. What brought you to that particular conclusion?" There is no bigger turn-off to communication than for you to yawn, look around the room aimlessly, or otherwise show that you are not interested in what is being said. The more interest you show your counterpart, the more interesting he or she becomes.

✔ **Maintain your focus:** People speak at the rate of approximately 150 words per minute. However, people *think* at approximately 500 words per minute. This gap leaves a lot of room for your mind to wander. Make a point of keeping your mind focused on listening to what the other person has to say. If your mind starts to wander, then rein it back in right away.

✔ **Ask questions:** If something is unclear or doesn't make sense to you, then ask questions to clarify the subject. Not only does this practice keep communication efficient and accurate, but it also demonstrates to the speaker that you are interested in what he or she has to say. *Reflective listening* — summarizing what the speaker has said and repeating it back to him or her — is a particularly effective way of ensuring accuracy in communication and demonstrating your interest. For example, you might say, "So you mean that it's your belief that we can sell our excess capacity to other firms?"

✔ **Seek the keys:** What exactly is your counterpart trying to tell you? It's easy for anyone to get lost in the forest of details of a conversation and to miss seeing the trees as a result. As you listen, make a point of categorizing what your speaker has to say into information that is *key* to the discussion and information that isn't really relevant. If you need to ask questions to help you decide which is which, then don't be shy — ask away! "What the heck does *that* have to do with meeting our goals?"

✔ **Avoid interruptions:** While asking clarifying questions or employing reflective listening techniques is okay, constantly interrupting the speaker or allowing others to do so is *not* okay. When you are having a conversation with an employee, he or she should be the most important thing in your life at that moment. If someone telephones you, don't answer it — that's what voice mail is for, after all. If someone knocks on your door and asks whether it's okay to interrupt, say no, but that it *will* be okay after you finish your current conversation. If your building is on fire, *then* it's okay to interrupt the speaker.

✔ **Listen with more than your ears:** Communication involves a *lot* more than the obvious, verbal component. According to the experts in this sort of thing, up to *90 percent* of the communication in a typical conversation is nonverbal! Facial expressions, posture, position of arms and legs, and much more add up to the nonverbal component of communication. Because this is the case, you must use all your senses when you listen — not just your ears.

✔ **Take notes:** Remembering all the details of an important conversation hours, days, or weeks after it took place can be quite difficult. Be sure to take notes when necessary. Taking notes can be a terrific aid to listening and remembering what was said. Plus, when you review your notes later, you can take the time to organize what was said and make better sense of it.

By practicing the preceding listening habits, you get the message, and your coworkers appreciate the fact that you consider them important enough to give them your full attention. So listen early and listen often.

The Power of the Written Word

At first glance, you may think that the information revolution has made the written word less important. Nothing is farther from the truth. Indeed, instead of making the written word less important, the information revolution has merely increased the variety of written media at your beck and call and increased the speed at which the written word travels. Writing well in business is more important than ever — you need to write concisely and with impact.

Regardless of whether you are writing a one-paragraph e-mail message or a 100-page report for your boss, business writing shares common characteristics. Review the list of writing tips that follows and don't forget to practice these tips every opportunity you get. The more you write, the better you get at it. So write, write, and then write some more.

✔ **What's the point?** Before you set pen to paper (or fingertip to keyboard), think about what you are trying to achieve. What information are you trying to convey, and what do you want the reader to do as a result? Who is your audience, and how can you best reach it?

✔ **Get organized:** Organize your thoughts before you start to write. Jotting down a few notes or creating a brief outline of your major points may be beneficial. Bounce your ideas off coworkers and business associates or find other ways to refine them and get the all-important reality check.

- ✔ **Write the same way that you speak:** Written communication and spoken communication have a lot more in common than many people think — the best writing most closely resembles normal, everyday speech. Writing that is too formal or stilted is less accessible and harder to understand than conversational writing, and you should avoid it at all costs.

- ✔ **Be brief and concise:** Every word that you write should have a purpose. Make your point, support it, and then move on to the next point. *Do not,* repeat, *do not* fill your memos, letters, and other correspondence with needless fluff simply to give them more weight or to make them seem more impressive. If you can make your point in three sentences, then don't write three paragraphs or three pages to accomplish the same goal.

- ✔ **Simplicity is a virtue:** Avoid the tendency to use a 50-cent word when a simpler one will do. Be alert to the proliferation of cryptic acronyms and jargon that mean nothing outside of a small circle of industry insiders and replace them with more common terminology whenever possible.

- ✔ **Write and then rewrite:** Few writers are able to get their thoughts into writing perfectly on the first try. The best approach is to write your first draft without worrying too much about whether it's done to perfection. Next, read through your draft and edit it for content, flow, grammar, and readability. Keep polishing your work until it shines.

- ✔ **Convey a positive attitude:** No one likes to read negative memos, letters, reports, or other business writing. Instead of making the intended points with their intended targets, negative writing often only reflects poorly on its author, and the message gets lost in the noise. Be active, committed, and positive in your writing. Even when you convey bad news, your writing can indicate that a silver lining follows even the worst storm.

Those of you who are interested in developing better writing skills can find plenty of books to help. However, Peter still swears by the time-worn, 1971-vintage printing of *The Elements of Style,* by William Strunk, Jr. and E.B. White, that he bought in 7th grade. The book's advice is timeless, the writing direct and compelling. Consider Rule 13:

> *Omit needless words.* Vigorous writing is concise. A sentence should contain no unnecessary words, a paragraph no unnecessary sentences, for the same reason that a drawing should have no unnecessary lines and a machine no unnecessary parts. This requires not that the writer make all his sentences short, or that he avoid all detail and treat his subjects only in outline, but that every word tell.

Making Presentations

While many people may dread the idea of standing up in front of a group of people, the ability to give oral presentations, speeches, and the like is a key skill for managers. Of course, some managers already know the value of being able to give effective presentations. Here's what management guru Tom Peters says in *The Pursuit of Wow!* about the power of having an audience hang on your every word: "Let me tell you about public speaking: If you have any sense of humility at all, it scares the hell out of you. There have been times when I held an audience in my hands. That's real power."

Preparing to present

When you see great speakers or presenters in action, you may think that because of their extraordinary skill, making a presentation takes little preparation on their part. This is kind of like saying that because an Olympic gymnast makes her floor routine look so perfect and so easy, she never has to practice it. What you don't see are the *years* of almost daily preparation that lead to her 90 seconds of glory.

Preparation is the key to giving a great presentation. The following tips can help you in preparing your presentation:

- **Determine what you are trying to accomplish:** Briefly outline the goals of your presentation. What exactly do you want to accomplish? Are you trying to convince decision-makers that they should give you a bigger budget or extend the amount of time that you have to design a product that actually works? Are you seeking to educate your audience or to train employees in a new procedure? Are you presenting awards to employees in a formal ceremony? Each kind of presentation requires a different approach, and you should tailor your approach accordingly.

- **Develop the heart of your presentation:** Build an outline of the major points that you want to communicate to your audience. Under each point, note any subpoints that are important to support your presentation. Don't try to accomplish too much; keep your major points down to no more than a few. Sketch out any visual aids that you need to reinforce and communicate the ideas that you are presenting verbally.

- **Write the introduction and conclusion:** After you finish the heart of your presentation, you can decide on your introduction and conclusion. The introduction should do three things: (1) tell your audience *what* they're going to gain from your presentation, (2) tell your audience *why* the presentation is important to them, and (3) get your audience's attention.

The conclusion is important as the final punctuation — the *period,* as it were — of your presentation. Your conclusion should do three things: (1) briefly summarize your key points, (2) refer your listeners back to the introduction, and (3) inspire your audience.

✔ **Prepare your notes:** Preparing notes to use as an aid in your presentation is always a good idea. Not only do notes help you find your way when you get lost — helping to build your confidence — but they also ensure that you cover all the topics that you planned to cover. Notes should be brief, but specific. The idea is for notes to trigger your thoughts on each key point and subpoint, not to be a word-for-word script of your remarks.

✔ **Practice makes perfect:** After you sketch out your presentation, practice it. Depending on your personal situation, you may be comfortable simply running through your notes a few times the night before the big event. Alternately, you may want to rehearse your presentation in front of a coworker or even a video camera so that you can review it at your leisure. Don't forget: The more presentations you make, the better you get at it.

You can never be *too* prepared for a presentation. Make the most of the time that you have before your presentation — doing so pays off in a big way when it comes time to get up in front of your audience and start your performance.

A picture is worth a thousand words

Studies show that approximately 85 percent of all information received by the human brain is received *visually.* Think about *that* the next time you make a presentation. While your spoken remarks may convey a lot of valuable information, your audience is likely to *get* more of the information when you present it to them visually.

Consider the following example. Once Peter was called upon to make a presentation to his company's executive team. Peter's task was to present the most recent financial performance of the company's Western Group. Faced with yards and yards of financial data stacked high to the ceiling, Peter realized that he had to find a way to present the essence of his message without getting himself and his audience lost in the details. Figure 11-1 illustrates what some of the financial data looked like in a spreadsheet format. As a little extra incentive, Peter had seen what happened to managers who tried to present and explain lots of numbers: They tripped over their tongues and then lost their way. Not a pretty sight!

Anyway, instead of developing an extensive spoken presentation, Peter had his controller develop a simple bar graph that summarized the piles of financial information visually. Then, he had the bar graph transferred to a transparency

Western Group Financials

	Past Year	Current Year
Direct Labor	$19,887,000	$21,896,000
Fringe Benefits	$7,504,000	$8,259,000
Overhead Applied	$9,945,000	$10,938,000
Cost of Money	$13,000	$14,000
Travel	$2,801,000	$1,952,000
Other Direct Cost	$278,000	$356,000
G&A Applied	$4,973,000	$5,475,000
Total	$45,401,000	$48,890,000

Figure 11-1: Financial data in spreadsheet format.

for projection onto a screen. The graph compared current year performance against past year performance, and it contained only the information essential to decision makers. Figure 11-2 shows the vastly improved bar graph version of the same financial information.

When Peter made his presentation, he kept his remarks brief, concentrating instead on walking his audience through the bar graphs. Sure, Peter could have given a highly detailed presentation of the numbers, but the results would have been more talk and less communication, a lot of wasted time, and a very numb group of executives! Instead, by using a simple visual presentation, Peter's audience was able to grasp his message quickly and easily, and they could concentrate on the message instead of the medium.

Here is the Nelson/Economy axiom of visual learning:

If you don't see it, you can't believe it (and you sure won't remember it!).

So how does this impact *your* presentations? Whenever possible, think of ways to present your information *visually*. The following are just a few of your options:

- ✔ Photographs
- ✔ Charts
- ✔ Displays
- ✔ Product samples
- ✔ Prototypes
- ✔ Role plays
- ✔ Graphs
- ✔ Maps

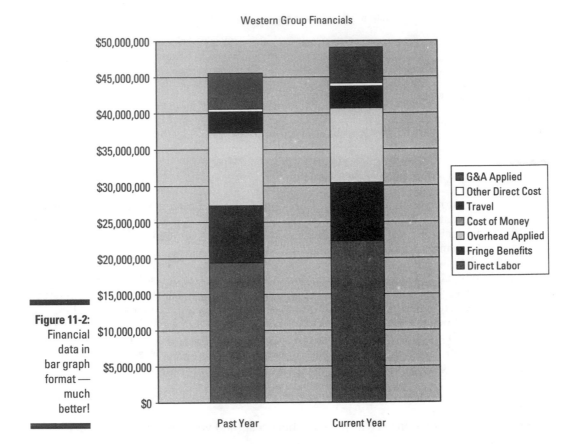

Figure 11-2:
Financial data in bar graph format — much better!

Presentation tools, visual aids, and other props serve several purposes. First, they convey your information much more quickly than do your spoken words. Second, people retain visual information longer than other kinds of information. Finally, presentation tools, visual aids, and other such props provide your audience with a welcome break from your oral presentation. Consider using the following presentation tools and props wherever and whenever possible:

✔ **Handouts:** Providing your audience with handouts of the information that you plan to cover is often helpful.

However, don't fall victim to the practice of providing handouts and then reading from them. Yuck! Nothing is more boring to an audience than following a presenter's handouts as he or she reads through pages and pages of text word for word. *Just say no!*

- ✓ **Transparencies:** For the modern, '90s kind of business person presentation meister, transparencies are probably just about the greatest thing since soap-on-a-rope. With your computer, a laser printer, a reducing/enlarging copier, and a box full of transparencies, you can turn most any information into compelling visual aids. Microsoft PowerPoint, WordPerfect Presentation, and Lotus 1-2-3 are all fantastic presentation software programs. The beauty of transparencies is that you can produce them quickly and easily and modify them anytime you want. Not only that, but you can scribble all over them during your presentation to emphasize your points.

- ✓ **Flip charts:** If you are presenting to a smaller group — say, up to about 30 people — flip charts are a handy way to present visual information. Flip charts are those *big* pads of paper that you can hang from an easel at the front of the room. You can set up your whole presentation on the flip charts *before* your presentation and, like transparencies, you can scribble notes on them for emphasis as you speak. Throw in a dash of fun (oh, boy!) by using *different* colors of markers throughout! *¡Caramba!*

- ✓ **Slides:** For presentations in front of *large* groups of people, 35 millimeter photographic slides are the choice of the pros (just ask Bob!). Not only are slides colorful, sharp, and inexpensive, but you can fit a hundred or more into a carousel about as big around as a medium pizza with anchovies. One danger with slides, however. What you see is what you get — you can't change them in the middle of your presentation or scribble notes all over them. On several occasions, Bob has been 3,000 miles away from the office when he discovered a major flaw in his slides the night before his presentation. Unfortunately, when this happened, there wasn't much that Bob could do to fix the problem.

- ✓ **White/chalk boards:** For smaller groups, white boards and chalk boards are great tools for making your points visually. You can write your main points on the board for emphasis as you proceed through your presentation and, if you make a mistake, you can simply erase and correct it.

When using visual aids, you should keep a couple of things in mind if you want to have a happy audience. First, don't try to jam too much information into each of your aids. Keep the type large, keep the quantity of words and numbers to a minimum, and use color to your advantage. Second, have everything ready well in advance of your presentation. Don't start your presentation by spending five minutes fumbling with setting up your projector or paging through a disorganized stack of transparencies. Your audience won't be impressed, and you won't exactly enhance your self-confidence. Finally, don't forget that *you* are the center of attention — not your visual aids. Use visual aids to *support* your presentation — don't use your presentation to support your visual aids!

Making your presentation

The waiting is over and your audience is gathered — raptly waiting to hear the pearls of wisdom that you're going to fling all about the room. At this point, all your hours of preparation pay off. Follow these steps as you begin your presentation:

- ✔ **Relax!** What do you have to be nervous about? You're thoroughly prepared for your presentation. Your notes are in order, your visual aids are positioned and ready to go, and your audience is sincerely interested in what you have to say. As you wait for the presentation to start, breathe deeply and stay alert.

- ✔ **Greet the members of your audience:** This is one of the pluses of arriving early. As the members of your audience arrive for your presentation, welcome them personally. Not only does this practice establish an initial level of rapport and interest, but getting a chance to talk to the members of your audience before you launch into your presentation helps you feel more at ease in front of the group.

- ✔ **Listen closely to your introduction:** Make sure that the facts are accurate, and listen for comments that you can incorporate into your initial remarks. For example, if the individual who introduces you mentions that, not only are you a brilliant manager, but that you are also an avid skier, you can work a humorous anecdote about skiing into the beginning of your presentation.

- ✔ **Wait for your audience's attention:** As a presenter, you must capture the full attention of your audience. One particularly effective technique is to stand in front of your audience and say nothing until everyone's attention is focused on you. Of course, if that doesn't do the trick, you can always resort to the old standbys: threats and intimidation!

- ✔ **Make your presentation:** Start at the beginning, finish when you're done, and have fun with everything in between! Remember Tom Peters's quote about speaking at the beginning of this section. This really is your opportunity to shine — make the most of it!

Test your new-found knowledge

What are the different kinds of business communication in order of importance?

A. Speeches, formal presentations, and memos

B. Business letters and phone conversations

C. Listening, speaking, writing, and reading

D. Formal and informal

What should the introduction to your presentation accomplish?

A. Tell your audience what they are going to gain; tell your audience why the presentation is important; and get your audience's attention

B. Make you appear knowledgeable and witty

C. Get you to the conclusion quickly

D. None of the above

Chapter 12
It's a Team Thing

In This Chapter

▶ Flattening the organization

▶ Empowering employees

▶ Categorizing teams

▶ Recognizing the advantages of teams

▶ Managing new technology and teams

▶ Making meetings work

A revolution is going on in business today. It's a revolution about who decides what work to do and how to accomplish it. It's a revolution about what goals an organization strives for and who is responsible for achieving them. It's a revolution that touches everyone in an organization — from the very top to the very bottom. What is this revolution? It's wet and wild! It's the ultimate in refreshment. It's the new Diet Pepsi! (Oops! Wrong commercial. We'll try again.) It's a revolution called *teams*.

What is a team? A team is two or more people who work together to achieve a common goal.

Why teams? Teams offer an easy way to tap the knowledge and resources of *all* employees — not just supervisors and managers — to solve the organization's problems. A well-structured team draws together employees from different functions and levels of the organization to help find the best way to approach an issue. Smart companies have learned (and not-so-smart companies are just now starting to figure out) that to remain competitive, they can no longer rely solely on management to guide the development of work processes and the accomplishment of organizational goals. The companies need to involve those employees who are closer to the problems and to the organization's customers as well. Guess who those employees are — the front-line workers!

Think about it. Who knows more about dealing with the needs of customers who walk in the front door of a business: a receptionist or the manager of the receptionist's department who is three levels removed from the front line?

Although some managers may disagree (sorry!), many observers, us included, conclude that the employee closest to the customer knows the customer's needs best.

Perhaps management expert Peter Drucker best answered the question "Why teams?" when he considered the importance of ranking knowledge over ego in the modern organization. According to Drucker, "No knowledge ranks higher than another; each is judged by its contribution to the common task rather than by any inherent superiority or inferiority. Therefore, the modern organization cannot be an organization of boss and subordinate. It must be organized as a team" (*Harvard Business Review,* September-October 1992). Wow. We're talking *profound* here.

This chapter discusses the changes in the American business environment that set the stage for the movement toward teams, the major kinds of teams and how they work, the impact of the new, computer-based technology on teams, and insights for conducting the best meetings ever.

The Obsolescence of Hierarchy

The '90s have seen a fundamental shift in the distribution of power and authority in organizations. Until recently, most organizations were vertical — that is, they had many layers of managers and supervisors between top management and frontline workers. The classic model of a vertical organization is the U.S. Army. In the Army, privates report to corporals, who report to sergeants, who report to captains, and so on, up to the top general. When a general gives an order, it passes down the line from person to person until it reaches the enlisted person or officer who is expected to execute it. *Ten hut!*

Until recently, large companies such as Ford, Exxon, and AT&T were not that different from this rigid, hierarchical model. Employing hundreds of thousands of workers, these companies depended — and in many cases still depend — on legions of supervisors and managers to control the work, the workers that did it, and when and how they did it. (Okay, perhaps today's legions are *smaller.*) The primary goal of top management was to command and control workers' schedules, assignments, and decision-making processes very closely to ensure that the company's objectives were met (and to ensure that workers weren't asleep at their desks!).

The downsizing of corporate America

The fundamental flaw of the hierarchical model is this: Many supervisors and managers made little or no direct contribution to the production of a company's products or services. Instead of making *things,* in many cases, managers merely managed other managers or supervisors served as liaisons between levels.

They did little more than push paper from one part of their desks to another. In the model's worst scenario, the levels of supervisors and managers actually impeded their organizations' capability to get things done — dramatically adding to the cost of doing business and slowing down the response time of decision-making. All those company-paid lunches added up. Although this problem was overlooked as the American economy continued to expand in the last half of the 20th century, the economic slowdown in the late '80s and early '90s made for quite a wake-up call to those companies (fat, dumb, and happy) with unproductive — or worse, counterproductive — middle management.

No company — no matter how large or how successful — seemed to be immune to the effects of the economic downturn. On January 2, 1996, AT&T announced the layoff of 40,000 employees. This layoff was in addition to previously announced layoffs at AT&T totaling 83,500 workers. A few years ago, Chrysler employed one salaried employee for every 25 hourly employees; the ratio is now one salaried employee for every 48 hourly employees. Chrysler expects the ratio to further increase to one salaried employee for every 100 hourly employees by the year 2000. In all, some 6 million workers lost their jobs because of the recession that rocked American business in the early '90s. Many of these workers were supervisors and middle managers.

Although the downsizing of corporate America in the early '90s had obvious negative effects on the employees who lost their jobs — and in many cases, their hopes for comfortable retirement — this dark cloud had a silver lining. In these new, flatter organizations, a new life (and quicker pace) came to the following important areas:

- **Decision-making:** Decisions, which might have taken weeks or even months to make in the old, bloated bureaucracy, are made in hours or minutes.

- **Communicating:** Instead of being intercepted and possibly distorted by middle managers at numerous points along its path, communication now travels a more direct — and much speedier — route from front-line workers to top management and vice versa. There's nothing like cutting six layers of management out of an organization to improve communication!

Also, this transformation from vertical to horizontal businesses has had a fundamental impact on financial and organizational elements:

- **Quantifiable benefits to the bottom line:** By cutting out entire layers of management employees, many companies saved money in the way of substantially reduced costs of personnel, facilities, and company-paid lunches.

- **Movement of authority and power:** From the very top of the organization down to the front-line employees who interact with customers on a day-to-day basis. With fewer middle managers to interfere, frontline employees are naturally granted more authority — and many accept it gladly.

The move to cooperation

More than ever before in American businesses, employees are being rewarded for *cooperating* with each other instead of competing *against* one another. This innovation in today's business environment is truly *amazing!* According to David Ehlen, chief executive officer with Wilson Learning, a management-training firm based in Eden Prairie, Minnesota, advancement in the new business world of teams "is measured not only by your individual contributions but by how effective you are as a collaborative team member" (*The Wall Street Journal,* Feb. 12, 1993).

Coupled with this shift of authority is a fundamental change in the way that many businesses structure their organizations. They are moving away from a structure of traditional, functional divisions that once separated departments from each other. In their place are *teams* — made up of employees from different departments — whose members work together to perform tasks and achieve common goals. Of course, most businesses still organize their operations by departments, divisions, and so forth, but smart managers now encourage, rather than discourage, their employees to cross formal organizational lines.

Following are benefits that your organization can reap from promoting cooperation:

- **Reducing unproductive competition:** Promoting a cooperative, team-oriented work environment reduces the chance that your employees can become overcompetitive.

    If allowed to continue unabated, overcompetitiveness results in the shutdown of communication between employees and, ultimately, reduced organizational effectiveness (as overcompetitive employees build and defended private fiefdoms). Besides, overcompetition among employees invariably leads to the release of *incredible* amounts of bad karma. *(Excuse me, but my karma just ran over your dogma!)*

- **Sharing knowledge:** Knowledge is power. If you are in the know, you have a clear advantage over someone who has been left in the dark — especially if *your* finger is on the light switch. In a cooperative work environment, teams members work together and thereby share their areas of knowledge and expertise.

- **Fostering communication:** The use of teams helps to break down the walls between an organization's departments, divisions, and other formal structures to foster communication between organizational units.

- **Achieving common goals:** The development of teams with members from various departments encourages workers from all levels and all parts of a company to work together to achieve common goals. Not only that, but they give you someone to hang out with on coffee breaks.

Team Empowerment

As we explained in the preceding section, with the flattening of organizational structures that accompanied downsizing, employees gained more authority and autonomy from top management. The result is better responsiveness to the needs of customers and the resolution of problems at the lowest possible level in the organization. The transfer of power, responsibility, and authority from higher-level to lower-level employees is sometimes called *empowerment*.

By empowering workers, managers place the responsibility for decision-making with the employees who are in the best position to make the decision. In the past, many managers felt that *they* were in the best position to make decisions that affected a company's products or customers. How wrong they were. Although this might have been true in some cases, their driving need to control workers and processes at all costs often blinded managers — so much so that control became more important than encouraging employee initiative.

The value of an empowered workforce

Effective managers today know the value of empowering their workers. Not only are customers better served, but by delegating more responsibility and authority to front-line workers, managers are free to pursue other important tasks that only they can do, such as coaching, marketing, long-range planning, walking the walk, and talking the talk. The result is a more efficient, more effective organization. And don't forget, tremendously good karma is all around. Companies can point to their successes when management is willing to give up responsibility for certain tasks and delegate them to frontline workers, as these quotes from the Feb. 12, 1993 edition of The Wall Street Journal show:

✔ All 80 employees at Techmetals, a small, Dayton, Ohio, metal-plating company, are involved in plant layout, scheduling, and delivery. According to Lee Watson, Techmetals's director of improvements, going to a team-based structure "simply made us a more efficient company, with better working conditions, and a more educated workforce."

✔ At the Country Cupboard, a Lewisburg, Pennsylvania, truck stop restaurant, the business's 350 employees have taken over many of the duties commonly reserved for management in other firms. According to co-owner Carole Baylor-Hamm, she is much better able to manage the business by assigning responsibility for making budgeting and planning decisions to her workers. With her workers taking over these time-consuming activities, Baylor-Hamm is now able to concentrate her efforts on the tasks that she is uniquely suited to perform.

Empowerment is also a great morale booster in an organization. Managers who empower their workers show that they trust them to make decisions that are important to the success of the company.

Eric Gershman, founder and president of Published Image, Inc., a small Boston, Massachusetts, newsletter publisher, struggled for a way to cure high employee turnover while boosting worker morale and improving customer service. According to Gershman, "We had a company whose employees believed their job was to please their boss instead of the customer. We needed to radically change the organization" (*The Wall Street Journal,* Sep. 26, 1994).

Gershman found his solution in the assignment of his employees to self-managing teams. Managers — now known as *coaches* — serve as advisors, while workers prepare budgets, set their schedules, and receive bonuses based on the performance of their teams. The result was a doubling of revenues, from $2 million in 1992 to $4 million in 1993, and an increase in profit margin, from 3 percent to 20 percent during the same period. Not only did Gershman achieve his financial goals for the company, but his employees are much more satisfied than they were before their assignment to teams. Not bad, eh?

What about quality?

Much has been made of the quality improvement movement in this country. Taking a cue from our Japanese business competitors — noted for their high-quality automobiles, consumer electronic products, and fugu (that tasty but deadly raw fish dish) — American business embarked on a quality quest in the '80s. American managers quickly discovered that the cornerstone of many Japanese programs was the empowerment of workers to make decisions regarding their work processes.

For example, quality circles — groups of employees who meet regularly to suggest ways to improve the organization — have become a much-copied Japanese technique of participative decision-making. A quality circle's suggestions carry great weight with management.

The management of Motorola considers employee teams to be a crucial part of its strategy for quality improvement. Self-directed teams at its Arlington Heights, Illinois, cellular equipment manufacturing plant not only decide on their own training programs and schedule their own work, but they also are involved in the hiring and firing of coworkers.

Advantages of Teams

Teams offer many advantages to firms that employ them. Some of these advantages include better decision-making, faster decision-making, and a higher degree of employee development. Those closest to a job tend to know best the needs and problems associated with that position. As a result, the probability of better decision-making increases when carried out by teams.

Not only does the potential exist for decisions to be better, but they can be made faster as well. Because team members are closest to the problems and to one another, a minimal amount of lag time exists due to communication channels or the need to get approvals from others in the organization.

Smaller and nimbler

Large organizations often have a hard time competing in the marketplace against smaller, more nimble competitors. Smaller units such as teams are better able to compete. The rate and scope of change in the global business environment has led to increased competitive pressures on organizations in most every business sector.

As customers *can* get products and services faster, they demand to *have* them so (those darn customers!). As they can get products more cheaply as a result of technology improvements or global competition, they expect lower prices as well (double-darn them!). And the expectation of quality in relation to price has dramatically increased over the years — especially with consumers' experience in obtaining more advanced electronics and computer technology for progressively lower prices. In short, customer values are changing so that they now want products and services "any time, any place." Not only that, but they want to pay less than they did last year.

Innovative and adaptable

Teams can also lead to increased innovation. According to then-Harvard economist Robert Reich in the *Harvard Business Review,* "As individual skills are integrated into a group, the collective capacity to innovate becomes something greater than the sum of its parts. Over time, as group members work through various problems and approaches, they learn about one another's abilities. They learn how they can help one another perform better, what each can contribute to a particular project, how they can best take advantage of one another's experience.
Each participant is constantly on the lookout for small adjustments that will speed and smooth the evolution of the whole. The net result of many such small-scale adaptations, effected throughout the organization, is to propel the enterprise forward."

Teams are also more adaptive to the external environment as it quickly or constantly changes so that the team's size and flexibility give it a distinct advantage over the more traditional organizational structure of competing organizations. Because the ability to compete in time is increasingly a significant competitive advantage, this is a major advantage for teams. As George

Stalk states, "Time is a more critical competitive yardstick than traditional financial measurements" (*Harvard Business Review,* July-August 1988). At Xerox and Hewlett-Packard, for example, design, engineering, and manufacturing functions are now closely intertwined in the development of new products — dramatically shortening the time from concept to production.

Teams used to be considered useful only for projects of short duration. However, this is no longer the case. According to Drucker, "Whereas team design has traditionally been considered applicable only to short-lived, transitory, exceptional task-force assignments, it is equally applicable to some permanent needs, especially to the top-management and innovating tasks" (*Harvard Business Review,* January-February 1974). Indeed, the team concept has proved itself to be a workable long-term solution to the needs of many organizations.

Setting Up and Supporting Your Teams

The first thing you need to consider when setting up a team is *what* kind of team to set up. Three major kinds of teams exist: *formal, informal,* and *self-managed* — that is, teams that combine attributes of both formal and informal teams. Each type of team offers advantages and disadvantages depending on the specific situation, timing, and needs of the organization.

Formal teams

A *formal team* is chartered by an organization's management and tasked to achieve specific goals. These goals can be anything of importance to the business — from developing a new product line to determining the system for processing customer invoices, to planning a company picnic. Types of formal teams include

- **Task forces:** Formal teams assembled on a temporary basis to address specific problems or issues. For example, a task force may be assembled to determine why the number of rejects for a machined part has risen from 1 in 10,000 to 1 in 1,000. A task force usually has a deadline for solving the issue and reporting the findings to management.

- **Committees:** Long-term or permanent teams created to perform an ongoing, specific organizational task. For example, some companies have committees that select employees to receive awards for performance or that make recommendations to management for safety improvements. Although committee membership may change from year to year, the committees continue their work regardless of who belongs to them.

> ✔ **Command teams:** Made up of a manager or supervisor and all the employees who report directly to him or her. Such teams are by nature hierarchical and represent the traditional way that tasks are communicated from managers to workers. Examples of command teams include company sales teams, management teams, and executive teams.

Formal teams are important to most organizations because much of the communication within an establishment traditionally occurs here. News, goals, and information pass from employee to employee via formal teams. And they provide the structure for assigning tasks and soliciting feedback from team members on accomplishments, performance data, and so on.

Informal teams

Informal teams are casual associations of employees that spontaneously develop within the formal structure of an organization. Such teams include groups of employees who eat lunch together every day, form bowling teams, or simply like to hang out together. The membership of informal teams is in a constant state of flux as members come and go and friendships and other associations between employees change over time.

Although informal teams have no specific tasks or goals assigned by management, they are very important to organizations for the following reasons:

> ✔ Informal teams provide a way for employees to obtain information outside formal, management-sanctioned communications channels.
>
> ✔ Informal teams provide a (relatively) safe outlet for employees to let off steam about issues that concern them and to find solutions to problems by discussing them with employees from other parts of the organization — unimpeded by the walls of the formal organization.

For example, a group of women employees at NYNEX Corporation, a large telecommunications firm, created *mentoring circles.* The purpose of these informal teams — developed outside the formal NYNEX organization — was to fill the void created by a lack of female top-level managers to serve as mentors for other women in the organization. Organized in groups of 8 to 12 employees, the circles provide the kind of career networking, support, and encouragement that mentors normally provide to their charges.

Ad hoc groups are informal teams of employees assembled to solve a problem with only those who are most likely to contribute invited. For example, you may form an ad hoc team when you select employees from your human resources and accounting departments to solve a problem with the system for tracking and recording pay changes in the company's payroll system. You wouldn't invite participants from shipping to join this informal team because they probably wouldn't provide meaningful input to the problem.

Self-managed teams

Self-managed teams combine the attributes of both formal and informal teams. Generally chartered by management, they often quickly take on lives of their own as members take over responsibility for the day-to-day workings of the team. Self-managed teams usually contain from 3 to 30 employees whose job is to meet together to find solutions to common worker problems. Self-managed teams are also known as *high performance teams, cross-functional teams,* or *superteams.*

To compress time and gain benefits, an organization's self-managing teams should be

- Made up of people from different parts of the organization.

- Small because large groups create communication problems.

- Self-managing and empowered to act because referring decisions back up the line wastes time and often leads to poorer decisions.

- Multifunctional because that's the best — if not the only — way to keep the actual product and its essential delivery system clearly visible and foremost in everyone's mind.

Self-managed teams of workers at Johnsonville Foods in Wisconsin increased productivity 50 percent between 1986 and 1990 — a much higher rate than chief executive officer Ralph Stayer had imagined possible. As a result of this dramatic productivity gain, Stayer decided to expand the company's sausage production facility.

The management of American automobile manufacturers and their union-dominated workforces have a long history of conflict — often violent and disruptive. However, at Saturn Corporation, the innovative subsidiary of General Motors, teams have helped to change this seemingly unchangeable tradition. Teams have led to cooperation between management and workers. Although differences of opinion still arise from time to time, according to Michael Bennett, president of Union Local 1853, "There is conflict, but it's managed differently. It's not adversarial. It's more advocacy in terms of finding a better solution or better opinions" (*Training*, June 1992).

Being a team member is not optional at Saturn: All employees belong to at least one. On the production floor, employees work in self-managed teams that make decisions regarding training, hiring, budgeting, and scheduling. Each team consists of 5 to 15 workers, and instead of being monitored by outsiders, the teams monitor themselves. Says Joseph D. Rypkowski, United Auto Workers (UAW) union vice president, in the June 1991 issue of *Personal Journal*: "Even though their piece of running the business may be relatively small, they gain a better appreciation for what the organization has to do and what it costs in dollars."

More and more, where management is willing to let go of the reins of absolute authority and turn them over to workers, self-managing teams are rising to the challenge and are making major contributions to the success of their firms. Indeed, the future success of many businesses lie in the successful implementation of self-managed teams.

The real world

Empowerment is a beautiful thing when it flourishes in an organization. However, real empowerment is still rare. Many plastic substitutes are out there *masquerading* as empowerment! While many managers talk a good story about how they empower their employees, few actually do it. When they are *real,* and not pale imitations, empowered teams typically

- ✔ Make the most of the decisions that influence team success.
- ✔ Choose their own leaders.
- ✔ Add or remove team members.
- ✔ Set their own goals and commitments.
- ✔ Define and perform much of their own training.
- ✔ Are rewarded as a team.

Unfortunately, this ideal of employee empowerment, for the most part, may be only an illusion. A survey of team members showed that plenty of room for change and improvement in the workings of teams still exists. Survey respondents clearly felt that the areas of intragroup trust, group effectiveness, agenda setting/meeting content, and role and idea conformity could use some improvement.

A recent study of managers, team leaders, and team members at nine different companies conducted by management expert Dr. Bob Culver discovered that real-world teams are more participative than empowered; that is, the *real* decisions are still being made by top management. Those pesky backsliders! Using Dr. Culver's study results as a basis, you can apply the following specific recommendations to counter the ineffectiveness of many teams:

- ✔ **Make your teams empowered, not merely participative:** That is, instead of just inviting employees to participate in teams, grant team members the authority and power to make independent decisions.
  - • Allow your teams to make long-range and strategic decisions, not just procedural ones.
  - • Let the team choose the team leaders.

• Let the team determine its goals and commitments.

• Make sure that all members of the team have influence.

✔ **Remove the source of conflicts:** Despite their attempts to empower employees, managers are often unwilling to live with the results. Be willing to start up a team, and then be prepared to accept the outcome.

• Recognize and work out personality conflicts.

• Fight turf protection and middle-management resistance.

• Work to unify manager and team member views.

• Minimize the stress of downsizing and process improvement tasks.

• Allow teams to make more decisions.

✔ **Change other significant factors that influence team effectiveness:** Each of these factors indicates that an organization has not yet brought true empowerment to its employees. You have the power to change this situation. Do it!

• Allow the team to discipline poorly performing members.

• Make peer pressure less important in attaining high team performance.

• Train as many team members as you train managers or leaders.

Although clear examples of companies where management has truly empowered its teams do exist (they're out there *somewhere!*), team empowerment doesn't just happen. Supervisors and managers must make concerted and ongoing efforts to ensure that authority and autonomy pass from management to teams. You can, too!

New technology and teams

According to a recent *Fortune* magazine article, the three dominant forces shaping 21st-century organizations are the following:

✔ A high-involvement workplace with self-managed teams and other devices for empowering employees.

✔ A new emphasis on managing business processes rather than functional departments.

✔ The evolution of information technology to the point where knowledge, accountability, and results can be distributed rapidly anywhere in the organization.

The integrating ingredient of these three dominant forces is *information.* Information technology and the way information is handled are increasingly becoming the keys to an organization's success.

But information can be tricky to manage. According to Peter Drucker in *Management: Tasks, Responsibilities, Practices,* "Information activities present a special organizational problem. Unlike most other result-producing activities, they are not concerned with one stage of the process but with the entire process itself. This means that they have to be both centralized and decentralized." Fortunately, information technology has overcome this challenge.

In a team environment, process management information moves precisely to where it's needed, unfiltered by a hierarchy. Raw numbers go straight to those who need them in their jobs because front-line workers, such as salespeople and machinists, have been trained in how to use that information. By letting information flow wherever it's needed, a horizontal self-managed company is not only possible, it's inevitable.

Information technology-enabled team support systems include electronic mail, computer conferencing, and videoconferencing that coordinate geographically, as well as across time zones, more easily than ever before. The development and use of computer software to support teams also is growing. An example is the expanding body of software called *groupware.* Groupware consists of computer programs specifically designed to support collaborative work groups and processes.

As organizations make better use of information technology, middle managers are less necessary for decision-making. As Drucker points out in the January-February issue of the *Harvard Business Review,* "When a company focuses its data processing capacity on producing information . . . it becomes clear that both the number of management levels and the number of managers can be sharply cut." Jobs, careers, and knowledge shift constantly. Typical management career paths are eliminated, and workers advance by learning more skills to be of greater value to the organization.

Those managers who remain need to take on new skills and attitudes to be more of a coach, supporter, and facilitator of those employees on the front line. Supervisors and managers no longer have the luxury of spending time trying to control the organization — instead, they change it. Their job is to seek out new customers at the same time as they respond to the latest needs of their established customers. Managers still have considerable authority, but instead of commanding workers, their job is to inspire workers.

Meetings: Putting Teams to Work

So what is a discussion about meetings doing in a chapter on teams? The answer is that *meetings* are the primary forum in which team members conduct business and communicate with one another. And with the proliferation of teams in business today, it pays to master the basic skills of meeting management.

Effective meetings pay off

Teams are clearly an idea whose time has come. As organizations continue to flatten their hierarchies and empower front-line workers with more responsibility and authority, teams are the visible and often inevitable result. This is good news to the burgeoning industry of consulting and seminars in business team building. *Cha-ching!* Consider the way the best companies run meetings to respond to this new, team-oriented business environment.

While other Fortune 500 companies were busy slashing their workforces and their earnings over the past decade, General Electric was busy finding new ways to grow. From 1984 to 1993, General Electric's revenues grew from $27.9 billion to $60.5 billion, while earnings jumped from $2.3 billion to $5.2 billion. Of course, these successes did not come easy — they required major changes in how GE and its managers and workers did business:

✔ Jack Welch, chairman of General Electric since 1981, determined that, if the company was going to be successful, it would have to move away from the old model of autocratic meetings and direction from top management. Welsh's solution was to initiate a town-hall concept of meetings throughout the entire organization. These meetings — called *work out* meetings — bring workers and managers together in open forums where workers are allowed to ask any question they want and managers are required to respond.

✔ The company's core business strategies are shaped in regular meetings of senior executives — each of whom represents one of GE's individual business units. In these high-energy meetings, attendees are encouraged to explore every possible avenue and alternative and to be open to new ideas. GE's recent ventures in Mexico, India, and China are a direct result of these meetings.

✔ At GE's Bayamón, Puerto Rico, lightning arrester plant, employees have been organized into teams that are responsible for specific plant functions — shipping, assembly, and so forth. However, instead of tapping only employees from shipping to be on the shipping team (for example), teams consist of employees from all parts of the plant. This enables representatives from *all* affected departments to discuss how suggested changes or improvements will affect their part of the operation. Hourly workers run the meetings on their own, and *advisers* — GE's term for salaried employees — intervene in meetings only at the request of the team.

Results of the Bayamón experiment have produced clear and convincing evidence that General Electric's approach is quite successful. A year after startup, the plant's employees measured a full 20 percent higher in productivity than their closest counterpart in the mainland United States. And if that weren't enough, management projected a further 20 percent increase in the following year.

Meetings that produce results such as these don't just happen by accident. Far too many meetings in organizations today are run poorly. Instead of contributing to an organization's efficiency and effectiveness, they actually make employees *less* efficient and *less* effective. How many times have you heard someone complain about getting stuck in one more useless meeting? With today's business imperative to get more done with less, making every meeting count is more important than ever.

What's wrong with meetings?

Unfortunately, most meetings are a big waste of time. Meeting experts have determined that approximately 53 percent of all the time spent in meetings — and this means the time that *you* spend in meetings — is unproductive, worthless, and of little consequence. And when you realize that most business people spend at least 25 percent of their working hours in meetings, with upper management spending more than double that time in meetings, you can begin to gain an appreciation for the importance of learning and applying effective meeting skills.

So what's wrong with meetings, anyway? Why do so many meetings go so wrong, and why can't you ever seem to do anything about it? Following are a few of the reasons:

- ✔ **Too many meetings take place:** When did you last say to yourself, "Gee, I haven't been in any meetings lately. I sure miss them"? Probably never. Indeed, the eternal lament of the manager is something more along the lines of "How am I supposed to get any work done with all these #@!%& meetings?" The problem is not just that too many meetings take place; it's that many meetings are unnecessary, unproductive, and a waste of your time.

- ✔ **Attendees are unprepared:** Some meetings happen prematurely, before a real reason to meet arises. Others are led by individuals who have prepared neither themselves nor the participants for the topics to be discussed. What often results is a long period of time where the participants stumble around blindly trying to figure out why the meeting was called in the first place.

- ✔ **Certain individuals dominate the proceedings:** You'll find one or two in every crowd. You know, the people who think that they know it all and who make sure that their opinion is heard loudly and often during the course of a meeting. These folks may be good for occasional comic relief, if nothing else, but they often intimidate the other participants and stifle their contributions.

- ✔ **They last too long:** Yes, yes, yes. A meeting should last no longer than it needs to. No less, no more. Despite this fact, most managers let meetings expand to fill the time allotted to them. So rather than let the participants leave after the business at hand is completed, the meeting drags on and on and on.

✔ **The meeting has no focus:** Meeting leadership is *not* a passive occupation. Many pressures work against keeping meetings on track and on topic, and managers often fail to step up to the challenge. The result is the proliferation of personal agendas, digressions, diversions, off-topic tangents, and worse.

The eight keys to great meetings

Fortunately, there is hope. Although many meetings are a big waste of time, they don't have to be. There's a cure for those dysfunctional meeting blues! And good news again: The cure is readily available, inexpensive, and easy to swallow.

✔ **Be prepared:** You need only a little time to prepare for a meeting, and the payoff is increased meeting effectiveness. Instead of wasting time trying to figure out why you're meeting *(uh, does anyone know why we're here today?)*, your preparation gets results as soon as the meeting starts.

✔ **Have an agenda:** An agenda is your road map, your meeting plan. With it, you and the other participants recognize the meeting goals and know what you're going to discuss. And if you distribute the agenda to participants *before* the meeting, you multiply its effectiveness many times over because the participants can prepare for the meeting in advance.

✔ **Start on time and end on time (or sooner):** You go to a meeting on time, and the meeting leader, while muttering about an important phone call or visitor, arrives 15 minutes late. Even worse is when the meeting leader ignores the scheduled ending time and lets the meeting go on and on. Respect your participants by starting and ending your meetings on time. You don't want them spending the entire meeting looking at their watches and worrying about how late you're going to keep them!

✔ **Have fewer but better meetings:** Call a meeting only when it is absolutely necessary. And when you call a meeting, make the meeting a good one. Do you *really* have to meet to discuss change in your travel reimbursement policy? Wouldn't an e-mail message to all company travelers do just as well? Or how about the problem you've been having with the financial reports? Instead of calling a meeting, maybe a phone call would do the trick. Whenever you're tempted to call a meeting, make sure that you have a good reason for doing so.

✔ **Think inclusion, not exclusion:** Be selective with whom you invite to your meetings — select only as many participants as needed to get the job done. But don't exclude people who may have the best insight into your issues simply because of their ranks in the organization or their lifestyles, appearance, or beliefs.

You never know who in your organization is going to provide the best ideas, and you only hurt your chances of getting those great ideas by excluding people for non-performance-related reasons.

✔ **Maintain the focus:** Ruthlessly keep your meetings on topic at all times. Although doing everything *but* talking about the topic at hand can be a lot of fun, you called the meeting for a specific reason in the first place. Stick to the topic, and if you finish the meeting early, participants who want to stick around to talk about other things won't have to hold the other participants hostage to do so.

✔ **Capture action items:** Make sure that you have a system for capturing, summarizing, and assigning action items to individual team members. Flip charts — those big pads of paper that you hang from an easel in front of the group — are great for this purpose. Have you ever come out of a meeting wondering why the meeting took place? A meeting with no purpose, no direction, no assignments or follow-up actions? Make sure that *your* meetings have purpose and that you assign action items to the appropriate people.

✔ **Get feedback:** Feedback can be a great way to measure the effectiveness of your meetings. Not only can you find out what you did right, but you also can find out what you did wrong and get ideas on how to make your future meetings more effective. Ask the participants to give you their honest and open feedback — verbally or in writing — and then use it. You can never see yourself as others do unless they show you.

Test your new-found knowledge

What are the three kinds of teams?

A. Formal, informal, and self-managed

B. Bad, worse, and worst

C. Actually, only two kinds of teams exist: official and unofficial

D. None of the above

What is the average amount of time wasted in meetings?

A. If I get to catch up on my sleep, none is wasted

B. Exactly 100 percent

C. Approximately 53 percent

D. Approximately 47 percent

Chapter 13

Politics in the Office

· ·

In This Chapter

▶ Assessing your political environment

▶ Creating a polished image

▶ Identifying the real side of communication

▶ Discovering the unwritten rules of your organization

▶ Defending your personal interests

· ·

*W*hen you mention the topic of office politics to a typical manager, you're sure to get one of two responses. The manager relates some personal anecdote about the horrors of office politics and how his or her career — or the career of an associate or friend — was trashed because of seemingly minor transgressions. Or you hear what a big-time operator the manager is in his or her political environment. Whether these feelings are *good* or *bad,* most people have strong feelings about office politics.

The simple fact is that office politics are generally a very positive force in an organization. At its best, *office politics* means nothing more than the relation-ships that you develop with your coworkers — both up and down the chain of command — that allow you to get things done, to be informed about the latest goings-on in the business, and to form a personal network of business associ-ates for support throughout your career. Office politics help to ensure that everyone works in the best interests of the organization and their coworkers. At its worst, office politics can degenerate into a competition, where employees concentrate their efforts on trying to increase their personal power at the expense of other employees — and their organizations.

Most managers know the power of spreading *positive* messages about others and making your boss and coworkers look good. In business, the universal law of *karma* — what goes around comes around — is in full effect. Those who spread *positive* messages about their bosses and coworkers throughout an organization are viewed positively in return. Conversely, those who spread *negative* messages about their bosses and coworkers eventually find them-selves the subject of negative messages.

Office politics, and the relationships that you develop with other employees in your organization, help you bridge the gap between the goals that you set for yourself and the outcomes that you achieve. As management guru Peter Drucker says, "Every decision has two elements: (1) what you ideally would like to do, and (2) what you are actually able to do." If you want to do more of the former, consider becoming an expert at working within your organization's political environment.

This chapter is about determining the nature and boundaries of your political environment, recognizing your image as an effective manager, understanding the unspoken side of office communication, unearthing the unwritten rules of your organization, and, in the worst-case scenario, becoming adept at defending yourself against political attack.

Evaluating Your Political Environment

How political is your office or workplace? As a manager, having your finger on the political pulse of the organization is particularly important. Otherwise, the next time you're in a management meeting, you might blurt out, "Why is it so difficult to get an employment requisition through human resources? You'd think it was *their* money!" only to learn that the owner's daughter-in-law heads up the human resources department. *Oops!* Have you ever wondered how far your head might roll if someone removed it for you? You may just be about to find out! With just a *little* bit of advance information, you could have approached this issue much more tactfully than you did. Getting in touch with your political environment will help you do just that.

Assessing your organization's political environment

Asking insightful questions of your coworkers is one of the best ways to assess the political environment of your organization. Such questions show you to be the polite, mature, and ambitious employee that you are, and they're a sure sign of your well-developed political instincts. Why don't you give these questions a try?

- ✔ "What's the best way to get a nonbudget item approved?"

- ✔ "How can I get product from the warehouse that my client needs *today* when I don't have time to do the paperwork?"

- ✔ "Is there anything else I can do for you before I go home for the day?"

On the other hand, questions such as those that follow show that you have a poorly developed political sense and that you need to return to the minor leagues for a while.

- ✔ "Who do I need to impress to get an immediate raise?"

- ✔ "How can I obtain a promotion in this organization without ruining my home life or staying past 5 p.m.?"

- ✔ "How long would it take me to become vice president if I didn't care how I did it?"

While asking politically savvy questions gives you an initial indication of the political lay of the land in your organization, you can do lots more to assess the political environment. Watch out for the following things while you're getting a sense for how things really work in your organization:

- ✔ **Learn how others who seem to be effective get things done:** How much time do they spend preparing higher-ups with phone calls before sending through a formal request for a budget increase? Which items do they delegate and to *whose* subordinates? When you find people who are particularly effective at getting things done in your organization's political environment, learn to model their behavior.

- ✔ **Observe how others are rewarded for the jobs they do:** Does management swiftly and enthusiastically give warm and personal rewards in a sincere manner to make it clear what behavior is considered important? Is credit given to *everyone* who helped make a project successful, or does only the manager get his or her picture in the company newsletter? By observing your company's rewards, you can tell what behavior is expected of employees in your organization. Practice this behavior.

- ✔ **Observe how others are disciplined for the jobs they do:** Does your management come down hard on employees for relatively small mistakes? Are employees criticized in public or in front of coworkers? Is everyone held accountable for decisions, actions, and mistakes even if they had no prior involvement? Such behavior on the part of management indicates that they do not encourage risk-taking; if this is the case, make your political style outwardly reserved as you get things done behind the scenes.

- ✔ **Consider how formal the people in the organization are:** When you are in a staff meeting, for example, you definitely show poor form if you blurt out, "That's a dumb idea. Why would we even consider doing such a thing?" Instead, buffer and finesse your opinions like so: "That's an interesting possibility. Could we explore the pros and cons of implementing such a possibility?" The degree of formality you find in your company indicates how you need to act to conform to the expectations of others. Act that way.

Identifying key players

So now that you've discovered that you work in a political environment (did you really have any doubt in your mind?), you need to determine *who* the key players are. Why? Because they are the individuals who can help make your department more powerful and effective and who can provide positive role models to you and your employees. Key players are those politically astute individuals who make things happen in an organization. You can identify them by their tendency to make instant decisions without having to refer them "upstairs," their use of the latest corporate slang such as *principled leadership, proactive,* and *learning organization,* and their affinity for always speaking up in meetings if only to ask, "What's our objective here?"

Sometimes influential people do not hold influential positions. For example, Jack, as the department head's assistant, might initially appear to be nothing more than a gofer. However, you may later find out that Jack is responsible for scheduling all his boss's appointments, that he sets agendas for department meetings, and that he can veto actions on his own authority. Because you can't get to your boss without going through Jack, you know that Jack has much more power in the organization than his title would indicate.

All the following factors are indicators that can help you identify the key players in your organization:

- ✔ Which employees are sought for advice in your organization?

- ✔ Which employees are considered by others to be indispensable?

- ✔ Whose office is located closest to those of the organization's top management and whose are located miles away. *(Have we arrived in Siberia yet?)*

- ✔ Who eats lunch with the president, the vice presidents, and other members of the upper management team?

As you figure out who the key players in your organization are, you'll start to notice that they have different office personalities. We believe that the following categories can help you figure out how to work with the different personality types of your organization's key players. Do you recognize any of these players in *your* organization?

- ✔ **Movers and shakers:** These individuals usually far exceed the boundaries of their office positions. For example, you might find a mover and shaker in charge of purchasing helping to negotiate a merger. Someone in charge of the physical plant might have the power to designate a wing of the building to the group of his or her choosing. Nonpolitical individuals, on the other hand, tend to be bogged down by responsibilities — such as getting their *own* work done.

- ✔ **Corporate citizens:** Diligent, hardworking, company-loving employees who seek slow but steady, long-term advancement through dedication and hard work. Corporate citizens are great resources for getting information and advice about the organization. You can count on them for help and support, especially if your ideas seem to be in the best interest of the organization.

- ✔ **The town gossip:** These employees always seem to know what's going on in the organization — usually before those individuals who are actually affected by the news know it. Assume that anything you say to these individuals will get back to the person about whom you say it. Therefore, always speak well of your bosses and coworkers when you are in the presence of town gossips.

- ✔ **Firefighters:** The individual who relishes stepping into a potential problem with great fanfare at the last conceivable moment to "save" a project, client, deadline, or whatever. Keep this person well informed of your activities so that you aren't the subject of the next "fire."

- ✔ **The vetoer:** This is the person in your organization who has the authority to kill your best ideas and ambitions with a simple comment such as, "We tried that and it didn't work." In response to any new ideas that you might have, the favorite line of a vetoer is, "If it's such a good idea, why aren't we already doing it?" The best way to deal with vetoers is to keep them out of your decision loop. Try to find other individuals who can get your ideas approved or rework the idea until you hit upon an approach that satisfies the vetoer.

- ✔ **Techies:** Every organization has technically competent workers who legitimately have a high value of their own opinions. Experts can take charge of a situation without taking over. Get to know your experts well — you can trust their judgments and opinions.

- ✔ **Whiners:** A few employees are never satisfied with whatever is done for them. Associating with them inevitably leads to a pessimistic outlook, which is not easily turned around. Or worse, your boss may think that *you're* a whiner, too. In addition, pessimistic people tend to be promoted less often than optimists. Be an optimist: It will make a big difference in your career and in your life.

Redrawing your organization chart

Your company's organization chart might be useful for determining who's who in the *formal* organization, but it really has no bearing on who's who in the *informal* political organization. What you need is the *real* organization chart. Figure 13-1 illustrates a typical *official* organization chart.

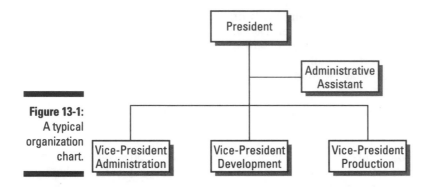

Start by finding your organization's official organization chart — the one that looks like a big pyramid. Throw it away. Now, from your impressions and observations, start plotting the *real* relationships in your organization *in your mind.* (You don't want someone to find your handiwork lying around in your office or in the recycling bin!) Begin with the key players whom you've already identified. Indicate their relative power by level and relationships by approximation. Use the following questions as a guideline:

✔ **Whom do these influential people associate with?** Draw the associations on your chart and connect them with solid lines. Also connect friends and relatives.

✔ **Who makes up the office cliques?** Be sure that all members are connected, because talking to one is like talking to them all.

✔ **Who are the office gossips?** Use dotted lines to represent communication *without* influence and solid lines for communication *with* influence.

✔ **Who are your competition?** Circle those likely to be considered for *your* next promotion. Target them for *special* attention.

✔ **Who are left off the chart?** Don't forget about these individuals. The way that today's organizations seem to change every other day, someone who is off the chart on Friday may be on the chart on Monday. Always maintain positive relationships with all your coworkers and never, *never* burn bridges between you and others within and without the company. Otherwise, you may find *yourself* left off the chart some day.

The result of this exercise is a chart of who *really* has political power in your organization and who doesn't. Figure 13-2 shows how the organization *really* works. Update your organization chart as you learn more information about people. Take note of any behavior that gives away a relationship — such as your boss cutting off a coworker in mid-sentence — and factor this observation into your overall political analysis. Of course, understand that you may be wrong. It's impossible for you to know the inner power relationships of every department. Sometimes, individuals who *seem* to have power may have far less of it than people who have learned to exhibit their power more quietly.

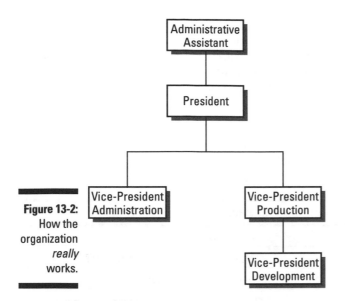

Figure 13-2:
How the organization *really* works.

Polishing Your Image

Your political image, or nonpolitical image as the case may be, needs careful attention throughout your career. If you ignore it, you may find yourself in the unpleasant position of being left out of the important decisions that affect your organization. So what can you do to keep your political image polished? First, be rational at all times. Second, do whatever you can to be knowledgeable about anything and everything that affects your business. Finally, avoid showing your emotions at work.

These points may seem petty, but depending on your organization's political environment, your career may very well depend on how you manage your own political image.

Being rational

The most fundamental and important aspect of a manager's political image is being rational. Your decisions and actions need to seem perfectly rational even if they aren't. Sure, people want their leaders to trust and empower them and to show human emotions such as compassion, empathy, and understanding, but ultimately, people want their leaders to be rational and in control. Irrational behavior on the part of managers in organizational environments is generally considered very inappropriate.

Beware of irrational behavior because you may seem that you are not in control.

The appearance of rationality is the main reason you'll never hear a company spokesperson defend a company's action by saying, "Oh, we just felt like it, no real reason to speak of." Likewise, no one is ever simply "having a cup of coffee" when not present for a phone call. The proper, rational response is, "He's on a conference call right now." Anything else is presumably unacceptable to the caller.

To have your actions perceived as legitimate, you must justify them with rational reasons and explanations. Table 13-1 shows some common reasons that managers give for doing whatever they feel like doing — or not doing — in an organization.

Table 13-1	Managers' Common Rational Responses
Why You Didn't	*Why You Did*
"We need more information."	"We didn't have time to get more information."
"The numbers didn't look right."	"The numbers looked right."
"It's not in the budget."	"I thought you'd approve this special need."
"It's not my responsibility."	"The customer requested it."
"We can't make an exception."	"We had to make an exception."

Being someone who knows

Another dimension of the rational image you want to cultivate is the appearance of being someone who knows. The importance of this aspect of your image increases as you rise in the organization and face an increasing lack of firsthand information. If others *see* a knowledgeable and confident exterior, they are more likely to assume that you *are* knowledgeable and confident.

Always smile and nod ever so slightly while conversing with others. Interject an occasional remark that alludes to events or to other information that shows that you are plugged in to the situation:

- ✔ "We found the same to be true when we looked at that problem. What else did you find?"

- ✔ "I couldn't agree more. In fact, that's just what I was telling Jacobs the other day."

- ✔ "I'm glad to hear your spin on this issue. It validates what I have been saying for the last month."

Unfortunately, after some managers get in positions of power, they blame any lack of knowledge (on their part) on those who work for them. Have you ever heard these kinds of statements uttered in your presence?

- "Why haven't I seen this report before?"
- "You expect me to wade through these numbers?"
- "How is this strategy any different from what the competition did in '95?"

If these kinds of comments are directed at *you*, be prepared to respond with a reasonable explanation:

- "I sent you a copy two weeks ago. Can I make you another?"
- "The summary is on page 2. I'll be glad to walk you through it right now."
- "It's a *lot* different. I have a presentation I developed that explains the differences. When would you like to view it?"

Avoiding emotional displays

If you are a normal person, inclined to a normal range of emotions such as anger, sadness, glee, or fear, you may have some problems in the corporate environment in which people are generally discouraged from showing emotion. Face it, business can be very sober stuff. Why else would gray and dark blue be the predominant colors chosen by those who dress for success? Unfortunately, in some organizations, displaying emotion openly is seen as a weakness — possibly a character flaw. The good news is that this attitude is changing in most organizations. However, before you publicly emote, first determine whether your organization encourages or discourages displays of emotion.

Be on the alert whenever you find yourself heading towards any of the following emotional outbursts. Take a time out, go to your office or the restroom, close the door, take 10 deep breaths, and turn to Chapter 14 to find out how to deal with your stress!

- **Anger:** Avoid showing anger toward the actions or inactions of your coworkers or employees. Instead, learn to grit your teeth and smile. If you're asked a question while you're gritting your teeth, simply nod.

- **Crying:** Definitely not a good career move. The preferred method of handling stress is to wait to cry on your commute home. No, really, the best thing to do is remove yourself from the situation and get it all out in the privacy of your office, a trusted associate's office, or the car.

- **Envy:** A definite no-no in any organization. Instead of showing hate, disgust, or any other related emotions, practice saying phrases like "Congratulations on your promotion," "Best of luck in your new job," or "Nice going on landing that new account."

✔ **Glee:** Happiness in business tends to come from pleasant surprises. Surprises indicate that something happened that wasn't planned. Unplanned activities indicate a lack of control. Do yourself a favor; save glee for the cake that your department gets you on your birthday.

Communication: What's Real and What's Not?

One of the best ways to determine how well you fit into an organization is to see how well you communicate. If you can casually banter and use the best of corporate lingo — peppering your conversation with popular business expressions and other jargon *(I really believe that we have to be proactive about this breakdown in organizational kaizen)* — you'll be well on your way to being a political player to be reckoned with.

Deciphering the *real* meaning of communication in an organization takes some practice. So how do you determine the real meaning of words in *your* organization? You can best get to the underlying meanings by observing behavior, reading between the lines, and — when necessary — knowing how to obtain sensitive information.

Tools for success?

No political image makeover is complete without the right accessories. For maximum power projection, choose among these items. Such trappings of power will surely enhance your perceived and therefore your real power. Not really. Unfortunately, some individuals really believe that these kinds of things create power. They *don't.* In fact, they may indicate a deep insecurity about not having any *real* power — the kind that comes from within an individual.

Cellular phone: Automatically rings anytime you have been in a meeting for more than five minutes. After you answer your phone, excuse yourself from the meeting, explaining that you have an important client on the line.

Antacid tablet container: Don't fake an ulcer when you can have the real thing! Show your commitment to the team with a large bottle of these chalk tablets on your desk. Collects many times its weight in first impressions.

Rolex watch face: Exchange the face of your no-name watch for one that commands attention. Two-tone 18K gold and stainless steel wristband, add $1,000.

Mont Blanc pen: An expensive pen ensures that every word you write is concise, witty, and important. (Or so you think.)

Political scorecard: This handy reference card helps you to easily remember who is in favor and who is out. Use for scoring points for political moves and deciding when you have enough points to make a move yourself.

Believing actions, not words

One way to decipher the real meaning of communication is to pay close attention to the corresponding behavior of the communicator. The values and priorities of others tend to come through more clearly in what they *do* rather than in what they *say*.

So, for example, if your manager repeatedly says he is trying to obtain approval for a raise for you, look at what actions he has taken toward that end. Did he make a call to his boss or hold a meeting? Did he submit the necessary paperwork or establish a deadline to accomplish this goal? If the answers to the above questions are "no," or if he is continually "waiting to hear," the action is probably going nowhere fast. To counter a situation like this, try to get higher up on your boss's list of priorities by suggesting actions that he or she can take to get you your raise. You may find that you need to do some or all of the footwork yourself. Alternatively, this may indicate that your boss is not a power player in the organization. Do everything you can to attract the attention of the power players in your organization who can suggest to your boss that you deserve a raise.

Reading between the lines

In business, don't take the written word at face value. Probe to find out the *real* reasons behind what is written. For example, here's a typical notice in a company newsletter announcing the reorganization of several departments:

> With the departure of J. R. McNeil, the Marketing Support and Customer Service department will now be a part of the Sales and Administration division under Elizabeth Olsen, acting vice president. The unit will eventually be moved under the direct supervision of the sales director, Tom Hutton.

Such an announcement in the company newsletter might seem to be straightforward on the surface, but if you read between the lines, you might be able to conclude:

> J. R. McNeil, who never did seem to get along with the director of sales, finally did something bad enough to justify getting fired. Tom Hutton apparently made a successful bid with the board of directors to add the area to his empire, probably because his sales were up 30 percent over last year. Elizabeth Olsen will be assigned as acting vice president for an interim period to do some of Tom's dirty work by clearing out some of the deadwood. Tom will thus start with a clean slate, 20 percent lower expenses, and an almost guaranteed increase in profits for his first year in the job. This all fits very nicely with Tom's personal strategy for advancement. (*P.S.: A nice congratulatory call to Tom might be in order.*)

Announcements like these have been reworked dozens of times by so many people that they appear to be logical and valid when you initially read them. By reading between the lines, however, you can often determine what is *really* going on. Of course, you have to be careful not to jump to the wrong conclusions. It may be that J.R. has simply gone on to better opportunities and that the company has taken advantage of that event to reorganize. It's important to validate your conclusions with others in the company to get the *real* story.

Probing for information

In general, you can get ongoing information about the organization by being a trusted listener to as many people as possible. Show sincere interest in the affairs of others, and they'll talk about themselves openly. After they begin talking, you can shift the topic to work, work problems, and eventually more sensitive topics. Ask encouraging questions and volunteer information yourself as necessary to keep the exchange equitable.

Even after you have developed such trusted relationships, you need to know how to probe to uncover the facts about rumors, decisions, and hidden agendas. Start by adhering to the following guidelines:

- Have at least three ways of obtaining the information.
- Check the information through two sources.
- Promise anonymity whenever possible.
- Generally know the answers to the questions you ask.
- Be casual and nonthreatening in your approach.
- Assume that the initial answer is superficial.
- Ask the same question different ways.
- Be receptive to whatever information you're given.

The Unwritten Rules of Organizational Politics

Every organization has rules that are never written down and seldom discussed. Such *unwritten* rules pertaining to the expectations and behavior of employees in the organization can play a major role in your success or failure. Because unwritten rules are not explicit, you have to piece them together by observation, insightful questioning, or simply through trial and error.

Interpreting the company policy manual

Even when written in black and white, an organization's policies are rarely what they appear to be. Most policies came about as a directive from the top to solve a particular problem. For example, if the company employed a single employee who preferred to wear gaudy jewelry, the individual could be confronted in a two- to three-minute discussion that would probably settle the matter. What is more often the case, however, is that management appoints a task force to develop a dress code and company plan for personal hygiene. Even after the policy is enacted, the targeted individual is likely to be oblivious to any perceived problem and might even wholeheartedly endorse the new code "for all those who need it" — that is, seemingly everyone except her.

A similar explanation can be made for most policies. To make the best use of a policy manual, consider using the following rules of thumb:

✔ Refer to the policy only when it clearly supports exactly what you want to do.

✔ Always assume that a policy that does not support what you want was intended for others.

✔ Claim an inability to equitably enforce policies you don't like by citing a rumored abuse or possible misinterpretation.

✔ When a conflict arises about policy implementation, argue that the policy is too specific (for general application) or too general (for specific circumstances).

✔ Argue that all policies should be considered flexible guidelines.

The point is that sometimes policies don't work. Your job is to recognize this and to work to change the policies that don't. For example, if you want to give your employees the flexibility to set their own work schedules, but company policy prohibits that, do whatever you can to get management to buy off on a new policy that accomplishes your goal.

Never underestimate the power of the unwritten rules of organizational politics. In many companies, they are just as important, if not more important, than the written rules contained in the company's policy manuals.

Be friendly with all

The more individuals you have as friends in an organization, the better off you are. If you haven't already done so, start cultivating friends in your immediate work group and then extend your efforts to making contacts and developing friendships in other parts of the organization. The more favorably you are viewed by your coworkers, the greater your chances of becoming their manager in the future. Cultivate their support by seeking advice or by offering assistance.

Remember: You never know who you'll be reporting to in the future. As the saying goes, *Be nice to people on the way up 'cause you might meet them on the way down.*

Build a network by routinely helping new employees who enter your organization. As they join, be the person who takes them aside to explain how things *really* work. As the new employees establish themselves and move on to other jobs in other parts of the organization, you have a well-entrenched network for obtaining information and assistance.

Knowing others throughout the organization can be invaluable for clarifying rumors, obtaining information, and indirectly feeding information back to others. An astute manager maintains a large number of diverse contacts throughout the organization, all on friendly terms. The following are excellent ways to enlarge your network:

- **Walk around:** Those who walk the halls tend to be better known than those who don't. Return telephone and e-mail messages in person whenever possible. Not only do you have the opportunity for one-on-one communication with the individual who left you the message, but you can stop in to see everyone else you know along the way.

- **Play company sports or games:** You can meet employees from a wide range of functions and locations by joining a company sports league. Whether bowling, golf, or softball is your cup of tea, surely something will catch your fancy. If you prefer, start or join a lunchtime bridge or chess group.

- **Join committees:** Whether the committee has been formed to address employee security or simply to determine who cleans out the refrigerator in the employee lounge, take part. You get to meet lots of new people in an informal and relaxed setting.

There's no interest like self-interest

A fundamental, unwritten rule of office politics is this: Getting what *you* want is easier when you give others what *they* want. Win the assistance of others by showing them what they stand to gain by helping you. When a benefit is not readily apparent, create or allude to one that might occur if they offer to help. Such benefits can include:

- **A favor returned in kind:** Surely, you can provide some kind of favor to your counterparts in exchange for their assistance. Lunch or the temporary loan of an employee are always popular options.

- **Information:** Don't forget: Information is power. You'll find that many of your coworkers crave the latest and greatest information in an organization. Perhaps you can be the one to give it to them.

✔ **Money:** Perhaps you have a little extra money in your equipment budget that you can allocate to someone's project in exchange for that person's help. Or maybe you have underrun your travel budget and your counterpart would really like to visit that customer in Sydney.

✔ **A recommendation:** The higher-ups trust your judgment. Your willingness to recommend a coworker for promotion to a higher position or for recognition for extraordinary performance is a valuable commodity. The right words to the right people can make all the difference to someone's success in an organization.

We're not suggesting that you do anything unethical or illegal here. When you provide these kinds of benefits to others in your organization, make sure that you are within your company's rules and policies. It's never worth violating your personal set of ethics or company policy to get ahead.

Don't party at company parties

Social affairs are a serious time for those seeking to advance within a company. Social events offer one of the few times when everyone in the company is supposed to be on equal footing. Don't believe it. Although social functions provide those at the top a chance to show that they're "regular" people and give those below a chance to ask questions and laugh at their bosses' jokes, they are also a time to be *extremely* cautious.

Beware of whom you talk to and, of course, what you say. Social functions such as holiday parties and company picnics are not the time to let loose and be the life of the party or to tell the division vice president exactly what you think of her — unless she has had more to drink than you. Managing most social encounters involves art and skill, especially those encounters that involve coworkers. Proper poise begins with proper mingling techniques.

✔ Powerful individuals stake out different corners of the room, and they know that the most prestigious locations face the entrance. Other great positions are near the food or the drinks, where people will look like they're interested in what you have to say even if they aren't. Beat everyone else to one of these spots, and you may just boost your *own* power rating.

✔ Use the middle of the room to intercept individuals that you especially want to speak to. As an alternative strategy for getting their attention, watch the hors d'oeuvres table or the punch bowl. Go for refills when the person you are seeking does so.

✔ During your conversations, make frequent compliments, congratulations, and expressions of gratitude. Keep discussion loose and light and avoid discussing work topics with anyone other than your boss. Try to move on before the person you're speaking to runs out of things to say and is overcome with a blank expression. *Don't* fawn or brown-nose. These behaviors are more likely to lose respect for you than to gain it.

✔ Leave the social function immediately after the departure of the highest ranking company official. If you are forced to leave before, let him or her know why.

Manage your manager

If you ever expect to play office politics with the best of them, you must be good at managing your manager. The idea is to try to get your manager to do the things that most directly benefit you and your staff. The following tried-and-true techniques for manager management have evolved through the ages:

✔ **Keep your manager informed of your successes:** "That last sale puts me over quota for the month."

✔ **Support your manager in meetings:** "Gadsby is right on this. We really *do* have to consider the implications of this change on our customers."

✔ **Praise your manager to those who are likely to repeat it back to him or her:** "Ms. Gadsby is probably the best manager I have ever worked for."

✔ **Quote your manager in tones of reverence:** "It was only last week that my boss, Ms. Gadsby — a woman devoted to putting us on top — stated, 'This company is more than a career to me, it's a way of life.'"

Although a well-controlled relationship with your manager is important, you need connections to those above your manager, too. A key relationship to develop is with your manager's manager — an individual who is likely to have a very big influence on your future career.

Volunteer for an assignment that happens to be a pet project of your manager's boss. If you do a good job, you'll more than likely be asked to do another project. If you don't have an opportunity like a pet project, try to find an area of common interest with your manager's boss. Bring up the topic in casual conversation and agree to meet later to discuss it in more detail. But be careful not to press your boss too hard on this. You don't want to appear *overly* anxious or like you're stalking your boss.

Move ahead with your mentors

Having a *mentor* is almost essential for ensuring any long-term success within an organization. A mentor is an individual — usually higher up in the organization — who provides advice and helps to guide your progress. Mentors are necessary because they can offer you important career advice, as well as become your advocate in higher levels of the organization — the levels that you don't have direct access to.

The person whom you select as your mentor (or who selects you, as is more often the case) should have significant organizational clout and be vocal about tooting your merits. If possible, get the support of several powerful people throughout the organization. *Sponsorships* (your relationships with your mentors) develop informally over an extended period of time.

Seek out a mentor by finding an occasion to ask for advice. If you find the advice extremely helpful, frequently seek more advice from the same person. Initially, ask for advice related to your work, but as time goes on, you can ask for advice about business in general and your career advancement specifically. Proceed slowly, or your intentions may be suspect. Always display tact and discretion in your approach to your mentor:

- ✓ **The wrong approach:** "Mr. Fairmont, I've been thinking. In the marketing department, a lot of bad rumors have been going around about you and Suzy. I could try to squelch some of them if I see something in it for me. You know: You take care of me, and I take care of you. What do you say?"

- ✓ **The right approach:** "Here's that special report you asked for, Ms. Smith. Correlating customer color preferences with the size of orders in the Eastern region was fascinating. You seem to be one of the forward-looking people in this organization."

Be trustworthy

Similar to having a mentor is being a loyal follower of an exceptional performer within the organization. Finding good people to trust can be difficult, so if you are trustworthy, you are likely to become a valued associate of a bright peer. As that person rises quickly through the organization, he or she can bring you along. However, whenever possible, hitch your wagon to more than one star: You never know when a star may fall and leave you all alone in the stardust.

Protecting Yourself

Inevitably, you'll find yourself on the receiving end of someone else's political aspirations. Astute managers take precautions to protect themselves — and their employees — against the political maneuverings of others. These precautions can also help if your own strategies go wrong. What can you do to protect yourself?

Document for protection

Document the progress of your department's projects and activities, especially when expected changes in plans or temporary setbacks affect your project. Documenting the changes or setbacks gives you an accurate record of your projects' history and ensures that these elements aren't *forgotten* (or inappropriately used against you) by individuals who don't have your best interests at heart. The form of the documentation can vary, but the following are most common:

- ✔ Confirmation memos
- ✔ Activity reports
- ✔ Project folders
- ✔ Correspondence files
- ✔ Notes

Don't make promises you can't keep

Avoid making promises or firm commitments for your employees or for yourself — especially when you don't want to or you can't follow through. If at all possible, don't offer a deadline, final price, or guarantee of action or quality. When you make such promises, you give up control and you become unnecessarily restricted. Instead, consider taking one of the following actions:

- ✔ **Hedge:** If forced to make a firm commitment to an action, hedge your promise as much as possible by building in extra time, staff, money, or other qualifier.
- ✔ **Buffer time estimates:** If you are forced to make a time commitment, buffer the estimate (that is, add extra time to what you think you'll really need) to give yourself room to maneuver. If your employees deliver early, they'll be heroes.

✔ **Extend deadlines:** As deadlines approach, bring any problems you or your staff encounter — even the most basic ones — to the attention of the person who requested that you do the project. Keeping people informed keeps them from being surprised if you need to extend your deadlines.

Be visible

To obtain the maximum credit for the efforts of you and your staff, first focus on receiving recognition for your department's successes. To ensure that credit is given where credit is due, do the following:

✔ **Advertise your department's successes:** Routinely send copies of all completed projects and letters of praise for every member of your staff to your manager and to your manager's boss.

✔ **Use surrogates:** Call on your friends in the organization to help publicize your achievements and those of your employees. Be generous in highlighting the achievements of your employees. If you mention too many of your own achievements, you may appear tactless and boastful.

✔ **Gain attribution by association:** Arrive and leave when the influential people do. Sit as close to top management as possible in meetings. Add your name or the name of key staff members to management distribution lists so that these names become better known to other managers.

Test your new-found knowledge

Name three kinds of key players.

A. Movers and shakers, salespeople, and firefighters

B. Presidents, vice presidents, and managers

C. Corporate citizens, vetoers, and administrative assistants

D. Firefighters, techies, and whiners

What are three good ways to document your work?

A. Confirmation memos, activity reports, and notes

B. Activity reports, hearsay, and innuendo

C. Selective amnesia, misplaced memos, and illegible notes

D. None of the above

Part V
Tough Times for Tough Managers

The 5th Wave   By Rich Tennant

"I've never been good at this part of the job, which is why I've asked 'Buddy' to join us. As you know business has been bad lately, and, well, Buddy has some bad news for you..."

In this part . . .

No one ever said that being a manager is easy. Rewarding, yes. Easy, no. In this part, we present strategies for managing change and stress in the workplace, disciplining employees easily and effectively, and conducting employee terminations.

Chapter 14

Keep Cool! Dealing with Change on the Job and the Stress It Creates

In This Chapter

▶ Dealing with crisis

▶ Putting up roadblocks to change

▶ Identifying stress

▶ Managing stress before it manages you

▶ Moving on with your life

*M*ore, more, more! Faster, faster, faster! Better, better, better! And while you're at it, can you cut the price in half?!? *I can get this same thing for 25 percent less from your competitor — why can't you cut the price?* The job of management has always had its own unique pressures — disciplining employees, setting and meeting goals, and making stuff happen. However, as long as U.S. companies dominated the world's marketplaces in a period of economic growth, domestic businesses had little need to worry about details such as quality, price, and delivery. *What quality problem?*

Or how about this scenario? Your employer — an American business icon and market leader since the beginning of time — announces a layoff of 30,000 employees during the course of the next year. And although your employer announces which divisions the layoff affects (your division, of course, is among them), several months may pass before you know exactly *who* is to be let go. *Hmmm . . .*

Times — and customer expectations — have changed . . . in a big way. If your customers want their goods yesterday, well, by golly, you better deliver the goods on the day *before* yesterday. If your customers want better quality, you must have the *best* quality. If your customers want 10 options, you need to give them 20. And all this at the best possible price. To survive, businesses must rise to the expectations of their customers. Being a faceless part of the business pack is no longer good enough — those *faceless* companies may all be out of business in a year or two. If your business is going to last past the year 2000, it must do its work better — much better than the competition.

So what does this forecast mean to you as a manager? Simply put, the pressures on managers to perform are greater than they've ever been before. In addition, most organizations have gone from being bastions of stability and status quo in the stormy seas of change to being agile ships, navigating the fluid and ever-changing seas in which they float. *Heywood, we have decided to reorganize the division. Starting tomorrow, you're in charge of our new factory in Singapore. I hope you like Chinese food!*

You see, employees naturally want to stay in their *comfort zones* — the places that they're familiar with and accustomed to. Pushing people out of their comfort zones creates stress as they grasp for familiarity in an ocean of change. After the change subsides and employees establish routines once again, the stress decreases, and life goes on.

The words *business* and *change* are quickly becoming synonymous. And the more things change, the more stress affects *everyone* in an organization. This chapter is about managing change and about working through the other pressures that cause managers and workers to get stressed out like never before.

What's the Rush?

What's *your* typical business day like? You get into the office, grab a cup of coffee, and scan your appointment calendar. Looks like a light day for meetings: two in the morning and only one in the afternoon. Maybe you'll finally get a chance to work on the budget goal you've been meaning to complete for the past few months, *plus* have some extra time to go for a walk at lunch to unwind. Wouldn't *that* be nice! Next, you pick up your telephone to check your voice mail. Of the 25 messages that have stacked up since you last checked, 10 are urgent. When you check your e-mail, you find much the same ratio.

As you begin to think how you can respond to these urgent messages, an employee arrives with his own crisis that needs your *immediate* attention. He tells you that the computer network has broken down, and until someone fixes it, the entire corporate financial system is on the *fritz*. While you are talking to your employee, your boss calls to tell you to drop *everything* because you have been elected to write a report for the president that absolutely *has* to be done by the close of business today.

So much for working on your budget goal. And you can forget that relaxing walk at lunch. This day is turning out to be just another day in paradise.

Legitimate urgency versus crisis management

Urgency has its place in an organization. The rate of change in the global business environment demands it. The revolutions in computer use, telecommunications systems, and information technology demand it. The need to be more responsive to customers than ever before demands it. In these urgent times, the winners are the companies that can provide the best solutions faster than anyone else. The losers are the companies that wonder what happened as they watch their competitors go streaking by.

However, an organization has a *real* problem when its managers fall into the behavior of *managing by crisis* and the trap of *reacting* to change instead of *leading* change. When every problem in an organization becomes a drop-everything-else-that-you-are-doing crisis, the organization is not showing signs of responsiveness to its business environment. Instead, the business is showing signs of poor planning and lousy execution. Someone (perhaps a manager?) isn't doing his or her job.

Recognizing and dealing with crises

Some crises are the legitimate result of outside factors beyond your control as a manager. For example, suppose that a vital customer requests that all project designs be submitted by *this* Friday instead of *next* Friday. Or perhaps the city sends you a notice that a maintenance crew plans to cut off the power to your plant for three days while the crew performs needed maintenance on switching equipment. Or a huge snowstorm in the Northeast cuts off all flights, in and out, for the rest of the week.

On the other hand, many crises occur because someone in your organization drops the ball, and now you (the manager) have to make things right. The following are avoidable crisis situations:

- ✔ Hoping that the need will go away, a manager avoids making a necessary decision. Surprise! The need didn't go away, and now he or she has a crisis to deal with.

- ✔ An employee forgets to relay an important message from your customer, and you're about to lose the account as a result. Another crisis.

- ✔ A coworker decides that informing you about a major change to a manufacturing process isn't important. Because of your experience, you would have quickly seen that the change would lead to quality problems in the finished product. When manufacturing grinds to a halt, you come in after the fact to clean up the mess. One more crisis to add to your list.

You can't afford *not* to be prepared to deal with externally generated crises. You have to be flexible, you have to work smart, and you have to work hard. But your organization can't afford to become a slave to internally generated crises. Managing by crisis forgoes one of the most important elements in business management. That element is *planning*.

You establish plans and goals for a reason: to make your company as successful as possible. However, if you continually set your plans and goals on a back burner because of the crisis of the day, you may as well not waste your time making the plans. And where does your organization go then? (See Chapter 8 for a discussion of the importance of having plans and goals.)

When you, as a manager, allow everything to become a crisis, not only do you sap the energy of your employees, but eventually, they lose the ability to recognize when a *real* crisis is upon them. Remember the old fable about the boy who cried "Wolf"? After the boy issued several false alarms in jest, the villagers didn't bother to respond to his cries when some wolves really appeared to attack his sheep. After responding to several manufactured crises, your employees begin to see the crises as routine, and they may not be there for you when you really need them.

Change Happens

Face it: Change happens, and you can do *nothing* about it. You can try to ignore it, but does that stop change? No, you only blind yourself to the things that are *really* happening in your organization. You can try to stop it, but does that keep change from happening? No, you are only fooling yourself if you think that you can stop progress — even for a moment. You can try to insulate yourself and those around you from the effects of change, but can you really afford to ignore it? No, to ignore change is to sign a death warrant for your organization and, quite possibly, for your career.

Unfortunately, from our personal observations, most managers seem to spend their entire careers trying to fight change: to predict, control, and harness change and its effects on the organization. However, fighting change is a losing battle. The casualties are all around you. Ulcers, heart attacks, burn out, premature graying, and catastrophic ego deflation are but a few of the symptoms that occur when people try to fight change and lose their resulting battle with stress.

The four stages of change

Change is not a picnic. Despite the excitement that change can bring to your working life — both good and bad — you've probably had just about all the change you can handle right about now, thank you. But as change continues, you go through four distinct phases in response to it:

1. **Deny it. When change happens, the first response you have (if you're like most people) is one of immediate denial.**

   Whose dumb idea was that? That's never going to work here. Don't worry, they'll see their mistake and go back to the old way of doing things! Operating with this attitude is like an ostrich sticking its head in the sand: If you can't see it, it'll go away. You wish!

2. **Resist it. At some point, you realize that the change is not just a clerical error; however, this realization doesn't mean that you have to accept the change lying down!**

   Nope, I'm sticking with the old way of doing that job. If that way was good enough then, it's good enough now. Resistance is a normal response to change — everyone goes through it. The key is not to let your resistance get you stuck; the quicker you get with the program, the better for your organization and the better for your career.

3. **Explore it. By now, you know that further resistance is futile and the new way of doing things just may have some pluses.**

   Hmmm . . . well, maybe that change actually does make sense. I'll see what opportunities can make the change work for me instead of against me. During this stage, you examine both the good and bad things that come from the change, and you decide on a strategy for managing the change.

4. **Accept it. The final stage of change is acceptance. At this point, you have successfully integrated the change into your routine.**

   Wow, this new system really works well. It beats the heck out of the old way of doing things! Now, the change that you so vigorously denied and resisted is part of your everyday routine; the change is now the status quo.

At the end of your change responses, you come full circle, and you're ready to face your next change.

Are you fighting change?

Are *you* fighting change? You may be fighting change and not even know it. Besides watching the number of gray hairs multiply on your head, how can you tell? Look out for these seven deadly warning signs of resistance to change:

✔ **You're still using the old rules to play a new game.** Sorry to be the ones to bring you this bad news, but the old game is gone, *kaput*. The pressures of global competition have created a brand new game with a brand new set of rules. For example, if you're one of those increasingly rare managers who refuses to learn how to use a computer (don't laugh — they *do* exist!), you're playing by the *old* rules. Computer literacy and information proficiency is the *new* rule. If you're not playing with the *new* rules, not only is this a warning sign that you're resisting change, but you can bet on being left behind as the rest of your organization moves along the path to the future.

✔ **You're ducking new assignments.** Usually, two basic reasons cause you to avoid new assignments. First, you may be overwhelmed with your current job and can't imagine taking on any more duties. If you're in this situation, try to remember that new ways of doing things often make your work more efficient or even wipe out many old things that you do. Second, you may simply be uneasy with the unknown, and so you resist change.

Ducking new assignments to resist change is a definite no-no. Not only are you interfering with the progress of the organization, but you are effectively putting your own career on hold.

✔ **You're trying to slow things down.** Trying to slow things down is a normal reaction for most people. When something new comes along — a new way of doing business, a new assignment, a new wrinkle in the marketplace — most people tend to want to slow down, to take the time to examine, analyze, and then decide how to react. The problem is that the newer things get, the slower these people go.

As a manager, you want to remain competitive in the new millennium; you don't have the luxury of slowing down every time something new comes along. From now on, the amount of *new* that you have to deal with is going to greatly outweigh the *old*. Instead of resisting the new by slowing down (and risking an uncompetitive and outmoded organization), you need to keep up your pace. How? When you are forced to do *more* with less, *focus* on less.

✔ **You're working hard to control the uncontrollable.** Have you ever tried to keep the sun from rising in the morning? Or tried to stop the dark clouds that drop rain, sleet, and snow on your house during a storm? Or tried to stay 29 years old forever? Face it: You just can't control many things in life — you waste your time when you try.

Are you resisting change by trying to control the uncontrollable at work? Perhaps you want to try to head off a planned corporate reorganization or stop your foreign competitors from having access to your domestic markets or delay the acquisition of your firm by a much larger company. The world of business is changing all around you, and you can do nothing about it. You have a choice: You can continue to resist change by pretending that you are controlling it (believe us, you *can't*), or you can concentrate your efforts on learning how to most effectively *respond* to change to leverage it to your advantage.

✔ **You're playing the role of victim.** Oh, woe is me! This response is the ultimate cop-out. Instead of accepting change and learning how to respond to it (and using it to the advantage of your organization and yourself), you choose to become a victim of it. Playing the role of victim and hoping that your coworkers feel sorry for you is easy to do. *(Poor Sam, she's got a brand new crop of upstart competitors to deal with. I wonder how she can even bring herself to come to work every morning!)*

But today's successful businesses can't afford to waste the time or money employing victims. If you're not giving 110 percent each day that you go to work, your organization will find someone who can.

✔ **You're hoping someone else will make things better for you.** In the old-style hierarchical organization, top management almost always took responsibility for making the decisions that made things better (or worse) for workers. We have a news flash: The old-style organization is changing, and the new-style organization that is taking its place has empowered *every* employee to take responsibility for decision-making.

The pressures of global competition and the coming of the Information Age require that decisions be made quicker than ever. In other words, the employees closest to the issues must make the decisions; a manager who is seven layers of the organization removed and 3,000 miles away can't do it. *You* hold the keys to *your* future. You have the power to make things better for yourself. If you wait until someone else makes things better for you, then you're going to be waiting an awfully long time.

✔ **You're absolutely paralyzed, like a deer in the headlights.** This condition is the ultimate sign of resistance to change and is almost always terminal. Sometimes change seems so overwhelming that the only choice is to give up. When change paralyzes you, not only do you fail to respond to change, but you can no longer perform your current duties. In today's organization, such resistance is certain death.

Instead of allowing change to paralyze you, become a *leader* of change. Here are some ideas how: Embrace the change *yourself.* Become its friend and its biggest cheerleader. Be flexible and be responsive to the changes that swirl all around you and through the corridors of your organization. Be a model to those around you who continue to resist change. Show them that they can make change work *for* them instead of *against* them. Focus on what you *can* do — not what you *can't* do. Finally, be sure to recognize and reward employees who have accepted the change and who have succeeded as a result.

If you notice any of these seven warning signs of resistance to change — in yourself or in your coworkers — you can do something about it. As long as you're willing to embrace change instead of fight it, you hold incredible value for your organization, and you'll be a survivor. Make responsiveness to change your personal mission: Be a leader of change, not a follower of resistance.

Identifying the Symptoms of Stress

No matter how hard you try to prevent it, some amount of stress in the workplace is inevitable. Although you may be doing a great job leading change in your organization and creating flexible plans that allow for the unexpected, you may have to work with many other employees who *aren't* doing such a great job. The presence of change and differences in individual working styles are bound to create stress for you and your organization.

And the stress that you experience on the job is multiplied by the stress that you bring with you from your everyday life. Is that house payment starting to weigh down your personal finances? Are you and your significant other embroiled in yet another conflict about how you squeeze your toothpaste out of the tube? Did you just get a call from the IRS about a little matter of auditing your tax records for the past three years?

So how do you know whether you're getting stressed out? The following list of stress indicators should help you identify the extent of stress in your business and personal lives. Because one affects the other, determining and dealing with the source of stress is important.

Table 14-1 shows a list of symptoms of stress with a place to check off the symptoms that you have. If you experience more than a couple of these symptoms, take a serious look at what creates the stress in your life. Quick! Do something about stress before it's too late!

Table 14-1	Symptoms of Stress
The Symptom	*Yes, I Have It!*
Aggression	❑
Hostility	❑
Headaches	❑
Indigestion	❑
Sleep disorders	❑
Defensiveness	❑
Poor judgment	❑

The Symptom	Yes, I Have It!
Nervousness	❏
High blood pressure	❏
Ulcers	❏
Fatigue	❏
Anxiety	❏
Depression	❏
Memory loss	❏
Inability to concentrate	❏
Mood swings	❏

Any one of these symptoms can indicate a stress problem, but the longer your list of symptoms, the greater is the damage being done to your mind and body. Fortunately, you can learn how to manage your stress. While you can't always prevent stress from entering your life, you *can* take definite steps to reduce the negative effects on your life. Learn how to take control of stress so that it doesn't take control of *you*.

Managing Your Stress

Have you ever wondered why so many organizations make such a big deal about stress management training? Organizations must deal with stress because, when employees allow stress to overcome them, they lose their effectiveness. And when employees lose their effectiveness, the organization loses its edge.

Most stress management training focuses on treating the symptoms of stress and not on curing its root causes within the organization. We see a problem with this approach. The training programs teach workers relaxation techniques to decrease their level of stress, but top management isn't forced to make better and faster decisions. The training shows employees how to use positive affirmations to reinforce their feelings of self-worth, but the lousy phone system that cuts customers off in mid-sentence isn't fixed. The program instructs the staff in better time management, but poor planning still leads to organizational crisis after organizational crisis.

These examples show that you can't wait for someone else to do something to reduce your stress. Learn to manage stress yourself. Fortunately, managing stress is not as hard as you may think. Effective stress management boils down to this: *Change* the things that you can change and *accept* the things that you can't change.

Changing the things you can change

You can do many things *right now* to change your work environment and decrease your stress. If they sound familiar, you've probably thought about doing them before, but you just couldn't seem to get around to it. Well, *now* is the time to get around to it! Don't delay and put it off until tomorrow. The life you save may be your own!

- **Get healthy:** You *know* that regular, vigorous exercise is one of the best things that you can do for yourself. Not only do you make your mind and your body stronger, but you work off tons of frustration and stress in the process. And when you're under stress, your body quickly becomes depleted of certain vitamins and minerals. Eat right. Don't forget your fruit and veggies! And this is doubly true when you're on the road. Don't forgo exercise and eating right just because you are making a business trip.

  Avoid the temptation to stop in at the Pizza Hut or Haagen-Daz outlet in your airline terminal while you're waiting for your flight. When you're traveling, you have to make an extra effort to stick with your diet and exercise routine. And those espresso mochas you've grown so fond of on the way to work each day? They have *at least* 10,000 calories apiece (well, okay, we're exaggerating a bit). Watch it!

- **Have fun:** If you're not having fun, why bother? Look, you're going to spend roughly a fourth to a third of your adult life at work. Sure, you need the money, and you need the psychological satisfaction that doing a good job brings with it, but you should never take work so seriously that you can't have fun with your job and your coworkers.

  Someday, when you retire, would you rather be remembered as the manager who kept an eye on the company's cash flow, or would you prefer to be remembered for touching the lives of all those around you and making their jobs more rewarding in the process?

- **Learn how to say *no*:** What's the old saying? "You can please some of the people some of the time, but you can't please all the people all the time." That is, recognize that you can't do it all. And when you try to do it all, the result is that it doesn't get done well. When you already have a full plate of work to do and someone tries to lay on more, you must be able to say *no*.

- **Relax:** Relaxation is an extremely important part of any program of stress management. When you relax, you give your brain a break, and you provide yourself with the much needed opportunity to recharge your batteries before going back into overdrive.

  Every minute counts. Do you remember what breaks are? You may not have taken one for a while, so you may be a little rusty at it. When you take a break to relax, make a *real* break from your routine. Get up from your desk and go someplace where you can remove yourself from the day-to-day business at hand. If you stay at your desk, the chances are that someone will call and you'll feel compelled to answer the phone *(maybe it's important!)* or someone will barge into your office and need your immediate attention. *(Sorry, Bob, I hope I'm not interrupting anything, but you've got to help me out here!)* Go for a walk outside your building. Smell some flowers. Listen to the birds. Relax!

✔ **Manage your schedule:** If you don't manage your own schedule, someone will more than happy to manage it for you. Get a personal planner or desk calendar and take charge of the meetings you attend and the appointments you keep.

If someone invites you to a meeting, don't automatically agree to go. Find out the topic of the meeting and your expected role. If you don't think that the meeting is worth your time to attend, don't! When you are pursuing your *own* goals and priorities, keeping the goals and priorities of others from intruding can be incredibly difficult. Steadfastly refuse to let someone else's crisis become yours! For *much* more information about managing your schedule, take a look at Chapter 2.

✔ **Streamline:** Why make things harder than they have to be? As a manager, you're in the perfect position to be on the lookout for ways to improve your organization's work processes and systems. Be brutal in reviewing everything that your department does and remove needless steps. Simplify, shorten, and condense. Fewer steps in a process translates into your workforce expending less effort, fewer things going wrong, and, ultimately, less stress for you to endure. *This* is good.

✔ **Look for silver linings:** Be an optimist. Look for the good in everything you do and everyone you meet. You'll be amazed by how much better you feel about your job, your coworkers, and yourself. And you'll be just as amazed by how much better your coworkers feel about *you* when they can depend on you to lift *their* spirits. Be an ambassador of optimism: You'll decrease your own stress and the stress of those around you, too.

Accepting the things you can't change

You just can't change certain things, no matter how hard you try. Instead of changing the unchangeable, you only end up stressed, defeated, or ill. And such an outcome is not good in anyone's book. When you can't change the unchangeable, you have one choice left: Change yourself.

✔ **Surrender:** Stop fighting change. To continue the fight simply causes your stress level to go up — along with your blood pressure and the number of bottles of Maalox that it takes to quell the fire in your stomach. Surrender to change, become one with it. Instead of trying to row against the swift currents of change, let yourself go and drift with them.

Understand that you can use change to your advantage. After you stop fighting change, you can concentrate on making change work for you and for your organization.

✔ **Don't take it personally:** Change doesn't affect just *you*. Everyone has to deal with change and the effects of change on the working environment. But the question is not how everyone else responds to change; the question is how *you* respond to change. Do you retreat into your shell? Do you get frustrated and angry? Or do you take charge?

✔ **Adjust your attitude:** Losing perspective is sometimes easy to do. After you've worked at a job for a few years, you can begin to get visions of grandeur. How would the organization survive without you? Before long, you become resentful when your opinion isn't given the widespread respect that you feel it deserves, and you begin to dislike performing the mundane tasks that are a part of your job. (And forbid that someone would ask you to do them — they'd better watch out!)

As you get hot under the collar about your current status, remember that most Americans are only a couple of paychecks away from bankruptcy. How long could you survive if you lost your job? And don't think that you can't. Who do you think would be let go first: Employees who willing do *whatever* they can to get the job done or employees who think that they're above all that? If you picked the former, you may be due for a major attitude adjustment; adjust your own attitude before someone adjusts it for you!

✔ **Don't be a victim:** In this world, you can be a hammer, or you can be an anvil. If you're a victim of change, you've stopped fighting change (which is *good*), but you've also stopped responding at all to the changes going on around you (which is *bad*). Don't give up and unplug yourself from the organization. Refuse to be a victim of change and, instead, become its biggest fan.

✔ **Control your anger:** Getting mad when things don't go your way may be expressive, but showing anger is not a productive use of your time and energy. Being angry about something you can do nothing to change saps your energy and distracts you from accomplishing the things that you *can* do something about.

What do you do when you get stuck in rush hour traffic? Do you stew and fume? Does your blood pressure go up as your face begins to take on the color of *borscht*? Does your anger help you go any faster or get you home any sooner? No! Instead of wasting time trying to change the unchange-able, catch up on some phone calls, relax to some new tunes, or listen to a book on tape. Exchange your anger for a productive activity, or the anger may eat you alive!

✔ **Don't sweat the small stuff:** Much of what happens during the course of a normal business day is *small* stuff. Filling out forms, pulling messages off your voice-mail system, poking at a few buttons on your computer key-board. The *big* stuff can be few and far between. We assume that some-thing like 80 percent of your time is spent getting 20 percent of your results. The point is: Most of what you do is small stuff, so don't sweat the small stuff! If you're going to worry, at least save it for something that's *really* important!

Specific stress reduction exercises

While you're out there changing the things you can change and accepting the things you can't change, you can use specific exercises to reduce your stress. These exercises are great because you can do them anywhere: at the office, at home, or in your car on the way to work. Not only that, but the exercises are effective on any kind of stress, whatever the source. The next time you feel your stomach tying itself into knots and your blood pressure starting to rise, give these exercises a try:

- **Breath control:** In. Out. In. Out. That's it. Take a deep breath. Hold it; don't let go. Now, exhale slowly. Feel the stress leave your body as you let go of your breath. Controlled breathing can have a calming effect.

  When you feel stressed, give this ancient yoga breathing exercise a try: Breathe in through one nostril for a count of one while placing a finger against the side of your nose to close your other nostril. Hold the breath for eight counts and then exhale through your other nostril for four counts. Then reverse the procedure starting with your other nostril and repeat the exercise for a total of four complete cycles. You should be as cool as a cucumber about now.

- **Positive affirmations:** Crowd the negatives out of your life with positive affirmations such as, "Gee, I have really got this customer's needs figured out," or "I did a great job on that last assignment. I can't wait for another one so I can do a great job on that one, too." Get positive. The more positive your life, the less stress you experience. (Plus you'll be a lot more fun to be around than those naysayers you have to work with.)

- **Progressive relaxation:** Believe it or not, this highly beneficial exercise was discovered by a guy who was bowling at the time. Apparently, his arm had gotten quite tired from lugging his big bowling ball around the lanes. Somebody called his name and he dropped the ball. Hmmm. Nice trick.

  Anyway, you can use progressive relaxation to benefit you when you're away from the bowling lanes. Lie down in a darkened room; starting with your feet, concentrate on tensing up your muscles for several counts and then let the muscles in your feet relax. Next, move to your calves. Tense your calf muscles for several counts and then let them relax. Keep moving up the rest of your body until you get to the top of your head. Finally, tense all your muscles at once, and then relax. The result is a general release of tension and increased relaxation.

- **Mental vacation:** Imagination is a very powerful tool. No matter where you are, you can take a vacation anywhere you want, anytime you want. When the crowd at your door is five deep, your phone is ringing off the hook, everyone has a problem instead of a solution, and your blood pressure erupts like Krakatoa east of Java, a mental vacation is definitely in order.

  Close your door, forward your phone to the operator or to voice mail, turn down your lights, kick your ergonomic chair back into its full relax mode, and let your mind float downstream. Picture yourself in a boat on a river with the sun shining and the birds chirping. Take yourself far, far away from the challenges of the day.

✔ **Laugh:** Don't take things so seriously that you lose your sense of humor. Having fun with your job and with your coworkers is an important way to reduce stress on the job. Don't forget the saying, "All work and no play makes Johnny a very boring guy." Not only does a good laugh provide you with a great way to release stress, but it reminds you that life is more than work, work, work. *Right?*

When All Else Fails

If you've done everything you can to reduce stress, become a leader of change, and take control of your business life, but you're still stressed out, you may be facing a much deeper issue that's not readily apparent on the surface.

When you read a book, do you ever wish that you had written it? When you go to a seminar, do you ever think that you could teach it? Have you ever wondered what owning your own business is like: to be your own boss and to be completely responsible for your company's profits or losses?

If you answered *Yes* to any of these questions, you may not be truly happy until you pursue your *own* dream. Maybe you would like to start a new career or move to a new company. Or perhaps you have an opportunity with your current employer to make a job change that will take you to your dream. Maybe you want to go back to school to pursue an advanced degree. Or maybe you just want to take a vacation or short leave of absence. Find your dream and give it all you've got! Don't dream it — be it.

Test your new-found knowledge

What are the four stages of change?

A. Grieve, counter, befuddle, and quit

B. Organize, label, date, and file

C. Blame, hide, wait, and go home

D. Deny, resist, explore opportunities, and accept

Should you sweat the small stuff?

A. Yes, there isn't much small stuff.

B. No, save your sweat for the big stuff.

C. Maybe; it depends on which side of the bed you woke up on today.

D. None of the above.

Chapter 15

Employee Discipline: Speak Softly and Carry a Big Stick

. . . .

In This Chapter

▶ Disciplining your employees

▶ Focusing on performance

▶ Following the twin tracks of discipline

▶ Writing a script

▶ Developing an improvement plan

▶ Putting an improvement plan into action

. . . .

*W*ouldn't it be nice if all your employees carried out their tasks perfectly all the time? Wouldn't it be nice if they all loved the organization as much as you do? Winning the lottery would be nice, too, but you probably shouldn't quit your day job just yet.

The fact is that your employees *will* make mistakes, and some of them will exhibit attitudes that are, shall we say, *poor.* Every organization has employees who exhibit varying degrees of these behaviors, and you shouldn't worry too much about it. However, when your employees make repeated, serious mistakes, when they fail to meet their performance goals and standards, or when it seems that they would rather be working somewhere (*anywhere!*) else but where they are now (and they prove it to you by ignoring company policies), you have to take action to stop the offending behaviors — immediate and decisive action.

Keeping to what is expected of you is known as *accountability.* Correcting the performance and behavior of employees who have strayed off the right path is called *discipline.*

Why bother disciplining your employees? Wouldn't it be better to avoid a potential confrontation and hope that things will work themselves out over time? No! Absolutely not!

Two main reasons for this exist.

First, when employees are not performing up to standard, or when they allow a poor attitude to overcome their ability to pull with the rest of the team, these employees *cost* your organization more than do the employees who are working at or above standard and pulling their share of the load. Poor performance and poor attitudes directly and negatively affect the efficiency and effectiveness of your work unit.

Second, if other employees see that you are letting their coworkers get away with poor performance, they have little reason to maintain their own standards. *Hey! If Marty can get away with it, I can, too!* Not only do you create more management headaches than you started with, but the morale and performance of your entire work unit decreases as a result. This situation is *not* good!

In this chapter, you can discover the importance of dealing with employee performance issues before they become major problems. You can find out why you should focus on performance, not personality, and you can see a system of discipline that is consistent and will work for you, regardless of your line of business.

Disciplining Employees

Employee discipline has gotten something of a black eye of late. Because of the abuses that more than a few overzealous supervisors and managers have committed, for many workers, the word *discipline* conjures up visions of crazed management tirades, embarrassing public upbraidings, and worse. What does discipline mean to you? What does discipline mean in your organization? Do your employees look forward to being disciplined? Do you?

The reality is that far too many employees confuse the terms *discipline* and *punishment* — considering them to be one and the same thing. This belief can't be farther from the truth — at least when discipline is done well. The word *discipline* comes from the Latin *disciplina,* meaning *teaching* or *learning* (no, *not* despicable). *Punishment,* on the other hand, is derived from the Latin root *punire,* which itself is derived from the Latin word *poena,* or *penalty.* Interestingly, the English word *pain* also found its beginnings in the Latin *poena.*

The whole point of this little digression is that employee discipline is supposed to be a *positive* thing. At least it should be when you do it the right way! Through discipline, you bring problems to the attention of your employees so that they can take actions to correct them *before* they become major problems. The primary goal of discipline is not to punish your employees; it is to help guide them back to satisfactory job performance. Of course, sometimes this will not be possible, and you will have no choice but to terminate employees who cannot perform satisfactorily.

Two main reasons to discipline your employees exist:

- **Performance problems:** All employees are required to meet goals as a part of their jobs. For a receptionist, a goal might be to always answer the telephone on the second ring or sooner. For a sales manager, a goal might be to increase annual sales by 15 percent. When employees fail to meet their performance goals, administering some form of discipline is required.

- **Misconduct:** Sometimes employees behave in ways that are unacceptable to you as a manager and to the organization. If an employee abuses the company sick leave policy, for example, you have a valid reason for disciplining that employee. Similarly, employees who sexually harass or threaten other employees should expect to be disciplined by their managers.

Discipline ranges from simple verbal counseling *("William, you turned in the report a day late. I expect future reports to be submitted on time.")* to termination *("Sorry, Mary, I warned you that I would not tolerate any further insubordination. You're fired.")*. Between these two extremes lie a wide variety of options, the use of which depends on the nature of the problem, its severity, and the work history of the employee involved. For example, if the problem is an isolated incident, and the employee normally performs well, the discipline will be less severe than if the problem is repeated and persistent.

Always carry out discipline as soon after the incident as possible. As with *rewarding* employees, your message is much stronger and relevant when it has the immediacy of a recent event. If too much time lapses between an incident and the discipline that you conduct afterward, your employee may forget the specifics of the incident. Not only that, but you send the message that the problem is not *that* serious because you don't bother doing anything about it for so long.

Managers practice effective discipline by catching performance shortcomings or misconduct *before* these problems become serious. Effective managers help to guide their employees along the right path. Managers who don't discipline their employees have only themselves to blame when poor performance continues unabated or acts of misconduct escalate and get out of hand. Employees need the active support and guidance of their supervisors and managers to know what is expected of them. Without that, it's no wonder that employees sometimes find it difficult to keep from straying from the right path.

And don't forget: You get what you reward. Take a close look at the behavior you're rewarding in your employees. You may be surprised to find that you are inadvertently reinforcing negative behaviors and poor performance.

Don't put off discipline. Don't procrastinate. Don't look the other way and hope that your employees' bad behavior will go away. If you do, you're doing a disservice to the employees who need your guidance; you're doing a disservice to the employees who are working at or above standard; and you're doing a disservice to your organization. Discipline your employees before it's too late. Do it now.

Focus on Performance, Not Personalities

You are a manager (or a manager-to-be). You are not a psychiatrist or psychologist — even if you feel that you sometimes do nothing *but* counsel your employees. Your job is not to analyze the personalities of your employees or to attempt to understand why your employees act the way they do. Your job is to assess your employees' *performance* against the standards that you and your employees agree to and to be alert to employee violations of company policy. If your employees are performing above standard, reward them for their efforts. (See Chapter 6 for complete information on rewarding and motivating your employees.) If, on the other hand, they are performing *below* standard, you need to discipline them.

This is not to say that you shouldn't be compassionate. Sometimes performance suffers because of family problems, financial difficulties, or other non-job-related pressures. Although you should give your employees the opportunity to get through their difficulties — you might suggest some time off or a temporary reassignment of duties — they eventually have to return to meeting their performance standards.

To be fair, and to be sure that discipline focuses on *performance* and *not* on personalities, ensure that *all* employees are fully aware of company policies and that you communicate performance standards clearly. When new employees are hired into your organization, do they get an orientation to key company policies? When your human resources representative drops off new employees at your door, do you or someone in your department take the time to discuss your department's philosophy and practices? Do you periodically sit down with your employees to review and update their performance standards? If you say *no* to any of these questions, *you* need to get to work!

You *must* apply discipline consistently and fairly. Although you should *always* discipline your employees soon after a demonstrated shortfall in performance or act of misconduct, rushing to judgment before you have a chance to get all the facts is a mistake. Although proving that an employee submitted a report a week late is simple, uncovering the facts in a case of sexual harassment may not be so simple. When you discipline employees, you *must* know the facts and you *must* act impartially and without favoritism for certain employees. If one employee does something wrong, you can't ignore the same behavior in your other employees. To do so certainly risks the loss of employee respect for your management, and it definitely invites lawsuits and other such unpleasantness.

Remember, although *your* job is to point out your employees' shortcomings and to help guide your employees in their efforts to perform to standard, *they* are ultimately responsible for their performance and their behavior. You can't, and you shouldn't, do their work for them, and you shouldn't cover for their mistakes and misdeeds. Sure, you can and should excuse an occasional mistake, but you *must* deal with an ongoing pattern of substandard performance or misconduct.

The Two Tracks of Discipline

As the beginning of this chapter explained, two key reasons for disciplining employees exist: performance problems and misconduct. The two-track system of discipline includes one set of discipline options for performance problems and another for misconduct. These tracks reflect the fact that misconduct, usually being a willful act on the part of the employee, is considered a much more serious transgression than a shortfall in performance. Performance problems are often not the direct fault of the employee and can often be corrected with proper training or motivation.

These two tracks reflect the concept of *progressive discipline.* Progressive discipline means that you should always select the least severe step that results in the behavior that you want. For example, if your employee responds to a verbal warning and improves as a result, great; you can move on to your next management challenge. However, if the employee doesn't respond to a verbal warning, you then *progress* to the next step — a written warning — and give that a try. The hope is that your employee will get the hint and correct his or her behavior *before* you get to heavy-handed steps such as reductions in pay, demotions, or (*gulp!*) terminations.

As you prepare to discipline your employees, first decide whether the behaviors you are trying to correct are performance related or the result of misconduct. After you figure that out, decide the best way to get your message across. If the transgression is minor — a lack of attention to detail, for example — you may need only to conduct a verbal counseling. However, if you catch an employee sleeping on the job, you may decide to suspend your employee without pay for some period of time. The choice is *yours.*

In any case, make sure that the discipline takes place as soon as possible after the transgression occurs. You want to correct your employee's performance *before* the problem becomes major. You definitely *don't* want to make discipline only an annual event by saving up all your employee's problems for his or her periodic performance appraisal. *Ouch!*

Note: Your organization's system for disciplining employees may be somewhat different from the one that we outline in this chapter. If you are dealing with union-represented employees, you likely are required to work within the system proscribed by the contract between the union and your firm. You may, for example, be required to allow a union representative to sit in on any discipline sessions that you conduct with union-represented employees. If this is the case, be sure to review your organization's policies and labor relations practices and procedures before you embark on the task of disciplining your employees.

Dealing with performance problems: the first track

If you have done your job right, each of your employees has a job description and a set of performance standards. The job description is simply an inventory of all the different duties that accompany a particular position. Performance standards, on the other hand, are the measurements that you and your employees agree to use in assessing their performance. Performance standards form the basis of periodic performance appraisals and reviews. They also make great filler for your personnel files.

Although every organization seems to have its own unique way of conducting performance assessments, employees usually fall into one of three broad categories: outstanding performance, acceptable performance, and unacceptable performance. When it comes to employee discipline, you are primarily concerned with correcting unacceptable performance. You always want to help your good employees become even better employees, but your first concern has to be to identify employees who are not working up to standard and to correct their performance shortcomings.

The following steps are listed in order of least to most severe. Don't forget: Use the least severe step that results in the behavior you want. If that step doesn't do the trick, move down the list to the next step:

- **Verbal counseling:** This form of discipline is certainly the most common, and most managers take this step first when they want to correct an employee's performance. It's not uncommon for a manager to verbally counsel a variety of employees many times a day. Verbal counseling can range from a simple, spontaneous correction performed in the hallway (*"Marge, you need to let me know when our clients call with a service problem."*) to a more formal, sit-down meeting in your office (*"Sam, I am concerned that you don't understand the importance of checking the correct address prior to shipping orders. Let's discuss what steps you're going to take to correct this problem and your plan to implement them."*). You usually don't document verbal counseling in your employees' files.

- **Written counseling:** When employees don't respond favorably to verbal counseling, or when the magnitude of performance problems warrants its use, you should consider written counseling. Written counseling formalizes the counseling process by documenting your employees' performance shortcomings in a written memo. Written counseling is presented to employees in one-on-one sessions in the supervisor's office. After the employees have an opportunity to read the document, verbal discussions regarding the employees' plans to improve their performance ensue. This documentation becomes a part of your employees' personnel files.

✔ **Negative performance evaluation:** If verbal and written counseling fail to improve your employees' performance, the situation warrants a negative performance evaluation. Of course, because performance evaluations are generally given only annually, if at all, they are not usually very useful for dealing with acute situations. However, if you give verbal and written counseling to no avail, negative performance evaluations are the way to go.

✔ **Demotion:** Repeated negative performance evaluations or particularly serious performance shortcomings may warrant demoting your employees to a lower rung on the organizational ladder. Often, but not always, the pay of demoted employees is also reduced at the same time. Face it: Some employees are hired or promoted into positions that they just can't handle. This situation isn't their fault, but you can't let your employees continue to fail if you have no hope of bringing performance up to an acceptable level with further training or guidance. Although demoralizing, demotions at least allow your employees to move into positions that they can handle. Before you resort to demotion, always first try to find a position at an equivalent level that the employee *can* handle. This will help to improve your employee's motivation and self-confidence and result in a situation that is a "win" for both the employee *and* the organization.

✔ **Termination:** When all else fails, termination is the ultimate form of discipline for employees who are performing unsatisfactorily. As any manager who has fired an employee knows, terminating employees is not fun. You should consider it as an option only after you exhaust all other avenues. Perhaps needless to say, in these days of wrongful termination lawsuits and multimillion-dollar judgments, you must document employees' performance shortcomings *very* well and support them by the facts. For further information on the ins and outs of this very important form of discipline, see Chapter 16.

Dealing with misconduct: the second track

Misconduct is a whole different animal from performance problems, so it has its own discipline track. Although misconduct and performance problems both can have negative effects on a company's bottom line, misconduct is usually considered a much more serious transgression than performance shortcomings because it indicates a problem with your employees' attitudes or ethical beliefs. And modifying performance behaviors is much easier than modifying workers' attitudes or belief systems.

Even the terminology of the different steps in the second track indicates that something serious is going on here. For example, while the first step on the first track is called verbal *counseling,* the first step on the second track is called verbal *warning.* You need to deal with misconduct more severely than you deal with performance problems.

The discipline that results from misconduct also has much more immediate consequences to your employees than does the discipline that results from performance problems. Although performance may take some time to bring up to standard, what with preparing a plan, scheduling additional training, and so forth, misconduct has to stop *right now!* When you discipline your employees for misconduct, you put them on notice that their behavior will *not* be tolerated. Repeated misconduct can lead quickly to suspension and termination.

As in the first track, the following discipline steps are listed from least severe to most severe. Your choice depends on the severity of the misconduct and the work record of the employee:

✔ **Verbal warning:** When your employees' misconduct is minor or a first offense, the verbal warning provides the least severe option for putting your employees on notice that their behavior will not be tolerated. *("John, it's my understanding that you have continued to pressure Susan into going to lunch with you — even though she has told you on numerous occasions that she is not interested. This is not acceptable. I expect you to stop this harassing behavior immediately.")* In many cases of misconduct, a verbal warning that demonstrates to your employees that you are aware of the misconduct is all that correcting the situation requires.

✔ **Written warning:** Unfortunately, not all your employees get the message when you give them a verbal warning. Also, the magnitude of the offense may require that you skip the verbal warning and proceed directly to the written warning. Written warnings signal to your employees that you are serious and that you are documenting their behavior for their personnel files. An employee's immediate supervisor gives the written warning.

✔ **Reprimand:** Repeated or serious misconduct results in a reprimand. A reprimand is generally constructed in the same format as a written warning, but instead of being given by an employee's immediate supervisor, it is given by a manager higher up in the organization. This is the last chance for an employee to correct his or her behavior before suspension, demotion, or termination.

✔ **Suspension:** A *suspension,* or mandatory leave without pay, is used in cases of very serious misconduct or repeated misconduct that has not been corrected as a result of other, less severe attempts at employee discipline. You may have to remove employees from the workplace for a period of time to ensure the safety of your other employees or to repair the morale of your work unit. Employees may also be given nondisciplinary suspensions while they are being investigated on charges of misconduct. During a nondisciplinary suspension, employees are usually paid while the manager, human resources representative, or other company official reviews the case.

✔ **Demotion:** Although you can demote an employee for misconduct, doing so is generally not recommended. Demotions are most appropriate for correcting poor performance when an expectation exists that an employee will be able to meet standards at a lower level of responsibility.

✔ **Termination:** In particularly serious cases of misconduct, termination may be your first choice in disciplining a worker. This rule is particularly true for extreme violations of safety rules, theft, gross insubordination, and other serious misconduct. Termination may also be the result of repeated misconduct that less severe discipline steps do not correct. See Chapter 16 for more information about terminating employees.

Disciplining Employees: A Suite in Four Parts

A right way and many wrong ways to discipline employees exist. Forget the many wrong ways for now and focus on the *right* way.

Regardless of which kind of discipline you select for the particular situation, the approach that you should take with your employees remains the same — whether you conduct verbal counseling or give a suspension or demotion (because of their finality, terminations are an exception here). Four steps should *always* form the basis of your discipline script. By following these steps, you can be sure that your employees understand *what* the problem is, *why* it's a problem, and what they need to do to correct the problem.

Describe the unacceptable behavior

Exactly what is your employee doing that is unacceptable? When describing unwanted behavior to an employee, make sure that you are excruciatingly specific. This is no time for mushy, amorphous statements such as "You have a bad attitude," or "You make a lot of mistakes," or "I don't like your work habits." *Huh?*

Always relate unacceptable behaviors to specific performance standards that have not been met or to specific policies that have been broken. Specify exactly *what* the employee did wrong and *when* the behavior occurred. And don't forget to focus on the *behavior* and not on the *individual. Just the facts, ma'am.*

Following are some examples for you to consider:

- ✔ "Your performance last week was below the acceptable standard of 250 units per hour."
- ✔ "You failed the drug test that you took on Monday."
- ✔ "The last three analyses that you submitted to me contained numerous computational errors."
- ✔ "You have been late to work three out of four days this week."

Express the impact to the work unit

When an employee engages in unacceptable behavior — whether his or her work doesn't meet standards or whether he or she engages in misconduct — a work unit is *always* affected negatively. When an employee is consistently late to work, for example, you may have to assign someone else to cover your employee's position until the offender arrives. Doing so takes your other employee away from the work that he or she should be doing, reducing the efficiency and effectiveness of the work unit. And if an employee engages in sexual harassment, the morale and effectiveness of the workers who are subjected to the harassment necessarily suffer.

Continuing with the examples that we started in the preceding section, following are the next steps in your discipline script:

- ✔ "Because of your below-standard performance, the work unit didn't meet its overall targets for the week."
- ✔ "This is a specific violation of our drug-free workplace policy."
- ✔ "Because of these errors, I now have to take extra time to review your work much more thoroughly before I can forward it up the chain."
- ✔ "Because of your tardiness, I had to pull Margeaux from her position to cover yours."

Specify changes required

Telling your employee that he or she did something wrong does little good if you don't also tell that employee what he or she needs to do to correct the behavior. As a part of your discipline script, tell your employee the exact behavior that you want him or her to adopt. The behavior should be in accordance with an established performance standard or company policy.

Following are some examples of the third part of your discipline script:

- ✔ "You must bring your performance up to the standard of 250 units per week or better immediately."

- ✔ "You will be required to set an appointment with the company's employee assistance program for drug counseling."

- ✔ "I expect your work to be error free before you submit it to me for approval."

- ✔ "I expect you to be in your seat, ready to work, at 8:00 a.m. *every* morning."

Outline the consequences

Of course, no discipline would be complete without a discussion of what is going to happen if the unacceptable behavior continues. Here's your big chance to give your employee fair warning of the consequences of continued performance or misconduct. Make sure that you get the message across clearly and unequivocally and that your employee understands it.

Finally, the icing on the pineapple upside-down cake that is employee discipline:

- ✔ "If you can't meet the standard, you will be reassigned to the training unit to improve your skills."

- ✔ "If you refuse to undergo drug counseling, you will be suspended from work without pay for five days."

- ✔ "If the accuracy of your work does not improve immediately, I will have to issue a written counseling to be placed in your employee file."

- ✔ "If you are late again, I will request that the general manager issue a formal reprimand in your case."

Putting it all together

After you develop the four parts of your discipline script, put them together into a unified statement that you deliver to your wayward employees. Although you will undoubtedly discuss the surrounding issues in some detail, this script should be the heart of your discipline session.

The four parts of the script work together to produce the final product as follows:

✔ "Your performance last week was below our standard of 250 units per hour. Because of your below-standard performance, the work unit didn't meet its overall targets for the week. You must bring your performance up to the standard of 250 units per week or better immediately. If you can't meet the standard, you will be reassigned to the training unit to improve your skills."

✔ "You failed the drug test that you took on Monday. This is a specific violation of our drug-free workplace policy. You will be required to set an appointment with the company's employee assistance program for drug counseling. If you refuse to undergo drug counseling, you will be suspended from work without pay for five days."

✔ "The last three analyses that you have submitted to me contained numerous computational errors. Because of these errors, I now have to take extra time to review your work much more thoroughly before I can forward it up the chain. I expect your work to be error free before you submit it to me for approval. If the accuracy of your work does not improve immediately, I will have to issue written counseling to be placed in your employee file."

✔ "You have been late to work three out of four days this week. Because of your tardiness, I had to pull Margeaux from her position to cover yours. I expect you to be in your seat, ready to work, at 8:00 a.m. *every* morning. If you are late again, I will request that the general manager issue a formal reprimand in your case."

Making a Plan for Improvement

Managers *love* plans: plans for completing projects on time, plans for meeting the organization's financial goals in five years, and plans to develop more plans. In the case of employee discipline, one more plan exists. The *performance improvement plan* is a crucial part of the discipline process because it sets definite steps for the employee to undertake to improve performance within a fixed period of time.

If your employee's performance transgressions are minor, and you are giving only verbal counseling, working up a performance plan is probably overkill. Also, because most instances of misconduct must by nature be corrected *right now or else,* performance improvement plans are generally not appropriate for correcting employee misconduct. However, if your employee's poor performance is habitual and you have selected counseling or more severe discipline, a performance plan is *definitely* what the doctor ordered. *Take two and call me in the morning!*

A performance improvement plan consists of the following three parts:

- ✓ **Goal statement:** The goal statement provides clear direction to your employees about what it takes to make satisfactory improvement. The goal statement — which should be tied directly to your employee's performance standards — might be something along the lines of "Completes all his assignments on or before agreed deadlines," or "Is at her station ready to work at exactly 8:00 a.m. every day."

- ✓ **Schedule for attainment:** What good is a plan without a schedule? It's sort of like eating an ice cream cone without the ice cream. Or like watching TV with the sound turned off. Every good plan needs a definite completion date with fixed milestones along the way if the plan for goal attainment is complex.

- ✓ **Required resources/training:** The performance improvement plan should also contain a summary of any additional resources or training that will be brought to bear to help your employee bring his or her performance up to snuff.

Here's a sample performance improvement plan for a worker who makes repeated errors in typed correspondence:

Performance Improvement Plan

Jack Smith

Goal statement:

- ✓ Complete all drafts of typed correspondence with two or fewer mistakes per document.

Schedule for attainment:

- ✓ Jack must meet the above goal within three months after the date of this plan.

Required resources/training:

- ✓ Jack will be enrolled in the company refresher course in typing and reviewing correspondence. This training must be successfully completed not later than two months after the date of this plan.

Implementing the Improvement Plan

After you put performance improvement plans in place, your job is to ensure that they don't just gather dust on your employees' shelves. Follow up with your employees to make sure that they are acting on their plans and making progress toward the goals that you both agreed to. Yes, following up on improvement plans takes time, but that time is *very* well spent. Besides, if *you* can't find the time to check your employees' progress on their improvement plans, you shouldn't be surprised if *they* don't find the time to work on them.

Are your employees following through with the goal statements that you agreed to? Do they even *have* the goal statements that you agreed to? Are they keeping to their schedules, and are they receiving the training and other resources that you agreed to provide? If not, you need to emphasize the importance of the improvement plans with your employees and work with them to figure out why they haven't been implemented as agreed.

One of the best things you can do to assist your employees in implementing their improvement plans is to schedule regular progress reporting meetings with them on a daily, weekly, or monthly basis. More extensive improvement plans necessitate more frequent follow-up. Progress meetings serve two functions. First, they provide you with the information that you need to know to assess the your employees' progress toward meeting their plans. Second, they demonstrate to your employees — clearly and unequivocally — that their progress is important to you. If you demonstrate that the plans are important to *you,* your employees will make the plans a priority in their busy schedules.

Set up performance improvement plans with your employees and stick with them. You'll be glad you did — and so will your employees.

Test your new-found knowledge

What are the two different tracks of employee discipline?

A. Performance problems and misconduct

B. Progressive discipline and termination

C. Counseling and coaching

D. None of the above

What are the three parts of a performance improvement plan?

A. Verbal counseling, written counseling, and negative performance evaluation

B. Written counseling, written warning, and reprimand

C. Goal statement, schedule for attainment, and required resources/training

D. Top, middle, and bottom

Chapter 16

Too Little, Too Late: Terminating Employees

. . . .

In This Chapter

▶ Understanding the kinds of termination

▶ Conducting layoffs

▶ Taking necessary precautions before terminating an employee

▶ Firing employees: a step-by-step approach

▶ Deciding at what time to terminate employees

. . . .

*B*eing a manager is a tough job. If people tell you that the job is easy, they're either joking or lying. Challenging, yes. Constantly changing, yes. Satisfying, yes. Easy, no. And of all the tough jobs that managers have to do routinely, firing employees has got to be the absolute toughest. No matter how many times you do it, it never gets any easier.

The mechanics of terminating employees — setting goals, gathering data, assessing performance, carrying out discipline, and completing the paperwork — aren't so tough. The tough part is all the emotional baggage that goes along with firing someone — especially someone you have worked with for some time and have shared good times and bad times with. However, no matter how difficult it is to take an employee aside and tell that employee that his or her services are no longer needed, sometimes doing so is your only option.

No matter how much you try to help someone succeed in your organization, sometimes that person's employment at your firm just isn't meant to be. The question is: Who is going to recognize the problem first, and who is going to take action?

You see, terminations aren't limited only to *your* discretion. Sometimes employees "fire" themselves. *I quit!* If you're lucky, you'll get two weeks' notice. If you're not so lucky, you'll get less. In any case, you're going to be awfully busy for a while as you work your way through the hiring process. See Chapter 5 for more information about hiring good employees.

This chapter deals with why employees are terminated, the different kinds of terminations, and exactly how you can carry them out. You discover the difference between a layoff and a firing as well as the importance of documentation to support your actions.

Terminations for Every Occasion

When you say the word *termination,* most people immediately think of the process of firing a worker who is not doing his or her job. Although firing is the most dramatic and potentially volatile form of termination (just ask any manager who has had to deal with an employee who exploded during a termination), terminations come in many different flavors, depending on the situation.

Two major categories of employee termination exist: voluntary and involuntary. The key difference between the two is that an employee undertakes a voluntary termination of his or her own free will, while involuntary terminations are carried out against the will of the employee — often with the employee kicking and screaming. The following sections describe each category of termination.

Voluntary terminations

Employees have many reasons to terminate their *own* employment. Yeah, we know — that *anyone* would voluntarily choose to leave your particular brand of workers' paradise is hard to believe, but leave they do, and for all kinds of reasons. Sometimes employees find better promotional or pay opportunities with another firm. Sometimes employees find themselves in dead-end work situations or leave because of personality conflicts with their manager or other employees. Sometimes employees leave because of emotional stress, family needs, chemical dependency, or other personal reasons.

In some cases of voluntary termination, you don't want your employees to leave; in others, you actively *encourage* them to go. And every once in a while, an employee actually stays with your firm long enough to retire. Because so few people seem to stay *anywhere* long enough to retire anymore, this phenomenon is always a shock to employees.

So the main reasons employees voluntarily leave are the following:

- ✔ **Resignation (not encouraged):** An unencouraged resignation occurs when an employee decides to quit his or her position with your firm with no prodding or suggestion to do so from you. Unfortunately, the best employees always seem to be the ones who resign. Although you can't force someone to stay with your organization forever (nor would you want to), you *can* make sure that people aren't leaving because problems in your organization are not being addressed adequately. A certain department experiencing a lot of turnover, for example, is a warning sign that work conditions are too stressful or that the supervisor or manager needs an attitude adjustment.

- ✔ **Resignation (encouraged):** An encouraged resignation occurs when you suggest to an employee that he or she quit his or her job. Such resignations are often used as face-saving measures for employees who are about to be fired; instead of firing your employees, you can offer them the opportunity to resign. This approach can help to dampen the hurt of being fired, plus it keeps a potentially damaging employment action off the employees' records.

- ✔ **Retirement:** Retirement happens when an employee reaches the end of his or her career and decides to terminate his or her employment finally and forever.

Involuntary terminations

Of course, not all terminations are as easy to deal with as the voluntary forms mentioned in the preceding section. Involuntary terminations are seldom pleasant experiences — for either manager or employee — and you really have to be at the end of your rope before you invoke this ultimate sanction against an employee. Involuntary terminations come in two types:

- ✔ **Layoffs:** A *layoff,* also known as a *reduction in force,* occurs when an organization decides to terminate a certain number of employees for financial reasons. If, for example, your company loses several key contracts and the revenue that was projected to come with them, to stay afloat, your firm may have no choice but to reduce payroll costs through layoffs.

  Every company has its own policy for determining the order of layoffs. In some organizations, the last employee hired is the first to go. In others, employee performance determines layoffs. Most organizations give hiring preference to laid-off employees if and when financial health is restored.

- ✔ **Firing:** Employees are fired when they have no hope of improving their performance or when they commit an act of misconduct that is so serious that termination is the only choice.

An 1884 Tennessee court decision (*Payne* v. *Western & A.R.P. Co.,* 81 Tenn. 507) established the termination-at-will rule. This rule said that employers have the right to terminate employees for any reason whatsoever — including *no* reason — unless a contract between employer and employee expressly prohibits such an action. However, more than 100 years of court decisions, union agreements, and state and federal laws have eroded the ability of employers to terminate employees at will. The federal government, in particular, has had the greatest effect on the termination-at-will rule, particularly in cases of discrimination against employees for a wide variety of reasons.

Federal regulations such as the Civil Rights Act of 1964, the Equal Employment Opportunity Act of 1991, the Age Discrimination in Employment Act, and others prohibit terminating employees specifically because of their age, race, gender, color, religion, national origin, and other federally mandated exclusions. To ignore these prohibitions is to invite a nasty and expensive lawsuit. Even the mere *appearance* of discrimination in the termination process (or anywhere else in your firm) can get you into trouble. In fact, most former employees who bring wrongful termination cases to court today win their cases.

Good reasons for firing your employees

As long as you aren't discriminating against your employees when you terminate them, you *still* have quite a lot of discretion as a manager. Although you generally have the right to terminate employees at will, you may find yourself on thin legal ice depending on the specific grounds that you select for firing your employees.

People generally agree, however, on certain behaviors that merit firing. Some of these behaviors are considered *intolerable offenses* that merit immediate action — no verbal counseling, no written warning, and no reprimand or suspension. Immediate and unequivocal termination. Right now! They include:

- **Verbal abuse of others:** Verbal abuse includes cursing, repeated verbal harassment, malicious insults, and other similar behaviors. Your employees have the right to do their jobs in a workplace that is free of verbal abuse. And verbal abuse of customers and other business associates is just plain bad for business. If your employees continue to verbally abuse others after you give them fair warning, you can fire them without fear of legal repercussions.

- **Incompetence:** Despite your continued efforts to train them, some employees just aren't cut out for their jobs. If you have tried to help them and they still can't perform their duties at an acceptable level of competence, parting ways is clearly in the best interest of both the employee and the firm.

- **Repeated, unexcused tardiness:** You depend on your employees to get their jobs done as scheduled. Not only does tardiness jeopardize the ability of your employees to complete their tasks on time, but it also sets a *very* bad example for your employees who are punctual. If your employees continue to be late to work *after* you warn them that you won't tolerate this behavior, you have clear grounds for termination.

✔ **Insubordination:** Insubordination — the deliberate refusal to carry out one's duties — is grounds for immediate termination without warning. Although it's not uncommon for supervisors to encourage their employees to question *why* a decision is made, after the decision is made, the employees must carry it out. If they are unwilling to follow your direction, the basic employer-employee relationship breaks down, and you don't have to tolerate it.

✔ **Physical violence:** Most companies take employee-initiated physical violence and threats of violence very seriously. Employees have the right to do their jobs in a safe workplace; employers have the duty to provide a safe workplace. Physical violence jeopardizes your employees' safety and distracts them from doing their jobs. If an employee threatens coworkers, clients, or others with physical violence or actually carries out a violent threat, you can safely fire that employee immediately.

✔ **Theft:** Theft of company property and the property of coworkers or clients is another big no-no. Most companies that catch employees engaging in this nasty little practice terminate them immediately and without warning. If you decide to terminate an employee for theft, and you have concrete proof that the employee carried out the crime, you can do so knowing that you are on firm legal ground.

✔ **Intoxication on the job:** Although being drunk or under the influence of drugs on the job is sufficient grounds for immediate termination, many companies nowadays offer their employees the option of undergoing counseling with an employee assistance program or enrolling in a program such as Alcoholics Anonymous. In many cases, employees can rehabilitate themselves and return to regular service.

✔ **Falsification of records:** Falsifying records is another big no-no that can lead to immediate dismissal. This category includes providing fraudulent information during the hiring process (fake schools, degrees, previous jobs, and so on) and producing other fraudulent information during the course of employment (fake expense reports, falsified timecards, cheating on examinations, and so on).

Reasons why some managers avoid the inevitable

As you know, terminating an employee is not a pleasant way to spend an afternoon. Most managers would prefer to do most anything else. *John, maybe we should go for a quick swim in the shark tank.* While the reasons for terminating employees listed in the preceding section are clear cut and relatively easy for managers to use as leverage in a termination, having that leverage doesn't make the task any easier.

Some managers avoid carrying out a termination because of these reasons:

- ✔ **Fear of the unknown:** Terminating an employee can be a frightening prospect — especially if you're getting ready to do it for the first time. Is your employee going to cry? Have a heart attack or stroke? Get mad? Punch you out? Don't worry, every manager has to experience a first time. Unfortunately, the last time never seems to come around until you retire.

- ✔ **Emotional involvement:** Considering that you likely spend from one-fourth to one-third of your waking hours at work, becoming friends with some of your employees is natural. Doing so is fine until you have to discipline or terminate one or more of your friends. Letting *any* employee go is tough enough, much less an employee with whom you have developed an emotional attachment.

- ✔ **Fear of a negative reflection upon yourself:** If you have to terminate one of your employees, what are you saying about yourself as a manager? In the case of a layoff, is it *your* fault that the organization did not attain its goals? If you are firing an employee, did *you* make the wrong choice when you decided to hire that person? Many managers would rather put up with performance problems in their employees than draw attention to their own shortcomings — whether real or perceived.

- ✔ **Possibility of legal action:** The fear of legal action is often enough to stop a bull moose in his tracks at 50 paces. In these days of runaway, sue-at-the-drop-of-a-hat (or spill-of-a-cup-of-coffee) litigation, it's no wonder that managers are scared witless to terminate their employees.

- ✔ **Hope that the problem will just go away:** Yeah, right. Don't hold your breath.

Conducting a Layoff

Call it what you like: a reduction in force, a downsizing, a rightsizing, a re-engineering, or whatever. The causes and results are still the same. Your *organization* needs to cut payroll and related personnel and facilities costs, and some of your *employees* need to go.

Layoffs, although understandably traumatic for those involved, are different from firings because the employees who are terminated are generally not at direct fault. They are usually good employees who follow the rules. They are productive and do their jobs. They are loyal and dedicated workers. The real culprits are usually *external* factors such as changes in markets, mergers and acquisitions, and pressures of a more competitive global marketplace.

When you are left with no alternative but to conduct a layoff of personnel, use the following step-by-step guide to help you through the process:

1. **Determine the extent of the problem and figure out which departments will be affected.**

   How deep is the financial hole that your organization has found itself in? Does the possibility that fortunes will change anytime soon exist? If certain products or services aren't selling, which departments are affected?

2. **Freeze hiring.**

   Hiring employees during a layoff process doesn't make sense unless the position is *absolutely* critical — for example, if a receptionist quits, and you still need someone to answer the phones and receive visitors. Not only do you risk laying off a new hire, but hiring at this time sends the wrong message to your employees: that you don't care about your current employees.

3. **Prepare tentative lists of employees to be laid off.**

   After you determine the extent of the problem and the affected departments, the next step is to determine *which* employees will be laid off. Of primary importance at this stage is figuring out which employees have the most skill and experience in the areas that the organization needs, and which employees have the least. The first employees to go in a layoff are usually those whose skills and experience don't mesh with the needs of the organization.

4. **Notify all employees of planned layoffs in advance.**

   Once the need for a layoff seems certain, get the word out to all employees *immediately* and well in advance of the planned layoff. Fully disclose the financial and other problems that your organization faces and solicit employee suggestions for ways to cut costs or improve efficiency. Sometimes employee suggestions can save you enough money to avert the layoff or at least soften its blow on the organization. Err on the side of overcommunication.

5. **Fully explore alternatives to layoffs.**

   Can you cut costs by improving processes or through attrition, demotions, or early retirement? Can employees be transferred to more financially healthy divisions? Can you find savings in discretionary expenses such as budgeted travel, facility improvements, or through deferral of capital purchases?

6. **Prepare a final list of employees to be laid off.**

   After you turn the organization upside down to find potential savings, you need to prepare a list of employees to be laid off. The list should be rank-ordered in the event of a change that might allow you to remove employees from the list. Most companies have standard procedures for ranking employees for layoff — especially if workers are represented by a union.

These procedures generally give preference to permanent employees over temporary ones and include seniority and/or performance in the formula for determining who stays and who goes. If you *don't* have a policy, it is up to you to determine the basis for laying off employees. In this case, you want to consider your employees' experience and how long they have been with their organization. Be careful not to discriminate against protected workers — older employees, for example — who are good performers.

7. **Notify affected employees.**

By now, many employees will be virtually paralyzed with the fear that they will be let go. As soon as you finish developing the layoff list, notify the affected employees. Private, one-on-one meetings are the best way to handle notification.

8. **Provide outplacement services to terminated employees.**

If time and money permit, provide outplacement and counseling support to the employees being terminated. Your organization can provide training in subjects such as resume writing, financial planning, interviewing, and networking, and allow the employees to use company-owned computers, fax machines, and telephones in their job searches. If you can help your employees by providing job leads or contacts, by all means do so.

9. **Terminate.**

Conduct one-on-one termination meetings with employees to finalize arrangements and complete termination paperwork. Explain the severance package, continuation of benefits, and any other company-sponsored termination programs as appropriate. Collect keys, identification badges, and any company-owned equipment and property. Escort your newly terminated, former employees out of the facility and wish them well.

10. **Rally the "survivors."**

Rally your remaining employees together in an "all-hands" meeting to let them know that, now that the layoffs are completed, the firm is back on the road to good financial health. Tell the team that, to avoid future layoffs, you will have to pull together to overcome this momentary downturn in the business cycle.

Warning: Before You Fire an Employee . . .

Although the concept of "at-will" employees isn't dead *yet,* it might as well be with all the strings that are now attached to firing. Firing an employee is unpleasant enough without having to get dragged through the courts on a charge of wrongful termination. The problem is that, although most organizations have clear procedures for disciplining employees, some managers still ignore these procedures in the heat of the moment. Seemingly minor oversights on the part of managers can lead to *major* monetary damage awards in favor of former employees.

Before you fire an employee for cause, make sure that you can meet the following criteria and your ducks are all lined up in a nice, neat row. Take our word for it: You'll be glad you did!

- ✔ **Documentation:** Remember the rule: Document, document, and then document some more. If you are firing an employee because of performance shortcomings, you better have the performance data to back up your assertions. If you are firing an employee for stealing, you better have *proof* that this employee is the thief. You can never have *too much* documentation. This rule is *always* true when you take personnel actions, and it's *especially* true when you terminate an employee.

- ✔ **Fair warning:** Were your employees' performance standards spelled out clearly to them *in advance*? Did you explain company policies and practices along with your expectations? Have you given your employees fair warning of the consequences of continued performance problems? Because of the American legal tradition of due process, terminating an employee without warning for *performance*-related behaviors is generally considered unfair. However, certain kinds of employee misconduct, including physical violence, theft, and fraud, are grounds for immediate termination without warning.

- ✔ **Response time:** Have you given your employees enough time to rectify their performance shortcomings? The amount of time considered reasonable to improve performance depends on the nature of the problem to be addressed. If, for example, the problem is tardiness, you would expect the behavior to be corrected immediately. However, if the employee is to improve performance on a complex and lengthy project, demonstrating improvement may take weeks or months for the employee.

- ✔ **Reasonableness:** Are your company's policies and practices reasonable? Are the performance standards that you set with your employees achievable by the average worker? Does the penalty match the severity of the offense? Put yourself in the employee's shoes. If *you* were being terminated, would you consider the grounds for termination to be reasonable? Be honest!

- ✔ **Avenues for appeal:** Does your firm offer employees ways to appeal your decision to higher-level management? Again, the tradition of due process requires that an avenue for terminated employees to present their cases to higher management exist. Sometimes a direct supervisor is too close to the problem or too emotionally involved, which can cause errors in judgment that someone who is not personally involved in the situation can see easily.

The Big Day: Firing an Employee in Three Steps

Don't forget: While your job is to point out your employees' shortcomings and help your employees perform to standard, the *employees* are ultimately responsible for their performance and behavior. When you arrive at the last disciplinary step prior to firing your employees, letting them know that the responsibility and choice are theirs and theirs alone is important; you can't do this critical thing for them. Your employees either improve their performance or leave. The choice is theirs.

Assuming that the employee has made his or her choice, and that choice is to continue the misconduct or below-standard performance, the choice is then *yours*. And your choice is to terminate before the employee does any more damage to your organization.

You should keep two key goals in mind when firing employees. First, provide a clear explanation for the firing. According to legal experts, many employees file wrongful termination lawsuits simply in hopes of discovering the *real* reason why they were fired. Second, seek to minimize resentment against your company and yourself by taking action to maintain the dignity of your employee throughout the termination process. The world is a dangerous enough place without incurring the wrath of potentially unstable former employees.

You should fire an employee in a one-on-one meeting in your office or other private location. The meeting should be concise and to the point; figure on setting aside approximately 5 to 10 minutes for the meeting. Termination meetings are not intended to be discussions or debates. Your job is to inform your employee that he or she is being fired. This meeting isn't going to be fun, but keep in mind that you are taking the best course of action for all concerned.

- ✔ **Tell the employee that he or she is being terminated.** State simply and unequivocally that you have made the decision to fire. Be sure to note that all relevant evidence was considered, that the decision was reviewed and agreed to by all levels of your organization's management, and that the decision is *final*. If you did your homework and used a system of progressive discipline in an attempt to correct your employee's behavior, the announcement should come as no surprise. Of course, no matter the circumstances, a firing shakes *anyone* to the core.

- ✔ **Explain exactly why the employee is being terminated.** If the firing is the result of misconduct, cite the policy that was broken and exactly what your employee did to break it. If the firing is due to a failure to meet performance standards, remind the employee of past counselings and attempts to correct his or her performance and the subsequent incidents that led to the decision to fire. Stick to the facts.

- ✔ **Announce the effective date of the termination and provide details on the termination process.** A firing is normally effective on the day that you conduct your termination meeting. Keeping a fired employee around is awkward for both you and your employee and should be avoided at all costs. If you are offering a severance package or other termination benefits, explain them to your employee as well as how he or she is to make arrangements for gathering personal effects from his or her office. Go through the termination paperwork with the employee and explain the handling of final wages due.

Termination can be quite traumatic for the employee on the receiving end of the news. Expect the unexpected. While one employee may quickly become an emotional wreck, another may become belligerent and verbally abusive. To help defuse these situations, consider applying the following techniques:

- **Empathize with your employee.** Don't try to sugarcoat the news, but be understanding of your employee's situation. The news you have just delivered is among the worst news that anyone can get. If your employee becomes emotional or cries, don't try to stop it — hand the person a tissue and go on.

- **Be matter of fact and firm.** Even if your employee becomes unglued, you must maintain a calm, businesslike demeanor throughout the termination meeting. Don't lead your employee to believe that he or she is participating in a negotiating session or that he or she can do something to change your mind. Be firm in your insistence that the decision is final and not subject to change.

- **Keep the meeting on track.** Although letting your employee vent his or her feelings is appropriate, don't allow the employee to steer the meeting from the main goal of informing him or her that the decision to fire has been made. If the employee becomes abusive, inform the employee that you will end the meeting immediately if he or she can't maintain control.

You might find it helpful to prepare a termination script to read during the termination meeting. A script is beneficial because it helps to ensure that you don't forget to mention an important piece of information, and it provides instant documentation for your employee's personnel file.

Here is a sample termination script for an employee with ongoing performance problems:

"Katie, we have decided that today is your last day of employment with the firm. The reason for this decision is that you are not able to maintain the performance standards that we agreed to when you were hired last year. As you know, we have discussed your failure to meet standards on many occasions over the past year. Specifically, the written counseling that I gave you on the 5th of October notified you that you had one month to bring your performance up to standard or you could be terminated. You did not achieve this goal, and I therefore have no other choice but to terminate your employment, effective today. Jenny from personnel is here to discuss your final pay and benefits and to collect your office keys and voice mail password."

When Is the Best Time to Terminate?

Any manager likely has his or her own idea of what day of the week and time of the day you should select to terminate your employees. Monday terminations are the way to go because of A, B, and C. Or Friday terminations are best because of X, Y, and Z. And is it better to carry out a termination the first thing in the morning, or should you wait until the close of business?

We think that carrying out terminations on Fridays rather than earlier in the week makes the most sense. Doing so allows your employee to take the weekend to sort out feelings, pick up the Sunday want ads, and immediately start looking for a new job. If you terminate an employee on a Monday, you totally disrupt his or her normal routine.

So what time is the best to terminate? Again, think in terms of "later is better." If you wait until a time at or near the close of business, fewer of the employee's coworkers will be around to question the events that transpire. Your employee will have the opportunity to clear out his or her belongings while retaining dignity and self-pride. Also, your employee will be less able to make nasty calls to your boss or poison the well with customers or coworkers.

If you terminate employees earlier in the day, they have to face their coworkers and explain why they are packing up their belongings and why the security guard is preparing to escort them off the premises. Your intent isn't to punish or embarrass your employees — you want to make the termination process as painless and humane as possible. Allow them to save face by scheduling the termination meeting at a time when you can avoid public display.

Test your new-found knowledge

What are the two kinds of involuntary terminations?

A. Retirement and resignation

B. Resignation and firing

C. Layoff and retirement

D. Layoff and firing

What are five good reasons for firing an employee?

A. Incompetence, insubordination, theft, intoxication on the job, and falsification of records

B. Bad attitude, speaking his or her mind, bucking authority, asking for a raise, and speaking before spoken to

C. Working too late, failing to take breaks, forgetting to turn off the office coffee pot, working on weekends, and taking work home

D. None of the above

Part VI
Tools and Techniques for Managing

The 5th Wave   By Rich Tennant

"The new technology has really helped me get organized. I keep my project reports under the PC, budgets under my laptop, and memos under my pager."

In this part . . .

Although you don't have to be a technical wizard to be a manager, it pays to be familiar with some of the key tools and technologies that drive business today. In this part, we consider the basics of accounting and budgeting and the importance of computers in the workplace. We also talk about how to develop employee skills and create a learning organization.

Chapter 17

Budgeting, Accounting, and Other Money Stuff

· ·

In This Chapter

▶ Creating your budget

▶ Applying professional budget tricks

▶ Understanding accounting basics

▶ Interpreting financial statements

· ·

*I*n any organization, money makes the world go around. No matter how great your department is, how exciting your products are, or what a swell bunch of workers you employ, you and your group are in big-time jeopardy if you don't have money. If profits are down and money is increasingly tight in your organization, you'd better take some actions to correct the situation (or revise your resume and reinitiate your personal network of business contacts).

As a manager, you need to understand the basics of budgeting and accounting. When your coworkers start throwing around such terms as *labor budget, cash flow, income statement,* and *balance sheet,* wouldn't you like to be able to do more than simply nod your head and respond with a blank stare? Here's some good news: You *don't* need an MBA to grasp these basics.

If computers and computer networks are the central nervous system of a business, accounting and finance (and the money that they measure and manipulate) are its lifeblood: its veins, arteries, platelets, and corpuscles. So what does it mean when your business is feeling a little queasy and the room starts to spin? That's right — you need a cash infusion!

In this chapter, we cover the importance of budgeting in an organization, as well as putting together a budget by using some of the professional tricks of the budget trade. We then introduce the *survival* basics of accounting. We aren't going to make you an accountant *(whew!),* but this chapter *can* help you to remove that quizzical look that gets pasted to your face every time someone starts talking balance sheets or cash flow. And don't forget: Although you may work for a governmental entity or nonprofit organization, and some of these concepts may not apply to you, you never know when you might find yourself in a new, private-sector job!

The Wonderful World of Budgets

Budgets provide the baseline of *expected* performance against which managers measure *actual* performance. The actual performance of an organization is provided by accounting systems that also generate reports to compare expected performance against actual performance. With this information, managers with budget responsibility act as physicians to assess the current financial health of their businesses.

The latest accounting report says that sales are too low compared to budget? Then the responsible manager (this means *you!*) needs to figure out why. Are prices too high? Maybe your sales force is having problems getting product delivered to customers quickly. Or perhaps your competition developed a new thingamajig that is taking sales away from your product. Are labor costs exceeding your budget? Perhaps your employees are working too much overtime. Maybe a reduction in production quality has led to an increase in the amount of rework required. Or employee pay simply could be too high.

Because change is the order of the day in American business, why should you bother having budgets? You go through all that work and then your budget is out of date the day after you finish it. Sure, planning becomes more difficult as the world changes all around you, but plan you must. Without a long-term plan and goals, your organization lacks focus and resources are wasted as employees wander aimlessly about. A budget is an educated guess that reflects your long-term plans and allows you to act on them. A budget tells you the cost of hiring needed employees, facilities and capital needs, and other resources. And you can change a budget anytime. The best budgets are flexible — not cast in concrete.

Those of you who are already experienced managers *know* the almighty importance of budgets. A *budget* is the total of the funding required to implement a company's plans. Budgets make plans *happen.* Through their interaction with lower-level managers during the budgeting process, upper management can have a tremendous impact on the direction that an organization and its employees take. Conversely, lower-level employees can also have a huge impact on the organization during the budgeting process by way of the budget requests that they submit to management for approval.

Budgets determine how many people you have on your staff and how much you pay them. Budgets determine the financial resources you have to improve your workplace or to buy necessary office equipment, such as computers and copiers. And budgets determine how much money you have available to support your efforts on projects. Not only that, but they give you something to do with all that expensive spreadsheet software that the company bought last year.

But budgets also fulfill another important purpose: They provide a baseline against which you can measure your progress toward your goals. For example, if you are 50 percent of the way through your fiscal year but have actually spent 75 percent of your budgeted operating funds, then you have an immediate indication that a potential problem exists if the extent of your expenditures should be approximately the same as the extent of the completion towards your goals. Either you have underbudgeted your expenses for the year, or you are overspending. Whenever *budgeted* performance and *actual* performance disagree, or are in *variance,* the job of the responsible manager is to ask *why.*

Another great thing about budgets is that they give you the opportunity to put together all kinds of snazzy graphs and charts to impress your employees and top management. Imagine yourself in the boardroom: lights dimmed, the attention of every audience member riveted to your presentation. Alternately projecting full-color, multilevel spreadsheets, and then beautiful three-dimensional bar charts and graphs. You're in command as you click the buttons on your remote control. There's nothing like numbers presented in an interesting way to get the attention of a group of managers!

Depending on the size of your organization, the budgeting process may be quite simple or, alternatively, very complex. Regardless of the size of an organization, you can budget most anything in it. Following are some examples:

- **Labor budget:** Labor budgets are made up of the number and name of all the various positions in a company along with the salary or wages budgeted for each position.

- **Sales budget:** The sales budget is an estimate of the total number of products or services that will be sold in a given period. Total revenues are determined by multiplying the number of units by the price per unit.

- **Production budget:** The production budget takes the sales budget and its estimate of quantities of units to be sold and translates those figures into the cost of labor, material, and other expenses required to produce them.

- **Expense budget:** Expense budgets contain all the different expenses that a department may incur during the normal course of operations. You budget travel, training, office supplies, and more as expenses.

- **Capital budget:** This budget is a manager's plan to acquire fixed assets (those with a long useful life) such as furniture, computers, facilities, physical plant, and so forth to support the operations of a business.

Doing a Budget

There's a right way and a wrong way to do a budget. The *wrong* way is simply to make a photocopy of the last budget and submit it as your new budget (*bad* form!). The *right* way is to gather information from as many sources as possible, review and check the information for accuracy, and then use your good judgment to guess what the future may bring. A budget is a *forecast* — a prediction of the future — and is only as good as the data that goes into it and the good judgment that you bring to the process.

So how do you actually put together a budget? Where does the information come from? Who should you talk to? The possibilities seem endless. However, experienced *budgetmeisters* know that once you understand your costs of doing business — and where they come from — the budgeting process is actually quite simple. Make a few phone calls. Have a couple of meetings. Look over some recent accounting reports. Crunch a few numbers. Bingo! Your budget is complete! Well, there may be a *little* more to it than that. Review the basic steps in putting together a budget:

- ✔ **Closely review your budgeting documents and instructions.** It's always a good idea to take a close look at the budgeting documents that you're working with *and* read any instructions that your accounting staff provides with them. Although your organization may have done something the same way for years, you never know when that procedure may change.

  Peter recently spent more hours than he would like to admit preparing an annual budget for his organization's liability and property insurance — something that he had routinely done year after year. At least until he read the budgeting instructions and discovered that this particular item no longer required his input. *Oops!*

- ✔ **Meet with staff.** When you are starting the budget process, meet with your staff to solicit their input. In some cases, you need the specific input of your employees to be able to forecast accurately. For example, you may need to know how many trips your salespeople plan to make next year and where they plan to go. In other cases, you can simply ask for employee suggestions. One employee might ask you to include a pay increase in the next budget. Another might inform you that the current phone system is no longer adequate to meet the needs of employees and customers and that a new one should be budgeted. Whichever the case, your staff can provide you with very useful and important budget information.

- ✔ **Gather data.** Pull copies of previous budgets and accounting reports and then compare budgeted numbers to actual numbers. Were previous budgets overrun or underrun? By how much? If no historical data is available, find other sources of information that can help guide the development of figures for your budget. How much business do you plan to bring in during the next budget period, and what will it cost you to bring it in? Consider whether you need to hire more people, lease new facilities, or buy equipment or supplies. Further, consider the possibility of large increases or decreases in sales or expenses and what effect they would have on your budget.

- **Apply your judgment.** Hard data and cold facts are very important in the budgeting process; they provide an unbiased, unemotional source of information on which to base your decisions. However, data and facts aren't everything — not by a long shot. Budgeting is part *science* and part *art*. As a manager, your job is to take the data and facts and then apply your own judgment to determine the most likely outcomes.

    For example, every year Peter budgets more for extraordinary maintenance of his office facility than he could ever justify on an item-by-item basis. He does this knowing that *something* will come up during the course of the year, and he needs to have enough money available in his budget to accommodate it. So when the big boss decides to build an additional 20 offices or redo the entire building in pink wallpaper, the money is available.

    When you are new to management, you have little experience on which to draw, so you have a natural tendency to rely more heavily on data. However, as you become more accomplished in management and budgeting, your personal experience and judgment come to the fore.

- **Run the numbers.** Depending on how your organization does business, either fill out your budget forms and send them to your budget folks for processing, or enter them in the budget model yourself. The result is a draft of your budget that you can review and modify before you finalize it. Don't worry if the draft is rough or is missing information. You'll have a chance to fill in the gaps soon enough.

- **Check results and run the budget again as necessary.** Check over your draft budget and see whether it still makes sense to you. Are you missing any anticipated sources of revenue or expenses? Are the numbers realistic? Do they make sense in a historical perspective? Are they too high or too low? Will you be able to support them when you present them to upper management? This is the fun part of budgeting: when you are able to play with your numbers and try different scenarios and what-ifs. When you are satisfied with the results, sign off on your budget and turn it in. Congratulations! You did it!

The accuracy of your budget hinges on two main factors: the quality of the data that you use to develop your budget and the quality of the judgment that you apply to the data you're working with. While judgment is something that comes with experience, the quality of the data you use depends on where you get it. You can use three basic approaches to develop the data for building a budget:

- **Build it from scratch.** In the absence of historical data, when you are starting up a new business unit, or when you just want a fresh view of things, you want to develop your budgets based strictly on current estimates. In this process, widely known as *zero-based budgeting,* you build your budget from scratch — determining the people, facilities, travel, advertising, and other resources that are required to support it. You then cost out each need, and the budget is complete. Perhaps not too surprisingly, the answer that comes out of building a budget from scratch is often *quite* different from one that results from using historical data. Funny how that works.

✔ **Use historical figures.** One of the easiest ways to develop data for your budget is to use the actual results from the preceding budget period. While the past is not always an indication of the future — especially when an organization is undergoing significant change — using historical data can be very useful in relatively stable organizations.

✔ **Use the combination approach.** Many managers use a combination of both preceding methods for determining which data to include in their budgets. To use this approach, gather historical data and compare the figures to the best estimates of what you think performing a particular function will cost. You then adjust historical data up or down, depending on your view of reality.

Pulling Rabbits Out of Hats and Other Budget Tricks

In any organization, a certain amount of mystery and intrigue — some would call it *smoke and mirrors* — hovers around budgets and the budgeting process. Indeed, whether your organization is a one-person operation or the federal government, you can use many tricks of the budget trade to ensure that you get all the resources you need and desire.

The top ten excuses for being over budget

Managers must use a million and one excuses for exceeding their budgets. Admittedly, trying to predict the future of a business that is going through dynamic change is not unlike trying to hit a gnat with a slingshot at 100 paces. Regardless, your boss expects you to stick to your budget, just as you expect your employees to stick to theirs. However, for those times when the future gets a little fuzzy, here are the top ten excuses for going over budget:

1. The accounting reports must be wrong.

2. Didn't you get my revised budget?

3. How was I supposed to know that it would *rain* (insert your own excuse here) this year?

4. You're not going to quibble over a measly couple of million dollars, are you?

5. Don't worry, we'll make it up next year.

6. My assistant worked up that budget — he must have messed it up.

7. It's an investment in our future.

8. *Cathy's* (insert name of another manager here) department didn't come through with the support that I was promised.

9. We're doing better than *last* year!

10. Well, two years out of three isn't bad, is it?

The budget game is a long-standing tradition in American business and government — in fact, the pros in Congress have raised the budget game to a whole new level. Managers who learn *how* to play the game prosper, as do the people who work for them. Managers who fail to learn how to play the game, and the employees who work for them, are doomed to always have to make do with insufficient resources, facilities, pay, and the other niceties of business life. If you're a manager, learning how the game is played is definitely in your interest.

Generally, the goal of the budget game is to build in enough extra money to actually be able to get the job done. In the worst case, you'll have enough resources available to protect your employees and vital functions when the business goes south. In the best case, you'll have money left over after you pay all your necessary expenses. Either you can turn the money back into accounting with much fanfare and accept the accolades from the powers that be for your expert resource management skills, or you can apply the money to the purchase of some much needed equipment or other department needs. *Gee, it's probably a good time to check up on our customer in Paris.* Of course, if you work for the government, this does not apply. *Your* goal is to spend every penny of your budgeted amounts so that your budget won't be decreased in the following year.

You can play the budget game up front, when you develop the budget, or during the course of the budget period. The following sections tell you how it's done.

Up-front budget maneuvers

Following are some of the games that the pros play when they develop budgets. While these techniques are most appropriate for new or unstable departments or projects, you can use them when developing *any* budget. While we may be exaggerating on some of these points, there is a lot of truth to most of them.

- ✔ **Do some selective padding.** Simple, but effective. The idea is to pad your anticipated expenses so that your budget targets are easy to achieve. You end up looking like a hero when you come in under your budget, *plus* you get some extra money to play with at the end of the year. This is what is known as a *win-win* situation.

- ✔ **Tie your budget request to your organization's values.** This is the *Mom and apple pie* approach to budgeting. If you want to beef up your budget in a particular area, just pick one of your organization's values — say, quality — and tie your request to it. When your boss asks you to justify why you have tripled your office furniture budget, just tell him that your employees can't do quality work without large walnut desks.

- ✔ **Create more requests than you need, and give them up freely.** You don't want to appear unreasonable in your budget demands — don't forget, you're a *team* player! When you draft your budget, build in items that you have no real intention of using. When your boss puts on the pressure to reduce your budget (and bosses *always* do), give up the stuff you didn't really want anyway. Doing so ensures that you get to keep the items that you do want.

✔ **Shift the time frame.** Insist that the budget items are an investment in the future of the company. The secret is to tie these investments to a *big* payoff down the road. *If we double our labor budget, we'll be able to attract the talent that we need to take us into the 21st century and beyond!*

✔ **Be prepared.** The best defense is a good offense. Know your budget numbers *cold* and be ready to justify each budget item in intimate detail. Don't rely on someone else to do this for you — it's your finest hour as a manager. Be a star — go for it!

Staying on budget

After your new department or project starts up, you need to closely monitor your budget to make sure that you don't exceed it. If your actual expenditures start to exceed your budget, you need to take quick and decisive action. Following are some of the ways that experienced managers make sure that they stay on budget:

✔ **Freeze discretionary expenses.** Some expenses, such as labor, benefits, and electricity, are essential to an operation or project and cannot be stopped without jeopardizing performance. Others, such as purchasing new carpeting, upgrading computer monitors, or traveling first-class, are discretionary and can be stopped without jeopardizing performance. Freezing discretionary expenses is the quickest and least painful way to get your actual expenditures back in line with your budgeted expenditures.

✔ **Freeze hiring.** Although you may have budgeted new hires, you can save a *lot* of money by freezing the hiring of new employees. Not only do you save on the cost of hourly pay or salaries, but you also save on the costs of fringe benefits such as medical care and overhead expenses like water, electricity, and janitorial services. And because you aren't messing with your current employees' pay or benefits, most everyone will be happy with your decision. Of course, some critical positions in your organization may need to be filled, budget problem notwithstanding. You can determine which positions in your own organization have to be filled if they become vacant, and which can be covered by the efforts of other employees.

✔ **Postpone products and projects.** The development and production phases of new products and projects can burn up a *lot* of money. By postponing the start-up and roll-out of these new products and projects, you can get your budget back on track. Sometimes it only takes a few weeks or months to make a difference.

✔ **Freeze wages and benefits contributions.** Now we're getting into the kinds of savings that directly affect your employees, and we can guarantee that they aren't going to like it one bit. Most employees are used to regular wage and benefits increases. Although increases aren't as generous as they were a decade ago, employees still consider them to be essential. However, if you have made cuts and still need to cut more, then you really don't have any choice but to freeze your employees' wages and benefits contributions (medical insurance, 401K matching, and so on) at their current levels.

✔ **Lay off employees and close facilities.** You are in business to make money, not to lose money. When sales aren't sufficient to support your expenses — even after enacting the cost-savings measures just mentioned, drastic action is in order. Action doesn't get much more drastic than laying off employees and closing facilities. However, if your budget is as far off as it must be if you reach this point, then cut you must. See Chapter 16 for more information on conducting employee layoffs.

Whether you are responsible for budgeting as a part of your managerial duties or not, you need to have a basic understanding of the process that your business goes through to account for the money it makes and the money it spends. In the section that follows, we present all the information that you need to know about accounting to achieve a basic level of understanding.

The Basics of Accounting

The accounting system that takes up gigabytes of storage space on your company's network server is dependent on a few very basic assumptions. These assumptions that comprise the basics of accounting determine how every dollar and cent that flows into and out of your organization is assigned, reported, and analyzed. (If you ever want to drive your accounting staff nuts, tell them that you noticed a two- or three-cent mistake in your accounting reports and want them to find the source.)

Some managers believe that they can skate by with little or no knowledge of accounting and finance. This attitude is a mistake. As a manager, you should be just as familiar with these accounting basics as are the employees who work in your accounting department. Not only does this knowledge help to ensure that *you* understand and control the financial destiny of your organization, but if you are in command of the financial side of your business as well as the technical side, then you are also much more likely to survive the next round of corporate layoffs.

No longer do you have to be dumbfounded when one of your fellow managers starts throwing around terms such as *ROI, accounts receivable,* and *retained earnings*. After you read this section, *you'll* be in the driver's seat!

The accounting equation

In every business, daily events affect its financial position. A manager spends cash to buy a stapler and is reimbursed out of the petty cash fund. The company taps its bank line of credit to pay vendor invoices. Checks are received from customers and deposited. Paychecks are distributed to employees. Each of these financial *transactions* and many, many more have their place in the accounting equation.

The accounting equation states that an organization's *assets* are equal to its *liabilities* plus its *owners' equity.* The accounting equation looks like this:

Assets = Liabilities + Owners' Equity

This simple equation drives the *very* complex system of accounting that is used to track every financial transaction in a business, provide reports to managers for decision-making, and provide financial results to owners, shareholders, lenders, the Internal Revenue Service, and other stakeholders.

So what exactly does each part of the accounting equation represent? Take a look at each part and what it comprises.

Assets

Assets are generally considered to be anything of value — primarily financial and economic resources — that a company owns. The most common forms of assets in a business include the following:

- **Cash:** This asset encompasses money in all its forms, including cash, checking accounts, money market funds, and marketable securities such as stocks and bonds. Every business likes to have lots of cash.

- **Accounts receivable:** This asset represents the money that customers who buy goods and services on credit owe to your company. For example, if your business sells a box of floppy disks to another business and then bills the other business for the sale instead of demanding immediate payment in cash, this obligation becomes an account receivable until your customer pays it. Accounts receivable are nice things to have unless the companies or individuals that owe you money skip town or decide to delay their payments for six months.

- **Inventory:** Inventory is the value of merchandise held by your business for sale, the finished goods that you have manufactured but have not yet sold, as well as the raw materials and work in process that are part of the manufacture of finished goods. Inventory usually becomes cash or an account receivable when it is sold. Inventory that sits around on a shelf forever is not the best way to tie up your company's assets. Keeping your inventory moving all the time is much better, because you are generating sales.

- **Prepaid expenses:** Prepaid expenses represent goods and services that your firm has already paid for but not yet used. For example, your company may pay its annual liability insurance premium at the beginning of the year, before the insurance policy actually goes into effect. If the policy is canceled during the course of the year, then part of the premium is refunded to your business.

- **Equipment:** This is the property — machinery, desks, computers, phones, and similar items — that your organization buys to carry out its operations. For example, if your company sells computer supplies to individuals and other businesses, you need to purchase shelves on which to store your inventory of computer supplies, fork lifts to move it around, and phone systems on which to take orders from your customers. As equipment ages, it loses value. You account for this loss through *depreciation,* which spreads the original cost of a piece of equipment across its entire useful lifetime. When in doubt, depreciate.

✔ **Real estate:** Real estate includes the land, buildings, and facilities that your organization owns or controls. Examples include office buildings, proving ranges, manufacturing plants, warehouses, sales offices, mills, farms, and other forms of real property.

Assets are divided into two major types: *current* assets and *fixed* assets.

Current assets can be converted into cash within one year. Such assets are considered to be *liquid.* In the preceding list of assets, cash, accounts receivable, inventory, and prepaid expenses are considered current assets. Liquid assets are nice to have around when your business is in trouble and you need to raise cash quickly to make payroll or pay your vendors.

Fixed assets require more than one year to convert to cash. In the preceding list of assets, equipment and real estate are classified as fixed assets. If your business gets into trouble and you need cash, fixed assets probably won't do you much good unless you can use them as collateral for a loan.

Liabilities

Liabilities are generally considered to be debts that you owe to others — individuals, other businesses, banks, and so on — *outside* the company. In essence, liabilities are the claims that outside individuals and organizations have against a business's assets. The most common forms of business liabilities include the following:

✔ **Accounts payable:** Accounts payable are the obligations that your company owes to the individuals and organizations from which *it* purchases goods and services: its suppliers and vendors. For example, when you visit your local office supply store to buy a couple of pencils and bill the purchase to your company's account, this obligation becomes an account payable. You can conserve your company's cash in times of need by slowing down payments to your vendors and suppliers, although you have to be very careful not to jeopardize your credit in the process.

✔ **Notes payable:** Notes payable are the portion of loans made to your organization by individuals, financial institutions, or other organizations that are due to be paid back within one year. If, for example, your firm takes a 90-day loan to increase its inventory of floppy disks to satisfy a rapid increase in customer demand, the loan is considered a note payable.

✓ **Accrued expenses:** These are miscellaneous expenses that your company incurs but that are not reimbursed. Examples include obligations for payroll, sick leave due to employees, taxes payable to the government, and interest due to lenders.

✓ **Bonds payable:** Some large companies issue bonds to raise money to finance expansion or achieve other goals. Bonds payable represents the money that a company owes to the individuals and organizations that purchase the bonds as an investment.

✓ **Mortgages payable:** When organizations purchase real estate, they often do so by incurring long-term loans known as *mortgages*. Mortgages differ from standard loans in that they are usually secured by the real estate that the mortgage finances. For example, if your company defaults in its payments on the mortgage used to purchase your office building, ownership of the office building reverts to the entity that originally issued the mortgage — usually a bank or investment group.

Like assets, liabilities are also divided into two major types: *current* liabilities and *long-term* liabilities.

Current liabilities are repaid within one year. In the preceding list of liabilities, accounts payable, notes payable, and accrued expenses are considered current liabilities.

Long-term liabilities are repaid in a period greater than one year. In the preceding list of liabilities, bonds payable and mortgages payable are both classified as long-term liabilities.

Owners' equity

All businesses have owners. In some cases, the owners are a few individuals who founded the company. In other cases, the owners are the many thousands of individuals who buy the company's stock through public offerings. Owners' equity is the *owners'* share of the assets of a business after all liabilities have been paid. The most common forms of owners' equity include the following:

✓ **Paid-in capital:** Paid-in capital is the investment — usually paid in cash — that the owners make in a business. For example, if your firm sells common stock to investors through a public offering, the money that your firm obtains through the sale of the stock is considered paid-in capital.

✓ **Retained earnings:** These earnings are reinvested by a business and not paid out in dividends to shareholders. A certain amount of earnings are retained in hopes of increasing the firm's overall earnings and also to increase the dividends that are paid to owners.

Double-entry bookkeeping

Double-entry bookkeeping is the standard method of recording financial transactions that forms the basis of modern business accounting. Invented in 1494 by Luca Pacioli, a bored Franciscan monk (he must have been *really* bored to invent accounting!), double-entry bookkeeping recognizes that every financial transaction results in a record of a *receipt* (also known as an *asset*) and a record of an *expense* (also known as a *liability*).

Consider this example: Your company buys $1,000 worth of computer floppy disks from a manufacturer to resell to your customers. Because your company has established an account with the floppy disk manufacturer, the manufacturer bills you for the $1,000 instead of demanding immediate cash payment. Do you remember the accounting equation that we discussed earlier in this chapter? Here's the double-entry version of the accounting equation illustrating the $1,000 purchase of floppy disks to stock in your inventory:

Assets	=	**Liabilities**	+	**Owners' equity**
$1,000	=	$1,000	+	$0
(Inventory)		(Accounts payable)		

In this example, assets (inventory) increase by $1,000 — the cost of purchasing the floppy disks to stock your shelves. At the same time, liabilities (accounts payable) also increase by $1,000. This increase represents the debt that you owe to your supplier of floppy disks. In this way, the accounting equation always stays balanced. Now, imagine the effect of the several hundreds or thousands of financial transactions that hit your accounting system on a daily, weekly, or monthly basis. Whew! And you wondered why your information systems manager is always complaining that the company's computer system isn't big enough or fast enough.

The Most Common Types of Financial Statements

An accounting system is a nice thing to have, but it's worthless unless it can produce data that is useful to managers, employees, lenders, vendors, owners, investors, and other individuals and firms that have a financial stake in your business. And believe us, a *lot* of people have a financial interest in your business.

The make-or-buy decision

One of the most common decisions made in business is whether to make — that is, build or perform with in-house staff — or buy goods and services that are necessary for the operation of a business. For example, say you decide that you need to assign a security guard to your reception area to ensure the safety of your clients. Do you hire someone new as an employee, or does contracting with a company that specializes in providing security services make more sense?

When you consider such a make-or-buy decision, the first thing to consider is the cost of each alternative to your firm. Say that in Case A, you hire your security guard as a full-time employee for $6.00 an hour. In Case B, a security services firm provides a guard for $8.00 an hour. On the surface, hiring a security guard as an employee seems to make the most sense. If the guard works 2,000 hours a year, then in Case A you spend $12,000 a year for your guard and in Case B you spend $16,000 a year. By employing the guard yourself, you stand to save $4,000 a year. Right?

Maybe not. See why.

Case A: Hire in-house security guard

Hourly pay rate
 $6.00

Fringe benefits rate @ 35%
 2.10

Overhead rate @ 50%
 3.00

Total effective pay rate
 $11.10

Hours per year
 x 2,000

Total annual labor cost
 $22,200

Annual liability insurance increase
 4,000

Uniforms/cleaning
 1,000

Miscellaneous equipment
 500

Total annual cost
 $27,700

Case B: Contract with security firm

Hourly pay rate
 $8.00

Total effective pay rate
 $8.00

Hours per year
 x 2,000

Total annual cost
 $16,000

Surprise, surprise. Instead of saving $4,000 per year by hiring an in-house security guard, you're actually going to spend almost $12,000 *more* each year because more costs are involved in hiring an in-house employee than just his or her hourly pay. You have to add all the fringe benefits, such as life insurance, medical and dental plans, and more, plus the employee's share of overhead — facilities, electricity, air conditioning, and so forth — to the basic wage rate to get a true picture of the cost of the employee to your organization. Not only that, but you need to purchase additional liability insurance, uniforms, uniform cleaning, and miscellaneous equipment such as a flashlight, Mace, and handcuffs.

On the other hand, when you contract with a security services firm, *the firm* bears the cost of fringe benefits, overhead, insurance, uniforms, and equipment. You simply pay the hourly fee and forget it. Not only that, but if the guard doesn't work out, you just make a phone call, and a replacement is sent immediately. No messy employee terminations or unemployment benefits to worry about.

Now, which deal do *you* think is the better one?

Would it surprise you to learn that almost *everyone* wants to know the financial health of your business? Well, they do. Managers want to know so that they can identify and fix problems. Employees want to know because they want to work for a company that is in good financial health and that provides good pay, benefits, and job stability. Lenders and vendors need to know your company's financial health to decide whether to extend credit. And owners and investors want to know because this knowledge helps them determine whether their investment dollars are being used wisely or are instead being frittered away.

Accountants invented *financial statements* for this reason.

Financial statements are nothing more than reports — intended for distribution to individuals outside the accounting department — that summarize the amounts of money contained within selected accounts or groups of accounts at a selected point in time or during a selected period of time. Each type of financial statement has a unique value to those people who use them, and different individuals may use some or all of an organization's financial statements during the normal course of business. The following sections review the financial statements that you are most likely to encounter during your career as a manager.

The balance sheet

The balance sheet is a report that illustrates the value of a company's assets, liabilities, and owners' equity — the financial position of the company — on a specific date. Think of it as a snapshot of the business. Although it can be prepared at any time, a balance sheet is usually prepared at the end of a definite accounting period — most often a year, quarter, or month.

Figure 17-1 shows a typical balance sheet.

As you can see, the balance sheet provides values for every major component of the three parts of the accounting equation. By reviewing the value of each item in the balance sheet, managers can identify potential problems and then take action to solve them. For example, in the balance sheet illustrated here, inventory is quite high relative to other assets. The experienced manager knows that when inventory is so high, the company is at some risk if an immediate need for cash — an asset in short supply in this particular balance sheet — arises.

The income statement

Assets, liabilities, and owners' equity are all very nice, thank you, but many people *really* want to see the bottom line. Did the company *make* money or *lose* money? In other words, what was its *profit* or *loss?* This job belongs to the *income statement.*

Sample Balance Sheet

	January 31, 2005
ASSETS	
CURRENT ASSETS	
Cash and cash equivalents	$458,000
Accounts receivable	$11,759,000
Inventory	$154,000
Prepaid expenses and other current assets	$283,000
Refundable income taxes	$165,000
TOTAL CURRENT ASSETS	$12,819,000
EQUIPMENT AND FURNITURE	
Equipment	$4,746,000
Furniture, fixtures, and improvements	$583,000
	$5,329,000
Allowance for depreciation and amortization	($2,760,000)
	$2,569,000
COMPUTER SOFTWARE COSTS, NET	$3,199,000
NET DEPOSITS AND OTHER	$260,000
	$18,847,000
LIABILITIES AND SHAREHOLDERS' EQUITY	
CURRENT LIABILITIES	
Notes payable to bank	$1,155,000
Accounts payable	$2,701,000
Accrued compensation and benefits	$2,065,000
Income taxes payable	$0
Deferred income taxes	$990,000
Current portion of long-term debt	$665,000
TOTAL CURRENT LIABILITIES	$7,576,000
LONG-TERM DEBT, less current portion	$864,000
DEFERRED RENT EXPENSE	$504,000
DEFERRED INCOME TAXES	$932,000
STOCKHOLDERS' EQUITY	
Common stock	$76,000
Additional paid-in capital	$803,000
Retained earnings	$8,092,000
	$8,971,000
	$18,847,000

Figure 17-1: A typical balance sheet.

An income statement adds all the sources of a company's revenues and then subtracts all the sources of its expenses to determine its net income or net loss for a particular period of time. Whereas a balance sheet is a snapshot of an organization's financial status, an income statement is more like a movie.

Figure 17-2 illustrates a simple income statement.

Revenues

Revenue is the value received by a company through the sale of goods, services, and other revenue sources such as interest, rents, royalties, and so forth. To arrive at net sales, total sales of goods and services are offset by returns and allowances.

Expenses

Expenses are *all* the costs of doing business. For accounting purposes, expenses are divided into two major classifications:

- **Cost of goods sold:** For a firm that retails or wholesales merchandise to individuals or other companies, this figure represents the cost of purchasing merchandise or inventory. By subtracting the cost of goods sold from revenue, you end up with the company's *gross margin* — also known as *gross profit*.

- **Operating expenses:** Operating expenses are all the other costs of doing business not already part of the cost of goods sold. Operating expenses are usually further subdivided into *selling expenses,* which include marketing, advertising, product promotion, and the costs of operating stores, and *general and administrative expenses,* which are the actual administrative costs of running the business. General and administrative costs typically include salaries for accounting, data processing, and purchasing staff and the cost of corporate facilities including utilities, rent payments, and so on.

Net income or loss

The difference between revenues and expenses (after adjustment for interest income or expense and payment of income taxes) is a company's net income (profit) or net loss. Also commonly known as a company's *bottom line,* net income or loss is the one number most often of interest to those who want to assess the financial health of a firm. Many corporate executives and managers have found themselves on the street when the bottom lines of their companies dipped too far into the loss side of the equation.

The cash flow statement

What's the old saying? *Happiness is a positive cash flow.* Cash flow statements show the movement of cash into and out of a business. It doesn't take an Einstein to realize that when more cash is moving out of a business than is moving into the business for a prolonged period of time, the business may be in *big* trouble.

Sample Income Statement

Twelve months ended

January 31,
2005

REVENUES

Gross sales	$58,248,000	
Less: Returns	$1,089,000	
Net Sales		$57,159,000

COST OF GOODS SOLD

Beginning inventory		$4,874,000
Purchases	$38,453,000	
Less: Purchase discounts	$1,586,000	
Net purchases		$36,867,000
Cost of goods available for sale		$41,741,000
Less: Ending inventory		$6,887,000
Cost of Goods Sold		$34,854,000

GROSS PROFIT $22,305,000

OPERATING EXPENSES

Total selling expenses	$8,456,000	
Total general expenses	$1,845,000	
Total operating expenses		$10,301,000
Operating income		$12,004,000
Other income and expenses		
Interest expense (income)	$360,000	
Total other income and expenses		$360,000
Income before taxes		$11,644,000
Less: Income taxes		$3,952,000
Net Income		$7,692,000
Average number of shares		3,500,000
Earnings per share		$2.20

Figure 17-2:
A simple
income
statement.

Using financial ratios to analyze your business

If you don't know exactly what you're looking for, analyzing a company's financial records can be quite a daunting task. Fortunately, over a period of many, many years, expert business financial analysts have developed ways to assess the performance and financial health and well-being of an organization quickly by comparing the ratios of certain key financial indicators to established standards and to other firms in the same industries.

Current ratio: This ratio is the capability of a company to pay its current liabilities out of its current assets. A ratio of 2 or more is generally considered good. Consider this example:

Current ratio = Current assets ÷ Current liabilities

= $100 million ÷ $25 million

= 4.00

Quick ratio: The quick ratio (also known as the *acid-test* ratio) is the same as the current ratio with the exception that inventory is subtracted from current assets. This ratio provides a much more rigorous test of a firm's capability to pay its current liabilities quickly than does the current ratio, because inventory cannot be liquidated as rapidly as other current assets. A ratio of 1 or better is acceptable.

Quick ratio = (Current assets − inventory) ÷ Current liabilities

= ($100 million − $10 million) ÷ $25 million

= $90 million ÷ $25 million

= 3.60

Receivables turnover ratio: This ratio indicates the average time that it takes for a firm to convert its receivables into cash. A higher ratio indicates that customers are paying their bills quickly. This

is good — *very* good. A lower ratio reflects slow collections and a possible problem that management needs to address. This is bad — *very* bad. Your boss isn't going to like it.

Receivables turnover ratio = Net sales ÷ Accounts receivable

= $50 million ÷ $5 million

= 10.00

You can gain one more interesting piece of information quickly from the receivables turnover ratio. By dividing 365 days by the receivables turnover ratio, you get the average number of *days* that it takes your firm to turn over its accounts receivable, which is commonly known as the *average collection period.* The shorter the average collection period, the better the organization's situation is, and the better your job security is.

Average collection period = 365 days ÷ Receivables turnover ratio

= 365 days ÷ 10.00

= 36.5 days

Debt-to-equity ratio: This ratio measures the extent to which the organization depends on loans from outside creditors versus resources provided by shareholders and other owners. A ratio in excess of 1 is generally considered unfavorable because it indicates that the firm may have difficulty repaying its debts. And nobody — especially cranky bankers or vendors — wants to loan money to companies that have problems repaying their debts. A particularly low ratio indicates that management *may* be able to improve the company's profitability by increasing its debt.

(continued)

(continued)

Debt-to-equity ratio = Total liabilities ÷ Owners' equity

= $50 million ÷ $150 million

= 0.33 or 33 percent

Return on investment: Often known by its abbreviation, *ROI,* return on investment measures the capability of a company to earn profits for its owners. Don't forget: Profit is *good* and loss is

bad. Because owners — shareholders and other investors — prefer to make *lots* of money on their investments, they like an organization's ROI to be as high as possible.

Return on investment = Net income ÷ Owners' equity

= $50 million ÷ $150 million

= 0.33 or 33 percent

Cash is sort of like gasoline. Your car requires a plentiful supply of gasoline to run. If you run out of gas, your car is going to stop dead on the highway. One minute, you're going 65 miles an hour; the next, you're going zero miles an hour. Similarly, if your company runs out of cash, it is going to stop dead, too. Without cash to pay employees' salaries, vendors' invoices, lenders' loan payments, and so forth, operations quickly cease to exist.

- ✔ **Simple cash flow statement:** The simple cash flow statement arranges all items into one of two categories: cash inflows and cash outflows.

- ✔ **Operating cash flow statement:** The operating cash flow statement limits analysis of cash flows to only those items having to do with the operations of a business, and not its financing.

- ✔ **Priority cash flow statement:** The priority cash flow statement classifies cash inflows and outflows by specific groupings chosen by the manager or other individual who requests preparation of the statement.

Test your new-found knowledge

Name three different kinds of budgets.

A. Activity budget, inactivity budget, and revenue budget

B. Labor budget, sales budget, and capital budget

C. Monthly budget, yearly budget, and infinite budget

D. None of the above

What is the accounting equation?

A. Cash + Credit = Total liabilities

B. Assets = Accounts receivable + Inventory

C. Owners' equity = Shares of stock × Price per share

D. Assets = Liabilities + Owners' equity

Chapter 18

Harnessing the Power of Technology

In This Chapter

▶ Finding out why computers are such a big deal

▶ The basics of computer hardware and software

▶ Choosing between the PC and the Mac

▶ Networking your organization

▶ Looking into the future of telecommuting

*Y*ou've *got* to love microcomputers (not the mini- and mainframe computers that are hidden away in some chilly room in the bowels of your corporate office — we're not addressing *those* computers in this chapter). Unfortunately, like everything else in life, computers have good points and bad points. With microcomputers, managers and workers alike have more ways to waste time than ever before. Sure, computers make great typewriters and wonderful adding machines (and a year after you buy them, boat anchors!), but do you *really* need the entire contents of the Library of Congress on a CD-ROM? Should you *really* spend half an hour typing, editing, spell checking, and laser printing a gorgeous, 64-shades-of-gray memo when a handwritten note or quick phone call would do just as well? Do you *really* need to exchange e-mail with a reindeer herdsman in Samiland?

We admit to admiring the amazing progress that computers have made in the last decade or so. About ten years ago, a desktop business computer was little more than a souped-up calculator (sort of like a '56 Chevy Belair with a 4-barrel carburetor in place of the original 2-barrel number). IBM's innovation, the personal computer, or *PC,* was expensive, bulky, and slow. And the software available at the time was really lousy. Remember WordStar and Visicalc? Bob does — believe it or not, he was one of the last surviving WordStar users until he upgraded his computer to Windows late last year! *Liebshen!*

Today, computers with anything less than a Pentium 133 MHz chip, 16MB RAM, and a 1GB hard drive are practically obsolete. Of course, part of the reason is that the programs you use in business — Microsoft Windows, Microsoft Word, Lotus Notes, Lotus 1-2-3, and so on — all require mega-megabytes of storage just to load onto your computer. For example, Peter's copy of Microsoft Office requires *85MB* of space on his hard drive. This requirement more than *doubles* the entire capacity of the 40MB hard drive installed in the first PC that Peter purchased in 1988.

In this chapter, we examine computers, software, and all those other things that make the world a better place to live. Yes, we know that computers aren't the end-all, be-all for today's managers — they *do* have their pitfalls. But overall, computers have helped to speed up business, as well as to make business more efficient and effective. As they say in the AT&T advertisement, *someday you will* (use a computer, that is). And when you do, someone will be standing there waiting to collect your toll on the Information Superhighway.

Computers: Where the Action Is

Are we imagining things, or do computers seem to be taking over the world? Certainly, computers have taken over in business. Even the most recalcitrant CEOs are finally taking the plunge *(I don't need a computer — never did and never will!)* and are signing onto the Information Superhighway in ever-increasing numbers. The managers that formerly relied on meetings and written memos to communicate with their employees now think nothing of dropping a couple thousand bucks to buy a microcomputer for an employee who has no other use for it than to send and receive electronic mail. Woe to the employees who are left out of the company's computer network. With such a lack of integration into company workings, these employees may as well be exiled to Elba. You *are* your e-mail address.

So what's with these computers? Why are they so essential to people's lives — both at work and away? Are we witnessing some sort of Venusian mind-control plot? The next step in the Trilateral Commission's plan for one-world government? Or simply a Madison Avenue ad executive's idea for creating massive new revenue streams where none existed before? To find out the answer to these questions and more, we need to explore what computers are: their essence, their heart, their soul — their *raison d'etre*.

What do managers do with their computers?

Think for a moment about the incredible progress of information technology just in your lifetime. With so many computerized tools at your fingertips, it's hard to believe that only two decades ago, the personal computer had yet to be introduced commercially. Whereas word processing used to mean a typewriter and a lot of correction fluid or sheets of messy carbon paper, computers have revolutionized the way in which business people can manipulate text, graphics, and other elements in their reports and other documents.

Computers are great at doing a lot of things — just ask anyone who has spent hours playing Solitaire or that great new 3-D pinball game that comes with Microsoft Windows. Ignoring those entertaining diversions for a moment, you as a manager can do two key things with your computer that result in measurable gains in productivity and efficiency:

✓ **Automate processes:** Not too many years ago, business processes were manual ones. For example, your organization's accounting and payroll system may have once been done entirely by hand with the assistance of only a ten-key adding machine. What used to take hours, days, or weeks can now be accomplished in minutes. Some of the other processes that are commonly automated are inventory tracking, customer service, call analysis, software bug-tracking, purchasing, and more.

✓ **Automate personal management functions:** As we describe in Chapter 2, more managers than ever are taking their calendars and personal planners and moving them onto computers. Although it's unlikely that paper-based planners will ever die, many managers are finding out that computers are much more powerful management tools than their unautomated counterparts. Managers also use computers to schedule meetings, track projects, analyze numbers, manage business contact information, conduct employee performance evaluations, and more.

However, before you run off and automate everything in sight, keep this one piece of information in mind: If your manual system is inefficient or ineffective to begin with, simply automating the system won't necessarily make your system perform any better. In fact, it can end up making your system perform *worse* than the manual version. When you make the move to automation, take the time to review the process in detail. Cut out any unnecessary steps and make sure that it is optimized for the new, automated environment. Believe us, the time you take now to improve your processes and functions will pay off big when you make the move to automation.

Do computers really make your organization more efficient?

The recent explosion of information technology accompanies the shift in American industry from old-line standards such as steel mills and petroleum refineries to companies producing semiconductors, computers, and related products. The personal computer industry, which did not exist two decades ago, has quickly grown into a market worth more than $50 billion in annual sales. More Americans work for computer-related companies than for the automobile, steel, mining, and petroleum industries combined. Can you believe it?!?

Over the last ten years, the average annual growth in sales of computer software has exceeded 25 percent. The growth of this particular piece of the computer industry has been so phenomenal that the market value of Microsoft Corporation (in 9th place), the world's largest producer of computer software, exceeds that of General Motors (in 23rd place), the world's largest manufacturer of automobiles.

The idea that business people who best manage information have a competitive advantage in the marketplace seems obvious enough. The sooner you receive information, the sooner you can act on it. The more effectively you handle information, the easier you can access that information when and where you need it. The more efficiently you deal with information, the fewer expenses you incur for managing and maintaining your information.

Management cites the preceding reasons, and others like them, as justification for spending obscenely huge amounts of corporate resources to buy computers, install voice mail and e-mail systems, and train employees to use these new tools of the Information Age. Have all these expenditures made your workers more productive? Unfortunately, for years, researchers found no evidence to prove that office automation resulted in measurable productivity gains. Despite the proliferation of computers and other digital business tools, only recently have studies shown a clear relationship between the implementation of office automation and increased productivity.

✔ Management at the Boeing Corporation studied the impact of electronic meeting software on 1,000 participants who attended 64 different meetings. According to the results of the study, Boeing saved an average of $6,700 per meeting — or $428,800 for all 64 meetings — primarily through savings in employee time. According to the study project manager, Brad Quinn Post, "The data show there are very clear opportunities to use these products to significantly improve business processes, to make our work cheaper, faster, and better" (*Fortune,* Mar. 23, 1992).

✔ By using information technology to provide employees with real-time information about orders and scheduling that cuts through the traditional walls within the organization, M.A. Hanna, a manufacturer of polymers, was able to reduce its working capital needs by one-third to achieve the same measure of sales. Impressive as this is, Martin D. Walker, CEO of M.A. Hanna, is convinced that his firm could further reduce its working capital by an equal amount simply by communicating with suppliers and customers through computer networks.

While the weight of evidence begins to swing toward productivity gains, studies indicate that merely installing computers and other information technology does not automatically lead to gains in employee efficiency and productivity. As a manager, you must take the time to improve your work processes *before* you automate them. If you don't, office automation can actually lead to decreases in employee efficiency and productivity. Instead of the usual lousy results that you get from your manual, unautomated system, you end up with something new: garbage at the speed of light. Don't let *your* organization make the same mistake!

Parts Is Parts: It's What's Inside That Counts

Every computer consists of two basic parts — hardware and software. *Hardware* is the term for all the electronic parts — the microprocessor, the wires, the keyboards, and so on — that physically represent the modern computer. When you say the word *computer,* you're usually talking about hardware.

Software is the set of instructions that tells the computer hardware what to do. These instructions, written in cryptic combinations of alphanumeric code, allow your computer to take the clicks of your mouse and the tip-tappings of your fingers on the keyboard and create whatever your heart (and your pocketbook) desires. Whether you're placing an order for flowers over the Internet or creating a daily menu for your restaurant, your computer would be a useless pile of junk without software to make it happen.

Hardware: Those boxes with the blinking lights and buttons you can push

Hardware is all the stuff that you see and touch when you use your computer. Computer hardware comes in different sizes and shapes. At your office, you might use a desktop computer that is linked to a large network server. While on the road, you might carry a battery-operated laptop computer in your briefcase. The size and kind of hardware that you select is now mostly a matter of personal preference. Even the smallest, most portable laptop systems are almost as capable as the most powerful desktop computers. Of course, this convenience comes at a price. While the more powerful Pentium desktop computers cost about $2,500, the equivalent laptop costs roughly double that.

Regardless of which computer you select, you find certain basic hardware elements in common:

✔ **Input devices:** You have to be able to get information into your computer so that you can slice, dice, and process that information. Input devices — keyboards, microphones, video cameras, the ubiquitous computer mouse, scanners, and the like — allow you to do just that.

- ✔ **Processing devices:** After you input the information into your computer, the processing devices perform the slicing, dicing, and processing of your information. Processing devices include microprocessors and random access memory (RAM) chips.

- ✔ **Storage devices:** Storage devices such as hard drives, diskettes, and CD-ROMs enable you to store computer software and files indefinitely. Back in the dark old days of the first personal computers (a decade ago), you had to load your computer programs onto your computer every time you wanted to use them. This step was a *major* pain in the neck.

- ✔ **Output devices:** Now that your computer has done its (slicing and dicing) thing, it needs some way to spit the results back out to you. Output devices — printers, video monitors, speakers, and the like — express the results of all that inputting, processing, and storage in ways that make sense to you, your employees, and your customers. At least you *hope* that the results make sense!

Software: Those expensive boxes full of air and cheap plastic disks

The most expensive, powerful computer hardware in the world is useless without the software to tell the hardware what to do. No matter what task you want to accomplish, typing a sales proposal for a client, sending an e-mail message to a vendor's plant in Singapore, or landing your make-believe F-14 fighter plane on the pitching deck of an aircraft carrier caught in a storm at night 1,000 miles out to sea, without software, you'd be staring at a blank screen.

If you've been in a computer superstore lately, filled to the brim with aisle after aisle of flashy software boxes, you know that your choices are virtually unlimited. The following sections give a synopsis of some of the most popular business software programs. (For further information on these software programs and how they work, IDG Books Worldwide offers an incredibly comprehensive variety of ...*For Dummies* guides on everything from *Windows 95 For Dummies* to *WordPerfect For Dummies* to *Visual Basic 3 For Dummies,* and much, much more.)

Operating systems

When you want to make your hardware work, operating systems are where the action is. Operating systems, such as Linux and Microsoft Windows, provide your computer with the basic operating instructions that enable it to process data. Operating systems tell your computer what to do with the click of your mouse, when to pull data from your hard drive, where to send that data, and so on.

Word processors

Where would the business world be without word processing software? Not only did word processing software cause the virtual extinction of the once-thriving American typewriter industry, but also it makes the production and storage of documents incredibly easy and flexible.

With word processing software, such as Microsoft Word or Corel WordPerfect, you can type a document, check for errors in spelling and grammar, make corrections, insert photographs, bar charts, or other graphical stuff, change the size and appearance of fonts, and lots more *before* you print the document. You can then save the document on your computer's hard drive or onto a floppy disk for future reference or to hand off to someone else.

Spreadsheets

Spreadsheet software such as Lotus 1-2-3 or Microsoft Excel has made many people's lives a *lot* easier. Complex financial analysis that formerly took hours (or even days) to complete is now a few mere keystrokes away. Peter can remember preparing annual budgets by hand many years ago. First, he had to work up several pages of numbers manually and then double-check them with a calculator. If he changed any of the figures, he had to go through the numbers to update any totals that changed as a result. After he completed the budgets, someone had to type them on a typewriter. And as with any other typewritten document, correcting mistakes was a real pain in the neck.

Now, Peter simply takes the budget template that Fiscal Services sends him each year via e-mail and fills in a few numbers on his computer, and the software does the rest. Numbers update themselves, formulas embed themselves, totals total, ratios change — all automatically and without fanfare. Minutes later, Peter retrieves his new, improved budget from the laser printer down the hall and submits it to his boss for approval. He then heads over to the local donut shop for a well-deserved break. Using a computer is *such* hard work!

Personal information management software

Personal information management programs such as Microsoft Outlook and Franklin Planner software for Windows combine the best features of personal planners, appointment books, address books, contact managers, and to-do lists into automated powerhouses of information for the busy business person. As a manager, you can use personal information management software to keep track of your daily appointments. And most of these programs enable you to set up and manage projects and to create extensive task lists.

Use personal information management software to change your personal information anytime you want. As an added benefit, you can print out the information from your office desktop computer or download the data to a notebook or laptop computer. In the case of Microsoft Schedule+, you can even send up to 70 entries to your Timex DataLink wristwatch. Now you'll never be without your schedule wherever you go.

Presentation software

Presentation software such as Harvard Graphics, Lotus Freelance Graphics, and Microsoft PowerPoint enables *anyone* to create tremendously powerful and professional-looking graphs and slides. A few years ago, most business people got pretty excited when they learned that they could use Xerox machines to photocopy typed bullet charts onto plastic viewgraphs; today, producing vivid and professional transparencies (that rival the best work of highly paid graphic artists) takes only a presentation software program, a PC, and a printer. You can even get a special adapter that projects the presentation's images directly from your laptop computer onto the screen. *C'est magnifique!*

Database programs

Database programs enable you to store and manipulate large quantities of data. Stand-alone database programs produced by Borland, Sybase, and Oracle dominate the market for large-scale corporate applications. But many word processing and spreadsheet packages offer integrated database applications that you can use effectively for smaller-scale applications.

If you need to organize data in many different ways, then database software is just what the doctor ordered. Say that you have approximately 125,000 active customers scattered all around the world. Your boss calls and asks you to prepare a list of all the company's French customers. As long as you have the information entered in a database program, you can sort and list all the French customers in seconds. Whether you want to sort your data alphabetically by name, by zip code, by total sales volume, or by any other data field, database programs make the task quick and easy.

Communications

Computers love to talk to each other. When Bob worked for Blanchard Training and Development (BTD), he could easily create a virtual office on his IBM laptop computer — located in whatever hotel he happened to be in that night. Using communications software, Bob could plug a phone line into his built-in modem, dial a toll-free number, and create an immediate electronic link with the BTD computer. Bob was able to pick up his e-mail messages, send replies, access and download work files, and then upload changes. He could even fax letters or text files to any fax machine in the world. Programs such as Symantec pcAnywhere and Procomm Plus make communicating between computers easy.

The Internet is taking the business world by storm. If your company hasn't yet established a site on the World Wide Web, then your competitors have already left you *way* behind. Business use of the Internet has exploded, and if you're not a part of the Internet yet, you'd better have plans to *be* a part of it soon. Internet browsers are specialized communications programs that enable you to transit the World Wide Web and the rest of the Internet with ease. Microsoft Internet Explorer and Netscape Navigator are examples of browsers that are hot right now.

PC versus Mac

Only a few years ago, business managers took the question of whether to buy PC (IBM-compatible personal computer) or Mac (Apple Macintosh personal computer) very seriously. While the Mac — with its intuitive, easy-to-learn operating interface, graphical icons, and computer mouse — was once vastly superior to its PC rivals, Microsoft Windows software changed all that. PCs using Microsoft Windows are virtually indistinguishable from Macintoshes in their ease of use, and they cost less to boot.

Although Apple almost crashed and burned a few years ago — threatening to take the Mac and its siblings along with it — the return of Steve Jobs to the company has led to a resurgence both in Apple and in the popularity of its hardware. And, while the Macintosh is still *the* standard for specific applications such as video, graphics and design, CNC milling shops, and musical composition, it is increasingly finding its way back into business — especially now that Apple prices its machines much more competitively than it did in past years.

Now that computer networks can accomodate both PCs and Macintoshes, you have really no reason to limit yourself to one or the other. Your accounting employees can be blazing away on their Pentium-based PCs while the graphics department happily designs and creates on their PowerPC-based Macs.

Who says that we can't all coexist peacefully? PC or Mac — the choice is yours.

Let's Network!

The personal computer began revolutionizing business a decade ago, shifting the power of computing away from huge mainframes and onto the desks of individual users. Now, computer networks are bringing about a new revolution in business computing. Although the personal computer is a self-sufficient island of information, when you link these islands together in a network, individual computers have the added benefit of sharing with *every* computer on the network.

So are there any good business reasons for networking? You bet there are! See what you think about these reasons:

✔ **Networks improve communication:** Computer networks allow anyone in an organization to communicate with anyone else quickly and easily. With the click of a button, you can send messages to individuals or groups of employees. You can send replies just as easily. Not only that, but employees on computer networks can access financial, marketing, and product information that they use to do their jobs from throughout the organization.

✔ **Networks save time and money:** In business, time *is* money. The faster you can get something done, the more things you can get done during the course of your business day. Computer e-mail allows you to create messages, memos, and other internal communications, to attach work files, and then to transmit them instantaneously to as many coworkers as you want. And these coworkers can be located across the hall or around the world.

✔ **Networks improve market vision:** Information communicated via computer networks is, by nature, timely and direct. In the old world of business communication, many layers of employees filtered, modified, and slowed the information as it traveled from one part of the organization to another. With direct communication over networks, no one filters, modifies, or slows the original message. What you see is what you get. The result is the transmission of better information more quickly throughout an organization. The sooner you get the information that you need and the higher its quality, the better your market vision.

Telecommuting: An Idea Whose Time Has Come?

With the proliferation of personal computers throughout the American landscape — both at work and at home — and with the availability of fast and inexpensive modems and communications software, the question is not *can* your employees telecommute. No, the question is will you *let* your employees telecommute. You see, the problem that telecommuting presents to managers is not a problem of technology, but a problem of managing people who aren't working in the office.

In the old-style office, most (if not all) of your employees are just footsteps away from your office. If you need their help, you can pop your head into their offices to make assignments. Oh, they're away for a break? No problem, you can hunt them down in the break room and personally realign their priorities.

Telecommuting has changed all that. When your employees work away from the office, they're no longer at your beck and call. Communication often becomes a long series of voice mail messages, e-mails, and faxes. Face-to-face communication decreases, as does the feeling of connectedness to the organization.

When her fiancé accepted a job in New Mexico, Amy Arnott, an analyst at Chicago-based Morningstar, Inc., was faced with a tough decision. Should she quit her job and move to New Mexico with her husband-to-be, or should she try maintaining a long-distance romance? Fortunately for Arnott, she didn't have to make the choice. Morningstar allows Arnott to telecommute each day from Los Alamos, New Mexico, to Chicago, Illinois — a journey of more than 1,000 miles each way.

It's new, it's exciting, it's the Intranet

If you thought that the Internet was the next big thing in business computing, guess again. Establishing a presence on the Internet is old news for most corporations. No, the next big thing in business is the *Intranet.* Some of America's largest corporations including Federal Express Corporation, AT&T, Levi Strauss, and Ford Motor Company, are building internal versions of the Internet *within* their organizations. At Silicon Graphics, for example, employees can access some 144,000 Web pages located on 800 different *internal* Web sites. Employees at DreamWorks SKG, the new entertainment conglomerate created by Steven Spielberg, Jeffrey Katzenberg, and David Geffen, use their company's Intranet to produce films and to take care of production details such as tracking animation objects, coordinating scenes, and checking the daily status of projects.

Intranets take the basic tools of the Internet — Web servers, browsers, and Web pages — and bring them *inside* the organization. Intranets are designed to be accessible strictly by employees and are not available to users of the Internet. For companies that have already made the investment in Web hardware and software, they are an inexpensive and powerful way to pull together an organization's computers.

Not only are Intranets revolutionizing the development of computer networks within organizations, but they're also democratizing them. Where most company computer networks are the sole province of a small staff of computer systems administrators and programmers, Intranets allow novices and experts alike to create Web pages. At Federal Express, for example, many of the company's 60 Web pages were created by and for its employees. According to Stephen Jobs, CEO of NeXT Computer, "The Intranet has broken down the walls within corporations." And Jobs ought to know. As co-founder of Apple Computer, he has broken down more than his share of walls.

(Source: *Business Week,* Feb. 26, 1996.)

While, according to Arnott, "Los Alamos isn't exactly a world financial center," she uses her computer and modem to tap into the Morningstar mutual fund database. Using the database, along with off-the-shelf word processing, spreadsheet, and e-mail software, Arnott performs her job just as well as if she were at her old office in Chicago. Well, meeting her coworkers in the hallway to chat about the latest goings-on within Morningstar *is* a little more difficult. (Source: *Business Week,* May 18, 1994.)

While the idea of virtual employees seems to be catching on in the world of business, you as a manager need to consider some pros and cons when *your* employees approach you with the idea of telecommuting.

Following are some pluses to telecommuting:

- ✔ Employees can set their own schedules.
- ✔ Employees can spend more time with customers.

✔ You can save money by downsizing your facilities.

✔ Costs of electricity, water, and other overhead are reduced.

✔ Employee morale is enhanced.

And following are some of the minuses to telecommuting:

✔ Monitoring employee performance is more difficult.

✔ Scheduling meetings can be problematic.

✔ You may have to pay to set up your employees with the equipment that they need to telecommute.

✔ Employees can lose their feelings of being connected to the organization.

✔ Managers must be more organized in making assignments.

According to Scott Bye of North Hollywood, "The prospect of being able to work out of my own home was much more appealing than merging onto the freeway each morning." While Scott still gets out of bed at about the same time as he did when he worked at a large corporate publisher, now his commute is a few steps down the hall instead of an hour and 15 minutes of bumper-to-bumper, smog-filled, stop-and-go traffic. By 9:30 a.m. — 15 minutes before his old starting time — Bye has already made several calls to his East Coast clients, sent a fax or two to publishing contacts overseas, and created a sales presentation on his computer. He sums up his new-found freedom in simple, but direct, terms: "Now that I've tasted the freedom of my own business in my own house, would I want to go back to the stuffed shirts and clocking in? Nah!" (*Microsoft Magazine,* Fall 1994).

Test your new-found knowledge

Name three different kinds of computer input devices.

A. Disk drive, keyboard, and microphone

B. Keyboard, video camera, and scanner

C. Monitor, speaker, mouse

D. Touchscreen, stylus, and printer

Does telecommuting make employees feel more or less connected to an organization?

A. More connected

B. Less connected

C. No change

D. None of the above

Chapter 19

Developing and Mentoring Employees

In This Chapter

▶ Understanding the importance of developing employees

▶ Building career development plans

▶ Developing employees

▶ Understanding the mentoring process

▶ Developing employees despite downsizing

*1*t's time for a quick pop quiz. What kind of manager are you? Do you hire new employees and then just let them go their merry way? *(Funny, I thought I recognized you from somewhere.)* Or do you stay actively involved in the progress and development of your employees, helping to guide them along the way? If you're a manager-to-be, do you know what it's like to have a mentor — someone who takes a personal interest in your career development?

In every organization, you have a lot to learn: internal and external office politics, formal and informal hierarchies, the *right* and *wrong* ways to get things done, which people you should ignore, and which people you should pay close attention to. And this list doesn't even take into account the skills that you need to know to do your job: mastering a particular spreadsheet program or learning to speak in front of large groups of people, for example. Of course, every time you progress to a new level in the organization or take on a new task, your learning process starts anew.

Employee development doesn't just happen. It takes a conscious, concerted effort on the part of both managers *and* employees. And beyond that, it takes *time* and *commitment.* When you do employee development right, you don't just talk about it once a year at your employees' annual performance reviews. The *best* employee development is ongoing and requires that you support and encourage your employees' initiative. Recognize, however, that all development is *self*-development; that is, you can really only develop yourself. You can't force your employees to develop. They have to want to develop themselves.

Why Help Develop Your Employees?

Many very good reasons exist for helping your employees to develop. However, despite all these good reasons, development boils down to one thing: As a manager, you are in the best position to provide your employees with the support that they need to develop in your organization. Not only can you provide them with the time and money required for training, but you also can provide them with unique on-the-job learning opportunities and assignments, mentoring, team participation, and more. You see, employee development involves a *lot* more than just going to a training class or two. In fact, approximately 90 percent of development occurs *on the job*.

The terms *training* and *development* can have two distinctly different meanings. *Training* usually refers to teaching workers the skills that they need to know *right now* to do their jobs. *Development* usually refers to teaching employees the kinds of skills that they will need in the future as they progress in their careers. For this reason, employee development is often known as *career development*.

Now, in case you don't have any inkling whatsoever why developing your employees is a good idea, the following list provides just a few reasons. We're sure that many more exist, depending on your personal situation.

- ✔ **You may be taking your employees' knowledge for granted.** Have you ever wondered why your employees continue to mess up assignments that you are certain they can perform? Believe it or not, it's quite possible that they don't know how to do those assignments. Have you ever actually seen your employee perform the assignments in question?

  Say you give a pile of numbers to your assistant and tell him you want them organized and totaled within an hour. However, instead of presenting you with a nice, neat computer spreadsheet, your employee gives you a confusing mess. No, your employee isn't necessarily a hack incompetent; your employee may well not know how to put together a spreadsheet on his computer. Find out! The solution may be as simple as walking through your approach to completing the assignment with your employee and then having him give it a try.

- ✔ **Employees who work smarter are better employees.** Simply put, smarter employees are better employees. If you can help your employees develop and begin to work smarter and more effectively — and doubtless you *can* — why *wouldn't* you? No one in your organization knows everything there is to know about everything he or she *needs* to know. Find out what your employees *don't* know about their jobs and then make plans with them about *how* and *when* they will learn what they need to know. When your employees have achieved their development goals, they will work smarter, your organization will reap the benefits in greater employee efficiency and effectiveness, and you'll sleep better at night.

✔ **Someone has to be prepared to step into your shoes.** Do you ever plan to take a vacation? Or get a promotion? Or retire? How are you going to do any of these things if you don't help to prepare your employees to take on the higher-level duties that are part of your job? We both know managers who are so worried about what's going on at the office when they are on vacation that they call the office to check on things several times a day. Whether they are in Niagara Falls, Walt Disney World, or at a beach in Hawaii, they spend more time worrying about the office when they are on vacation than they do enjoying themselves.

The reason that many managers don't have to call their offices when *they* are on vacation is because they make it a point to help develop their employees to take over when they are gone. You can do the same thing, too; the future of your organization depends on it. Now, how about another mai-tai?

✔ **Your employee wins, and so does your organization.** What a great way to spend your scarce budget dollars! When you allocate funds to employee development, they win by learning higher-level skills and new ways of viewing the world — and your organization wins because of increased employee motivation and improved work skills. When you spend money for employee development, you actually double the effect of your investment because of this dual effect. It's a better deal than going to Vegas! And most important, you prepare your employees to fill the roles into which your organization will need them to move in the future.

✔ **Your employees are worth your time and money.** New employees cost a lot of money to recruit and train. And not only do you have to consider the investment in dollars, but you and the rest of your staff also have to make an investment in *time*.

A year or two ago, Peter's secretary accepted a promotion to another department. The result was a parade of three or four different temporary employees until Peter could recruit, interview, and hire a replacement. To say that this parade disrupted his organization is an understatement. After investing hours and hours of the staff's and his own time in training the temp in the essentials of the job, a new one would suddenly appear in her place. Then it was time for another round of training. Again and again.

When employees see that you have their best interests at heart, they are likely to want to work for you and learn from you. As a result, your organization will be able to attract talented people. Invest in your employees now, or waste your time and money finding replacements later. The choice is yours.

Working in the coal mine

Many jobs that were formerly the province of relatively less educated blue-collar workers are becoming increasingly technical. For example, in coal mining, career development used to mean learning how to use a new type of pickax or pneumatic drill. Now, however, miners are using laptop computers to monitor water quality and equipment breakdowns. At the Twentymile Mine, located near Oak Creek, Colorado, employees of Cyprus Amax Mineral Company have many skills to master in addition to wielding a shovel or driving a tractor. According to an executive of the firm, Cyprus Amax Mineral is looking for employees with "high math skills, more technical background, more comfort with electronics." Indeed, workers at the Twentymile Mine have an average of two years of college under their belts.

(Source: *Business Week,* Oct. 17, 1994.)

✔ **The challenge is stimulating to your employees.** Face it: Not every employee is so fortunate as to have the kind of exciting, jet-setting, make-it-happen job that you have. *Right?!?* For this reason, some employees occasionally become bored, lackadaisical, and otherwise indisposed. Why? Simply, employees constantly need new challenges and new goals to maintain interest in their jobs. And if *you* don't challenge your employees, you're guaranteed to end up with either an unmotivated, low-achievment workforce or employees who jump at offers from employers who *will* challenge them! Which option do *you* prefer?

Creating Career Development Plans

The career development plan is the heart and soul of your efforts to develop your employees. Unfortunately, many managers don't take the time to create development plans with their employees, instead trusting that, when the need arises, they will find training to accommodate the need. This kind of *reactive* thinking ensures that you will always be playing catch-up to the challenges that your organization will face in the years to come.

Why wait for the future to arrive before you prepare to deal with it? Are you *really* so busy that you can't spend a little of your precious time planting the seeds that your organization will harvest years from now? No! While you *do* have to take care of the seemingly endless crises that arise in the here and now, you also have to prepare yourself *and* your employees to meet the challenges of the future. To do otherwise is an incredibly short-sighted and ineffective way to run your organization.

All career development plans should contain at minimum the following key elements:

- ✔ **Specific learning goals:** Say, for example, that your employee's career path is going to start at the position of junior buyer and work its way up to manager of purchasing. The key learning goals for this employee might be to learn material requirements planning (MRP), computer spreadsheet analysis techniques, and supervision.

  When you meet with your employees to discuss their development plans, you identify specific learning goals for each employee. And don't forget: Each and every employee in your organization can benefit from having learning goals. Don't leave *anyone* out!

- ✔ **Resources required to achieve the designated learning goals:** After you identify your employee's learning objectives, you have to decide how he or she will reach them. Development resources include a wide variety of opportunities that support the development of your employees. Assignment to teams, job shadowing, stretch assignments, formal training, and more may be required. Formal training might be conducted by outsiders, by internal trainers, or perhaps in a self-guided series of learning modules. If the training requires funding or other resources to make them happen, identify those resources and make efforts to obtain them.

- ✔ **Required date of completion for each learning goal:** Plans are no good without a way to schedule the milestones of goal accomplishment and progress. Each learning goal has to have a corresponding date of completion. The dates you select should not be too close that they are difficult or unduly burdensome to achieve, nor so far into the future that they lose their immediacy and effect. The best schedules for learning goals allow employees the flexibility to get their daily tasks done while keeping ahead of the changes in the business environment that necessitate the employees' development in the first place.

- ✔ **Standards for measuring the accomplishment of learning goals:** For every goal, you must have a way to measure its completion. Normally, the manager assesses whether the employees actually use the new skills they have been taught. Whatever the individual case, make sure that the standards you use to measure the completion of a learning goal are clear and attainable and that both you and your employees are in full agreement with them.

The career development plan of our junior buyer might look like this:

Career Development Plan

Sarah Smith

Skill goal:

✔ Become proficient in material requirements planning (MRP).

Learning goal:

✔ Learn the basics of employee supervision.

Plan:

✔ Complete class "Basics of MRP" not later than the 1st quarter of FY 97. ($550 plus travel costs.)

✔ Successfully complete class "Intermediate MRP" not later than the 2nd quarter of FY 97. ($750 plus travel costs.)

✔ Shadow supervisor in daily work for half-days, starting immediately.

✔ Attend quarterly supervisor's update seminar on the 1st Wednesday of January, April, July, and October. (No cost: in-house.)

As you can see, this career development plan contains each of the four necessary elements that we described. A career development plan doesn't have to be complicated to be effective. In fact, when it comes to employee development plans, simpler is definitely better. Of course, the exact format that you decide on is not so important. The most important thing is that you *do* career development plans at all.

Helping Employees to Develop

Contrary to popular belief, employee development doesn't just happen all by itself; it takes the deliberate and ongoing efforts of employees with the support of their managers. If either party drops the ball, then employees *won't* develop, and the organization will suffer the consequences of not having the employees needed to meet the challenges that the future will bring. This outcome is definitely not good. As a manager, you want your organization to be ready for the future, not always trying to catch up to it.

The role of employees is to identify the areas where development will help to make them better and more productive workers in the future and to relay this information to their managers. After further development opportunities are identified, managers and employees work together to schedule and implement them.

As a manager, your role is to be alert to the development needs of your employees and to keep an eye out for potential development opportunities. Those of you who are in smaller organizations may have the assignment of determining where the organization is going to be in the next few years. Armed with that information, you are responsible for finding ways to ensure that employees are available to meet the needs of the future organization. Your job is then to provide the resources and support required to develop employees so that they will be able to fill the organization's needs.

To develop your employees to meet the coming challenges within your organization, follow these steps:

1. **Meet with your employees about their careers.**

   After you assess your employees, meet with them to discuss the places in the organization you see for them and also to find out where in the organization *they* want to go. This effort has to be a joint one! Having elaborate plans for an employee to rise up the company ladder in sales management is not going to do you any good if your employee *hates* the idea of leaving sales to become a manager of other salespeople.

2. **Discuss your employees' strengths and weaknesses.**

   Assuming that, in the preceding step, you discover that you are on the same wavelength as your employee, the next step is to have a frank discussion regarding his or her strengths and weaknesses. Your main goal here is to identify weaknesses or new skills that your employees need to develop to allow their continued upward progress in the organization and to meet the future challenges that your business faces. You should focus the majority of your development efforts and dollars here — in the future.

3. **Assess where your employees are now.**

   The next step in the employee development process is to determine the current state of your employees' skills and talents. Does Joe show potential for supervising other warehouse employees? Which employees have experience in doing customer demos? Is the pool of software quality assurance technicians adequate enough to accommodate a significant upturn in business? If not, can you develop internal candidates, or will you have to hire new employees from outside the organization? Assessing your employees provides you with an overall road map to guide your development efforts.

4. **Create career development plans.**

   Career development plans are agreements between you and your employees that spell out exactly what formal support (tuition, time off, travel expenses, and so on) they will receive to develop their skills and when they will receive it. Career development plans contain milestones for the achievement of learning goals and descriptions of any other resources and support needed to meet the goals that you agree to.

5. **Follow through on your agreements, and make sure that your employees follow through on theirs.**

   Don't break the development plan agreement! Make sure that you provide the support that you agree to provide *when* you agree to provide it. And make sure that your employees uphold their end of the bargain, too! Check on their progress regularly. If they miss schedules because of other priorities, reassign their work as necessary to ensure that they have time to focus on their career development plans.

So when is the best time to sit down with your employees to discuss career planning and development? The sooner the better! Unfortunately, many organizations closely tie career discussions to annual employee performance appraisals. On the plus side, doing so ensures that a discussion about career development happens at least once a year; on the minus side, development discussions become more of an afterthought than the central focus of the meeting. Not only that, but with the current rapid changes in competitive markets and technology, once a year just isn't enough to keep up. Planning for career development only once a year is like watering a plant only once a year!

Conducting a career development discussion twice a year with each of your employees is not too often, and four times a year is even better. Each discussion should include a brief assessment of the employee's development needs and what he or she believes can be done to fill them. If those needs require additional support, now is the time to determine what form this support will take and when it should be scheduled. Career development plans are adjusted and resources are redirected as necessary.

The top ten ways to develop employees

#1 Be a mentor to an employee.

#2 Let an employee fill in for you in staff meetings.

#3 Assign your employee to a team.

#4 Give your employee assignments that stretch his or her capabilities.

#5 Increase the scope and difficulty of an employee's assignments.

#6 Send your employee to a seminar on a new topic.

#7 Bring an employee along with you when you call on customers.

#8 Introduce your employee to top managers in your organization and arrange to have him or her perform special assignments for them.

#9 Invite an employee to sit in on an off-site management meeting.

#10 Allow an employee to shadow you during your work day.

Find a Mentor, Be a Mentor

When you are an inexperienced employee working your way up an organization's hierarchy, having someone with more experience to help guide you along the way is invaluable. Someone who has already seen what it takes to get to the top can advise you about the things that you should do and the things that you shouldn't do as you work your way up. This someone is called a *mentor.*

Isn't that what a *manager* is supposed to do? *No.* A mentor is most typically an individual high up in the organization who is *not* your boss. The job of a manager is clearly to coach and help guide employees, and though managers certainly can act as mentors for their own employees, mentors most often act as confidential advisers and sounding boards to their chosen employees and are therefore not typically in the employee's direct chain of command.

The day that a mentor finds you and takes you under his or her wing is a day for you to celebrate. Why? Because not everyone is lucky enough to find a mentor. And don't forget that someday you will be in the position to be a mentor to someone else. When that day comes, don't be so caught up in your busy business life to neglect to reach out and help someone else find his or her way up the organization.

Mentors provide definite benefits to the employees they mentor, and they further benefit the organization by providing needed guidance to employees who might not otherwise get it. Here are some of the reasons why mentors are a real benefit, both to your employees and to your organization:

- **Explain how the organization really works.** Mentors are a great way to learn what's *really* going on in an organization. There's usually a *big* difference between what is formally announced to employees and what *really* goes on in the organization — particularly within the ranks of upper management. Your mentor quite likely has intimate knowledge of the workings of the organization behind the formal pronouncements, and he or she can convey that knowledge to you (at least, the knowledge that isn't confidential) without your having to learn it the hard way.

- **Teach by example.** By watching *how* your mentor gets things done in the organization, you can learn a lot through his or her example. Your mentor has likely already seen it all, and he or she can help you discover the most effective and efficient ways to get things done. Why reinvent the wheel or get beat up by the powers that be when you don't have to?

- **Provide growth experiences.** A mentor can help guide you to activities above and beyond your formal career development plans that are helpful to your growth as an employee. For example, though it's not identified in your *official* development plan, your mentor might strongly suggest that you join a group such as Toastmasters to improve your public speaking skills. Your mentor makes this suggestion because he or she knows that public speaking skills are very important to your future career growth.

✔ **Share critical knowledge.** Wouldn't it be nice to know that your position is a dead end on the organization's promotional ladder? Or that your boss has a history of firing people who don't agree with her? Mentors can often give you that kind of critical information and more. Although not everything that a mentor tells you is going to have a life-or-death impact, and it is not appropriate for a mentor to disclose confidential information, occasionally the information that you learn makes a *big* difference in your career choices and in the kinds of training and career development that you seek.

✔ **Provide career guidance.** Your mentor has probably seen more than a few employees and careers come and go over the years. He or she will know which career paths in your organization are dead ends and which offer the most rapid advancement. This knowledge can be *incredibly* important to your future as you make career choices within an organization, and it is one of the most important bits of advice that your mentor can offer to you.

The mentoring process often happens when a more experienced employee takes a professional interest in a new or inexperienced employee. Employees can also initiate the mentoring process by engaging the interest of potential mentors while seeking advice or working on projects together. However, recognizing the potential benefits for the development of their employees, many organizations — including Merrill Lynch, Federal Express, and the Internal Revenue Service — have formalized the mentoring process and make it available to a wider range of employees than the old informal process ever could. If a formal mentoring program isn't already in place in your organization, why don't *you* recommend starting one?

Development and Downsizing

You've seen the numbers: x thousand employees laid off at IBM, y thousand employees laid off at AT&T, and z thousand employees laid off at General Motors — all within the last few years. Maybe *your* organization has felt the sharp knife of reengineering, downsizing, or reductions in force. If so, you may ask, "Isn't employee development too difficult to perform when everything is changing so fast around me? My employees might not even *have* careers next year, much less the need to plan for developing them."

Actually, nothing could be farther from the truth. While businesses are going through rapid change, employee development is more important than ever. As departments are combined, dissolved, or reorganized, employees have to be ready to take on new roles — duties that they may never have performed before. In some cases, employees may have to compete internally for positions or sell themselves to other departments to ensure that they retain their employment with the firm. In this time of great uncertainty, many employees feel that they may have lost control of their careers and even their lives.

Career planning and development provides employees in organizations undergoing rapid change with the tools that they need to regain control of their careers. The following list tells what some of the largest American companies have done to help their employees get through massive corporate downsizings and reorganizations:

- ✔ As a result of dramatic organizational changes, General Electric provided targeted career training for its crucial engineering employees. The firm also scheduled informal follow-up meetings with graduates of this engineering career training.

- ✔ Raychem, a maker of industrial products located in Menlo Park, California, offers its employees the services of an in-house career center. At this center, employees can take courses in resume writing and interviewing techniques and search for transfer or promotional opportunities within their company. Raychem CEO Robert J. Saldich said in the October 17, 1994 issue of *Business Week,* "We get a person who is fully engaged, who is excited about what he or she is doing — a much more productive, dedicated employee."

- ✔ At AT&T, management offered special three-day career development seminars to its employees nationwide in response to dramatic staff reductions.

- ✔ IBM overhauled the career plans of thousands of employees who transitioned from staff positions to sales positions as a result of a massive corporate reorganization.

Despite the obvious negative effects of downsizing on employee morale and trust, these times of change provide managers with a unique opportunity to shape the future of their organizations. For many managers, this will be the first time that they have such an opportunity to help "remake" the organization.

Employee development is more important than ever as employees are called upon to take on new and often more responsible roles in your organization. Your employees need your support now — make sure that you are there to provide it. This just might be one of the most valuable gifts that you can give to your employees.

Test your new-found knowledge

What are the four elements of a career development plan?

A. Learning goals, resources required, completion dates, and standards of measurement

B. Learning goals, class syllabus, dates of attendance, and grade transcripts

C. Description of intent, summary of commitment, specific resources allocated, and likely outcomes

D. Specific, motivating, attainable, and time-based

Is continuing employee development during organizational downsizing important?

A. Yes, the future of the organization depends on it.

B. No, things are changing too fast anyway.

C. No, it's better to wait until things calm down again.

D. None of the above.

Chapter 20

Quality and the Learning Organization

• •

In This Chapter

▶ Building quality into your organization

▶ Understanding systems thinking

▶ Unblocking obstacles to learning

▶ Making your organization a learning organization

• •

During the past decade, the focus of American business has been on *quality.* You can't seem to find any organization that doesn't have some sort of quality program in place. Both the private and public sectors embraced a new lexicon of management techniques with names such as *quality circles, total quality management, total quality leadership, continuous improvement,* and the *Deming method.* At Ford Motor Company, quality was (and still is) Job 1. Approximately 60 percent of midsized and large American businesses are providing these types of quality training to their employees.

In the United States, people create numerous new businesses every year. According to a study published in *Organizational Dynamics* magazine, after 5 years, only 38 percent survive. Only 21 percent of American businesses see their 10th birthday, and only 10 percent make it to their 20th birthday. Guess how many firms are around after 50 years? Not many — only 2 percent make it that far. And we're not just talking about the little mom-and-pop pizza joints on the corner here. Large, long-established firms are not invincible either. Of the Fortune 500 industrial firms listed in 1970, one-third were gone by 1983.

Why do so many businesses fail? Sure, an organization can blame its failure on any number of factors: changing markets, a lousy location, insufficient financing, unfair foreign competition, a militant union, or a wide variety of other handy excuses. However, the failure of many businesses seems to come down to one critical factor: a failure of the organization's management, and of the organization as a whole, to learn. Although the organization may have implemented progressive management programs such as quality improvement and employee empowerment, it may not have incorporated this new knowledge into its *culture* (or daily operations!).

For example, Peter's organization implemented a quality program to much fanfare several years ago. The program — which chartered cross-departmental quality teams to focus on organizational process improvements — was centered on five key beliefs similar to Dr. W. Edwards Deming's 14 Points (see the sidebar in this chapter). To make a long story short, this progressive management program ultimately failed, because the top management of the organization did not support it. Once the novelty of the program wore off, it was gone. The program failed because it was not incorporated into the *culture* of the organization.

As Dr. W. Edwards Deming, the father of the modern quality movement, put it, "The biggest problem that most any company in the Western world faces is not its competitors nor the Japanese. The biggest problems are self-inflicted, created right at home by management that are off course in the competitive world of today" (Mary Walton, *The Deming Management Method*).

Despite the comings and goings of endless flavor-of-the-month management programs marketed with the promise of curing any and all organizational ills, few organizations actually make the fundamental process and structural changes required to truly transform the organization. After the novelty of the program wears off — often only a few short weeks or months after its introduction — the organization goes back to business as usual.

Learning organizations, on the other hand, pick out the best approaches from the wide variety of innovative practices — both externally and internally — that are available, try them, and if they work, actually *make* the changes necessary to transform the business.

In this chapter, we consider how today's organizations are implementing quality improvement programs, we uncover the *real* obstacles to change and their solutions, and we discuss the importance of the learning organization to the future of business and how to set one up in *your* organization.

The Quality Movement

Before the Industrial Revolution, almost every product that anyone wanted to buy was produced substantially by hand. Skilled artisans built furniture, sewed clothing, constructed wagons, and so on — few mechanized processes existed at that time. However, after the Industrial Revolution took hold, machines began to take over people's roles in the production process. Machines created products, and workers' roles shifted to the operation of the machines that created the products.

Scientific management

In the early 1900s, researchers sought new ways to make production more efficient. Their efforts led to the blossoming of the field of *scientific* management. In his ground-breaking work, Frederick Winslow Taylor proposed that organizations could use well-defined rules and work standards to control worker performance. Taylor accomplished this by studying worker activities. He identified, defined, measured, timed, and refined each step in the production process. Armed with this information, managers could develop work procedures that were simple, direct, and efficient.

Taylor's work led to positive and long-lasting improvements:

- New workers — often recent immigrants with no factory experience — could be trained quickly and easily, because each employee's task was tightly circumscribed.
- Work processes became quite efficient, American industry boomed, and the country prospered.

However, this particular coin had two sides:

- Because these step-by-step work procedures defined workers' tasks so strictly, they stripped away worker creativity, initiative, and power.
- Workers became little more than machines themselves — performing the same repetitive tasks over and over, day after day, year after year. Not exactly a mind-expanding experience.

Indeed, scientific management *did* help the United States become an industrial powerhouse, tipping the balance of power in World War II and producing rivers of consumer goods — washing machines, toasters, televisions — to fuel the American dream in the 1950s and '60s. Unfortunately, with the drive for efficiency at any cost and the emphasis on *quantity,* something was lost. This something was *innovation.*

As long as the United States dominated world markets with its products, the loss of innovation wasn't a problem. No other country had a chance to compete with the wide variety of consumer and industrial goods that American industry produced. It seemed that American business would ride this wave of prosperity forever. However, on the other side of the Pacific Ocean — unnoticed by the American industrial powers that were flush with cash and confidence — a revolution was occurring. Not a revolution in government, but a revolution in business.

Japan: the rising sun

World War II decimated Japan's highly developed industrial base. In the early 1950s, Japan underwent the tortuous process of rebuilding its businesses and industries. Because everything — facilities, processes, management hierarchies, and so on — had been wiped away by the war, Japanese business leaders were able to start with a clean slate.

During Dr. W. Edwards Deming's early visits to Japan, he gained the attention of Japanese business leaders. In 1950, Deming was invited to give a course in quality-control methods to a group of Japanese engineers, managers, and researchers. The rest is history. Japanese industry adopted Deming's philosophy of statistical control and management, and production shot up along with the quality of the finished products. Before long, the label "Made in Japan" — once a sure sign of a shoddy piece of merchandise — became a symbol of quality: one that consumers the world over desired.

The shocking thing about the Deming saga is that while Deming was embraced as a national hero in Japan, his theories were generally ignored back home in the United States. Despite his success helping the Japanese get their industries back on track, and despite ongoing attempts to convince American managers of the compelling need for them to implement quality improvements, Deming and his theories remained relatively unknown in the United States. This changed in the 1980s when large American firms such as Ford discovered Deming and his teachings.

Dr. Deming's work with Ford resulted in the development of a corporate mission, the identification of corporate values, and a set of guiding principles to direct the actions of employees from day to day — all essential pieces in Ford's new quality philosophy. The following from Walton's *The Deming Management Method* are the guiding principles that Ford created:

- ✔ Quality comes first. To achieve customer satisfaction, the quality of our products and services must be our number one priority.

- ✔ Customers are the focus of everything we do. Our work must be done with our customers in mind, providing better products and services than our competition.

- ✔ Continuous improvement is essential to our success. We must strive for excellence in everything that we do: in our products, in their safety and value — and in our services, our human relations, our competitiveness, and our profitability.

- ✔ Employee involvement is our way of life. We are a team. We must treat each other with trust and respect.

- ✔ Dealers and suppliers are our partners. The Company must maintain mutually beneficial relationships with dealers, suppliers, and our other business associates.

Deming's 14 Points

Although the Japanese must be applauded for their success in creating affordable, high-quality products, you must not forget that much of the management innovation that laid the foundation for Japan's success is due to an American: Dr. W. Edwards Deming. Deming, who died in 1993, was a relentless management innovator and an obsessive proponent of quality. Peter had the good fortune to view Deming at a week-long satellite teleconference in 1992. Despite his age — Deming was 92 at the time — he radiated an excitement and energy about his life's work that many people half his age would be hard-pressed to rally.

Dr. Deming is particularly well known for his "14 Points," an item-by-item prescription for curing the ills of modern management practice. Many of these points are a routine part of many American businesses today, but this was not the case when Deming first put his points in writing some 30 years ago. If you aren't using them in your organization, why don't you give them a try?

"1. Create constancy of purpose toward improvement of product and service, with the aim to become competitive and stay in business, and to provide jobs.

2. Adopt the new philosophy. We are in a new economic age. Western management must awaken to the challenge, must learn their responsibilities, and take on leadership for change.

3. Cease dependence on inspection to achieve quality. Eliminate the need for inspection on a mass basis by building quality into the product in the first place.

4. End the practice of awarding business on the basis of price tag. Instead, minimize total cost.

5. Improve constantly and forever the system of production and service, to improve quality and productivity, and thus constantly decrease costs.

6. Institute training on the job.

7. Institute leadership. The aim of leadership should be to help people and machines and gadgets to do a better job. Leadership of management is in need of overhaul as well as leadership of production workers.

8. Drive out fear, so that everyone may work effectively for the company.

9. Break down barriers between departments. People in research, design, sales, and production must work as a team, to foresee problems of production and in use that may be encountered with the product or service.

10. Eliminate slogans, exhortations, and targets for the work force asking for zero defects and new levels of productivity. Such exhortations only create adversarial relationships, as the bulk of the causes of low quality and low productivity belong to the system and thus lie beyond the power of the work force.

11. (a) Eliminate work standards (quotas) on the factory floor. Substitute leadership. (b) Eliminate management by objective. Eliminate management by numbers, numerical goals. Substitute leadership.

12. (a) Remove barriers that rob the hourly worker of his right to pride of workmanship. The responsibility of supervisors must be changed from sheer numbers to quality. (b) Remove barriers that rob people in management and in engineering of their right to pride of workmanship. This means . . . abolishment of the annual or merit rating and of management by objective.

13. Institute a vigorous program of education and self-improvement.

14. Put everyone in the company to work to accomplish the transformation. The transformation is everybody's job."

(Source: Peter Scholtes, *The Team Handbook*.)

> ✔ Integrity is never compromised. The conduct of our Company worldwide must be pursued in a manner that is socially responsible and commands respect for its integrity and for its positive contributions to society. Our doors are open to men and women alike without discrimination and without regard to ethnic origin or personal beliefs.

Clearly, Ford's new philosophy led to great success for the company. According to the Hoover online company profiles found on America Online, five of the top eight best-selling cars and trucks in the United States are built by Ford, including the #1 car, the Ford Taurus, and the #1 truck, the Ford F-series pickup.

Following are a few more stories of companies that have successfully implemented quality programs:

> ✔ To provide its workers with the tools to improve quality, Motorola built an 88,000-square foot employee training facility at a cost of $10 million. Motorola also initiated more than 4,000 quality teams throughout the organization. According to Bill Smith, Motorola's vice-president and Senior Quality Assurance Manager, "Empowered to change the way they work, these teams are the backbone of Motorola's quality movement."
>
> ✔ Federal Express has improved quality by implementing an annual employee attitude survey. FedEx uses the surveys to determine where problems exist in the organization. Shortly after the results are distributed each year, managers arrange meetings with their employees to address and solve the problems that the surveys bring up.
>
> ✔ Monsanto Chemical Company trained its 15,000 workers in quality techniques and then gave them the power to make improvements in specific work processes by granting them the necessary freedom, resources, and authority. As a result, workers at Monsanto's LaSalle manufacturing facility increased the accuracy of the plant's inventory system from under 75 percent to over 99 percent and raised gross profit by $3 million in one year.

(Source: Stoner, Freeman, and Gilbert, *Management*.)

Unfortunately, although companies such as Ford, Motorola, and others have made quality, continuous improvement, and employee empowerment an integral part of their corporate cultures, many other companies give quality a try and then abandon their efforts after a short while. For many firms, quality improvement is nothing more than a fad, and their management teams are unwilling to make the fundamental reorganization of processes and structures that results in a capability to respond to the constant changes in global markets and competition.

For every company that adopts quality and makes it a permanent part of the organization, many, many more give it up shortly after implementing their programs. Workers, at first heartened by the empowerment that the quality movement promised, are left disappointed and demoralized as yet another management fad comes and goes. And the companies that once touted the benefits of jumping on board the quality bandwagon are left no better off than before — and perhaps a little worse.

The problem isn't within the quality movement itself; it is within the managers who for one reason or another fail to change their fundamental ways of doing business. They may tout the benefits of continuous improvement or total quality management in staff meetings, and perhaps even launch quality teams or steering committees. However, after the initial novelty wears off, many managers go right back to their old ways of doing business. In other words, they don't *learn*. The concept of the learning organization was developed and nurtured as a result of the observation of this phenomenon.

Starting a quality improvement program

In our years as managers, we have seen many quality improvement programs come and go. Despite the best intentions, and despite managers' and workers' tremendous interest in making improvements in their organizations, many quality improvement programs just don't *stick*. Starting a quality program takes a lot of work. And keeping it going takes even more work.

There are probably as many different models for instituting quality improvement programs as there are stars in the sky. The key to success is to be organized and to have a definite plan and procedure in place before you launch your program. Nothing kills a quality program faster than rolling it out prematurely before all the pieces are in place.

Follow these five steps to establish a basic quality improvement program in *your* organization:

1. **Secure top management buy-in.**

   For a quality improvement program to enjoy long-term success, you have to have the active support of your organization's top management team. Because quality programs empower workers by giving them the ability to make suggestions for organizational improvements — often across departmental lines and boundaries — some managers worry that they lose some amount of power in the process. In this crucial first step, your job is to sell top management on the benefits in real dollars-and-cents terms.

2. **Establish a quality steering committee.**

   This steering committee, which should consist of employees from different levels and parts of the organization, develops systems and procedures for soliciting improvement suggestions from employees and then analyzing them and making recommendations for disposition. In a small organization, the committee might consist of only one individual or a small group of two or three people. In a larger organization, the committee might be made up of 20 or more individuals. To ensure that your quality improvement program has clout (which is critical to the success of your efforts), make sure that the committee reports directly to someone on your organization's top management team, who can provide support and guidance as well as clear organizational obstacles.

3. Develop guidelines and procedures.

Although many models of successful programs exist, most have several basic elements in common:

- **Solicit employee quality improvement suggestions.** You do this via a form specifically developed for the purpose. On this form, the employee writes down the area needing improvement and a specific suggestion for making the improvement. Encourage employees to write their names on the suggestions so that you can question them in the event that you need more information about the problem. Then you route the suggestions directly to the quality steering committee for evaluation. Encourage employees to concentrate on suggestions that are within their own departments or work teams so that they can participate directly in developing solutions.

- **Review suggestions and determine disposition.** The quality steering committee reviews all suggestions and then determines where each suggestion should go from there. If the suggestion has merit, it can be routed to a manager for action or, for more complex issues, a cross-departmental team can study the issue and develop specific recommendations. If the committee needs more information before determining disposition, the suggestor can be called in to provide it. Return suggestions that don't have merit to the suggestor with a note thanking the person for the submission and explaining why no action was taken. All suggestors should receive a note of thanks, whether the suggestion is acted upon or not.

- **Track progress.** The steering committee should issue a regular report that summarizes the suggestions that have been received and the status of each one. This report should be distributed to all employees at least once a month. This system has two benefits: First, you can keep an eye on the nature of the suggestions and see whether your organization has specific problem areas. If, for example, all the suggestions are coming out of your payroll operation, either payroll is in trouble or your other employees aren't being open and honest with *their* problems. Second, the report *shows* employees that the quality improvement has been working.

4. Inform your employees.

Your employees need to know that they have been given the power to help make real changes in their organization. Most organizations communicate this important news in company newsletters, at staff meetings, via videos, or through many other means. To have the greatest impact on all employees, the person at the top of your organization — the president, general manager, director, or whoever — should make the formal announcement. This ensures that your employees get the message that quality improvement is a priority in your organization. The announcement should be followed closely by the distribution of the written guidelines and procedures developed in step 3 to all employees.

5. Review program results.

What good is a quality program if you can't measure the results? Shaky, at best. Periodically review the results of your program to determine whether employees are participating, to see whether certain departments seem particularly troubled, and to ensure that action is being taken on the suggestions referred to managers or other individuals or teams. If you can quantify the benefits of the improvements in terms of money saved, hours cut, customer service improved, or other similar factors, so much the better.

Systems Thinking

In the old style of organization, the focus of management is to solve specific problems as they arise. An employee isn't working up to standard? Better discipline the employee and fix the problem. Quality defects are up? Better increase the number of inspectors to ensure that problems are caught before the product ships. Whenever something breaks — a product, a machine, or a worker — the manager's job is to fix it. *If I just fix this one last problem, everything will be okay.*

The fundamental predicament with this style of management by crisis is that it doesn't fix the underlying problems that lead to the breakdown in the first place — it only puts a patch on the immediate issue. Usually with a short-term fix that covers up the problem temporarily. Managing in this manner is sort of like a doctor who treats the symptoms of a brain tumor with aspirin. The aspirin may relieve some of the symptoms for a short while — the headaches and the generalized pain — but the underlying cause is left unidentified and untreated. If the doctor doesn't bother to take the steps necessary to discover the underlying cause of the symptoms, the patient will surely die. Similarly, the manager who treats the symptoms of organizational failure without addressing the underlying cause risks a comparable fate.

Many managers are now aware that solving organizational problems involves more than merely treating the symptoms of failure. The term *systems thinking* has developed to describe the awareness that one cannot consider events in an organization in isolation. Any change to one part of an organization, whether positive or negative, affects someone or something in another part of the organization. Managers must see how one event affects the entire organization, not simply how individual events affect things on a local, departmental level.

In his pioneering work on the learning organization, MIT management theorist Peter Senge offers the following five key skills for managers to use in applying the concept of systems thinking:

- ✔ **Seeing interrelationships, not things, and processes, not snapshots:** Many managers tend to see isolated incidents and problems, not series of actions or steps. The result is a narrowing of focus and a failure to see how changes in one step of a process affect all others, and how changes in one part of an organization affect the rest of the organization. Systems thinking requires that you step back and look at the big picture.

- ✔ **Moving beyond blame:** Most organizational problems result from bad *systems* or *processes* — not bad *employees.* This being the case, blaming or punishing employees for performance that doesn't meet your expectations does no good because the employee can do nothing about the performance problem. Instead of blaming employees, managers who practice systems thinking closely examine their organizations' systems to find the root of the problem.

- ✔ **Distinguishing detail complexity from dynamic complexity:** Systems thinking involves two kinds of complexity: detail and dynamic.

    - • *Detail* complexity refers to the kind of complexity that results from a large quantity of different variables. Most managers are referring to this kind of complexity when they say that an issue is *complex.*

    - • *Dynamic* complexity arises when the cause of an action and its ultimate effect are located some time into the future, and the impact of managerial interventions are not obvious to most employees. In systems thinking, the greatest gains are to be found in a system's dynamic complexity.

- ✔ **Focusing on areas of high leverage:** A high leverage area is one where the greatest gains can be made with the least amount of effort. In many cases, the most obvious solutions result in the least improvement while smaller, less obvious solutions result in much greater gains. Systems thinking leads managers to always seek the solutions that they can accomplish with the least effort but that result in the greatest and longest-lasting gains to the organization.

- ✔ **Avoiding symptomatic solutions:** Treating the *symptoms* of organizational disease rather than the underlying causes results only in short-term fixes, not long-term cures. Managers constantly have to fight the pressure to make the quick fix and instead focus on discovering solutions that address the underlying causes and result in lasting improvement.

(Source: "The Leader's New Work: Building Learning Organizations," *Sloan Management Review,* Fall 1990.)

Obstacles to Learning

What do you think the greatest obstacle to learning is in most any organization? Is it workers' desire to maintain the status quo? Employees certainly like to have stability and predictability in their lives, but that's not it. Is it the stacks of written policies in those big, black vinyl binders that haven't been updated since the last millennia? Sure, excessive policies that aren't kept up to date with changes in the organization's environment and all the red tape that they represent often do little more than to stifle innovation and hamstring the efforts of workers to make positive changes in their workplaces. Or maybe the assistant to the vice president for sales? No, even though he may be the biggest pain in the neck in the entire organization, he's not the problem, either.

No, although all these things — and many others — may contribute to an organization's resistance to learning and ultimate doom to failure in the rapidly changing global business environment, one thing has the greatest impact on the capability of an organization to learn.

The greatest obstacle to learning in your organization is your organization's top management team.

Think about it for a moment. When an organization is in crisis and the ongoing efforts of the current management team fail to turn the organization around, what happens? The first thing you see is an article in *The Wall Street Journal* or your favorite business weekly announcing the "resignation" of the company's president and the installation of a new person at the helm. And the next announcement is usually the one the new president makes when he or she removes the rest of the top management team and installs his or her own selections in these posts.

When an organization is in trouble and top management can do nothing to turn things around, the organization has to *unlearn* its bad habits — and fast! — to get back onto the track for success. So how does an organization unlearn the things that once made the firm successful but that are now dragging it down? The quickest way to accomplish this task is to remove the top management team so that the organization can *learn* new habits that enable it to succeed. You see, old habits are sometimes very hard to break. When a company president or other executive or manager has had success in an organization, there is little reason for him or her to change the things that made success possible. If it worked in the past, why wouldn't it work in the future? Instead of embracing change, such executives fight it. The easiest way for the organization to learn is to remove a recalcitrant executive team.

Take the recent case of Apple Computer, for example. On February 2, 1996, the board of directors of Apple Computer, Inc., fired chief executive officer Michael Spindler. Why? When Spindler took Apple's reins in 1993, revenues for the year were $7.9 billion, gross margin was at 34 percent, and the market share of the company's personal computers stood at 14 percent. However, although

Spindler made dramatic cuts in product prices and production costs and laid off 2,000 employees, and although revenues in 1995 climbed to $11 billion, gross margin was down to 15 percent and the personal computer market share for the year fell to 7.8 percent (7.1 percent in the fourth quarter of 1995). Investors were not happy.

The key thing that always separated Apple's products from the ocean of less expensive and less capable IBM PC clones that flooded the personal computer market was its leadership in technological innovation. According to Apple cofounder Steve Jobs, who was himself ousted from his position as Apple's chief executive officer in 1985, Apple once enjoyed a ten-year jump on its PC competitors. However, says Jobs, something happened — or rather, didn't happen. "Apple didn't fail. The trouble with Apple is it succeeded beyond its wildest dream. The rest of the world became just like it. The trouble is, the dream didn't evolve. Apple stopped creating," he said (*San Jose Mercury-News* on America Online, downloaded 3/20/96). As a result, most customers no longer had a reason to pay Apple's premium prices. As PCs using Microsoft Windows became more like Apple's products, the technology advantage that Apple enjoyed for many years slowly evaporated.

So although Spindler slashed prices, trimmed production costs, and laid off 2,000 employees — creating a sizable sales boost in 1994 — his management team botched several attempts to sell the company to big players such as IBM and Hewlett-Packard; corporate buyers — increasingly nervous about Apple's long-term viability — began delaying orders and switching over from Apple personal computers to IBM PC-compatibles; and Standard & Poor's lowered its rating of a portion of Apple's debt to "junk."

Clearly, it was time for a change. At an emergency meeting on January 31, 1996, Apple's board gave Spindler the news: His services were no longer required. Two days later, Spindler cleaned out his desk and Gilbert Amelio, chief executive officer of National Semiconductor and a member of Apple's board, was installed as Apple's new chief executive. Shortly after his appointment, Amelio announced the hiring of a new chief administrative officer and chief financial officer from outside the company. Then, in March 1996, Amelio created a new position in the firm, Vice President of Internet Platforms, to coordinate Apple's nacent Internet strategy. In a few short days, the board of directors transformed the organization and created a situation in which it could unlearn by removing the company's chief executive officer. At the same time, Apple learned new, hopefully more successful habits by hiring a new chief executive.

Now, wouldn't finding a way to enable the organization to learn new ways of responding to change be better than having to *unlearn* — by removing the top management team — every so many years? Yes, it would! Not only would managers feel more secure about their job stability and workers less insecure about possible layoffs, but the organization would also waste less money, time, and energy in transitioning from management team to management team.

Fortunately, you *do* have a way to accomplish this: by creating a learning organization.

Creating a Learning Organization

A *learning organization* is an organization that can effectively develop and use knowledge to make change for the better. Ever since Peter Senge's groundbreaking book *The Fifth Discipline* was published in 1990, the question of how to create and lead organizations in which continuous learning occurs has been at the top of many managers' lists of management techniques to consider.

The problem with the old, command-and-control way of doing business is that it is built on the premise that the world, and all that goes on within it, is a predictable place. If you can just build a model that is large and complex enough, you can anticipate *any* eventuality. There's only one problem with that particular view of things: The world is *not* predictable. The global world of business is chaos — what is true today will surely be washed away tomorrow as the next wave of change hits. The *only* thing that is predictable in today's organizations is that they do change. And change. And change again.

The idea of the learning organization is designed around the assumption that organizations are going through rapid change and that managers should *expect* the unexpected. Indeed, managers who work for learning organizations welcome the inevitable unexpected events that occur within an organization, because they consider them to be opportunities, not problems. Instead of static organizations that are strictly hierarchical, learning organizations are flexible and less hierarchical than traditional organizations. This structure makes managers much better able to *lead* change instead of merely reacting to change.

So exactly how do you go about designing a learning organization? Several characteristics are particularly important as you consider turning your *own* organization into a learning organization. The more of each characteristic that your organization exhibits, the closer it is to being a learning organization — one that thrives in times of rapid change (such as *right now!*).

- **Encourage objectivity.** Over the course of our careers, we have seen managers make *many* organizational decisions simply to please someone with power, influence, or an incredible ego. Such subjective decisions — reached not through a reasoned consideration of the facts but through emotion — are rarely as good as decisions made in an *objective* review of the facts. As a manager, you should both encourage objectivity in your employees and coworkers *and* practice objectivity in your own decision-making.

- **Seek openness.** For an organization to learn, employees have to be willing to tell each other the truth. To make this openness possible, you must create safe environments for your employees to say what is *really* on their minds and to tell you, their manager, bad news without fear of retribution. Driving fear out of the organization should be a top priority of every manager who wants to build a learning organization.

✔ **Insist on teamwork.** Deploying employee teams is a very important part in the development of learning organizations. You would be hard pressed to name any learning organization that hasn't implemented teams widely throughout the organization. When an organization relies on individuals to respond to changes in its environment, one or two individuals may pick up the torch and run with it; however, when an organization relies on teams to respond to change, many more employees are mobilized much more quickly. Not only that, but the best solution will more likely be reached because the team obtains the benefits of *all* its members. And this can mean the difference between life and death in the ever-changing global business environment.

✔ **Create useful tools.** Managers in learning organizations need the tools that enable employees to quickly and easily obtain the information that they need to do their jobs. Computer networks, for example, have to be set up with access for *all* employees, and they have to provide the kinds of financial and other data that decision-makers need to make the *right* decisions. The best tools are those that get the right information to the right people at the right time.

✔ **Consider the behavior you are rewarding.** Remember the phrase, "You get what you reward." What actions are you rewarding, and what behaviors are you getting in return? If you want to build a learning organization, rewarding the behaviors that help you create a learning organization is essential. Stop rewarding behaviors that are inconsistent with building a learning organization such as subjectivity and individualism. The sooner you accomplish this mission, the better.

Test your new-found knowledge

Which of the following is one of Deming's 14 points?

A. Always take the path of least resistance.

B. Remember the golden rule.

C. Don't worry, be happy.

D. Drive out fear so that everyone can work effectively for the company.

What is systems thinking?

A. The awareness that one cannot consider events in an organization in isolation.

B. Always seeking the equilibrium of systems.

C. It doesn't really matter.

D. None of the above.

Part VII
The Part of Tens

"WE OFFER A CREATIVE MIS ENVIRONMENT WORKING WITH STATE-OF-THE-ART PROCESSING AND COMMUNICATIONS EQUIPMENT; A COMPREHENSIVE BENEFITS PACKAGE, GENEROUS PROFIT SHARING, STOCK OPTIONS, AND, IF YOU'RE FEELING FUNKY AND NEED TO CHILL OUT AND RAP, WE CAN DO THAT TOO."

In this part . . .

These short chapters are packed with quick ideas that can help you become a better manager. Read them anytime you have an extra minute or two.

Chapter 21

Ten Common Management Mistakes

Yes, it's true: Managers make mistakes. Mistakes are nature's way of showing you that you're learning. Edison once said that it takes 10,000 mistakes to find an answer. As Peter's instructor once asked him at a frosty (32 degrees *below* zero at 9:00 a.m., no wind chill) ski school in Quebec, "Is that your nose lying there on the snow?" No, actually, Fritz's lesson was much more profound than that: "If you're not falling down, you're not learning." Bob's driver's education teacher taught him a similar lesson in the 11th grade, just before he wrecked the family car: "If you're not crashing, you're not learning." You get the idea.

This chapter lists ten traps that new and experienced managers alike can fall victim to.

Not Making the Transition from Worker to Manager

When you're a worker, you have a job and you do it. Although your job likely requires you to join a team or to work closely with other employees, you are ultimately responsible only for yourself. Did you attain *your* goals? Did *you* get to work on time? Was *your* work done correctly? When you become a manager, everything changes. Suddenly, you are responsible for the results of a *group* of people, not just for *yourself*. Did *your employees* attain their goals? Are *your employees* highly motivated? Did *your employees* do their work correctly?

Becoming a manager requires the development of a whole new set of business skills: *people* skills. Some of the most talented employees from a technical perspective become the *worst* managers because they fail to make the transition from worker to manager.

Failing to Delegate

Despite the ongoing efforts of many managers to prove otherwise, you can't do everything by yourself. And even if you could, doing everything by yourself is not the most effective use of your time or talent as a manager. You may very well be the best statistician in the world, but when you become the manager of a *team* of statisticians, your job changes. Your job is no longer to perform statistical analyses, but to manage and develop a group of employees.

When you delegate work to employees, you multiply the amount of work that you can do. A project that seems overwhelming on the surface is suddenly quite manageable when you divide it up among 12 different employees. Not only that, but when you delegate work to employees, you create opportunities to develop their work and leadership skills. Whenever you take on a new assignment or work on an ongoing job, ask yourself whether one of your employees can do it instead.

Not Setting Goals with Employees

Do the words *rudderless ship* mean anything to you? They should. Effective performance starts with clear goals. If you don't set goals with your employees, the result is often an organization that has no direction and employees who have few challenges and therefore have little motivation to do anything but show up for work and collect their paychecks. Your employees' goals begin with a vision of where they want to be in the future. It is then up to you as a manager to meet with your employees to develop realistic, attainable goals that guide them in their efforts to achieve the organization's vision. Don't leave your employees in the dark. Help them to help you, *and* your organization, by setting goals and then by working with them to achieve those goals.

Failing to Communicate

In many organizations, it's a miracle that anyone knows anything at all about what's *really* going on in the organization. Information is power, and some managers use information — in particular, the *control* of information — to ensure that they are the most knowledgeable and therefore the most valuable individuals in an organization. Some managers shy away from social situations and naturally avoid communicating with their employees. Others are just too busy. They simply don't make efforts to communicate information to their employees on an ongoing basis, either letting other, more pressing business take precedence or "forgetting" to tell their employees.

Whatever the reason, the widespread dissemination of information throughout an organization, and the communication that enables this dissemination to happen, is essential to the health of today's organizations — especially during times of change (translation: *all* the time). Employees *must* be empowered with information so that they can make the best decisions at the lowest possible level in the organization: quickly and without the approval of higher-ups.

Failing to Learn

Most managers are accustomed to success, and they initially learned a lot to make that success happen. Many were plucked from the ranks of workers and promoted into positions as managers for this very reason. Oftentimes, however, they catch a dreaded disease — *hardening of the attitudes* — after they become managers, and they only want things done *their* way.

Successful managers find the best ways to get things done and accomplish their goals, and then they develop processes and policies to institutionalize these effective approaches to doing business. This method is great as long as the organization's business environment doesn't change. However, when it does, if the manager doesn't change with it — that is, doesn't *learn* — the organization suffers as a result.

This situation can be particularly difficult for a manager who has found success by doing business a certain way. The model of manager as an unchanging rock that stands up to the storm is no longer valid. Today, managers have to be ready to change the way they do business as their environments change around them. They have to be constantly learning, experimenting, and trying new things. To do otherwise dooms a manager to extinction — just like that big Tyrannosaurus Rex in the movie *Jurassic Park.*

Resisting Change

If you think that you can stop change, you're fooling yourself. You may as well try standing in the path of a hurricane to make it change its course. Good luck! The sooner you realize that the world — *your* world included — is going to change whether you like it or not, the better. Then you can concentrate your efforts on taking actions that make a positive difference in your business life. This means learning how to adapt to change and use it to your advantage rather than fighting it.

Instead of reacting to changes *after* the fact, proactively anticipate the changes that are coming your way and make plans to address them *before* they hit your organization. Ignoring the need to change does not make that need go away.

Not Making Time for Employees

To some of your employees, you are a resource. To others, you're a trusted associate. Still others may consider you to be a teacher or mentor, while others see you as a coach or parent. However your employees view you, they have one thing in common: All your employees need your time and guidance during the course of their careers. Managing is a "people" job — you need to make time for people. Some workers may need your time more than others; it's important that you assess the needs of each of your employees and address them.

Although some of your employees may be highly experienced and require little supervision on your part, others may need almost constant attention when they are new to a job or task. When an employee needs to talk, make sure that you are available. Put your work aside for a moment, ignore your phone, and give your employee your undivided attention. Not only do you show your employees that they are important, but when you focus on *them,* you *really* hear what they have to say.

Not Recognizing Employee Achievements

In these days of constant change, downsizing, and increased worker uncertainty, finding ways to recognize your employees for the good work that they do is more important than ever. The biggest problem is not that managers don't want to reward employees — most managers agree that rewarding employees is important — it's that many managers don't *take the time* to recognize their employees.

Although raises, bonuses, and other perks have largely evaporated in many organizations, you can do many things that take little time to accomplish, are easy to implement, and cost little or no money. In fact, the most effective reward — personal and written recognition from one's manager — doesn't cost a thing. You should never be so busy that you can't take a minute or two to recognize your employees' achievements. Your employees' morale, performance, and loyalty will surely improve as a result.

Going for the Quick Fix Over the Lasting Solution

Every manager loves to solve problems and fix the parts of his or her organization that are broken. The constant challenge of the new and unexpected (and that second-floor, corner office) attracts many people to management in the first place. Unfortunately, in their zeal to *fix* problems quickly, many managers neglect to take the time necessary to seek out long-term solutions to the problems of their organizations.

Instead of diagnosing cancer and performing major surgery, many managers perform merely what amounts to sticking on a Band-Aid. Although it's not as fun as being a firefighter, you have to look at the entire system and find the *cause* if you really want to solve a problem. After you find the cause of the problem, you can develop real solutions that have lasting effect. Anything less isn't really solving the problem; you're merely treating the symptoms.

Taking It All Too Seriously

Yes, business is serious business. If you don't think so, just see what happens if you blow your budget and your company's bottom line goes into the red as a result. You quickly learn just how serious business can be. Regardless — indeed, *because* — of the gravity of the responsibilities that managers carry on their shoulders, you must maintain a sense of humor and foster an environment that is fun, both for you *and* your employees. Invite your employees to a potluck at the office, an informal get-together at a local lunch spot, or a barbecue at your home. Surprise them with special awards for things such as the strangest tie or the most creative workstation. Joke with your employees. Be playful.

When managers retire, they usually aren't remembered for the fantastic job that they did in creating department budgets or disciplining employees. Instead, people remember that someone who didn't take work so seriously and remembered how to have fun brightened their days or made their work more tolerable. Don't be a stick in the mud. Live every day as if it were your last.

Chapter 22

Ten Great No-Cost Ways to Recognize Employees

· ·

*A*re you giving your employees the recognition they deserve? We certainly hope so! Why? Because recognizing your employees for doing a good job is one of the best ways to keep them motivated and engaged in their work. And not only that, but you don't have to break your budget to do it. There are countless ways to thank and appreciate employees for doing a good job, and many of them require little if any money to do. No, you don't need to send your employees to the Bahamas or give them $1,000 bonuses or gold-plated coffee warmers. Ironically, no-cost forms of recognition such as the ten that follow can be among the most motivating to employees. Don't believe us? Try them and see for yourself!

Interesting Work

Although some of the tasks that you personally perform day in and day out may have long ago become routine for you, these very same tasks may be *very* exciting and *very* challenging for your employees. When your employees excel at their assignments, reward them by delegating some of *your* duties to them or by designing interesting projects for them to work on. It doesn't cost you a dime, and your employees are stimulated at the same time that they develop their work skills. Your employees win, and your organization wins, too.

Visibility

Everyone wants to be recognized and appreciated for doing a good job. One of the easiest and most effective ways to reward your employees for no cost is to recognize them publicly for their efforts. You can gain visibility for your employees' efforts by announcing their accomplishments in staff meetings, sending out e-mail messages that congratulate your employees for their fine work — with copies to all the other employees in the department or organization — submitting articles about your employees' efforts to the company newsletter, and many other similar approaches. Give it a try. What have you got to lose? This technique is free, easy, and *very* effective.

Time Off

Another great, no-cost way to reward your employees is to give them some time off. In today's busy business world, time off from work has become an increasingly valuable commodity. People want to spend more time with their friends and families and less time in the office. Of course, the effect of downsizing and reengineering has been to give everyone *more* work to do, not *less*. Whether you give an hour off or a day off, your employees will be pleased to be able to get away from the office for a short while to take care of personal business, go fishing, or just *relax*. They will return refreshed from the time off and grateful for the recognition that you gave for their efforts.

Information

Your employees *crave* information. However, some managers hoard information and guard it as though they were in charge of all the gold in Fort Knox. Instead of withholding information from your employees, share it with them. Fill them in on how the organization is doing and what kinds of things are in store for the future — both for the organization as a whole *and* for your employees. By giving your employees information, you not only empower them with the tools that they need to make more informed and better decisions, but you also demonstrate that you value them as people. Isn't that what *everyone* wants?

Feedback on Performance

Employees want more than ever to know how they are doing in their jobs. The only one who can *really* tell them how they are doing is you, their manager. Ask them to join you for lunch or to get a soda. Ask them how things are going and whether they have any questions or need help with their work. Provide them with feedback on their performance. Thank them for doing a good job. You don't have to wait until your employees' annual performance review to give them feedback. Indeed, the more feedback you give your employees, and the more often you give it, the better able they are to respond to your needs and to the needs of the organization.

Involvement

Involve employees — especially in decisions that affect them. Doing so shows your employees that you respect their opinions, and it also ensures that you get the best input possible in the decision-making process. Employees who are closest to a work process or a customer are often in the best position to see the best solution when a problems arises. Your employees know what works and what doesn't — perhaps even better than you do. Unfortunately, many workers are never asked for their opinion, or if they are, their opinions are quickly discarded. As you involve other employees, you increase their commitment to the organization and at the same time help to ease the implementation of a new idea or organizational change. The cost? Zero. The payoff? Huge.

Independence

Employees highly value being given the latitude to perform their work the way they see fit. No one likes a supervisor or manager who always hovers over employees' shoulders, reminding them of the exact way something should be done and correcting them every time they make a slight deviation. When you tell employees what you want done, provide them with the necessary training, and then give them the room to decide *how* they get their work done, you increase the likelihood that they will perform to your expectations. Not only that, but independent employees bring additional ideas, energy, and initiative to their jobs, too.

Celebrations

Birthdays, company anniversaries, the highest average number of units produced, the longest unbroken safety record, and many, many other milestones are terrific reasons to celebrate. Buy a few Twinkies and throw a party! (Okay, so this idea isn't exactly *no* cost.) *Your employees* will appreciate the recognition, and *you'll* appreciate the improved performance and loyalty that you get from your employees in return.

Flexibility

All employees appreciate having flexibility in their jobs. Although some jobs, such as receptionists, retail clerks, and security guards, clearly require strict schedules and work locations, many other jobs — computer programmers, technical writers, financial analysts, for example — aren't so tied to the clock or to your established workplace. Giving your employees flexibility in determining their own work hours and their own workplace can be very motivating to them. In organizations where giving employees *this* much flexibility is not possible, you can still empower your employees with the authority to make day-to-day decisions about exactly how they perform their work or how they respond to customer service issues.

Increased Responsibility

Most employee development happens on the job. This development comes from the new learning opportunities that you provide to your employees, as well as the chance to gain new skills and experience in an organization. Few employees are satisfied with going nowhere — most hope to learn more, to be involved in higher-level decisions, and to progress in both responsibility and compensation. Giving your employees new opportunities to perform, learn, and grow is therefore *very* motivating. It shows your employees that you trust and respect them and that you have their best interests at heart. You aren't going to motivate your employees by building a fire *under* them. Instead, find ways to build a fire *within* them to make work a place where your employees want and are able to do their best.

Chapter 23

Ten Classic Business Books You Need to Know About

● ●

An incredible variety of business books is available for you to read and to buy. Becoming bewildered by all the choices is easy, and sorting out which books are of the greatest benefit to managers is difficult.

In the list that follows, we have already done the heavy lifting for you. Every manager should buy and read these ten classic business books (plus a bonus 11th) before reading any other business book (except this one, of course!).

Managing for Results

Peter F. Drucker (Harper & Row, 1964)

In this book — a real classic in the field of management — Drucker takes the development of his management theories a step further by showing readers what they must do to create an organization that will prosper and grow. Drucker does this by encouraging readers to focus on opportunities in their organizations rather than on problems. The book also suggests that managers must take a hard look at an organization's strengths and weaknesses to develop effective plans and strategies.

The Human Side of Enterprise

Douglas McGregor (McGraw-Hill, 1960)

The first wake-up call for managers everywhere, this book proclaims that (gasp!) people play a big part in the success of any business. Specifically, a manager's assumptions about the people that work for him or her dictate many of the results that ultimately follow. This book produced the birth of Theory X and its negative assumptions of human behavior (for example, "People are lazy") and Theory Y, which focuses on the positive assumptions of human behavior (for example, "People want to do a good job"). McGregor argues that relying on authority as the primary means of control in industry leads to "resistance, restriction of output, indifference to organizational objectives, the refusal to accept responsibility and results in inadequate motivation for human growth and development." Still relevant reading for managers today who just don't get why employees are so important.

The Peter Principle

Dr. Laurence Peter and Raymond Hull (Morrow, 1969)

The Peter Principle says that in a hierarchy, every employee tends to rise to his or her level of incompetence. This book is an amusing look at how hierarchies work in organizations and what managers can do to ensure that employees aren't assigned to tasks beyond their capabilities. A must!

Up the Organization

Robert Townsend (Knopf, 1970)

This book, written by the former CEO of Avis, offers up some pithy advice for business people everywhere. Townsend discusses the strategies that helped drive Avis's success in a fun, readable format. The book includes such gems as: "Don't hire Harvard MBAs" (they just want to be CEOs anyway, so they focus on that as their main goal) and "Fire the human resources department" (Townsend believes that this function should be the job of every manager).

The One Minute Manager

Kenneth Blanchard and Spencer Johnson (Morrow, 1982)

Written in a unique parable format, this book became an instant business classic. Even today, it is a perennial resident on most business best-seller lists. *The One Minute Manager* teaches readers three very simple but important management skills (One Minute Goal Setting, One Minute Praisings, and One Minute Reprimands), and it does so in an entertaining but informative way. A true classic.

In Search of Excellence

Thomas Peters and Robert Waterman (Harper & Row, 1982)

In this groundbreaking work, Peters and Waterman distill the practices of America's best companies into eight basic practices that are characteristic of successful companies:

- They have a bias for action.
- They stay close to the customer.
- They encourage autonomy and entrepreneurship.
- They seek productivity through people.
- They are hands-on and value-driven.
- They stick to their knitting.
- They have a simple form and a lean staff.
- They hold simultaneous loose-tight properties.

One of the best parts of this book is the wealth of real-life examples of how America's best companies got where they are — and what they will do to stay there.

The Goal

Eliyahu Goldratt and Jeff Cox (North River Press, Second Edition, 1992)

This well-paced novel — a business parable — features Alex Rogo, a UniCo plant manager in fictional Bearington, U.S.A. Alex has big problems: He has been given three months to turn his plant around or face shutdown. Suddenly, Alex encounters his kindly old physics professor, Jonah, who sets him on an almost mystical quest for "the goal." Along the way, he learns that the real lesson is to avoid orthodoxies of all kinds and accept the need for constant reexamination of every process. Woven into this narrative is much valid information about various weighty concepts — among them, just-in-time manufacturing, total quality management, and computer-integrated factories.

Leadership Is an Art

Max Du Pree (Doubleday, 1989)

When Max Du Pree wrote this book, he was chairman of the board of furniture manufacturer Herman Miller — a firm well known for being a management innovator. Du Pree's main premise is that leadership isn't a science or a discipline; it's an art. For this reason, leadership has to be experienced, created, and felt. This perspective is quite different from the old-style model of management that depends on strict rules and policies and the measurement of results.

The Fifth Discipline: The Art and Practice of the Learning Organization

Peter Senge (Doubleday/Currency, 1990)

This book started the learning/systems fad in business, which is still going strong. It encourages organizations to view systems thinking, personal growth, and work from a new perspective. Senge argues that organizations should make learning a continuous process rather than treat it as a series of distinct, unrelated events. He claims that everyone in an organization has a responsibility to help create a learning organization, with top managers playing a crucial role in the process. He also encourages organizations to realize the importance of reflection, as opposed to action, in business. (Yeah, but who's going to help the customer?)

The Wisdom of Teams

Jon R. Katzenbach and Douglas K. Smith (Harvard Business School Press, 1993)

Katzenbach and Smith define a team as "a small number of people with complementary skills who are committed to a common purpose, performance goals, and [an] approach for which they hold themselves mutually accountable." The authors analyze teams broadly, dividing them by function into those that do things, those that recommend things, and those that run things. This analysis helps people understand why the meetings of an operational team, an advisory board, and a quality team are often so different in purpose and format. (But who's in charge of bringing the donuts?)

This book argues that team learning is the most important kind, and that "the same team dynamics that promote performance also support learning and behavioral change, and do so more effectively than larger organizational units or individuals left to their own devices."

The Game of Work

Charles Coonradt (Deseret, 1984)

Coonradt observes that the same workers who complain about something in the workplace — office temperature, for example — will ignore the fact that the external environment is even worse to participate in some form of recreation, such as golf or tennis. In *The Game of Work,* Coonradt shows the reader how to get employees to use the same motivation in the workplace that they bring to their recreational pursuits. Using this principle, the author claims that anyone in an organization can achieve better results — and make work fun in the process!

Index

●●●

• A •

accountability. *See* responsibility
accounting
  assets, 280–281
  as cumulations of transactions, 279
  double-entry bookkeeping, 283
  example of make-or-buy decision, 284
  importance of understanding, 279
  liabilities, 281–282
  owners' equity, 282
  See also budgeting; financial statements
accounts payable, 281
accrued expenses, 282
ACT (contact management software), 40
ad hoc groups as team efforts, 197
adaptability. *See* flexibility
Adler, Mark, 177
agendas for meetings. *See* meetings
ambush-style evaluations, 162
Amelio, Gilbert, 326
America Online, 175
American Express, 104
Apple Computer, 325–326
appointment calendars. *See* personal planners
appraisals. *See* performance evaluations
Arnott, Amy, 300–301
ASCEND (contact management software), 40
assets, 280–281
associations, professional, for potential employee referrals, 83, 90
AT&T, 301, 313
attitude
  as factor in hiring decisions, 80
  as factor in stress reduction, 240, 241–242, 335
  hardening of, and failure to learn, 333
  humor as aid to stress reduction, 242, 335
  implications of employee misconduct, 245, 249–251
authority
  impact of teams upon, 191, 199–200
  as issue in delegation, 52, 55
  negatives of reliance upon, 342
automation
  and myths of increases in efficiency, 293, 295
  See also computers

• B •

balance sheet, 285, 286
bar or Gantt charts, 147–148
Baylor-Hamm, Carole, 193
Bennet, Michael, 198
Berdahl, James, 68
Bing, Stanley, 69
Blanchard, Ken, 25, 71, 72–75, 109, 342
Blittle, Lonnie, 68
Boeing Corp., 294
Bolles, Richard Nelson, 85
bonds payable, 282
bookkeeping, double-entry, 283
Borland database software, 298
bottom line, 287
budgeting
  capital, 273
  creation of budgets, 273–276
  excuses for overruns, 276
  expense, 273
  gathering data (from scratch and/or history), 274, 275–276
  importance and purposes of, 271, 272–273
  labor, 273
  padding amounts or numbers of items, 277
  preliminary draft of, 275
  production, 273
  rechecking and rerunning, 275
  reviewing documents and instructions, 274
  role of judgment and intuition, 275
  sales, 273
  shifting time frames, 278
  soliciting input from employees/staff, 274
  types of, 273
  value of intimate knowledge of, 278
  See also accounting; financial statements
budgets, staying within
  closing facilities, 279
  freezing expenses, 278
  freezing hiring, 278
  freezing wages/benefits, 278
  laying off employees, 279
  padding amounts or numbers of items, 277
  postponing products or projects, 278
Burke, Lori, 39
Burnham, Whitey, 118
Bye, Scott, 302

• *C* •

calendars, 33–34
  See also personal planners
career planning. *See* developing employees
cash, 280
cash flow statement, 287, 290
celebrations as rewards, 340
cellular phones, 171, 172, 177–178
change
  creating stress, 229–230
  managing stress, 237–240, 334
  organizational, 15–16, 17, 23
  recognizing resistant attitudes or behaviors,
    233–236, 333–334
  recognizing symptoms of stress, 236–237
  seeking, 242
  shaping 21st-century organizations, 200–201
  stress reduction exercises, 241–243
  typical reactions (denial, resistance,
    exploration, acceptance), 233
  See also communications, technological
    advances; learning organizations; techno-
    logical change
Chrysler, 65, 191
coaching, 73–74, 109–118, 334
  See also developing employees; support;
    training; vision
command teams, 197
commitment
  avoiding unkeepable promises, 224–225
  to employee development, 303
  to goals, 131
  job stability as factor in hiring decisions, 80
  as key to successful delegation, 55, 62
  to rewards programs, 101
  to suggestion programs, 322–323
committees as team efforts, 196. *See also*
    team efforts
CommSuite communications software, 298
communicating
  across departmental barriers, 100, 192
  critical importance of, 169
  as facet of leadership, 66–67, 338
  failure to, 332–333
  frequency of use versus training for, 170
  goals, 128–131
  impact of flattened organization structures
    upon, 191
  importance for all employees, 99, 100
  improving writing skills, 170, 181–183
  increasingly technological means of,
    169, 171–172
  interpreting underlying meanings, 216–218
  as key to successful delegation, 55, 61
  listening, 24–25, 115, 117, 170, 179–181
  as manager's function, 22–23

communications software, 298
communications, technological advances
  cellular phones, 171, 172, 177–178
  e-mail, 31, 171, 174, 292, 294
  fax machines, 171, 174
  laptop computers, 40, 41, 176
  networks, 299–300
  pagers, 172, 176, 177
  PDAs (personal digital assistants), 32, 39–40,
    42, 175–176
  telecommuting, 40, 298, 300–302
  toll-free numbers, 177–178
  videoconferencing, 178–179
  voice mail, 30, 31, 171, 172, 176, 177, 294
comparisons of employees in performance
    evaluations, 159
compensation. *See* salary considerations
competing
  detriment to organizational goals, 192
  impact of teams, 195
CompuServe, 175
computers
  advantages for managers, 292–293
  as aids to getting organized, 40–42
  connectivity, 176
  hardware, 295-296. *See also* hardware for
    computers
  laptops, 40, 41, 176
  modems, 300
  myth of "automation equals efficiency improve-
    ments," 293–295
  networking, 299–300
  PCs versus Macs, 299
  phenomenal pace of change in, 291–292
  and scheduling software, 40–42
  software, 295, 296-298. *See also* software
  See also communications, technological advan-
    ces; e-mail; technological change; voice mail
conferences. *See* meetings
confidence
  in management, signs of lack of, 10
  as politically advantageous, 214–215
  as trait of leaders, 63, 70
confidential or sensitive circumstances, not to be
    delegated, 59
connectivity of computers, 176
control issues in delegation, 50
  See also authority
Cook, Paul M., 66
Coonradt, Charles, 345
Corel WordPerfect, 297
cost considerations
  of digital alternatives to calendars, 38
  See also budgets
cost of goods sold, 287
counseling
  for employees not working up to standard, 248

as means of handling failed delegation, 60, 62
not to be delegated, 58
upon failure to achieve goals, 151
Country Cupboard, 193
Covey, Stephen R., 42
Cox, Jeff, 343
CPM (critical path method), 149
Crisafulli, Steve, 129
crisis management, 45–46
importance of pursuing goals despite crises, 232
problem of short-term fix versus lasting solution, 335
recognizing and dealing with problems, 231–232
cross-functional teams, 198
culture of organizations, 315–316
Culver, Dr. Robert, 199
current liabilities, 282
current ratio, 289
customer service
exceptional, importance of providing, 18
motivating employees to provide, 19
Cyprus Amax Mineral Co., 306
Cyrix Corp., 173

• D •

daily planners, 34–37
See also personal planners
Data Link watches by Timex and Microsoft, 42–44, 297
database software, 298
Day Runner, Inc., 34
debt-to-equity ratio, 289
decision-making
impact of teams upon, 191, 193, 194–195, 200
involvement in process as reward for good work, 339
decisiveness
as trait of leaders, 72
versus indecision, 24, 72
delegating
advantages for fostering personal involvement by employees, 48–49
control issues, 50
correcting problems, 60
detail work, 56
as facet of leadership, 75
future tasks, 57–58
handling of junk mail, 46
impact of teams upon, 193
importance of, 47, 48
inability to, 24, 26, 47, 332
information gathering, 56–57
meetings with fill-ins as surrogates, 57
monitoring progress, 59–62
prioritizing items for, 32
repetitive tasks, 57
steps for, 55

types of jobs not to delegate, 58–59
untrue reasons not to, 49–54
Delrina CommSuite communications software, 298
Deming, Dr. W. Edwards, 316, 318, 319
The Deming Management Method, 316
demotion
for misconduct (not recommended), 251
for repeated negative performance evaluations, 249
developing employees
assessment of present skills and talents, 309
career planning, 154, 163–165, 306–308, 309
coaching, 73–74, 109–118, 334
following through, 310
importance in face of downsizing, 312–313
making time for, 334
meetings and discussions, 309, 310
mentoring, 311–312
performance evaluations as aspect of, 154, 163–165
reasons for, 304–306
ten top ways to, 310
versus training, 304
See also support; training
Diamond Fiber Products example of performance measuring and monitoring, 145–146
digital organizers, 37–39
directing, as facet of leadership, 73
disciplinary action
describing unacceptable behavior, 251–252
explaining impact on work unit or team, 252
goal statements, 255
importance of promptness in, 245
as matter of accountability, 243–244
misconduct, 245, 249–251
not to be delegated, 58
overview of steps to correct, 251–256
performance improvement planning and implementation, 254–256
performance problems, 245, 246, 248–249
personalities not at issue, 246
potential for positivity: learning, not punishment, 244
progressive, 247
schedules for improvement, 255, 265
specifying changes required, 252–253
specifying consequences of continuing unacceptable behavior, 253
training or resources required for improvement, 255
for union-represented employees, 247
See also performance evaluations; terminations
discrimination
avoiding in hiring decisions, 93
avoiding in job interviews, 88
do-and-learn technique for managers, 25
documentation. *See* written records
Domenik, Steve, 173

double-entry bookkeeping, 283
downsizing, 190–191
    how to conduct layoffs, 259, 262–265
    importance of developing employees, 312–313
DreamWorks SKG, 301
Drucker, Peter, 63, 105, 143, 190, 196, 201, 341
drug abuse, 261
Du Pree, Max, 344

• E •

Eaton, Robert, 16
Ehlen, David, 192
800 and 888 telephone numbers, 178
electronic meetings (videoconferencing), 178–179
The Elements of Style, 182
e-mail
    convenience of, 171, 174
    described, 174
    expanding use of, 292, 294
    problem of unwanted, 31
    See also computers
emergencies, prioritizing handling of, 32
employee motivators
    credibility, 108
    critical importance of, 95
    desire to do good work and succeed
        (Theory Y), 11, 66, 342
    empowerment, 16, 17, 65, 67, 193–194, 199–200
    energizing, 19–20
    fear and intimidation (Theory X), 11, 15, 25, 67,
        102–103, 342
    giving employees benefit of doubt, 103
    high expectations for employees' abilities, 103
    jellybean theories, 97–98
    as manager-determined, 108
    manager-initiated recognition, 102, 106, 107, 334
    merit bonuses, 105
    money as overrated, 104–106
    most effective, 106–107
    negative impact of favoritism, 108
    positive reinforcers (praise), 96, 102–103
    rewards versus punishment, 95–96
    smaller successes more likely than large,
        103–104, 113–115
    trust, 18–19
    value of asking employees what motivates
        them, 99
    varied nature of, 98–99
    See also rewarding employees
employee suggestion programs, 322
employees
    as assets, 100
    demoting, 249, 251
    developing. *See* developing employees
    disciplining. *See* disciplinary action

evaluating performance. *See* performance
    evaluations
hiring. *See* hiring
measuring performance. *See* performance
    measuring and monitoring
terminating. *See* terminations
employment agencies, 83
empowerment
    as employee motivator, 16, 17
    impact of teams upon, 193–194, 199–200
    as manager's function, 20–22
energizing employees
    with announcements of goals, 130, 132
    as manager's function, 19–20
environment
    coach's job to enhance, 111
    considerations for conducting job interviews, 86
    management's job to enhance, 12
    supportive as ideal, 22, 99–100
Envoy PDA by Motorola, 39–40, 173
equipment, 280–281
ethics
    handling employee misconduct, 245, 249–251
    integrity as trait of leaders, 71
    as principle of organizations, 80
    as quality desired in employees, 80
Excel, 297
expenses, 287
experience, as factor in hiring decisions, 80

• F •

facilitating, as facet of leadership, 67–68
falsification of records, 261
favoritism, negative effects of, 108
fax machines, 171, 174
fear and intimidation as employee motivators
    (Theory X), 11, 15, 25, 67, 342
Federal Express, 159, 301, 320
feedback
    essential for employees, 157, 339
    from meetings, 205
    provided by coaches, 111
*The Fifth Discipline: The Art and Practice of the
    Learning Organization,* 327, 344
financial ratios, 289–290
financial statements
    balance sheet, 285, 286
    cash flow statement, 287, 290
    cost of goods sold, 287
    expenses, 287
    financial ratios, 289–290
    importance of, 285
    importance of understanding, 279
    income statement, 285, 287, 288
    net income/loss, 287

operating expenses, 287
revenues, 287
See also accounting; budgeting
firings. *See* terminations
Fisher, George, 112
500 numbers, 178
flexibility
   adaptability enhanced through team efforts,
      195–196
   as issue in delegation, 53
   as reward for good work, 340
flip charts as visual aids to presentations, 186
flowcharts, 148–149
following through
   checking progress in delegated tasks, 59–62
   as facet of coaching, 115
   on effectiveness of rewards systems, 101
   on employee development plans, 310
   on employee performance improvement, 256
Forbes, Kenneth S. III, 177
Ford Motor Co., 301, 318, 320
formal teams, 196–197
Franklin Quest Co.'s planning systems, 33, 34, 36, 40
friendliness and participation as politically
      advantageous, 219–220

• G •

The Game of Work, 345
Gantt charts, 147–148
General Electric, 202, 313
General Motors, 294
Gershman, Eric, 194
getting organized
   to achieve goals without distractions, 133
   as aid to stress reduction, 239
   concentrating on what's important, 30–32
   crisis management, 45–46
   daily prioritizing, 45
   delegating handling of junk mail, 46
   first steps, 27–30
   importance of, 27, 30
   making time for employees, 334
   saying "No!" to distractions, 133
   taking advantage of technology. *See* communi-
      cations, technological advances
   winding down and tying up loose ends, 46
   workspace, desk, etc., 27–28, 29
   See also personal planners
The Goal, 343
goal-setting
   activity versus results, 132
   attainable, 125
   in career development plans, 307
   communicating, 128–131
   employee input to, 144
   employee-related, 126

examples of successful, 124, 143–145
failure to, 332
focused, 128, 132
forms and uses of power to achieve, 133–135
for improvement of poor performance, 255
measurable, 125
not to be delegated, 58
as part of coaching, 110
as primary function of management, 121
prioritized, 131–133
reasons for, 123
relevance, 125, 128
revisiting and updating, 128
schedules and deadlines, 125
simplicity, 126, 144
specificity, 125, 144
team efforts toward, 192
value-based, 126
See also performance measuring and
      monitoring
Goldratt, Eliyahu, 343
Graham, Dr. Gerald, 102, 106
gross margin/profit, 287
groupware (software for collaborative work), 201
Grove, Andrew S., 174
gunnysacking, 161

• H •

Hallmark Cards, Inc., 131
halo effect in performance evaluations, 159
handouts accompanying presentations, 186
Hanna, M. A., 294
hardware for computers
   input devices (keyboard, scanners, etc.), 295
   modems, 300
   output devices (printers, speakers), 296
   processing devices (microprocessors, memory
      chips), 296
   storage devices (floppies, hard disks,
      CD-ROMs), 296
Harvard Graphics presentation software, 298
Hatz, Bruce, 85
Hauptfuhrer, Robert, 67
headhunters (employment agencies), 83
health considerations, 235
   See also stress
Hewlett, Bill, 66
Hewlett-Packard, 196
hierarchical model of organizations, 190, 342
high performance teams, 198
hiring
   advantages of outlines for job interviews, 81
   deciding whom to hire, 92–94
   defining desired qualities, 80–81
   evaluating candidates, 88–92
   falsification of application information, 261

hiring *(continued)*
  freezing in anticipation of layoffs, 263
  importance and difficulties of, 79, 91
  importance of objectivity plus intuition, 92–93
  interviewing candidates. *See* job interviews
  job definition process, 81
  making job offer, 92
  or promoting/replacing from within, 83
  ranking of candidates, 92
  reference checks, 88–90
  referrals, 83
  through employment agencies (headhunters), 83
  through Internet ads, 84
  through professional associations, 83, 90
  through temp agencies, 83
  through want ads, 84
Hockaday, Irvine O., 131
Holtz, Lou, 118
Hull, Raymond, 342
The Human Side of Enterprise, 341–342
humor
  as aid to stress reduction, 242, 335
  See also attitude
Hyatt Hotels' rooms equipped with computer-
    ized workspace, 172

• I •

Iacocca, Lee, 65
IBM, 313
icons used in this book, 4–5
In Search of Excellence, 343
inability to delegate. *See under* delegating
incentives. *See* employee motivators
income statement, 285, 287, 288
income/loss, 287
incompetence, 260
  See also performance evaluations
indecision, 24, 72
independence as reward for good work, 339
informal teams, 197
information
  forcing change upon organizations, 200–201
  sharing with employees, 338
  See also communicating
initiative, as factor in hiring decisions, 80
innovation, 195–196, 317
inspiring action
  as facet of coaching, 111
  as facet of leadership, 65–66
insubordination, 261
integrity. *See* ethics
intelligence, as factor in hiring decisions, 80
Internet
  browsers, 298
  communications by, 171
  described, 175

  opportunities for wasting time, 31
  for recruiting new employees, 84
interviews. *See* job interviews
intoxication, 261
Intranets, 301
intuition, role in hiring decisions, 93
inventory, 280
involvement in decision-making as reward, 339

• J •

Japan and quality movement, 318
job descriptions
  reviewing before attempting to hire for, 81, 86
  with standards for measuring performance,
    155–156
job interviews
  advantages of outlines for, 81
  avoiding power trips, 86
  environment for, 86
  familiarity with job description, 81, 86
  importance of, 84
  note-taking during, 87, 91
  overview of key steps, 89
  questions not to ask, 87–88
  questions to ask, 85–86
  resume checks before, 86
  second and third rounds of, 91–92
  See also hiring
job stability, as factor in hiring decisions, 80
Jobs, Stephen, 301, 326
Johnson, Spencer, 342
Johnsonville Foods, 198

• K •

Katzenbach, Jon R., 344
Kennedy, John F., 65
knowledge
  as politically advantageous, 214–215
  as power, 134
Kodak Co., 112
Kovac, Frederick, 16

• L •

laptop computers, 40, 41, 176
layoffs, 259, 262–265, 279
leadership
  as coaching, 73–74, 109–118, 334
  communicating, 66–67. *See also* communicating
  compared to management, 64-65. *See also*
    management
  confidence, 63, 70
  decisiveness, 72
  delegating, 75. *See also* delegating

directing, 73
inspiring action, 65–66
integrity, 71. *See also* ethics
optimism, 63, 70
scarcity of, 63
Situational, 72–73, 109
supporting and facilitating, 67-68, 74-75.
    See also support
Leadership Is an Art, 344
learning organizations
    creating, 327–328
    *The Fifth Discipline: The Art and Practice of the
        Learning Organization,* 327, 344
    objectivity, 327
    obstacles to, 324–326
    openness, 327
    results of failure to become, 315–316, 321, 333
    rewards systems, 328
    support and resources, 328
    teamwork, 328
learning techniques for managers
    doing and learning, 25
    looking and listening, 24–25
legal considerations
    creating reluctance to terminate unsatisfactory
        employees, 262
    documenting decisions not to hire (notes taken
        during job interviews), 81, 87, 91
    of failure to evaluate and document employee
        performance, 154–155
    job interview questions *not* to ask, 88
    personal planners subject to subpoena, 37
    reference checks and supervisors' true
        opinions of former employees, 90
    of terminations for age, race, gender, etc., 260
Leonard, Darryl Hartley, 16
Levi Strauss & Co., 159, 301
liabilities, 281–282
listening
    frequency of use versus training for, 170
    tips for improving skills, 179–181
    value of, 24–25, 115
    while coaching employees, 115, 117
    See also communicating
long-term liabilities, 282
look-and-listen technique for managers, 24–25
Lotus 1-2-3, 297
Lotus Freelance Graphics presentation software,
    298

• *M* •

McGregor, Douglas, 341
Macintosh computers versus PCs, 299
McNealy, Scott, 116
Madden, John, 118

make-or-buy decision example (security
    services), 284
management
    compared to leadership, 64–65
    defined, 9, 11–14
    Leadership Is an Art, 344
    people as focus, 12
    politics. *See* politics in offices
    problem of quick fixes, 12–14
    using power, 133–135
management challenges
    change, organizational and technological,
        15–16, 68
    getting organized. *See* getting organized
    handling stress, 229–230, 236–240, 241–243
    managing instead of doing, 14–15, 331
    transitioning to management from
        non-management, 331
management functions
    attend meetings. *See* meetings
    budgeting. *See* budgeting
    coaching employees, 73–74, 109–118, 334
    communicating, 22-23. *See also* communicating;
        listening
    considering legalities of actions. *See* legal
        considerations
    considering political ramification of actions.
        See politics in offices
    counseling employees. *See* counseling
    crisis management, 45–46, 231–232, 335
    discipline. *See* disciplinary action
    documentation. *See* written records
    eat, meet, punish, obstruct, and obscure, 21
    employee development. *See* developing
        employees
    empowering employees, 20–22
    energizing employees, 19–20
    firing employees. *See* terminations
    follow-up. *See* following through
    fostering teamwork. *See* team efforts
    getting organized. *See* getting organized
    giving presentations, 135, 170, 183–188
    goal-setting, 121. *See also* goal-setting
    hiring. *See* hiring
    interviewing job candidates. *See* job interviews
    motivating employees. *See* employee motivators
    performance evaluations. *See* performance
        evaluations; performance measuring
        and monitoring
    quality improvement, 317, 318–324
    rewarding employees. *See* rewarding employees
    supporting employees' efforts. *See* support
management styles
    compromise, 11–12
    nice guy (Theory Y), 11
    reactions to good *and* bad news, 99

management styles *(continued)*
  tough guy (Theory X), 10–11, 342
  See also employee motivators
Managing for Results, 341
Marmot Mountain, 129
Mayer, Jeffrey, 32
measurements. *See* performance measuring and
    monitoring
Meek, Catherine, 68
meetings
  agendas for, 204
  to discuss goals, 130–131
  maximizing effectiveness of team efforts, 201–205
  for performance evaluations, 158
  savings through use of scheduling software, 294
  for termination of unsatisfactory employee,
    266–267
  videoconferencing, 178–179
  virtual, 179
  as waste of time and energy, 21, 24, 203–204
  ways to improve, 204–205
mentors and sponsors, 223, 311–312
micromanagers, 47
Microsoft, 294
Microsoft Excel, 297
Microsoft PowerPoint presentation software, 298
Microsoft Project (project planning software), 150
Microsoft Schedule+ (contact management
    software), 40–42, 297
Microsoft Windows, 296, 299
Microsoft Word, 297
Microsoft/Timex Data Link watches, 42–44, 297
mirroring in performance evaluations, 159
misconduct, 245, 249–251
mobility, computer technology aiding, 40, 298,
    300–302
money as motivator, 104–106
monitoring. *See* following through
Monsanto Chemical Co., 320
Moody, Roy E., 181
Morningstar, 300–301
mortgages payable, 282
Mosaic Internet browser, 298
motivators. *See* employee motivators
Motorola, 124, 194, 299, 320
  Envoy personal intelligent communicator,
    39–40, 173

• N •

net income/loss, 287
Netscape Navigator Internet browser, 298
networking, 299–300
nice-guy/gal syndrome in performance
    evaluations, 160
Nieman, Andrea, 67
Nordstrom, Inc.'s employee manual, 18

norms used in performance evaluations, 155–156
Norton pcANYWHERE communications software,
    298
notes payable, 281
note-taking
  documenting changes or setbacks for
    self-protection, 224
  during job interviews, 87, 91
NYNEX Corp., 197

• O •

objectivity
  importance in hiring decisions, 92–93
  importance in learning organizations, 327
OmniGo by Hewlett-Packard, 38, 39
1001 Ways to Reward Employees, 107
The One Minute Manager, 342
openness, 22, 327
operating expenses, 287
operating system software, 296
optimism
  as aid to stress reduction, 239
  as trait of leaders, 63, 70
  See also attitude
Oracle database software, 298
organization charts, "real" or "political," 211–213
organizational change, 15–16, 23
  and changes in employee attitudes, 17
  See also change
organizations, culture of, 315–316
organizing. *See* getting organized; getting
    organized, importance of
OS/2 Warp, 296
outplacement services, 264
overmanaging, 24
owners' equity, 282

• P •

pagers, 172, 176, 177
paid-in capital, 282
Part of Tens
  classic books on business, 341–345
  common management mistakes, 331–335
  described, 4
  ways to recognize employees' contributions,
    337–340
patience, as principle of ethical power for
    organizations, 71
pay. *See* salary considerations
Payne v. *Western & A.R.P. Co.* (termination-at-will
    rule), 260
pcANYWHERE communications software, 298
PCs. *See* computers
PDAs (personal digital assistants), 32, 39–40, 42,
    175–176

peak performers, 75
Peale, Norman Vincent, 71
people
  as focus of management, 12, 342
  skills as essential to managers, 331
performance evaluations
  ambush-style, 162
  as aspect of career development, 154, 163–165
  common mistakes to avoid, 159–163
  communicating, 154
  critical importance of, 153, 154–155
  as feedback, 157, 161
  formal documentation of achievements or
      failings, 154
  goal-setting, before and after, 154, 157, 158
  gunnysacking, 161, 162
  improvement planning and implementation,
      254–256
  of managers by employees, 159
  negative, 249
  not to be delegated, 58, 158
  as ongoing, not annual, process, 161, 163
  reasons for all-too-frequent failure to conduct,
      153, 161
  360-degree evaluations, 159
  using norms and standards, 155–156, 157
  in writing, 158
  See also disciplinary action
performance measuring and monitoring
  action sequencing and relationships, 142
  action specificity, 141, 145
  bar or Gantt charts, 147–148
  caution on short-sighted "counting" instead of
      measuring, 143
  comparing results to goals, 150
  critical importance of, 137–138
  examples of successful cases, 143–146
  flowcharts, PERT charts and CPM, 148–149
  MARS (milestones, actions, relationships,
      schedules) system, 140
  positive feedback, 139, 144
  quantifying by key indicators, 138
  recognizing incremental progress, 139
  rewards for success, counseling for failure, 151
  scheduling, 142
  setting checkpoints and milestones, 140–141
  software, 149–150
  value of openness, 140
performance-based measures, 101–102
  smaller successes more likely than large, 103–104
persistence, as principle of ethical power for
    organizations, 71
personal assignments from bosses, not to be
    delegated, 59
personal digital assistants (PDAs), 32, 39–40, 42,
    175–176
personal information management software, 297

personal planners
  advantages, 29, 32–33, 45
  calendars, 33–34, 45
  choosing, 44
  computers and scheduling software, 40–42
  daily planners, 34–37
  Data Link watch, 42–44, 297
  digital organizers, 37–39
  PDAs (personal digital assistants), 32, 39–40,
      42, 175–176
  subject to subpoena, 37
  for tracking delegated task completion, 61
  See also getting organized
personal power, 134
perspective, as principle of ethical power for
    organizations, 71
PERT charts, 149
Peter, Dr. Laurence, 342
The Peter Principle, 342
Peters, Thomas, 17, 172, 343
Petersen, Donald, 66
Phillips, Bum, 118
physical violence, 261, 265
Pierce, Lisa, 177
pitchfork effect in performance evaluations, 159
planners. See personal planners
Poling, Harold A., 65
politics in offices
  advantages of mentors, 223, 311–312
  advantages of working within, 207–208
  avoiding unkeepable promises or commit-
      ments, 224–225
  deciphering communications and understand-
      ing underlying meanings, 216–218
  documenting changes or setbacks for
      self-protection, 224
  evaluating environment, 208–209
  failure of "policies" designed to solve
      problems, 219
  friendliness and participation, 219–220
  identifying key players, 210–211
  knowledge and confidence, 214–215
  managing bosses, 222
  mutual favors, 220–221
  personal image polishing, 213–216
  "political" organization charts, 211–213
  rationality, avoiding emotional displays,
      213–214, 215–216
  sensitive situations not to be delegated, 58–59
  socializing with extreme caution, 221–222
  trustworthiness, 223
  unwritten rules of conduct, 218–223
  visibility, 225
position power, 134
positive reinforcers
  as employee motivators, 96, 102–103
  as facet of coaching, 115

positive reinforcers *(continued)*
  measuring and monitoring toward achievement
    of goals, 139
Post, Brad Quinn, 294
power
  derived from relationships, 134
  derived from tasks, 135
  impact of flattened organization structures
    upon, 191
  of knowledge, 134
  personal, 134
  positional, 134
The Power of Ethical Management, 71
prepaid expenses, 280
presentation software, 298
presentations
  delivering, 187–188
  frequency of giving versus training for, 170
  importance of visual aids and handouts, 184–187
  improving skills through Toastmasters, 135
  preparing, 183–184
pride, as principle of ethical power for organiza-
    tions, 71
ProCOMM Plus communications software, 298
Prodigy, 175
professional associations, for potential employee
    referrals, 83, 90
profit/loss, 287
promoting/replacing from within, 83
Published Image, Inc., 194
purpose, as principle of ethical power for
    organizations, 71

• *Q* •

quality circles, 194
quality improvement
  beginnings of movement in scientific manage-
    ment, 317
  Deming as developer, 318–321
  steps to creating program, 321–323
  success stories, 320
  systems thinking, 323–324
  widespread adoption of, 194, 315
quick ratio, 289

• *R* •

Raben, Chuck, 116
rationality and unemotionality
  as aid in stress reduction, 240
  as politically advantageous, 213–214, 215–216
Raychem, 313
reading, frequency of use versus training for, 170
real estate, 281
Rebholz, Dave, 16
recognition. *See* rewarding employees

reference checks on potential employees, 88–90
references on good business practice, 341–345
referrals as source of new hires, 83
Reich, Robert, 195
relationship power, 134
relaxation as aid to stress reduction, 238–239, 241
resignations, 259
resources. *See* support
responsibility
  failure to show accountability as matter for
    disciplinary action, 243–244
  as reward for good work, 340
  sense of, as factor in hiring decisions, 80
results
  described in *Managing for Results,* 341
  See also goal-setting; quality improvement
resume checks of job candidates, 86
retained earnings, 282
retirement, 259
return on investment (ROI), 290
revenues, 287
reverse (upward) evaluations, 159, 164
rewarding employees
  as cardinal principle of employee motivation,
    96–97
  with celebrations, 340
  with feedback, 339
  with flexibility, 340
  for good suggestions, 322
  importance of, 328, 334
  importance of planning systems for, 100–101
  with increased responsibility, 340
  with independence, 339
  with information, 338
  with interesting work, 337
  with involvement in decision-making, 339
  as issue in delegation, 53
  for performance, 101–102, 339
  for successful performance on delegated tasks,
    62
  with time off, 338
  with visibility, 338
  See also employee motivatorsROI (return on
    investment), 290
rules of conduct, for survival of politics in offices,
    218–223
Rypkowski, Joseph D., 198

• *S* •

salary considerations
  bonuses as entitlements, not incentives, 105–106
  as employee motivator, 105
  freezes to stay within budgets, 278
  handling in job interviews, 86
  as part of performance evaluation process,
    163–164

Saldich, Robert J., 313
Samsung, 124
Saturn Corp., 198
Schedule+ (contact management software) by
    Microsoft, 40–42, 297
schedules
    for employees' career development steps, 307
    for improvement of poor performance, 255, 265
    See also getting organized
scheduling software, 40–42
security services example of make-or-buy
    decision, 284
self-improvement programs, 135
self-managed teams, 198–199
Senge, Peter, 323, 327, 344
Silicon Graphics, 301
simplicity
    as aid to stress reduction, 239
    as benefit in goal-setting, 126, 144
Situational Leadership, 72–73, 109
slides as visual aids to presentations, 186
Smith, Bill, 320
Smith, Douglas K., 344
socializing
    with extreme caution, 221–222
    value of, 335
software
    communications programs, 298
    database programs, 298
    groupware for collaborative work, 201
    Internet browsers, 298
    for meeting scheduling, 294
    operating systems, 296
    for performance measuring and monitoring,
        149–150
    personal information management programs, 297
    presentation programs, 298
    spreadsheet programs, 297
    word processors, 297
speaking
    frequency of use versus training for, 170
    improving skills through Toastmasters, 135
    See also presentations
Spindler, Michael, 325
spreadsheet software, 297
Spry Mosaic Internet browser, 298
Stalk, George, 195–196
standards
    importance for employee disciplinary action, 248
    as key to successful delegation, 55
    for measuring employees' career development
        steps, 307
    used in performance evaluations, 155–156
Stayer, Ralph, 198
stereotyping in performance evaluations, 159
Stoodley, Martha, 85

stress
    caused by change and uncertainty, 229–230
    exercises for reducing, 241–243
    managing, 237–240
    recognizing symptoms of, 236–237
subpoena. *See* legal considerations
suggestion programs, 322
Sun Microsystems, 116
superteams, 198
support
    by top management, of quality improvement
        programs, 316
    for employee development, 307
    as facet of coaching, 111, 117
    as facet of leadership, 67–68, 74–75
    as key to successful delegation, 55
    as manager's function, 22
    See also developing employees; training
supportive workplace environment, 22, 99–100
suspension upon discovery of employee
    misconduct, 250
Sybase database software, 298
systems thinking, 323–324

• T •

"talking the talk," 69
tardiness, 260–261
task forces as team efforts, 196
task power, 135
Taylor, Frederick Winslow, 317
team efforts
    ad hoc groups, 197
    advantages, 189–190, 344–345
    coaching, 111, 116, 117–118
    command teams, 197
    committees, 196
    cooperation and collaboration, 192
    corporate downsizing, 190–191
    empowerment of workers, 193–194, 199–200
    formal versus informal, 196–198
    fostering, as part of coaching, 111
    high performance, cross-functional, and
        superteams, 198
    importance of, 22, 328
    information handling, 200–201
    innovation and adaptability, 195–196
    interdepartmental, 192
    maximizing effectiveness of meetings, 201–205
    obsolescence of hierarchy, 190
    self-managed, 198–199
    task forces, 196
    The Wisdom of Teams, 344
Techmetals, 193
technological change, 16
    disadvantages of deluge of information, 30
    giving edge over competitors, 173–174

technological change *(continued)*
  Internet, 31
  in means of communicating, 23, 169, 171–172, 230
  online services, 175
  See also change; computers
telecommuting, 40, 298, 300–302
temp agencies, 83
terminations
  announcing, 266–267
  appeals from, 265
  disagreeableness of, 257–258, 261–262
  for intolerable offenses, 260–261
  for misconduct, 251
  and termination-at-will rule, 260
  timing of, 268
  for unsatisfactory performance, 249
  voluntary, 258–259
  wrongful, 260, 262, 264–265, 266
  See also layoffs
theft, 261
Theory X management (fear and intimidation), 11, 15, 25, 102–103, 342
Theory Y management (encouragement), 11, 66, 342
360-degree evaluations, 159
Time Management For Dummies, 32
time off, as reward for good work, 338
Timex DataLink watches, 297
Toastmasters, 135
toll-free numbers, 177–178
The Tom Peters Seminar, 172
tough guy management style, 10–11
Townsend, Robert, 342
training
  directing and coaching, 73–74, 109–118, 334
  to give marginal job candidates better qualifications, 93
  importance of, 18
  for improvement of poor performance, 244, 255
  management functions, giving training, 18, 73–74, 93, 244, 255
  See also developing employees; support
transparencies as visual aids to presentations, 186
trust
  as employee motivators, 18–19, 100, 313
  as issue in delegation, 50, 54–55
trustworthiness as politically advantageous, 223
turning points
  coaching employees through, 114–115
  cumulative nature of, 114
  as opportunities for small successes, 113
Twentymile Mine, 306

• *U* •

Union Pacific Railroad, 172
Up the Organization, 342
upward (reverse) evaluations, 159, 164

• *V* •

verbal abuse of others, 260, 267
videoconferencing, 178–179
violence, 261, 265
visibility
  as politically advantageous, 225
  as reward for good work, 338
vision
  goal-setting growing from, 121, 128
  goal-setting not to be delegated, 58
  as issue in delegation, 54
  perspective as principle of ethical power for organizations, 71
voice mail, 30, 31, 171, 172, 176, 177, 294

• *W* •

Walker, Martin D., 294
"walking the walk," 69
Walsh, Mike, 172
want ads, 84
warnings upon discovery of employee misconduct, 249, 250, 265
watches, Timex Data Link, 42–44, 297
Waterman, Robert, 343
Watson, Lee, 193
Welch, Jack, 25, 65, 202
What Color Is Your Parachute?, 85
white/chalk boards as visual aids to presentations, 186
Wilson Learning, 192
wireless communications, 176
The Wisdom of Teams, 344
Wooden, John, 118
word processors, 297
WordPerfect, 297
work hours and flexibility, 340
"work out" meetings at GE, 202
working environment. *See* environment
writing
  frequency of use versus training for, 170
  tips for improving skills, 181–183
written records
  of counseling given employees for poor performance, 248, 265
  documenting changes or setbacks for self-protection, 224
  falsification of, 261
  note-taking during job interviews, 87, 91
  of reprimands and warnings given to employees for misconduct, 250, 265
  See also communicating; performance evaluations
wrongful terminations, 260, 262, 264–265, 266

• *X* •

Xerox, 196